MULTICULTURALISM AND MINORITY RELIGIONS IN BRITAIN

Krishna Consciousness, Religious Freedom, and the Politics of Location

CURZON STUDIES IN NEW RELIGIOUS MOVEMENTS

Editor: Judith Coney

This Series is interested particularly in any innovative religious group that has established itself in the last fifty years. We welcome high-quality, original research contributions from across the globe, based on sensitive, in-depth research methods. Preference is given to the publication of material on religious groups which have not so far been documented. All the books in the Series address the theme of religion and society. The Series is mainly comprised of monographs exploring and extending existing theories about religion and society. It also includes edited collections designed to focus, in particular, on cross-cultural themes and draw together research findings from across the world.

Proposals or scripts for the Series will be welcomed by the Series Editor or by the Chief Editor, Curzon Press.

MULTICULTURALISM AND MINORITY RELIGIONS IN BRITAIN

Krishna Consciousness, Religious Freedom, and the Politics of Location

Malory Nye

Routledge
Taylor & Francis Group
LONDON AND NEW YORK

First Published in 2001
by Curzon Press

Published 2015 by Routledge
2 Park Square, Milton Park, Abingdon, Oxfordshire OX14 4RN
711 Third Avenue, New York, NY 10017

First issued in paperback 2015

Routledge is an imprint of the Taylor and Francis Group, an informa business

Typeset in Sabon by LaserScript Ltd, Mitcham, Surrey

British Library Cataloguing in Publication Data
A catalogue record of this book is available from the British Library

Library of Congress Cataloguing in Publication Data
A catalogue record for this book has been requested

ISBN 13: 978-1-138-86253-1 (pbk)
ISBN 13: 978-0-7007-1392-9 (hbk)

For Alex … and Micah and Martha

CONTENTS

PREFACE AND ACKNOWLEDGEMENTS

Sometimes books seem to take on a life of their own. This is not the book I intended to write: events and ideas have pushed and pulled me through various writing stages, often in quite surprising ways. As with many research projects, the circumstances that eventually take on a seemingly concrete existence as printed texts are always so much more nebulous in their early stages. This book is about a number of things: minority religions, 'new religions', Hindu and 'new' Hindu forms, law, religion, multiculturalism, place, power, etc. Some of these things were fundamental issues in my previous book (*A Place for our Gods*), when I wrote on the construction of a religious place among a minority Hindu group in Scotland. But the conflict at Bhaktivedanta Manor, the campaign, the legal disputes, and the final resolution all came up on me as if by surprise – first suggested to me by some brief conversations and a rummage through archives in the Centre for New Religions at King's College London. As an anthropologist working in a religious studies department I would never have imagined that I could possibly find something to say about planning legislation, whilst the enactment of legislation on the European Convention on Human Rights again took my interests in another unexpected direction. All these things, I hope, add up to a book that is a lot more interesting and relevant than the book I had once imagined would come out of my research.

This is a book that I hope contributes to several debates, not only those that go on within scholarly 'New Religions' circles, but also the wider ones that these come out of (and feed into). That is, the role of religious minorities, religious practice, and 'religion' within contemporary multicultural western cultures is not something which can be reduced or explained by any simplistic idea – whether that be secularisation, globalisation, ethnicity, postcolonialism, or whatever. Questions about the 'role of religion' in the 'modern world' cannot be answered without reference to specifics, to use a (perhaps unfortunate) common phrase 'the devil is in the detail'. My engagement with a particular religious organisation (ISKCON), who happen to be involved in networks and cultural areas in which I had previously located my research (British Hindus), has led me to present a series of arguments and a critical analysis which I hope speaks to and beyond these particularities. There is not one single audience that I expect to reach with this book, but rather a number of different groups and people: students, researchers, teachers, commentators, law practitioners, and decision makers, and indeed anybody who may be challenged to pursue an interest in issues of culture and religion within contemporary multicultural contexts.

In writing this book, there have, of course, been many people who have inspired, guided, and supported me in various ways and so deserve mention and credit. In particular, I am very grateful to the Curzon New Religions series editor Judith Coney (now Judith Fox), not only for her very insightful and encouraging comments and suggestions on the book, but also for our long discussions at the beginning of the project. I have also gained a great deal from the various colleagues with whom I have worked over the years, first at Kings College London, particularly Peter Clarke, Sue Hamilton, and Elisabeth Arweck. And then, since 1995, in the department of religious studies at Stirling, particularly Jennifer Haswell, Mary Keller, Mary Maaga, Scott Matthews, Clare Palmer, and Abd al-Fattah El-Awaisi.

Comments from those people kind enough to listen to or read various papers, presentations, and drafts that I have made from this material over the years have helped to shape and direct my work. Those that come most readily to mind are Rohit Barot, Andrea Baumeister, Peter Edge, Jonathan Freedman, Kim Knott, Nicole Bourque, Marion Bowman, Robert Exon, Martin Baumann, Richard Gale, Simon Coleman, Sanda Ducaru, John Hinnells, Werner Menski, Roger Ballard, Eileen Barker, Margit Warburg, and Nurit Zaidman-Dvir. In addition, I have much to thank in various ways from Ian Reader, Steve Sutcliffe, Ali Wardak, and my students (both undergraduate and postgraduate) who have endured the various courses I have taught in London and Stirling. My always challenging and thoughtful doctoral students are constantly an inspiration to my work, including Kerry Huntly, Cat McEarchern, Aislinn Jones, and Judith Macpherson.

There are many people within ISKCON, and others beyond the organisation within wider Hindu circles, who helped to shape and inform my knowledge and understanding of this material. Of these I would like to make special mention of: Rasmandala das, Shaunaka rishi das, Akhandadhi das, Bimal Krishna das, Damodar das, Prabhupada Vani das, Hari Jones, and Hariprasad Haria.

I was very fortunate to receive funding from several sources to help cover my travel and other expenses at various stages of researching and writing this book. These were a British Academy Small Grant (1995), a Carnegie Trust Grant (1998), University of Stirling Research Funds (1996), and a King's College London School of Humanities Research Grant (1994). I am very grateful to all these organisations for helping to financially support this research.

Various parts of this book have been tried out in various (and quite different) forms in other places, over the years in which I have been writing. These include the *Journal of Contemporary Religion* (1995), the *Journal of Church and State* (1999), and ISKCON *Communications Journal* (1998).

Finally, my greatest thanks go to my wife Alex, with whom I have shared so many fun and rewarding years, which have not always been too dominated by my obsession to complete this book. And I also owe so much to our children Micah and Martha, who are still too young to read or discuss this book, but who have both contributed so much to the writing of it, and together with Alex have made life such a pleasure, despite its moments of tragedy and farce. It is to these three people that this book is dedicated, with thanks, appreciation, and love.

GLOSSARY

acharya	religious leader and teacher
ahimsa	principle of non-violent behaviour
ashram	religious community
ashramadharma	the 'life order', in which one performs certain duties according to the stage at which one is living: as a student, a householder, a renouncer, or an ascetic
avatar	incarnation/human embodiment of Krishna
bhajans	religious songs
brahmacharinis	young female ascetics/devotees
brahmacharis	young male ascetics/devotees
darshan	form of worship through sight of *murtis*
dham	the abode of the temple deity, an area around a *mandir*
Gaudiya Math	Chaitanya based organisation founded in Bengal in 1918 by Bhaktisiddhanta Saraswati
goshala	cow sheds, a place in which cows are cared for, worshipped, and their products taken for use in the temple
gurukul	religious school for children of devotees
Harinam	a form of public witness and devotion, usually through the soliticing of literature
Janmasthami	festival in August/September in celebration of Krishna's birthday
japa	meditation, usually through chanting of the *mahamantra* around a *mala*
Kali Yug	the 'Dark Age' of history, the last of the four ages in the cycle of time
karmis	people who live in body-consciousness instead of soul-consciousness, generally used as a slang term to describe non Krishna devotees
kirtan	religious songs
Krishna-lila	dramas enacting the pursuits of Krishna

mahamantra	the Hare Krishna 'chant' (Hare Krishna Hare Krishna, Krishna Krishna, Hare Hare, Hare Rama, Hare Rama, Rama Rama, Hare Hare)
mala beads	a string of 108 beads, usually kept in a cloth bag, on which the *mahamantra* is chanted
mandirs	Hindu temple or buildings of worship
math	a teaching institution, used for the training of *pujaris* and also for worship
maya	the illusion of reality which lies between the devotee and Krishna consciousness
murtis	statues (or pictures) in temples in which the deities are manifest and embodied
padayatra	a 'walking pilgrimage'
parampara	the tradition of guru succession, through a line from guru to disciple
prasad	'blessed' food, which has been offered to a deity and comes back for consumption as 'grace'
pujaris	temple 'priests', devotees who have been trained to perform complex rituals in service of the deities
Rathayatra	a public procession of temple deities through streets on a large chariot
sanatan dharm	literally translated as the 'eternal religion', a self-definitional expression for the broad Hindu tradition
sankirtan	public worship by devotees, usually in bands who play music, sing and dance as a form of witness
shika	top-knot of hair that is left to grow on men's otherwise shaven heads
tilak	mark on the forehead, taking a particular form of parallel vertical lines for followers of Krishna
tirtha	a place of pilgrimage
tulsi	the Indian basil plant, which is worshipped as an embodiment of Krishna

PART ONE

CHAPTER ONE

Multiculturalism, Minority Religions, and ISKCON

Historical introduction

In 1973 George Harrison (a former 'Beatle') donated a country house in the village of Letchmore Heath, Hertfordshire to the International Society of Krishna Consciousness (ISKCON, or more popularly known as the 'Hare Krishnas'). At that time ISKCON was a small but growing 'new' religious movement, already well known for their public chanting and dancing in public places (such as on Oxford Street in London). The house was renamed Bhaktivedanta Manor (in honour of the Indian guru who founded ISKCON), and was converted into a place to educate people into the complex theology and practice that was integral to the Hare Krishnas. As part of this conversion, a large room was turned into a temple and regular worship became a central feature of the activities at the Manor.

In the early 1970s, around the time that Bhaktivedanta Manor was founded, ISKCON was primarily known as a 'new' religion from India which was actively converting white people to a 'strange' set of ideas. Although the founder was Indian, most Hare Krishna devotees were considered to be white people wearing Indian clothes. Despite this image, however, the temple at Bhaktivedanta Manor became very popular with the large community of Hindus of Indian descent living in nearby north west London, many of whom had only recently arrived in the country as refugees expelled from Idi Amin's Uganda. These Hindus found much to satisfy their religious needs at the Manor, and within a short time large numbers were using the temple on a regular basis.

But the Manor was situated in the heart of a small village, which was an oasis of peace in the Green Belt, on the fringe of London. Residents in the village suddenly found on their doorsteps long traffic queues of Hindus trying to get into the grounds of the Manor, and the roads were becoming blocked by cars being parked in the village itself. Complaints were made to the local council, who reminded ISKCON that they did not have planning permission to allow large scale public worship in the building. When

ISKCON took over the Manor the planning agreement had been for the place to be used as a 'theological college for the promotion of Krishna consciousness'.

During much of the 1980s and the 1990s ISKCON were involved in a series of complicated legal disputes. These were primarily with the local council, but also with the national government, taking their sense of a violated freedom of religion to every available court including the European Court of Human Rights in Strasbourg. Despite a number of legal defeats, ISKCON finally achieved their goal in 1996 of having Bhaktivedanta Manor given full planning permission as a place of public worship, following a proposal to construct a new access driveway to the temple which bypassed the narrow lanes of the local village. With this road now in place ISKCON have finally achieved a secure base at Bhaktivedanta Manor, and the Manor is a major site for pilgrimage for all Hindus across Britain.

This dispute focused on a particular religious building, belonging to a rather small (albeit well known) religious group. In many respects it was a quite unspectacular case of litigation proceeding in the main through the normal channels of English planning law. However, the dispute went far beyond the small number of residents at the Manor: it brought in a population of Hindus in Britain numbering up to half a million, it involved a legal dispute that attempted to test the place of religious liberty within British law, it provided the first instance of a criminal prosecution in England for religious worship for several centuries, and it was only resolved in the mid nineties following intense lobbying at the national political level. In these respects, as well as a number of others, it provides an interesting and enticing case study for examining a number of issues within the study of religiosity in contemporary Britain.

Locating minority religious groups in multiculturalism

The extended analysis of the Bhaktivedanta Manor dispute which I am offering in this book opens up some very significant areas of debate within areas of contemporary British cultural identity and practice. ISKCON's campaign touched upon issues such as religious freedom and basic human rights, the place of 'new religious' organisations, multiculturalism and diversity, and in particular the ways in which the British nation-state responds to and implements these issues through legislation such as planning policies. ISKCON argued that they had a *right* to freedom of religion, to free access for their devotees to worship in the place of their choice, and that within a *multicultural* and tolerant society the state should make allowances for cultural and religious diversity. As it happened, despite a significant lack of any policy or legislative framework for implementing either of these two ideals, ISKCON were eventually successful in their challenge, winning their case *because* they were a religious minority group.

Very soon after the resolution of the Bhaktivedanta Manor campaign, however, a significant shift in the British political landscape resulted in a fundamental constitutional change: Tony Blair's new Labour government introduced legislation in 1997 for the incorporation of the European Convention on Human Rights (ECHR) into British law. This *Human Rights Act 1998* (HRA) meant that (following its full implementation in 2000) it would become possible for British citizens to appeal within British courts if they considered a public authority to have violated any of the freedoms set out in the ECHR. Prior to this Act, the ways in which religious practice (particularly among those regarded as minority or non-mainstream) has been dealt with by the courts has been remarkably ad hoc and unspecific – apart from the well contested blasphemy laws which overtly privilege the Anglican Christianity of the Established Church of England (and exclude other religious groups). The ECHR, however, has a specific article which outlines the principle that 'everyone has the right to freedom of expression, conscience, and religion' (Article 9), and so puts issues of religiosity quite explicitly into legal discourses in Britain. Although the ways in which the ECHR and the HRA will actually be interpreted by the judiciary have yet to be determined, this development could create a significant change in legal and cultural discourses over the place of religion in contemporary British life. What is fairly certain is that it will provide a public forum in which many of the debates about religious pluralism and practice will be closely scrutinised and most likely change.

Anticipating some of these debates, I argue that questions of what is actually meant by 'religion' (both within the general public discourses on religious liberty, as well as within the particular legal interpretation of Article 9 of the ECHR) needs to be discussed and re-evaluated. One purpose of this book is to open up a particular debate: by asking what exactly it is that needs to (or should) be protected by Article 9. That is, I do not wish to put forward or discuss any particular definition of religion as such, but rather I am arguing that the processes of using the term 'religion' to distinguish particular types of activity, practice, and organisation come out of political strategies that could be made more transparent by rethinking the basic terms of the equation. Rather than articulating the debate in terms of which groups are 'religions' or 'religious' (and thus creating 'league-tables' of 'religions' which include and exclude on political and theological criteria), the interpretation of the ECHR should instead work on an assumption of religion as practice which makes clear the implicit idea that such practice is privileged by law as a public good, unless such practice can be shown to be otherwise. Thus within such a framework, for example, the widespread discussions (in Britain and elsewhere) of whether the Church of Scientology should be classified 'as a religion' could be reconfigured into a less theological debate which does not get bogged down in questions about the 'beliefs' and teaching of the group ('are they theistic of not?'), nor indeed whether the commercial activities of the organisation undermine its claims to qualify for the status of a 'religion' ('is it a religion *or* a business?'). Instead, the questions that should be asked revolve around whether the practices of Scientology are substantially of enough public benefit for the organisation to be given certain privileges, such as the protections outlined in Article 9 of the ECHR. I am not suggesting that this makes the processes of decision making any simpler, but it does, I think, make the political nature of majoritarian decision making a little bit more transparent, instead of (as currently often seems to happen) cultural, religious, and political prejudices being hidden behind seeming abstract and neutral questions of definition of the term religion.

The focus of this book on ISKCON very much locates the material within the academic (mainly sociological) debates about new religious movements (or 'NRMS'). Although this is perhaps unavoidable, one of my intentions in this volume is to challenge this all-to-easy classification, but in terms which I think open up the issues that I am discussing to a wider audience. Academic debate on the 'Hare Krishnas' usually takes place within discussion of a list of a number of other 'similar' new religious groups (such as the Unification Church, The Family, Brahma Kumaris, Neo-Pagans, New Agers, and indeed the Church of Scientology, etc.), and one result of such a classification is that discourses on these groups are often removed or separated from another set of discourses on ethnic minority religious groups (i.e. those who are identified in some way as Hindus, Sikhs, or Muslims, etc.). Many of those who are identified with the latter category are 'new' just as much as those which are labelled as NRMS, even though they may predominantly be groupings that resulted from large scale migration rather than conversion.

Discussion of ISKCON does sometimes cross-over this divide, so that the participation of Hindus of Indian ancestry within ISKCON in Britain (and elsewhere) has been acknowledged by a number of writers. But I argue that the fact ISKCON steps over this divide highlights a flaw in academic attempts to categorise (into NRMS/ethnic religions). It is certainly true that there may be sociological differences between religious groups that have formed following conversion and those that were created following migration/transplantation and settlement. Thus sociologically there are some generic differences between (mainly ethnically white) alternative religiosities and (mainly minority ethnic) religiosities such as British forms of Islam. But the sociological differences within each of these categories are equally important, and if any particular sociological distinction needs to be emphasised it is that *all* of these are social, religious and cultural *alternatives* and *minorities*. At the same time, though, it is not at all clear *what* they are alternatives to. But the plurality between and within practitioners and groups is probably more significant than any dividing line based on colour (which is indeed what seems to mark out NRMs from ethnic religion). Indeed the academic tendency to allow this (one could say apartheid) distinction seems to foster a divide and rule approach which encourages states to favour some groups (such as Sikhs and Jews, and Hindus – as this case shows), while disadvantaging others such as Moonies, Scientologists, other 'cults', and – to a certain extent – Muslims).

The most obvious framework which this could be placed within, therefore, is that of multiculturalism, and it appears to me that one of the challenges faced both by the judges who make the case law on the HRA and academics who write about new and alternative forms of religiosity is to determine how and where diversity of religious groups and practices can be located within the politics of multiculturalism. The ideology of multiculturalism (which extends ambiguously into multireligiosity, or religious plurality) is one reason why certain religious organisations (and individuals) are favoured more than others. In terms of 'race' or 'ethnicity' British law (through the *Race Relations Act 1976*) has allowed a favouring of religious groups which are clearly identified as 'racial' or 'ethnic' (particularly Sikhs and Jews) over others (particularly Muslims). Many 'cults' or 'NRMs' are indeed quite ethnically homogenous (that is, predominantly white), yet have likewise failed to find protection under race relations legislation. 'New' religious groups have managed to make this situation work for them, particularly ISKCON who decided to play the 'race' card by stressing their Indian support over and against the stereotyping of them as an NRM. But this only became possible for them because of their substantial following of people from 'non-white' backgrounds.

The politics of multiculturalism creates an ambiguous set of discourses, making it unclear where religious groups should or could fit in – mainly because of a static and essentialistic view of the cultures that make up cultural diversity. The HRA could provide a means by which this is challenged, since it is assumed that free religious practice should allow religious as well as cultural diversity. But this would have fairly limited consequences if a static view of cultures becomes bound up with a static and essentialistic view of religions. In this case, the multireligionism that is produced becomes a matter of recognising different religions, with the implication that some religions can be included in this recognition whilst others are excluded. I argue that both culture and religion need to be thought through further: to consider practice in a more fluid sense, and so the politics of recognition becomes a matter of accepting a diversity of fluid religious identities, configurations, and practices. Thus I would like to stress my earlier point that such a multicultural perspective does not result in the production of league tables of religious groups, or rigid classifications (not to say academic empires) such as NRMs v. ethnic religions. The questions that academics should be asking about locating religion in multiculturalism are not so much related to where a particular religious group should be mapped within a particular multicultural situation, but rather which political interests are produced and maintained by particular discourses of multiculturalism and religious diversity.

The ISKCON case that I discuss in this book shows how certain elements of British legal processes are extremely ambiguous with regard to place and placing of religious groups and practices. That is, the 'planning system' is part of the mechanism of state control over the use of land and buildings, and thus is a crucial part of regulation of the state by a wide range of social and individual activities. Minority religious practices can be extremely curtailed by planning regulations: collective or public worship at a particular place is subject to permission by the state (that is through the granting of planning permission for a place to be used for worship). In ISKCON's case the problem was eventually resolved in their favour, but only after more than fifteen years of legal disputes, which entailed considerable expense on the part of both ISKCON and the local authority with which they were in conflict. This in itself raises the question of whether or not the planning system can be made more applicable to a political landscape in which there is obvious multicultural diversity, and more generally, of how do the discourses of planning effect and shape the practices which planners have the power to control.

Although this book is about ISKCON, a large part of the discussion is using the case study of ISKCON's campaign and experiences as a starting point for examining these general questions of how scholars (and others) should think about issues of religious diversity and multiculturalism. But I am also seeking to examine in this book the changes that have happened within ISKCON in Britain (and more widely as an international movement) through the experiences of this campaign. In the remainder of this chapter I will pursue such an examination of where ISKCON have come from, and how they have developed, whilst in Part Two of the book I will look in depth at how ISKCON and their supporters dealt with the threat of closure of Bhaktivedanta Manor and the specific issues thrown up along the path they travelled to 'save the temple'.

History of ISKCON

The International Society for Krishna Consciousness is simultaneously a *new* religious organisation, and part of an ancient religious tradition. For years ISKCON have striven to dissociate themselves from the label of 'new religion' (or NRM), but the roots of the movement within their present (predominantly western) context do not go back much more than thirty years, to 1965. In that year, a sixty nine year old Bengali holy man, called A.C. Bhaktivedanta Swami Prabhupada made a passage to New York from India with the express purpose of introducing to the USA the teachings and devotional practices of the Gaudiya Math (which follows the Vaishnava tradition formulated by the sixteenth century mystic Chaitanya).[1] Prabhupada had for many years followed a life of devotion and service to these teachings in India (particularly in the north Indian town of Vrindaban), waiting for the opportunity to fulfil the instructions of his own guru Bhaktisiddhanta Saraswati to take the message of Chaitanya to the west. These instructions themselves were an encouragement to Prabhupada to enable the fulfilment of the prophesy by Chaitanya that one day the name of Krishna would be said in 'every town and village' (Brooks 1989:82; Goswami 1983:42–44). On arriving in the USA, therefore, he worked hard to introduce this message to the people he met, and soon he gathered a group of young men and women into a religious group which he incorporated as the organisation ISKCON in 1966. This *international* organisation, with himself at its head, gradually developed and spread from New York first to San Francisco to other major cities in north America, and then onto Europe. Administration of the growing movement was transferred in 1972 to a group of twelve important devotees called the Governing Body Commission (GBC).[2] Very soon before Prabhupada's death in 1977 he separately initiated eleven 'initiating gurus', who were to take on elements of the spiritual leadership of the movement after he had departed (Knott 1986:37–40, Shinn 1987:48–50).

In the short space of time between Prabhupada's arrival in New York in 1965 as an almost penniless religious preacher from India, and his death twelve years later, he succeeded in attracting thousands of new devotees – mostly from white western backgrounds – to his religious outlook. In doing this he achieved something which was radically new and quite unique: the creation through conversion of a Hindu derived religious community, spanning a number of western countries, with high levels of orthodoxy and practice. In one sense Prabhupada merely intended to internationalise the Gaudiya Math, the religious movement in India to which he belonged, taking it beyond the ethnic, cultural, and geographical constraints that linked it to a certain part of India (Bengal) and to those who were born as 'Hindus'. But in doing so he created a new group, a new religious organisation, albeit as something that was derived from a tradition that went back much further than 1965.

Prabhupada's attachment and devotion to Gaudiya Vaishnavism derived from developments in eastern India (particularly Bengal and Orissa) in the late nineteenth century. At that time Bhaktivinod Thakur, a civil servant and judge who had been educated in English medium missionary schools, worked very prominently to revive the devotional tradition of the sixteenth century mystic Chaitanya Mahaprabhu. Chaitanya, who was considered to be an *avatar* (incarnation) of the supreme deity Krishna left a tradition of spiritual succession (*parampara*) after his death which continued down to the nineteenth century, but was very much in decline at the time of

Bhaktivinod. Through his writing and teaching, Bhaktivinod not only revived this spiritual lineage and created an effective organisation to propagate the teachings and practices of Chaitanya, in doing so he also provided a religious response which was appropriate to the context of the colonial world in which he and other Bengalis lived. His success came partly from his ability to use the technology and organisational culture that had been introduced to India by the British colonialists – using the printing press for reproducing ancient religious texts, and a magazine for the exposition of religious ideas. In doing so, he recreated the Chaitanya tradition for his modern era, providing an intellectual and practical response to the significant cultural and religious changes that had been imposed onto Bengali culture through colonial rule. In this sense, Bhaktivinod effected a religious reform in eastern India that was comparable to the achievements of other religious leaders of his time in other parts of India, such as Swami Dayanand creation of the Arya Samaj in northern India (see Jones 1976). Unlike Dayanand, however, Bhaktivinod saw his role as an exponent of the teachings of a relatively recent predecessor (that is, Chaitanya) and thus he did not attempt to be innovative with philosophy and theology but instead sought innovative means of getting that message across to a new generation and a new social context.

Following Bhaktivinod Thakur's death in 1914, his son Bhaktisiddanta Saraswati took over the role of spiritual leader of this revival of Gaudiya Vaishnavism. One very important development instituted by Bhaktisiddanta was the creation in 1918 of an actual organisation, the Gaudiya Math, which would be the vehicle for the religious teachings and revival brought about by his father. It was Bhaktisiddhanta who introduced Prabhupada (or Abhay Charan De, as he was then called) to the movement in 1922, giving him the instructions to take Krishna consciousness to the west (in fact he sent, unsuccessfully, other disciples to England and Germany in the 1930s with a similar mission). However, when Bhaktisiddanta Saraswati died in 1937 he left no obvious spiritual heir to be the head of the Gaudiya Math. As a result a bitter and unresolved battle ensued between a number of senior religious leaders in the organisation, each trying to assume overall control. Prabhupada himself was not a party to this power struggle, but his experience of it from within the Gaudiya Math taught him a strong lesson in the potential problems of redistributing authority within an organisation that had no obvious historical precedents.

Having taken initiation in 1932 from his spiritual master Bhaktisiddhanta, and then later renouncing world attachments in 1956, Prabhupada (under the name of Bhaktivedanta) lived in the holy city of Vrindaban in Uttar Pradesh for a number of years, a place which was not only strongly associated with the human manifestation of Krishna, but was also a major centre of the Gaudiya Math, having been rediscovered by Chaitanya in the sixteenth century. In Vrindaban, Prabhupada prepared himself for his goal of taking Krishna consciousness to the English speaking world, setting up a magazine called *Back to Godhead*, and working on translations and commentaries of important Gaudiya Vaishnava sacred texts, such as the *Bhagavad Gita* and the *Bhagavata Purana*. Eventually in 1965 he managed to persuade the director of the Bombay based Scindia Steamship Company to allow him a free passage on the freight ship Jaladuta to New York, and this was how (despite having two small heart attacks whilst on board) he finally arrived in the USA to begin his mission and found ISKCON.

ISKCON in Britain

In 1968 Prabhupada sent six of his disciples to London to set up a mission and eventually a temple for Krishna consciousness. These devotees managed to make contact with the pop group the Beatles, and they spent some time in the company particularly of John Lennon and George Harrison (Knott 1987:33–37; Goswami 1983:158–174). In 1969 Harrison helped ISKCON devotees to record the Hare Krishna *mahamantra*,[3] which soon became a pop chart success. Perhaps a more significant achievement by these early founders of Krishna consciousness in Britain was the establishment of a temple in Bury Place, central London. This temple, situated in a small flat, was dedicated to Krishna and his consort in the form of Radha Londoniswara. This, in fact, was one of the first Hindu temples to be created in Britain, and it was formally dedicated by Prabhupada on his first trip to Britain in September 1969.

During the early 1970s Krishna consciousness grew in Britain, where it had a high public profile following the early support given to it by the Beatles, and also because of the prominent religious activities of its devotees. They took their message to the streets of London (and other cities) in the form of dancing, chanting, and book selling (a tradition inaugurated by Chaitanya in sixteenth century Bengal, and which had been successfully put to practice by ISKCON devotees in New York, San Francisco, and elsewhere).

The foundation of Bhaktivedanta Manor

In 1973 it became possible for the movement to create a new temple in the London area, when George Harrison decided to donated a large building which could be adapted for such use. He enlisted the help of some ISKCON devotees, and eventually they decided to take on a mock-Tudor house called Piggotts Manor in a small country village called Letchmore Heath near Watford in Hertfordshire. This house, which was built in 1884, had in previous years (since 1948) been used as a nurses' training college by St Bartholomew's hospital (of central London). The surroundings of the

Manor were a very tranquil village in the heart of an area protected by government Green Belt policy to ensure it retained a rural character, despite its location on the fringe of the urban sprawl. Indeed, its location within the upper middle class commuter belt only fifteen miles north west of London made it a very popular residential area and therefore under great pressure for development. Such factors were not considered too important by ISKCON at the time that they took over the house. This was a donation that they felt was too good to turn down: a large house that was very convenient for London but also set in idyllic surroundings which were very conducive to meditation.

The house was renamed Bhaktivedanta Manor in honour of the movement's founder, who used it regularly when he visited Britain. In fact, Prabhupada chose it as the base for his final visit to Europe before his death in 1977. The Manor was intended to become a centre for the training of devotees, not only into the complex philosophy of Gaudiya Vaishnavism, but also into the fine details of the rituals associated with the maintenance of the growing number of ISKCON temples throughout the world (such as the one in central London). In the words of Prabhupada 'the Society's aim is to build men and women of character and knowledge'.[4] What Bhaktivedanta Manor was effectively intended to become was a *math*, a place of religious teaching and spiritual development.

Therefore the building was converted to accommodate these needs of the movement. Rooms were set aside as dormitories for the students who came to the college, teaching and meditation rooms, a *gurukul* (school) for the children of the teaching staff, a kitchen and dining area. Importantly, two adjacent rooms were also given over to a temple where deities were to be worshipped. In Hindu traditions there is usually such a temple in all homes, that is a place where members of a family can worship together each day. In a theological college it was therefore natural that such provisions be made for the students to worship.

To this end, therefore, statues carved by skilled craftsmen in Jaipur, Rajasthan were brought over from India and the traditional dedication rituals of *murti stapana* and *pran pratishta* were performed on them by Prabhupada himself. In doing so, these statues were permanently 'placed' within the temple, and 'breath' (*pran*) was infused in them to give them life. That is, the statues (*murtis*) were made to become living embodiments of the Deities, who forever after should be given the greatest respect by their devotees.

For ISKCON the supreme god is Krishna, who is manifest in many forms such as the person Krishna (who taught the *Bhagavad Gita*, one of the most influential Hindu religious texts), Ram, and Chaitanya himself. Lord Krishna as the one single god (the Supreme Personality of Godhead) is also comprised of a female part, Radha, and it is these two figures together that ISKCON devotees usually worship, as Radha-Krishna. When Radha-Krishna become physically manifest in temples as *murtis* they take a particular embodied form which is localised to the temple and the area (*dham*) around it. The *murtis* that Prabhupada ritually installed into the temple within Bhaktivedanta Manor took the form of two statues of Radha and Gokulananda (the latter being a form of Krishna). Therefore the worship by devotees at the theological college was to be directed in a personal manner towards the supreme god Krishna through the particular embodied forms of Radha-Gokulananda. Such an idea may appear confusing to the reader, and gives the impression of what is otherwise known as polytheism. But the school of philosophy to which ISKCON belongs places a strong emphasis on conceptualising a single, monotheistic deity (unlike some other strands of Hindu tradition), and the worship of Krishna in forms such as Radha-Gokulananda does not compromise this idea. Indeed, it is considered by devotees to give expression to it.[5]

Following the installation of these deities, it became imperative that the daily activities of the Manor should include regular worship of the deities, to show them the respect and devotion that they deserve as manifestations of god. Through assisting in the numerous acts of devotion that take place in the temple throughout the day between 3.45am and 10.30pm devotees learn the complexities of such actions, and after a number of years become skilled *pujaris*, who are then learned and responsible enough to be temple priests. The standard of this training for serving the needs of the *murtis* is very high, and the authenticity of the worship is scrupulous – following the principles set down in the sixteenth century by Sanatan Goswami (a follower of Chaitanya) in the work called *Hari Bhakti-Vilas*, which was itself based on the classical scripture called *Narada Pancaratra* (AdPE:37).

Therefore the Manor required the presence of these deities for it to be an effective 'theological college' for the training of Krishna conscious 'priests'. Once they were installed as *murtis*, these deities needed to be continually worshipped by residents at the Manor. The perceived high standard of service by devotees to these murtis has made the temple a very significant place for many Hindus. It is felt that the continual service to Radha-Gokulananda which has been performed throughout the day, every day of the year, for over twenty five years has made these deities show great favour on those who take such trouble. The significance of this development will be considered later, since it is a very important element in the popularity of the temple.

In short, Bhaktivedanta Manor was intended to be a place of great spiritual importance for the ISKCON movement right from the time of its foundation as a theological college in 1973. Not only would new converts to the movement receive training in the scriptures and teachings of Krishna consciousness, they would also become highly trained priests, capable of serving the needs of the *murtis* in the growing number of temples that Prabhupada was establishing throughout the world. On a more local level, the temple at the heart of the college would become a space in which great spiritual power was felt to be manifest – and although this was primarily to be the domain of the immediate users of the college (staff and students) would not necessarily be limited to them.

Post-samadhi ISKCON

For most people, both within and outside of ISKCON, there are two very distinct phases of the development of the movement: that is, the years when Prabhupada was alive and in control of ISKCON, and the subsequent years in which existing and new devotees had to come to terms with his lack of presence. The continuities and discontinuities between these stages have produced a large part of the dynamics of ISKCON at the international level, as well as particularly within Britain. It would be speculation to suggest that the development of ISKCON in Britain would have been much different if Prabhupada had remained alive and actively leading the movement beyond the time of his death in 1977. In particular it is impossible to know if the conflict over the Manor could have been averted or avoided if he had been able to make an intervention, or even whether he would have thought it wise to support such a long running and potentially negative campaign. What can be argued more confidently, however, is that the organisation of ISKCON within Britain has been very much shaped by developments within the movement that have sprung directly and indirectly from Prabhupada's death, and a number of these developments have helped to feed into how the campaign has been presented as well as fought.

At the highest level of ISKCON, the loss of Prabhupada left a very obvious gap within the leadership of what was then a very new organisation. Although his declining health in the months before his actual demise helped to prepare his closest followers, it was inevitable that the actual physical loss of Prabhupada would transform the movement. ISKCON depended to a very large extent on his enterprise and ability, and so for it to survive and continue to grow devotees had to find new ways of relating to Prabhupada's teachings and incorporating his charisma. Prabhupada had himself been aware of the potential for disaster that his death would create: he had after all seen fission and dispute overwhelm the Gaudiya Math following the death of Bhaktisiddhanta Saraswati. According to Prabhupada's secretary Tamal Krishna Goswami

> Prabhupada's solitary voyage to the West was as much due to his disgust at seeing his guru's institution [the Gaudiya Math] fracture as to the missionary order he had received from him. He was determined that the society he formed would not repeat the failure of succession that had befallen the mission of his guru. But given the strangeness of his religious and cultural message as well as the youth of his first

> followers, the same problems of succession were practically inevitable. (T.K Goswami 1997:14–15)

Prabhupada resolved that no single person should take over his role as spiritual leader of ISKCON, and that instead this very difficult task should be shared by a number of core devotees (eleven in total) who would assume the status of 'initiating gurus'. Alongside this, the Governing Body Commission (GBC) would be the administrative and legislative head of the organisation, although there were no clear guidelines for how the initiating gurus and the GBC should share power over the movement as a whole. In fact, all of the eleven gurus were people who had been brought into ISKCON after his arrival in the US, and so none had more than eleven years of devotional service, and were on the whole still quite emotionally immature, as well as having fairly limited experience of what was expected of them as Vaishnavite leaders. The failures of a significant number of these gurus is well known: Jayatirtha in Britain was dismissed in 1982 for advocating the use of LSD and sex as means of spiritual development; Hamsadutta in western USA raised money through arms dealing; and Kirtananda in West Virginia was implicated in murder, as well as arms smuggling, drug dealing, and illegal merchandising. Alongside this, each of the eleven gurus took responsibility for certain geographical areas, in which they assumed complete spiritual authority. This 'zonal acharya system' created a series of blocs within ISKCON, each of which acted as a separate movement, and which if left unchecked could have led to a breaking down of ISKCON into these constituent units. Furthermore, as the only centralising organisation of ISKCON, the GBC, was dominated by the zonal/initiating gurus there were no checks in the system to prevent such a break up.

It took until the mid 1980s, when a revolt from a lower level of devotees (mainly temple presidents in north America) forced the GBC to face up to the danger of disintegration, with the result that in 1987 the organisation of ISKCON was radically changed (see T.K. Goswami 1997:24; R.S. das 1994). The number of initiating gurus was considerably expanded, as was the membership of the GBC, and the 'zonal system' was broken down, with gurus being allowed to initiate in any part of the globe where they were requested. Together with the interventions that the GBC had been forced to make with Hamsadutta, Jayatirtha, and Bhagwan, these developments created a power structure within ISKCON where the authority of each guru was not absolute, but was in fact 'tied to the GBC, thus re-establishing Prabhupada, through the GBC, as the head of ISKCON' (T.K. Goswami 1997:24). Thus the transfer of power following Prabhupada's death was not a straightforward guru to guru(s) transmission – as had indeed been the expectation of many of his followers. Instead it was (eventually) a process of routinising his charismatic authority into the bureaucratic institution of the GBC, which would be the only effective machinery for preventing the disintegration that had occurred within the Gaudiya Math following Bhaktisiddhanta's death.

Although such a process sounds simple and relatively routine, Prabhupada was faced with the major problem that the organisation that he had created was (at all levels) inexperienced and underdeveloped, and so was more than likely to make mistakes as it tried to manage this change after his death. The decisions that he took, and the instructions that he gave, are now considered by most devotees to be the best that he do with the rather inadequate human resources he had at his disposal. Such a viewpoint does, of course, give a rationalisation for what could otherwise be seen as Prabhupada's mistakes. According to Ravindra Svarup das, an initiate of Prabhupada, and one of the leading players in the 1980s reform movement (and now one of ISKCON's leading contemporary scholars):

> We can be sure that [Prabhupada] knew his own disciples better than they themselves; he had no illusions about their spiritual qualifications. Yet they were pressing for a selection of successor gurus, the ultimate position to the ambitious ... Yet Srila Prabhupada clearly did not want to give his sanction to unfit people, a spiritual error. So he selected them without endorsing them ... He expected them to become 'regular gurus' in the future, but there was no 'hand-picking of successors', no laying on of hands or anointing with oil ... He also knew that some, like Kirtananda, would initiate with or without his sanction, so he named them. If not there would likely have been a schism in 1978 instead of 1987. To me, Srila Prabhupada's solution was brilliant, the best that could have been done under the circumstances. The result would depend on Krishna. (R.S. das 1994:32).

In Britain the problems continued after the dismissal of Jayatirtha: the guru who was found to replace him, Bhagwan Maharaj, brought back a measure of calm and confidence for a few years, but was then himself dismissed for (mainly sexual) misconduct in 1986. One result of Bhagwan's removal was that many devotees who had been initiated by him were left feeling that not only had they been betrayed by their spiritual master, but even their initiations as Krishna followers were invalid. A significant number (but by no means all) left the movement rather than face the pain of choosing whether to continue under these circumstances or finding a new spiritual master to put their trust into. Meanwhile Jayatirtha attempted to create a reformed Krishna consciousness movement, advocating the use of narcotic drugs as a means of achieving spiritual liberation. However, in 1988 one of his disgruntled followers decided that Jayatirtha had gone too far and murdered his one time spiritual master by beheading him in the back room of a shop in north London. By this time Jayatirtha and his followers were clearly separate from ISKCON, and so the negative publicity produced by this bizarre and gruesome death did not become too strongly associated with the mainstream ISKCON organisation. But Jayatirtha's death, following fairly soon after Bhagwan's dismissal and of course's Jayatirtha's own fall from power, all created an atmosphere of despondency and perpetual crisis in the movement from which devotees have spent much of the 1990s trying to get away.[6]

Reconstructing ISKCON in Britain

Prabhupada's death, along with the failures of his successors, thus impinged very much both sociologically and psychologically on devotees. Alongside this, however, there were slower and less dramatic developments within ISKCON as devotees began to explore new and alternative ways to make Krishna consciousness and Gaudiya Vaishnavism work for them within the particular British or other non-Indian contexts. It seems that it gradually became clear to devotees that the model of Krishna consciousness that they had envisaged (or imagined) at the time of initial conversion needed to be contextualised within a wide and very rich picture of social development that was rooted in Bengali society and Hindu/Vaishnavite theology and philosophy. The task of transplanting this beyond India to create a sustainable religious organisation was something that Prabhupada had only just been able to begin. The challenge was for his spiritual successors to make it work for themselves. The responses that ISKCON leaders evolved were to become an integral part of the campaign to keep open the Manor, which involved remaining true to Prabhupada's directions, the wider Gaudiya tradition, and also the contemporary needs of ISKCON in the here-and-now. The most obvious manifestations of these changes were the development of ISKCON as a communal and congregational as well as a monastic organisation and the increasing emphasis on communication and public presentation of Krishna consciousness to the 'outside world'. Both of these factors were pivotal to the successful conclusion of the campaign for the Manor.

The obvious question that arises is whether or not the ISKCON of 1990s Britain – which fought and won the campaign – was the same as, or comparable with the ISKCON that was first created in New York in 1966. How much was the early ISKCON (particularly from 1966 through to 1975) a true reflection of what Prabhupada intended, and how much has it come to be truer to his vision after his death? On first registering ISKCON in 1966 Prabhupada laid out the principal aims of the movement as such:

1. to systematically propagate spiritual knowledge to society at large, to educate all people in the techniques of spiritual life in order to check the imbalance of values in life and to achieve real unity and peace in the world.

2. to propagate a consciousness of Krishna as He is revealed in the Bhagavad-Gita and Srimad-Bhagavatam.
3. to bring the members of the Society together with each other and nearer to Krishna, the Prime Entity, thus to develop the idea within the members and humanity at large that each soul is part and parcel of the quality of Godhead, Krishna.
4. to teach and encourage the sankirtana movement, congregational chanting of the holy name of God, revealed in the teachings of Lord Sri Caitanya Mahaprabhu.
5. to erect for the members and the society at large a holy place of transcendental pastimes dedicated to the Personality of Krishna.
6. to bring the members closer together for the purpose of teaching a simpler and more natural way of life.
7. with a view towards achieving the aforementioned purposes to publish and distribute periodicals, magazines, books, and other literature.

Prabhupada saw the world (western countries, and his own native India) as very much bound up with a pursuit of (and devotion to) materialism, which he framed as attachment to *maya*, or illusion. The purpose of Krishna consciousness, as set out by Chaitanya and the Vaishnava tradition, was to develop a rich spiritual life that led the individual soul 'back to Godhead'. Through service and devotion individuals could overcome their attachment to the material world (and to their material bodies) and let their souls return to their rightful home, to the supreme deity Krishna. This could only be achieved through effective preaching and teaching, and through an organisation which could allow such teaching to reach across the globe. This organisation also needed to be robust enough to take in and direct those devotees who were introduced to Krishna through the teaching programme. Thus ISKCON was to be the social means by which Krishna consciousness could be taken to 'all people' and in doing so (it was expected) the world would be transformed.

In effect, this produced a collectivity that was on one level extremely outward looking. ISKCON started as, and has remained, a strongly missionary religious group, and it is Krishna devotees' activities as preachers and missionaries that have given them such a recognisable profile. Devotees are expected to literally get out onto the streets and convince non-devotees of the significance of the message of Krishna, by exposition, by example (through chanting and dancing), and also through the sale of Krishna consciousness literature (mainly the commentaries and translations written by Prabhupada). As a religious community who were brought together by conversion, ISKCON devotees derived a sense of imperative to extend their religious grace to others and to go out and change the world. Ironically, however, despite this outward orientation, the culture of ISKCON in many countries developed a strongly exclusive and insular attitude, considering those in the 'outside world' to be so enmeshed in *maya* and materialism as to be beyond Krishna's grace.[7] Thus although *harinam* (book selling or distribution) and *sankirtan* (public performances of religious chanting and dancing) took devotees into direct contact with non-devotees, Krishna followers developed a strong sense of their own unique spiritual place in the world, and tended to categorise others as *karmis*, that is as people so bound up with their bodies and the fruits of their non-Krishna oriented actions to be unable to appreciate the truth and importance of Prabhupada's and Chaitanya's message.

It was because of this institutional culture that Roy Wallis chose to include ISKCON within his typology of 'world rejecting' in his influential monograph *The Elementary Forms of the New Religious Life* (Wallis 1984). Indeed, ISKCON appeared to be have become one of the classic examples of a 'new religious' group in the west who set themselves up in distinction to 'the world', that is to mainstream society and culture. The external and internal message of ISKCON was that 'the world' was a dangerous place, and that the teachings and practices of Krishna consciousness should take the devotee away from the material and harmful things of the world, to true spiritual bliss and enlightenment. Thus the expectations of devotee practice, such as early rising at four o'clock each morning, a vegetarian diet, intense chanting of the *mahamantra* each day, and particularly the four regulative principles (no gambling, no intoxicants, no flesh eating, and no illicit sex), all seemed to take away from the devotee, and set her/him up against, the pleasures and rewards of contemporary culture.

The intense lifestyles of devotees also required institutional support, so devotees were expected to live (usually unmarried) in temple dormitories, where they would almost constantly serve Krishna and spend their time in the company of other devotees (even, or especially, when out in public doing *sankirtan* and *harinam*). Thus devotees would live a life of seclusion from 'the world', despite their requirement to change the world by taking part in it. This strong orientation of 'world rejection' was a predominant element of ISKCON life for many years, both during the time of Prabhupada, and for more than a decade after his death. It was not altogether encouraged by Prabhupada, whose activities in the late 1960s showed an intensity of interaction with 'the world', such as through the contemporary alternative culture (counter culture) of the time – interacting with significant figures such as Allen Ginsberg, John Lennon, and George Harrison. Prabhupada, and indeed many devotees themselves, had an extremely ambivalent attitude to 'the world', which is somewhat glossed over by Wallis' typology (1984) – they wanted to transform all people, and to bring 'real unity and peace in the world', but at the same time seemed to despair of doing anything more than recruiting enough devotees to maintain the movement. From the late 1960s to the mid 1980s it was certainly very difficult for devotees to live a life of Krishna consciousness anywhere but in a residential temple community. But at a later stage, in the 1980s, these same devotees still found it relatively straightforward to change their attitudes and living conditions when they chose to move out from the temples to go and live *and* work 'outside', in 'the world'.

This shift in the development of ISKCON – what one of their leading British thinkers Rasamandala das has labelled as a shift from 'the temple to the congregation' (R. das 1994) – is perhaps one of the most important sociological changes that has occurred within ISKCON. On one level the shift reflected the maturation of a significant number of devotees. They found that as they matured, married, and their families grew it became more and more difficult to live the intense life of the temple, and so decided that a move to more independent accommodation would be the most effective way of maintaining their Krishna conscious lifestyle. However, the shift of emphasis to 'the congregation' was also a response to a related but rather distinct development, that is the increasing number of people who had lived for a time as 'full time' temple devotees, and who had decided to leave ISKCON but who still kept in touch on an occasional basis. For a long time, these occasional worshippers were considered by those within the temple as bad as any other *karmis* who did not live in the temple,[8] but as the years went on the congregation of former devotees still wishing to attend ISKCON temples grew larger and larger. What had been clear from the very early days of the movement was that although recruitment rates could be extremely high, drop out rates could also run at the same levels, as many who initially found a great deal of satisfaction in the life in the temple 'blooped' and chose to leave.[9] But many of these drop-outs still felt a strong attachment to the ideals of Krishna consciousness, and so wished to remain in touch with their local temple. It was the demographic growth of this new congregation of 'part time' devotees (which for many years went unnoticed, or was deliberately ignored), which played such a strong role in the eventual recognition of an ISKCON congregation that extended beyond the immediate vicinity of the temples. A particular motivating factor behind this recognition, beyond the maturity and skills which many of these congregational devotees could bring to their temple, was the fact that many were in salaried employment ('in the world'), and so were potential financial benefactors who could made a strong impression on local temples' budgets.

At the same time as this movement of devotees from the 'core' (temple) to the 'congregation' (life outside the temple), a change in recruitment patterns led to the encouragement of new devotees to remain within their communities, rather than rush to live as *bramacharis* and *bramacharinis* in a temple (R. das 1994:84). New organisations were developed within ISKCON to administer and nurture these new non-temple devotees – initially FOLK (Friends of Lord Krishna), which developed into the Nama Hatta programme, organised on a central basis in Britain, but liaising with individuals and local groups to encourage the practice of Krishna consciousness within the contexts of people's daily lives. These Nama Hatta groups have been a useful means of developing ISKCON in places where there has been no easily accessible temple (as well as serving in some cases as the basis for the development of a temple), and have both acted as a useful form of low level recruitment and as feeders of devotees into more committed core membership. Yet the creation of a fairly autonomous and unsupervised level of devotees in the Nama Hatta groups (in comparison with temple devotees) has not been without its problems, not only in terms of intragroup dynamics and conflicts (c.f. K. das 1994), but also in regard to the question of how temple residents should relate to Krishna followers who manifest a 'lower level' of development and commitment to themselves.

As part of the response to these problems, Rasamandala das (former head of ISKCON Education Services, and head of the Vaishnava Training and Education division) has described a new stage of development of the movement which deals more effectively with the ambiguities of status between the various manifestations of commitment (R. das 1994:88–89). Whilst still accepting the temple devotee community as an important (if not necessarily central) element of the movement, he distinguishes between the neophyte *bramacharis* and *bramacharinis* (who live a monastic lifestyle in temple *ashrams*) from the married and renunciate householder devotees, even if the latter are actively participating in the devotional and practical life of a temple. Such householders are called the 'clergy', and are the mature and spiritually developed members of the community who should take the lead in 'actively spreading Krishna consciousness' to the *bramacharis* and *bramacharinis*, to the congregation, and to the 'outside world'. The role of the congregation is to financially and socially support the temples and core activities of the movement, as well as being the source of new *bramacharis* and *bramacharinis*. However, at the same time the congregation is one of the places where former temple residents should be expected to go following their training in a temple if they decide to not take on a leadership role within the 'clergy'. The crucial principle of this scheme is that 'anyone "joining the temple" (or more precisely the student ashram) does not stay there indefinitely . . . Student life is a temporary allocation . . .' and temples '. . . are places one almost always passes through . . .' for the purposes of training to progress onto full service to Krishna and to ISKCON (ibid.:88).

On one level this model dispels the outsider (anti-cultist) idea of ISKCON temples as 'black holes' where vulnerable youngsters are ensnared by brainwashing and forced to remain forever out of touch with their families and society (unless rescued and deprogrammed by exit counsellors). Instead the expectation is that new recruits live *outside* of temples as part of the congregation for a while (as a 'cooling off period' to prepare them for the demands of temple life), and that their short time as a 'student' (that is, as a *bramachari* or *bramacharini*) will be a three or four year training for a life of active service to Krishna in the world. In this regard, temple communities have a stable layer of functionaries or leaders (the 'clergy') and a transitory student population, and so begin to resemble small residential colleges or universities. In suggesting (and trying to bring about) this change, Rasamandala das is thus attempting to resolve a significant popular misrepresentation of ISKCON as a total (and totalising) institution, whilst at the same time to rationalise current practice and in so doing build up internal organisation and relations that approximate more obviously to what is considered the 'true Vedic' model of *ashramadharma*.[10] On one level, this suggestion is more radical than it may appear, since it attempts to dismantle (or reformulate) the temple structures that were put in place during the era of Prabhupada's leadership, and perhaps even more significantly it is based on the principle that householders should support (financially) *bramacharis* and *bramacharinis*, and not the other way around. For over thirty years of ISKCON history it has been young temple devotees who have generated the primary financial income of the movement, primarily through the distribution (and sale) of Krishna consciousness books and other literature. The requirement to distribute books was strongly endorsed and encouraged by Prabhupada on a number of occasions, and has been a primary element of service by all devotees, helping to spread the message of Krishna as well as generating money for temple support and development.[11] Thus the suggestion that new students should be prevented from (or relieved of) carrying out this duty goes substantially against a central part of ISKCON culture, even though such fund raising produces 'debilitating constraints' on students (ibid.:91 fn29).

It is unlikely that street bookselling will ever be removed entirely from the curriculum of new Krishna students, partly because distribution is such an important part of the group, and it tends to be younger members who have the enthusiasm (and time) for doing this. But what is being called for (and indeed implemented) is a change in emphasis that ensures that the main activity of *bramacharis* and *bramacharinis* is training, and that their time spent at the temple *ashram* is primarily taken up with classes and learning. To this effect, a European Working Party on Vaishnava Training and Education produced a syllabus in 1994 to be implemented at European training colleges (particularly Bhaktivedanta Manor) which gave a systematic programme of introductory, foundational, and advanced/specialised courses with fixed entry dates (VTE 1994, A. das 1994). This syllabus was implemented at Bhaktivedanta Manor that same year (two leading participants in the VTE group, Akhandadhi das and Rasamandala das were also in positions of leadership at the Manor), and has subsequently been the training route of all new devotees in England.

The introduction of the VTE programme has therefore marked a strong shift towards the routinisation of the training of devotees, and is an important element in the development of the organisation and developmental models envisaged for ISKCON by Rasamandala das.

As Kim Knott (n.d.) has noted, this development of the internal organisation and training of devotees has been mirrored largely by a change in the ways in which ISKCON relate to outsiders. That is, from approximately 1985 onwards there has been a growing awareness of the need by ISKCON to effectively communicate with people outside of the movement – not only to put across the message of Krishna consciousness, but also to promote a positive profile of the group and to develop effective and friendly relations with interested parties. Thus the European and English communications offices have taken a pro-active role in contacting media groups and academics; the *ISKCON Communications Journal* has been developed as a significant vehicle for discussion not only between leading ISKCON figures, but also with a wider community;[12] ISKCON have taken a very active role in interfaith dialogue (particularly with Christian groups); and ISKCON Educational Services have built up a strong profile in relation to educationalists at all levels of teaching in British schools and universities. Some of the impetus for the development of this focus on communication has come from the problems they faced in the past, particularly arising from the 'cult' images put on them by diverse media and anti-cultist groups, as well as the need to win the public battle over the future of the Manor (which I will discuss in more depth in later chapters). But, in agreement with Knott, I would also argue that this move into new forms of communication is also something that has been fairly inevitable for a group that was created to communicate a new message to a new audience (that is, Prabhupada's mission to take Krishna consciousness to the west), and is indeed a 1990s development of the process that Bhaktivinod Thakur began when he used British printing presses to produce and publish his Gaudiya Vaishnava literature for late nineteenth century Bengal.

Bhaktivedanta Manor and the Hindu community

Another very substantial component in the development of contemporary ISKCON has been the growing participation of people of Indian ancestry at all levels of the devotional and administrative life of the movement. This has been a gradual process, which has its beginnings in the arrival of ISKCON, and particularly Prabhupada in London in the late 1960s, but which developed particularly with the coinciding of the opening of Bhaktivedanta Manor in 1973 with a wave of migrations of South Asian Indians (many of whom were Hindus) to Britain around that same time from the former British colonies of East Africa.

Women and men from South Asia had begun to settle in East Africa in large numbers at the end of the nineteenth century. Most of them had migrated across the Indian Ocean from Gujarat, on the west coast of India, to take advantage of trading opportunities that were newly opening up with the British expansion into Kenya and then Uganda. The Asians almost followed in the wake of the British, primarily up the line of the Kenya-Uganda railway as it made its way into the hinterland from Mombasa, settling in favourable areas along its route. For example, the city of Nairobi developed with the influx of large numbers of Indian settlers. This large scale migration from India to East Africa, which continued well into the twentieth century, was actively encouraged by the British colonial authorities, who were able to use the Asians as an effective level of middle ranking administration between themselves and the indigenous Africans.[13]

The British colonial encouragement of Indian settlement in East African left the population extremely exposed when these countries gained Independence in the 1960s. Following Independence the new republic of Kenya under the leadership of Jomo Kenyatta followed a policy of 'Africanisation', which sought to place more of the agencies of government, administration, and commerce in the hands of the indigenous Africans (and away from the Asians, who had taken these positions under British rule). This put a great deal of pressure on the Indian communities, and many left Africa during the 1960s in fear of losing their livelihoods. The most dramatic exodus of Asians from Africa, however, occurred in 1972 when President Idi Amin of Uganda ordered that all non-Ugandan passport holding Asians in that country would have to leave within ninety days, taking with them no more than fifty pounds worth of possessions. This expulsion precipitated a major international crisis, as countries across the world were pressured into finding homes for the many thousands of refugees (Twaddle 1975; Melady & Melady 1976).

Rather reluctantly Britain agreed to honour the British passports of a number of these refugees, and in September and October 1972 approximately 28,000 Ugandan Asians arrived in Britain.[14] The policy of the British government was to lessen the impact of such a large number of migrants on the political landscape of post-Enoch Powell Britain,[15] and so there were attempts to prevent concentration of the new arrivals in certain popular 'red' areas where there were already existing Asian populations. Such initiatives generally failed – many made their own way to the areas where their family and friends were living (Kuepper et al. 1975:60–84). One such 'red area' which proved to be extremely popular was north west London, around the areas of Wembley, Willesden, and Harrow. Therefore, in the early 1970s there arrived – almost out of the blue – a large population of Hindus from East Africa in the urban areas within close proximity of Bhaktivedanta Manor.

There is no clear documented evidence to show how or why some of this large concentration of Hindus in north west London began to make use of Bhaktivedanta Manor as a regular place of worship. At that time the facilities for public Hindu worship were very poor – the population of Hindus had only recently arrived and had little money available to spend on temple buildings (Burr 1984:246). The public chanting of white western Hare Krishna devotees on the streets of central London were gaining them attention, as were ISKCON's yearly Rathayatra bullock cart processions through London in which *murtis* were paraded. It is possible that it was through such means that Hindus began to learn about ISKCON, and also of the presence of Bhaktivedanta Manor. This is borne out by a Hindu interviewed by Sean Carey in the mid 80s, who reminisced:

> We first heard of Hare Krishnas in the papers [around 1972]. The police were objecting to them chanting on the street and it was through that that we got to know where the London temple was. I can tell you we were surprised to find such a nice temple. We couldn't believe it. We were very impressed. (Carey 1987:87)

This interest in Bhaktivedanta Manor began very soon after it was founded. Indeed, ISKCON's records show that at the Janmasthami festival in September 1973 (when Prabhupada installed the Radha-Gokulananda deities) there were 'unexpected large attendances'. According to a document on 'Indian community' involvement in ISKCON in Britain, written in 1982:

> When in 1973 invitations were sent out to life members for the first big festival [at the Manor] about a hundred guests were expected, but over a thousand turned up. Chaos reigned on that first Sunday – not enough food, too many cars, no planned order of events. (ICAP)

This occurred again in November that year for Diwali and for those two festivals the following year (AdPE:155). At the Diwali festival in November 1974 there were around 9,000 visitors at the Manor (AgHBC/A:33).

At this time it is very likely that the visitors were curious to see the facilities that the temple had, since the majority of them would have had very little knowledge of the ISKCON tradition. As a modern version of Gaudiya Vaishnavism, the roots of Krishna consciousness in Bengal, on the eastern side of the Indian subcontinent, are quite distant from the predominantly Gujarati (western Indian) roots of East African Hindus of north west London. Even though such Gujaratis often belong to Vaishnava traditions, these are very different to those promoted by ISKCON. The traditions of Gujaratis were particularly influenced by the Vallabacharya Pushtimarg, and less directly by Swaminarayanism.[16] In both these traditions Krishna is given a high degree of devotion, and most Gujaratis consider Krishna to be one of their favourite deities. Therefore Gujaratis would have been likely to take an interest in the facilities for worship at Bhaktivedanta Manor because of the presence of the *murtis* of Radha and Krishna (Radha-Gokulananda). At that time, they were very unlikely to have known much about the theology of ISKCON, nor about its history.

Over the next few years, however, the connections between these Gujarati Hindus and ISKCON developed and strengthened. ISKCON were themselves aware of the potential support that this population could offer the movement, as was noted by one of their officers in 1982:

> In Britain, in particular, there was clearly a need to make a very special effort to reach the large Indian community, who, by virtue of their religion and culture were so much closer to Krishna consciousness than the rest of the population ...
>
> The work really began in 1970 when Srila Prabhupada introduced the life membership scheme in India ... When in 1972 the life membership programme was started in Britain, the devotees found that it was also a familiar pattern in the Hindu communities here.[17] Prabhupada had said to the devotees: 'Go to the Indian businessmen, show them our books, explain our work and ask them to become life members.' At first, the devotees were a little apprehensive, but in practice they found it remarkably easy. (ICAP)

The easy accessibility of the Manor made it a convenient place to visit by car at the weekend, and the rural location was an obvious incentive to Hindus living in urban areas. A visit to the temple made a pleasant day out of London in the countryside, especially in the summer when the weather was good. More particularly, though, Hindus found at the temple a quality of worship which could not be matched in any other temple in Britain.[18] The emphasis that Prabhupada placed on the training of devotees to high standards of *murti* service, and the regular daily activities directed towards Radha-Gokulananda were (and are) very impressive.

Many casual visitors liked what they saw and decided to return again. Others asked questions of the temple devotees, to hear what they had to say about their beliefs, and discovered a group of people who were very articulate at explaining and preaching their religion. Prabhupada's mission to the west to teach Krishna consciousness had relied on such articulation on the part of devotees, and so this came in useful when Indian Hindus turned to the devotees with their questions. Prabhupada had also created a large collection of literature, which included not only translations of sacred scriptures such as the *Bhagavad Gita*, but also commentaries and explanations of Gaudiya Vaishnavism. These also helped the Hindu visitors to learn in more depth of the distinctive philosophy and theology that lay behind the temple.

The ethnicity of the white western devotees also proved an ironic attraction. The fact that these people had actually taken the trouble to *become* Hindus proved a challenge to the Indian visitors. In the words of Carey's informant: 'In fact I felt ashamed that it was Westerners who were so enthusiastic. I felt that they were running towards God and we Asians were running away from him' (Carey 1987:87). Similarly an elderly Indian women was reported as saying to ISKCON devotee in the early 1970s: 'Look at what they [ISKCON] are doing. We've come to this country, but we're doing nothing, but they are working so hard for our religion. They've got temples and are establishing young programmes, so we must do something to help them' (ICAP). Time and again I have heard similar comments from Hindus that I have spoken to at the Manor.

It was not merely the fact that these were westerners who had taken up the symbols of Indian culture – such as the shaved heads, the *tilak* and *shika*, and the Indian clothes. Visitors found the devotees' knowledge of Sanskrit particularly impressive, along with their understanding of (this particular strand of) Hindu philosophy, and their devotion to the deities in the temple. Such a reaction from Indians was anticipated by Prabhupada: in fact he believed that his successes in taking Krishna consciousness to the west would in fact help to spread this message to the Hindus of his native India.

Hinduisations of ISKCON

Whether he intended to do so or not, one significant development of ISKCON has been the gradual realignment of the movement to be seen as a sectarian *part of* the broader religious category of 'Hinduism'. This development was not only a theological or categorical shift, but has also had very important political consequences – particularly in terms of the way in which in the 1980s and 90s ISKCON and their supporters presented Bhaktivedanta Manor as a *Hindu* temple. However, as Charles Brooks shows in his book on *The Hare Krishnas in India* (Brooks 1989), interaction between ISKCON and Indian Hindus has been a fundamental part of the Krishna consciousness movement almost from its beginning, and one of the substantial ethnic bases for ISKCON on the international level is the support it receives from Indians in the subcontinent. ISKCON has major temples in Delhi, Bombay, and many other Indian cities, as well as international pilgrimage sites in Vrindaban in Uttar Pradesh and at Mayapur in Bengal, which is the birthplace of Chaitanya. In all of these Indian ISKCON centres the membership (both within the temples, and the wider community/ congregational support) is dominated by Indians. This notwithstanding, it is fair to say that ISKCON's situation in England is uncommon, in that it is quite unusual to find such a highly developed and intense set of links between ISKCON and other Hindu groups. Most ISKCON temples do not have such a sizeable Indian Hindu population in easy travelling distance as Bhaktivedanta Manor has, and many are located in states or countries where there is no substantial settlement of Hindus of Indian ancestry. However, there are other ISKCON centres outside of India where interaction has grown up because of similar populations of Hindu settlers, in places such as Nairobi in Kenya and Durban in South Africa.

Nurit Zaidman-Dvir (1998, n.d.) describes a similar situation in Philadelphia, USA where there is also considerable interaction at the ISKCON temple between predominantly white western devotees and Indian Hindus. The picture painted by Zaidman-Dvir is of a Krishna temple in which there is a high degree of support from the local Indian Hindu community, but there is also a large degree of negotiation and indeed fluidity between the ISKCON temple management and the non-ISKCON Hindus. What she observed in Philadelphia was that the temple management were prepared to turn a blind eye to some of the cultural and religious practices of the Hindu worshippers, even these were obviously falling outside of the expectations of Gaudiya Vaishnavite theology and philosophy. In particular Zaidman-Dvir draws attention to the worship of Durga in a hired hall within the temple, even though for Krishna devotees Durga is a *devi*, i.e. demi-god, who is subordinate to the supreme deity Krishna. ISKCON take the attitude that so long as the temple itself is not violated by such incorrect worship, they are happy to maintain the links that they have established with the Hindu population, even though those Hindus still have a long way to go before they are properly Krishna conscious.

The situation at Bhaktivedanta Manor both differs from and mirrors the Philadelphia case. In some respects, ISKCON in London find themselves with a Hindu population who have religious expectations and practices which differ from those that are normative for Gaudiya Vaishnavism. For example, many Gujarati Hindus who use the Manor also have a strong attachment to Durga, and other *devis*, there are many who eat meat (which is considered to be murder by ISKCON devotees), and a number often smoke tobacco (which is prohibited), even within the grounds of the temple. The teachings of Krishna consciousness show an acceptance of the view that it is difficult for people to follow Krishna properly, since after all the present time is the *Kali Yug* (the 'dark age') when the natural state is immorality. Thus there is a large degree of tolerance for those who (even though they are Hindu) have still not realised the correct way to approach Krishna. However, unlike the Philadelphia temple, at Bhaktivedanta Manor the devotees and temple management have followed a policy of very strict orthodoxy and orthopraxy. There would be no suggestion of formal *devi* worship at the Manor (even if only in a meeting hall), it is expected that Hindus who visit the temple should accept the complete package of what ISKCON have to offer.

Rather unsurprisingly, however, there is still some measure of leeway even at the Manor. No matter how much they feel they should, ISKCON devotees are unable to police their visitors' actions (let alone thoughts) at all times, and it is inevitable that some non-Gaudiya Vaishnavite practices do still slip into temple activities, almost when the temple devotees and pujaris are not looking. I recall that once on a visit to the Manor I was offered some *prasadam* (i.e. a meal) by Arjuna das [a pseudonym], a senior temple devotee. As I had an appointment elsewhere, and the food was taking a long time to come through to the dining room, Arjuna tried to arrange a plate of food for me to take away and eat on the way to my appointment. He slipped into the temple kitchens, to return a few minutes later with a plate of food and an anxious look on his face. 'I think I must have stepped on someone's ancestors in there,' he said, referring to the upset which he had obviously caused by taking food which was being prepared by a group of elderly Gujarati women, and which had not gone through a ritualised dedication to these women's ancestors. All Krishna devotees are expected to take extreme care when preparing food, especially if it is to be offered as *prasadam*, and part of the preparation is the offering of the food to Krishna before anyone else takes a taste. However, the offering of the food to personal, human, ancestors is an act of devotion and respect which is not associated with strict Gaudiya Vaishnavism. Arjuna was obviously upset to have been given a row by the elderly women, and to have been assertive with women old enough to be his grandmother. However, he chose to turn his feelings into a joke that demonstrated his relaxed toleration of their own personal devotions which neither he nor ISKCON shared. However, some transgressions of ISKCON philosophy and practice are not so easily tolerated: at most festival times, and indeed at times of sizeable gatherings, some of the visitors openly smoke cigarettes in the grounds of the Manor. This activity is totally unacceptable to Krishna devotees, and indeed some devotees take on the duty of (gently) informing such visitors that there should be 'no-smoking at the temple please'.

The vigour with which devotees at the Manor seek to ensure the correct standards and attitudes of true Krishna consciousness are both an attraction and a hindrance for Hindus. As I mentioned above, many Indian Hindus respect the devotion and sincerity of the white western devotees, feeling rather guilty that they themselves have not been able to follow such a religious life (despite having been raised in a Hindu/Vaishnavite family). The ability of ISKCON devotees to formulate philosophy and to teach and explain complicated theological ideas is often seen as extremely impressive, especially to parents who are wondering how they can teach their children anything about 'the Hindu tradition', or to teenagers who want to 'find out about Hinduism' but can get no sense out of their parents or their local temple priest. The total package of Krishna consciousness is easily available at the Manor, in English, Gujarati, and Sanskrit, and in recent years ISKCON have made a lot of effort to show how one can live and practise Krishna consciousness in the home (ISKCON n.d.).

At the same time, however, what ISKCON offers can very often be seen as too rigid and fixed, and too narrowly focused. Some Indian Hindus would even argue that ISKCON's approach amounts to 'fundamentalism', particularly in their teachings on religious philosophy and lifestyle. The philosophy of the ISKCON movement is very clearly set out in Prabhupada's writings,[19] and every new devotee is expected to learn in depth exactly what s/he is taking on before s/he is initiated by a guru. Because of this there is a high degree of orthodoxy in ISKCON (there have been intense theological debates, but in most cases the terms of these debates have tended to be quite rigid[20]). This is fairly unusual for Hindu movements and certainly comes as something of a shock to many non-sectarian Hindus in Britain who are used to a more fluid type of religiosity in which the individual has a greater degree of choice of belief and practice. As I already indicated, this can also be seen as a strength for ISKCON, since the certainties can give a high measure of security for young Hindus interacting with the fluidity of British cultural forms. But on the other hand, if the majority of Hindus in Britain wish to maintain a sense of 'unity in diversity' within their concept of what their Hindu religiosity is about, then ISKCON's particularity is only likely to be accepted by a minority.

There are, however, arguments put forward from a number of perspectives that quite clearly place the religious practices of ISKCON as *outside* of Hinduism. Most ISKCON devotees tend to be happy enough with the label of 'Hinduism' as a description of their religiosity, as a loose translation of what they feel is the more correct term '*sanatan dharm*' in Hindi. But there is within ISKCON a minority of devotees who do not like the term Hinduism, which they feel has a lot of connotations which are irrelevant to them. Many of these non-Hindu (and non-Indian) devotees wish to retain the internationalism of ISKCON, and see the primary purpose of the ISKCON *yatra* (organisation) as being to preach to and convert the indigenous white population of Britain. This perspective is largely justified by passages of Prabhupada's own teachings, in which he makes a clear point about distinguishing ISKCON from Hinduism, clearly stating that Krishna consciousness is *not* Hindu (Prabhupada 1977:117–23). For him, this 'Hinduism' was a hodgepodge, a *khitchari* of religious beliefs and practices which misrepresent and distort the Vedic teachings.

In a recent analysis of Prabhupada's writing, Jan Brzezinski (1990) shows that the basic problem behind Prabhupada's rejection of a Hindu religious identity was not (as is often cited) the etymological origins of the word 'Hindu'. Rather, Hindu for Prabhupada referred to something that he considered to be a 'culture' rather than a 'religion'. Thus 'culture is not religion. Religion is a faith whereas culture is education and advancement of knowledge' (letter written in July 1970, quoted in Brzezinski 1998:34). In this sense, it was not a matter of ISKCON not being Hindu, Prabhupada recognised that there are many Hindu aspects in Krishna consciousness, but

Krishna consciousness is *more* than Hinduism. As a religion, Krishna consciousness is primarily focused on 'the loving service of the transcendent Lord' (Brzezinski 1998:31, from *Srimad Bhagavatam* 1.2.6) or more specifically the 'laws of God' (ibid.:34). Aside from this theological distinction, he also used the term strategically – in particular considering it counter productive to his mission in the west to be identified as Hindu, and thus alien (ibid.:41). Interestingly, however, he was happy to receive support from the Hindu nationalist Jan Sangh party in India in a campaign to save the Bombay (Mumbai) temple at Juha, who testified that ISKCON was a 'bona fide Hindu organisation' (ibid.:42).

Thus as a native Indian, brought up and practising his faith within religious traditions that many (both non-Indians and fellow Bengalis) would call 'Hindu', Prabhupada's comments on the relationship between Hinduism and Krishna consciousness need to be treated carefully. His distinction of Hinduism as an 'ism' and thus as less than a proper religion is of course an important means by which he could promote Krishna consciousness as the right and true spiritual path. But at the same time it glosses over the fact that there is also what could be called an 'ISKCON culture', which shares a great deal in common with other Indian cultural forms – in terms of food, dress, and many points of reference – which is also hybridised through the performance of this culture by converts from a range of backgrounds (including north Americans, British, Eastern Europeans, Scandinavians, Africans, and also Indians). Although the processes of 'Indianisation' identified by Sean Carey among ISKCON in Britain in the 1980s has emphasised the Indian-ness of this cultural ethos, it is this same Indian-ness (or Hindu-ness in Prabhupada's terms) that has been so important ever since the creation of the movement in New York in 1966. After all, the initial attraction of ISKCON came from within the emerging hippy generation who were already looking towards India for solutions to social, spiritual, and psychic disaffection. In this sense, the reliance by ISKCON on Indian populations, in Britain, and other places such as Philadelphia, in Africa, and India has not significantly 'Indianised' the movement, but rather has involved a substantial breaking down of a cultural barrier that early ISKCON devotees (along with Prabhupada) wished to erect between Krishna consciousness and the broad descriptive category of 'Hinduism', whilst still maintaining the claims of spiritual superiority for the religion that ISKCON are offering.

If one looks at the distinctions between Hinduism and Krishna consciousness in terms of strategies, therefore, it is clear that in recent years there has definitely been a large effort made by ISKCON in Britain to engage with the idea of Hinduism, and to identify themselves as part of the *sanatan dharm*. And rather than distinguish the terms *sanatan dharm* and Hinduism, ISKCON leaders have instead promoted an interpretation that they are (almost) synonymous, and that Krishna consciousness can be definitely placed within this religious culture. In the majority of their public statements ISKCON have been very clear in saying that they are most definitely Hindu, and point to the large level of support that they receive from Indian Hindus as proof of their authenticity as Hindus. On the level of public discourse this has had the two successful objectives of promoting ISKCON within Hindu populations and promoting ISKCON to outsiders, particularly to the politicians, media, judges, and bureaucrats, on whom the future of Bhaktivedanta Manor depended. As Prabhupada had himself done in Mumbai in the early 1970s, ISKCON in Britain found in the 1980s and 90s that the task of saving a Krishna consciousness temple could be made easier, if it was also designated as 'Hindu'.

Within these debates, therefore, are some interesting reformulations of ISKCON identities, that are produced by the specific histories of Prabhupada's mission to the US and other western countries, and so led to the creation of ISKCON, and other histories which separately resulted in the establishment of large populations of British Indians. The reformulations of these identities in Britain have been most strongly influenced by (and also helped to shape) the development of the conflict over Bhaktivedanta Manor, and in later chapters I will be examining the interactions between Hinduism as a minority religious identity and ISKCON as a 'new religion' within the context of the campaign to keep the Manor open. In the next two chapters, however, I will be looking more particularly at the role of the Manor as a place, serving as a site for the construction and localisation of ISKCON within a British context, and the ways in which such a placing of Hinduism is mediated through (and very much influenced by) the political control exercised by the state through planning policies.

Notes

1 For a description of the history of ISKCON see Judah (1977), Knott (1986), and Shinn (1987).

2 This GBC was subsequently increased over the years to twenty four members (Subhananda das 1985), and in 2000 has 34 members (see GBC web site <http://iskcon.org/txt-only/main/address/boss.htm>).

3 '*Hare Krishna, Hare Krishna, Krishna Krishna, Hare Hare. Hare Rama, Hare Rama, Rama Rama, Hare Hare*'.

4 Letter by Prabhupada to the President of Bhaktivedanta Manor in 1973, quoted by Akhandadhi das (in AdPE:27).

5 For a discussion of the relationship between image and deity within worship at a South Indian temple see Fuller (1984:6–17), and for a specific discussion of the philosophy and theology of *murti* worship in Gaudiya Vaishnava traditions, see Deadwyler (1995).

6 Burke Rochford (1999), writing in the late 1990s about a survey he conducted amongst worldwide ISKCON communities in 1996 talks in detail about the continuing problems of low morale and lack of trust among devotees in many different communities.

7 As Ravindra Svarup das points out, this anti-society viewpoint was probably more a legacy of the early devotees' counter-cultural roots than anything that they took out of Gaudiya Vaishnavism (R.S. das 1994:48).

8 Ravindra Svarup das describes how such 'fallen' devotees were labelled as 'fringies' who were 'the shadow of ISKCON'. Such 'fringies' were frequently shown anger, resentment, and sarcasm by the devotees who remained within the temple (R.S. das 1994: 50).

9 ISKCON are by no means unusual in this respect. Many other small religious organisations which expect such high levels of commitment from new converts often experience similar problems with high drop out rates (see for example Barker's analysis of conversions and recruitment to the Unification Church [Barker 1984]).

10 That is, the 'traditional' Hindu life developmental model in which a person progresses through the four stages of 'student', 'householder', 'renunciate', and 'ascetic'.

11 The extent to which Krishna consciousness has been judged by success in book distribution can be seen through the over-enthusiasm of some individual devotees – and sometimes whole temple communities – leading to conflicts with the markets that are targeted by this distribution. For example, Burke Rochford provides a careful examination of the controversies that ISKCON faced in the late 1980s following widespread dissatisfaction with their work in airports and particularly their technique of 'changing up' (Rochford 1988).

12 The scope of the ICJ was most obviously demonstrated when it included a serious article in 1998 detailing experiences of child abuse in ISKCON temples in the 1970s and 80s (Rochford and Heinlein 1998; B.S. das 1998). The combination of the sensationalist exposé of past sexual misdemeanours in a 'new religion' combined with the frankness of ICJ itself to be the medium for this revelation led to the details of the article being reported on the front page of the *New York Times* (Rochford 1998). Indeed the frankness of ISKCON's communications appeared to create more of a story than the sexual abuse itself, thus the *New York Times* article began by asking 'Why did the Hare Krishnas come forward with this story about child abuse in their own journal? Why would they tell the world about such a troubling part of their past?' (quoted in ibid.:65).

13 The history of Asians in East Africa is recorded in a number of very good sources. See in particular Ghai & Ghai (1970), Gregory (1971), Hollingsworth (1960), Mangat (1969), and Morris (1968).

14 Figure given by Humphrey & Ward (1974:151), Kuepper et al (1975:111).

15 Powell himself had been inspired to make his 'Rivers of Blood' speech in 1968 in reaction to the influx of Asians from Kenya in the late 1960s.

16 See Michaelson (1987), Nye (n.d.2:109–20), Williams (1984). Although both of these traditions appear to have influenced general forms of Gujarati Vaishnavism, very few followers of Swaminarayan have any involvement with ISKCON.

17 The life membership programme involved a devotee making a one-off payment which would then give him (as the male head of a household) and his family the opportunity to enjoy many benefits, such as free accommodation in any ISKCON temple throughout the world. For ISKCON as a developing movement, the immediate benefits of substantial sums of money were extremely attractive, as were the prospects of easy and free access to ISKCON resources for devotees. However, the UK life membership scheme (UKLM) proved to become a liability fairly soon after its first flush of success. Many 'life members' soon found that

their financial commitments were not honoured outside of the UK (for example, they were required to pay for staying at temples in Europe and India), and resentments grew up between life members and the movement. Eventually, in the 1980s the scheme was gradually phased out to be replaced by the Manor Foundation, which continues to work on the basis of members pledging to give a certain sum (at present £1,008) every year.

18 ISKCON's only significant 'rival' in this respect has been the Swaminarayan Hindu Mission temple, in Neasden, north west London. However, this temple was not opened until 1995.

19 In particular, Prabhupada's translation and commentary on the *Bhagavad Gita* (Prabhupada 1983), but also a number of other translations and commentaries of Vaishnavite sacred writings, along with many other writings, lectures, and interviews.

20 See, for example, T.K. Goswami (1997:25–38) on the *ritvik* and *jiva* debates, which have raged over the issues of disciplic succession and the relationship between souls and the godhead.

CHAPTER TWO

Sacred Space and Locality: Creation, Location, and Contest

Locating religion

In the next couple of chapters I intend to explore the various ways in which the particularities of Bhaktivedanta Manor as a place – as a religious (or sacred) site – provide some means by which Krishna consciousness, and Hinduism, have been embodied within an English context. As a means of exploring this, I intend to pursue a set of questions relating to how the manifestation of ISKCON as a religion can be understood through a theoretical analysis of practices of space and locality, which I wish to show are central to the embodiment of culture and religious forms.

In academic studies, as well as in popular discourses, it is a common occurrence to hear religion being talked about in abstract terms, as if 'it' is a 'thing' or an entity, which yet is not a thing at all, since the entity which religion is held to be is an abstraction of something else. Thus the concept of religion is often thought of as a metaphor for thinking about a principle or a basic inclination of human beings, or as (if anything) the vehicle through which ideas of deity, or ideas of holiness, or the numinous become manifest. In this regard, the concept of religion is extremely unclear and indeed unhelpful – in fact, one could argue that the assumption that religion is such an abstracted entity is very close to a theological or faith perspective (c.f. Fitzgerald 1995).

Any observation or practice of 'religion' is primarily concerned with religious manifestation. That is, religion is *manifest*: embodied and placed in particular persons, or roles, or material objects, or in particular locations. It may be philosophically possible to argue for the existence of an 'essence' of religion, or religiosity, which goes beyond these particularities of manifestation, but this quest for an essence is tangential to the more obvious (or empirical) embodied practices which make up the lived experiences of what westerners call religion. In fact, a great deal of twentieth century studies of religion have focused on such religious embodiment (either directly or indirectly), through discussion of religious persons (such as Christ, Buddha, Mohammed, Gandhi, etc.), discussion of religious objects or artefacts (a classic example would be of *tjurungas*, and more generally symbols), places (mainly sacred centres and pilgrimage sites), religious actions (rituals), or texts, have all given scholars a means of discussing 'religion' as religious manifestations. What has been left largely unexamined, however, is to what extent the manifestation is the same as the phenomenon, or to put this another way, is the scholar studying (the) 'religion' or particular religious manifestations? The classic attempt by Mircea Eliade (1963) to deal with this question provides the most explicit answer: manifestations (whether they be persons, places, or any other material thing) are locations and vehicles for the religious reality of 'the sacred' which goes beyond the human, and it is this other reality which is the true concern both of religious practitioners and religion scholars. Such a perspective, although still very popular in some areas of academic religious studies, only causes more problems than it solves, and Eliade's theories have been subject to very scathing criticism for the largely theological agenda which underwrote them (Fitzgerald 1995, Gill 1998, Wiebe 1999).

The recognition that religion is embodied is, therefore, a simple but also radical perspective to take. On the one hand, this opens the door to the exciting possibilities of studies of 'religion and the body', which ask, more precisely, how scholars can attempt to understand religious phenomena by locating practice within embodied (that is, human body) contexts.[1] In conjunction with the application of the practice theory of Pierre Bourdieu (1977, 1992), writers such as Bell (1992) have shown how the study of ritual should be reconfigured as a means of understanding how bodies are used by actors/agents in certain types of 'religious' (as well as non-religious) action, called ritualisation, which express relations and conceptions of power. In this sense, the perspective that takes into account the embodiment and manifestation of religions is not a theory or answer in itself. It is simply a starting point for developing new means of contextualising action and giving new forms of critical analysis on the study of religion.

What I am particularly concerned with in this book is not so much the embodiment of religion within actual bodies, but rather the siting or placing of religion (c.f. Olwig & Hastrup 1997), or to put this another way, the practice of religious places. Bodies do, of course, come into this picture, since it is bodies that make use of religious sites: they queue to enter temples, they eat *prasad*, and they sit in cars on their way to temples. Indeed, an analysis of the roles and expressions of body consciousness within ISKCON would make a fascinating study – developing the analysis began by Angela Burr nearly twenty years ago (Burr 1984), and below I make a few tentative remarks in this regard.

However, another form of embodiment of religiosity is concerned with how a set of religious ideas becomes located in particular geographical sites or places. A place gives a useful point of academic reference: it helps scholars to see how religiosity is manifest through a particular type of embodiment, as well as giving some access to seeing how actors themselves view and create their own relations to that embodiment (both thinking with a place, and placing their 'beliefs'). The placing of religiosity in a site does not only give a direct and physical expression of certain values and practices, it also creates a space for development, for debate, and for contest (Chidester and Linenthal 1995).

Manifesting Krishna consciousness

Questions of religion and body, and the placing of religion are very clearly manifest in a certain paradox about ISKCON: that is, on one level bodies are significantly unimportant for devotees, and yet a large part of the history of ISKCON has depended on very particular embodiments. Followers of Prabhupada's and Chaitanya's teachings live by a very strong adherence to the idea that the person 'is not the body' (c.f. Burr 1984), and that the body (and physicality) are external manifestations which obscure rather than reveal reality. However, the success of ISKCON has relied very much on its embodiment in particular locations, obviously through the physical survival of Prabhupada's aged body beyond seventy years (despite having three heart attacks at the beginning of his mission, between 1965–67), but also through the embodiment of Prabhupada's teachings in the bodies of 'white western' men and women. Much of the novelty and distinction about ISKCON (particularly in the first decade of 1966–76) was the juxtaposition of 'white bodies' and a cultural religiosity normally associated with 'other' bodies, that is Asian Hindus. On the other hand, the body consciousness of gender, that is the separation of roles into male and female (which in Krishna consciousness philosophy are part of the material body and not the integral soul) has been very much part of ISKCON devotees' experiences even though it goes against the grain of the idea that the body is unimportant (c.f. Knott 1996).

But the non-corporeal philosophy of ISKCON has not only been spread through manifestation in particular bodies, it has also had to be manifest through being placed, and its placement has mirrored the novelty of its embodiment. That is, ISKCON has become ISKCON by Prabhupada relocating a cultural perspective on religiosity from his native Bengal to western countries such as the USA and Britain. Prabhupada himself had to relocate as a cultural migrant in order to create ISKCON, and recreate his image of the Gaudiya Math (as his own guru had commanded him). And Prabhupada's success was in his successful placement in certain peoples within New York and San Francisco (and elsewhere) of his vision of how a Gaudiya Vaishnava should behave and act, as well as the creation of particular places (the Second Avenue temple in the lower East Side in New York, and the Haight-Ashbury temple in San Francisco), where devotees could gather and manifest their newly found religiosities. In doing so, this relocated Vaishnavism became embodied, as an organisation called ISKCON, which itself became the vehicle and obvious manifestation for the spread of Prabhupada's teachings across the globe. Thus Prabhupada's message (following Chaitanya) of non-embodiment was very largely mediated through substantial embodiment in persons and places.

Furthermore, popular images of ISKCON have very much drawn on what devotees do with their bodies: from general presentation (men without hair except the *shika*, women with long hair, both dressed in 'Indian style' clothes, Vaishnava forehead marks, etc.), to bodily actions (dancing in public places), and bodily regulation (control of diet through strict vegetarianism). Likewise, an ISKCON devotee is challenged to learn how to live in his/her body – despite being spiritually detached from it – not only through the strict diet, but also by controlling his/her bodily patterns (for example, waking at four am each morning), and learning very regulated bodily actions (such as the repetitive *japa* meditational action of going through 108 *mala* beads with the right thumb and middle finger whilst chanting the *mahamantra*). In many respects, therefore, Krishna consciousness is a realisation of ultimate non-corporeality which can only be realised through a particular embodiment.

The embodiment of such a religious perspective in Britain has similarly relied on certain physical developments, such as the physical presence of Prabhupada in London in September 1969, the manufacture of the 'Hare Krishna' pop single, and later the attraction to ISKCON of a different body of people (Indian Hindus), and the placing of the group at the house and estate which came to be known as Bhaktivedanta Manor. As with many such embodiments, the siting of Krishna consciousness at the Manor was not a final resolution of Prabhupada's desire to place ISKCON in Britain, it was instead the source of a long and important conflict over placement, which became an important part of the negotiation of the place of Krishna in British cultural life.

Placing religiosity

Space, place, and location

As Kirsten Hastrup and Karen Olwig (1997) have recently argued, the role of place within the production and experience of culture has long been taken for granted by anthropologists and other cultural theorists. Traditional practices of anthropology, particularly through the methodological framework of ethnography, have been conducted with regard to specific *places* (that is, fieldwork sites), and the resulting products of research have been (to some degree or other) limited in their analysis of how the space occupied by the anthropologist in his/her research is the same as the space occupied by those s/he is researching, and how in general the construction and use of space goes far beyond the physical constraints of a particular research project (see also Appardurai 1986, Clifford 1997, Marcus 1995). The recognition of the fluidity of place within constructions and expressions of culture also points towards the rather different perspective that the people that anthropologists study are also very much involved with their own conceptualisations of place in the working out of their cultures, or that the practice of culture is also the practice of place.

Thus one of the objectives of cultural study should be an attempt to make 'an exploration of the "place" of culture in both the experiential and discursive spaces that people inhabit or invent ...' (Hastrup and Olwig 1997:3). Neither culture, space, or indeed religiosity, are static entities to be observed, noted, and described in monographs, but are instead in fluid relations with each other, and what are observed are particular manifestations of people's projections and experiences, which can be crystallised around particular 'focal points' such as important cultural sites. Thus, as Pamela Graves argues: 'social space is created through social practice ... The creation and reproduction of particular kinds of knowledge are integral to the reproduction of ... social relations and hence to the maintenance of authority in given contexts' (Graves 1989:297). However, the identification between a person or group with a particular cultural site should not obscure the fact that the production of the site, and the experience of the persons or groups are still to themselves located within 'a complex of relations of global as well as local dimension' (ibid.:11).

Precisely what these terms 'place' and 'space' signify is not altogether clear, nor is there any straightforward means of distinguishing space from place, nor indeed either of these terms from location. It is in fact the case that many critical discussions of space, place, and power tend to use the two terms fairly interchangeably, with no real discussion of how they could or should be distinguished (see for example Gupta and Ferguson 1997, Keith and Pile 1993). However, it may be worthwhile trying to distinguish some sense of difference, if only to clarify the ways in which space and place can be reconceived. For example, according to Smith and Katz, geographers make distinctions between location, position, and locality:

> '*location*' fixes a point in space, usually by reference to some abstract co-ordinate system such latitude and longitude. Location may be no more than a zero-dimensional space, a point on a map. '*Position*', by contrast, implies location *vis-à-vis* other locations and incorporates a sense of perspective on other places, and is therefore at least one-dimensional. '*Locality*' suggests a two-(or more) dimensional place, and within which multiple and diverse social and natural events and processes take place. (Smith and Katz 1993:69, emphasis added)

Taking a rather different set of reference points, Arjun Appardurai argues that location needs to be conceived as a phenomenon of social production, making a distinction between locality and neighbourhood:

> I view *locality* as primarily relational and contextual rather than as scalar or spatial. I see it as a complex phenomenological quality, constituted by a series of links between the sense of social immediacy, the technologies of interactivity, and the relativity of contexts. This phenomenological quality ... expresses itself in certain kinds of agency, sociality, and reproducibility ... In contrast, I use the term *neighborhood* to refer to the actually existing social forms in which locality, as a dimension or value, is variably realized. Neighborhoods, in this usage, are situational communities characterized by their actuality, whether spatial or virtual, and their potential for social reproduction. (Appardurai 1996b:178–79)

Thus much social life (including practices which are identified as ritual and religious) is concerned with the production of locality through cultural activity, as well as the counter process of locating subjects within the localities, and specific neighbourhoods, so produced.

In what is the strongest statement in this respect, however, Michel de Certeau makes the distinction between what he sees as static and univocal 'space' (*lieu* in French) and the multivocality of practices which is expressed by the term 'place' (*espace*):

> A place (*lieu*) is the order ... in accord with which elements are distributed in relationships of co-existence. It thus excludes the possibility of two things being in the same location (*place*) ... A place is thus an instantaneous configuration of positions. It implies an indication of stability.
>
> A *space* exists when one takes into consideration vectors of direction, velocities, and time variables. Thus space is composed of intersections of mobile elements. Space occurs as the effect produced by the operations that orient it, situate it, temporalise it, and make it function in a polyvalent unity of conflictual programs or contractual proximities. In short, *space is a practiced place.* (de Certeau 1984:117, emphasis in original).

In making this distinction he is usefully contrasting place as a point of reference, and space as activity which is part of social, cultural, and personal practice and discourse. However, the problem I find with these terms is that to me the English word 'place' suggests more than the univocality of a fixed location, particularly because its active form (i.e. *placing*) makes a stronger statement of practice than is possible with 'space'. Furthermore, this attempt to distil the two terms down into a fairly rigid dichotomy seems to me to be going against the grain of showing the dynamism of the ways in which spaces (and places) are actively constructed and practised. Thus although I agree with de Certeau's formulation of space as a constructed and practised entity, I also feel quite comfortable using the term 'place' interchangeably with this, and indeed would be happy to read his phrase as 'space is a practised location'.

The possibilities of this approach are to a degree expressed well by Doreen Massey's critique of Ernesto Laclau's formulation of space as the realm of stasis, as the antithesis of the temporal (time as *dis*location). Like de Certeau, Massey argues for a conceptualisation of space in dynamic and temporal terms:

> 'Space' is created out of the vast intricacies, the incredible complexities, of the interlocking and the non-interlocking, and the networks of relations at every scale from local to global ... [S]pace is by its very nature full of power and symbolism, a complex web of relations of domination and subordination, of solidarity and co-operation. (Massey 1993:155–56)

Thus space is not 'dead' but is an active location, which is not dualistically opposed to time, but is itself produced by and produces temporality (or to put this another way, space has a temporal dimension, and time has a spatial dimension). As Lefebvre argues 'space may be said to embrace a multitude of intersections, each with its assigned location', which can be mapped onto a conceptual triad of space which is composed of spatial practices, representations of space, and representational space (Lefebvre 1984:33).[2] Space (and place) are 'an active constitutive component of hegemonic power: an element of the fragmentation, dislocation and weakening of class power, both the medium and message of domination and subordination. It tells you where you are and it puts you there' (Keith and Pile 1993:37).

In many cases this space is discursive and metaphorical: talk of space is often concerned with representational space, giving a means of thinking about and symbolising (as well as practising) relationships. Thus academic discourses in cultural, social, and literary theory make extensive use of spatial metaphors, to the extent that Smith and Katz argue that these initially grounded spaces have become 'virtually free-floating abstractions' (1993:80), which are in many ways metaphorical spaces within metaphorical space. The reliance of languages (in particular late twentieth century English) on spatial metaphors relies on such representational space as a means of thinking, and such metaphors are also a substantial element of storytelling (c.f. de Certeau 1984:118).

But not all representations are merely ungrounded simulacra. Sometimes places (or spaces) are represented through the simulacra of what Lefebvre calls representational space, and sometimes 'as they are' (or as they are imagined) in terms of spatial practices. The ways in which particular places (or locations) are represented and thus practised (and thus in de Certeau's terms become spaces) is my concern in this book, with specific reference to the particular place of Bhaktivedanta Manor as a place that is represented as religious or sacred. In this respect, it is worth asking what is the extent to which the designation of 'religious' makes a difference to the practice of a place?

Religious places

With respect to religious practice and place, the role of place can on one level be taken as 'a given': a temple, or a church, or any other 'sacred site' is located in a particular place that is easily identifiable and which (with a good enough map[3]) can be found without too much trouble. In some senses, this is what de Certeau talks of as 'place' (as a fixed point), Merleau-Ponty describes as 'geometrical space' (c.f. de Certeau 1984:117), and for Smith and Katz (1993:75–76) is 'absolute space'. For example, when I first visited Bhaktivedanta Manor in November 1993 I followed general directions given to me by the temple president, in conjunction with my road map, and had no problem in finding the place – the place has a fixed set of references with regard to other places (it does not move). This, of course, is the common experience of thousands of devotees, worshippers, and visitors (past and present) who have made their way through the Hertfordshire countryside to the Manor.

However, two observations must be made with regard to this ease of finding a religious place (or indeed any other place). Firstly, that particular place (the Manor) has not always been there, less than thirty years ago Bhaktivedanta Manor did not exist: the building which now goes by that name was once a nurses' training college called Piggott's Manor. For it to become Bhaktivedanta Manor required a deliberate *placing* of the organisation of the religious group in that particular site, locating at the Manor both the bodies of the devotees and the physical manifestation of Krishna (the Radha-Gokulananda *murtis*). This goes back to Massey's point, noted earlier, that a particular space must be understood in temporal as well as spatial terms – although as absolute space there is no discernible fluidity, if the temporal dimension is recognised the Manor (and any other place) is not quite so solidly fixed.

Secondly, the experience of the Manor depends very much on the perspective of the person who makes the visit. For some people going to the Manor is like 'going home to Krishna', for others it is a place of great spiritual importance, whilst for others it is 'just' a former country house used for other purposes. These views, of course, comes down to personal perspective – a devotee inevitably experiences the place in a different way to a non-devotee, especially if the non-devotee views the concept and practice of Krishna consciousness with hostility. But as views, the experience of place are mediated and practised – the seemingly absoluteness of the location of the place tends to hide the fact that the same place is subject to a variety of subjectivities.

In this regard, therefore, although places may appear to be fixed and given, in practice a place or site is a dynamic cultural manifestation. A place has a history, or histories (and potential futures), it has meanings which are assigned to it, groups and persons who use it in their own particular, and sometimes conflicting ways, and acts as an embodiment of various discourses, some of which may be explicit and generally accepted (for example, no one disputes the name 'Bhaktivedanta Manor'), whilst others may be strongly contested (not everyone will accept that Krishna actually abides at the place). This view of place is intended to de-essentialise static conceptions of place, and to direct attention to the discourses and relationships through which places are experienced. Thus, according to Smith and Katz, the seemingly commonsensical and universal perspective of absolute space 'is only one of the many ways in which space can be conceptualized' (1993:75), which, despite the supposedly abstract neutrality of this perspective it is, in fact, 'politically charged in its contemporary implications as much as in its historical origins' (p. 76).

Coming from this there are, according to David Chidester and Edward Linenthal (1995), three general characteristics of (or perspectives on) the production of sacred space which can be identified. That is: space as ritualised embodiment, space as a location of interpretation and the production of meaning, and space as a locus of the play of power relations. As embodied space, a particular place (particularly if it is considered to be of religious importance), is a location of bodily practice, often in the form of ritualisation (c.f. Bell 1992). In this regard, a place can be seen as a particular form of Bourdieu's concept of *habitus* (c.f. Bourdieu 1977, 1992), where 'through embodiment, the ritualized *habitus* ... is produced and reproduced as a dynamic spatial ordering of knowledge and power' (Chidester and Linenthal 1995:10). This observation does, in some respects, follow de Certeau's (1984) attempt to locate such *habitus* in space and spatial-symbolic metaphors.[4]

Bourdieu's concept of *habitus* is, of course, a two way process in which practice and meaning are embedded in each other, acting as 'a matrix of perception, appreciations and actions' (Bourdieu 1977:95) which are 'structured structures predisposed to function as structuring structures ... which generate and organize practices and representations ...' (Bourdieu 1992:53). Therefore as a location for embodying practice, a place is also the space of generating and grounding meanings. Thus 'the meaning objectified in things or places is fully revealed only in practices structured according to the same schemes which are organised in relation to them (and vice versa)' (Bourdieu 1977:90). In Chidester and Linenthal's words:

> sacred places focus a classification of persons, carving out a place for a human identity ... [which also] focus more general orientations in space and time that distinguish center from periphery, inside from outside, up from down, and a recollected past from a meaningful present or an anticipated future'. (Chidester and Linenthal 1995:12)

Such meanings are not, however, homogeneous or uncontested since as Michel Foucault argues 'space is fundamental in any exercise of power' (Foucault 1984:252, quoted in ibid.:15). Issues of ownership of a sacred place, its use and organisation, and the various interpretations of it are all mediated through and produced by dynamic power relations, and so are subject to contestation and conflict. 'In this respect, a sacred space is not merely discovered, or founded, or constructed; it is claimed, owned, and operated by people advancing specific interests' (Chidester and Linenthal 1995:15). So it should not necessarily come as a surprise to find that many significant sacred or religious places are contested.

The construction and maintenance of such a place is the product of often immense symbolic and actual labour, and the ownership of such a site carries with it also the 'ownership of the symbolic capital (or symbolic real estate) that signifies power relations' (p. 16). And even when ownership and control of an important site is relatively uncontested, the way in which it is used and perceived may be subject to fierce debate, since how it is viewed will not be limited by its spatial limits or its regulated use. Similarly, Sallnow and Eade argue that pilgrimage shrines, as a particular type of religious place, provide 'a ritual space for the expression of a diversity of perceptions and meanings which the pilgrims themselves bring to the shrine and impose on it' and so are best characterised as a 'realm of competing discourses' (Sallnow and Eade 1991:10). Thus, a religious site becomes a place of contest because it is where 'spatially scarce resources are transformed into a surplus of signification' in which 'no appropriation can be can ever be final [and] no exclusion can be total ... In this respect, a space or place is perhaps revealed at its most sacred when people are willing to fight, kill, or die over its ownership and control' (Chidester and Linenthal 1995:18–19).

The fluidity and contestability of the many 'meanings' that are attached to a single religious place are most obvious at the times when that place is being constructed (or reconstructed). Every place needs to at some stage *become* a place, and every site (even and especially those that are long established) needs to be *re*-placed, through being re-established for each generation and each social-political context (or *habitus*). Although there will be very definite points at which a place is constructed or dedicated, the placing of religious and cultural practice within a site is always an ongoing process. As Pamela Graves observes in her discussion of medieval English churches, the consequences of the fluid and creative processes of construction are often ignored in favour of what appears as the finished product of a particular place, especially when that place consists of constructed buildings.

> Architectural history tends to concentrate on the final product of a building programme, on stylistic qualities and influences. What of the consequences of construction as a practice? ... [T]he liturgical space of a parish church went through long periods of *creation*, through acts of patronage, rather than existing as a finite entity. The building programme acted as a means of 'presencing' the authority of the lord of the manor. (Graves 1989:311, emphasis in original).

This creation of the practice of a place and the 'presencing' of certain power relations occurs in a number of ways, through contest within the group or groups using the place, as well as through contest with outsiders. Sometimes the metaphor of construction, or reconstruction, can be used explicitly to describe social and cultural (re)formulations, whilst in other contexts it may be used as an implicit agenda. These processes of contest and construction are very obvious means by which a place becomes an embodiment of certain political and cultural forms, and both form a very important part of the practice of place.

A caveat that needs to be added to this discussion of sacred or religious place is whether or not the designation of sacredness makes any difference to the ways in which it is used? Chidester and Linenthal leave the application of sacredness largely unexplored in their analysis, in so much as they assume that it is a useful descriptive category to use, within which they are referring to a constructed quality which reflects both the 'poetics and politics' of cultural life (p. 5–9). In drawing out their analysis of sacred places, they are ready to include within this category not only places such as traditional Hawaiian burial grounds and Buddhist temples, but also the Pearl Harbour national shrine and the Mount Rushmore monument. Clearly, what they intend by the term 'sacred' refers to more than normative western ideas of what is 'religious'. In this sense a discussion of 'religious space' appears to be more limiting than of 'sacred space'.

In a later chapter (chapter seven) I will be discussing some of the political contexts of applying a definition of religion, and the problems involved in identifying certain practices or places as religious. For my analysis I am not wishing to make too strong a distinction between a religious and a non-religious place, but at the same time I think that the designation of 'sacred' or 'sacredness' is as equally problematic as 'religious' (see Stanner 1967 and Stirrat 1984 for discussion of some of the problems of using the term sacred). What both terms (religious and sacred) indicate most effectively, however, is the production of a 'surplus of signification' that Chidester and Linenthal highlight as such an important element within the politics of the use of place. In fact, if any meaning should be attached to what constitutes the religiosity or sacredness of a place, it is precisely this, rather than any more specific definition which refers to the sacred as 'set apart' (c.f. Durkheim 1964[1915]) or manifesting the supernatural (c.f. Eliade 1963, Paden 1991).

Of course in the actual practice of a place as a religious place, there are important contextual factors which are bound up with the designation of religiosity. That is, the use of Bhaktivedanta Manor as a temple as a site of Krishna's embodiment, and hence as a religious place, are very important factors to the devotees and worshippers who visit it. Even non-devotees will consider, use, and thus construct the place in a certain way because of this designation of religious-ness (indeed, as I will discuss in chapter six, this was a crucial element in the resolution of the conflict). But for the outsider, one has to tread with care around such a designation: the placing of a religious site is also the placing of a cultural site, and as the boundary between the two (religiosity and culture) is extremely unclear, even unnecessary, the analytic application of such a boundary can often create problems rather than resolve any. What I intend to argue here is that a site such as the Manor involves the placing of important cultural practice, as *habitus*, through which actors also create a focus for context. The examples that I am using happen to be associated with *religious* practice, as defined by the actors themselves, and my description of them as such intends to use this self-designation as a part of the cultural production of place, rather than imposing and extending any expectation that religious sites are phenomenologically different to non-religious sites. In brief, what I am looking at is how the discourses and practices of religiosity are bound up within the production of place and the siting of cultural manifestations.

In an earlier work I discussed the various ways in which a particular religious and cultural place was constructed and used by a minority group, that is a temple which was being created by a Hindu community in Edinburgh (Nye 1995). In that case, the temple was the site of the (literal) locating of Hindu discourses and practices within a western (particularly Scottish) context and which provided the space (symbolic and actual) for placing certain reconstructed identities of a displaced collection of people (Hindus of Indian origin). Although my analysis in this book takes up and continues some of the themes, my concern here is not so much on the intra-group dynamics that so often play a large part in the constructions of concepts of space, place, culture, and identity, but rather on ways in which the placing of a different type of temple has 'spilled out' into wide cultural discourses in Britain. Thus although there is undeniably a range of contests within the groups and persons who worship at Bhaktivedanta Manor, I am more concerned here with the conflict that grew up between the various Krishna followers and those outside of this group, and the ways in which this conflict have been part of the process by which ISKCON have placed Krishna consciousness (and Hinduism) in a British cultural milieu.

Placing Hindu practice in multicultural Britain

Although *mandirs* (temple buildings) are by no means the only places in Britain where religious practice is manifest by Hindus,[5] they are certainly of great importance as a public demonstration of the location of this new form of religiosity in British culture. It is at *mandirs* that communities (generally ethnic and Hindu) can focus their activities and thus *become* communities (c.f. Nye 1993a). But a *mandir* can also be used as a metaphor for how Hindus think about themselves and what Hinduism 'is', and also for how others (outsiders) think about Hinduism. The creation of a *mandir* requires *physical* construction: every *mandir* is placed within a particular location and neighbourhood and becomes part of that social and cultural environment.

The majority of *mandirs* are located in converted buildings (such as former houses or churches) which do not obviously show their new function, although there are also a number of buildings which are built either to specific Indian Hindu architectural specifications (the most obvious being the Swaminarayan Hindu Mission temple in Neasden), or at least in imitation of such styles. But even in cases of an unmodified house conversion, the *mandir* building is altered in some way to show some obvious sign of its new use. For example a large *aum* sign may be painted or carved above the entrance, or the identity of the building may be written in Hindi, Gujarati, or some other (non-English) script to be noticeable to passers-by. When I lived in south London, the nearby *mandir* displayed its title in a very visible sign which read 'Greenwich Hindu Mandir' written in Devanagari script. Someone able to read this script can discern the direct message which is intended, whilst the majority of non-Indians will see just a piece of 'foreign writing'.

Beyond these obvious, presentational signs of use, there are many other ways in which *all mandirs* have interaction with their surrounding environment. In particular it is through the use that worshippers and other visitors make of the building that local residents become aware of a place, and thus it is the ways in which worshippers use such a building that tend to determine how local residents perceive the place, and perhaps – on a general level – what they consider to be Hinduism. Thus the placing of Hindu practice in a building as a *mandir* does more than just create a space for Hindus actors/agents themselves. It also acts as a manifest means of locating an 'alien' religious tradition within British cultural life.

For Hindus a *mandir* is in many respects a *sacred space*: the creation of a *mandir* requires a high degree of ritualisation, that is special ritual work (particularly *murti stapana* and *pran pratishta*) to place and embody the deities in the space of the *mandir* and the *murti* statues in particular,[6] and through doing so the *mandir* becomes the home of the deities. In his discussion of the foundation of a particular Hindu *mandir* (a Sri

Venkateswara temple) in the USA, Fred Clothey describes this process as involving a 'pacification of space' (1983:195), carving out a civilised niche in the wilderness. As Clothey also notes, this is a useful idea for Hindus living in the 'wilderness' of western culture. The ambiguity of this pacification, or colonisation, of space is significant in an almost negative way too, for as Bernard Faure has argued: 'A new religious place in becoming a centre *dis*places a previous spatial frame, thus it becomes at the same time a concrete space and yet functioning as a kind of negative field, ruled as it was by the law of emptiness' (Faure 1987:346, emphasis in original). Neither the new space and what was there previously (and still surrounds it) are absolute. They exist in relation to each other, being constructed through the conceptualisations of both those who are already living in the 'wilderness' and those for whom the new place is sacred.

Once the *mandir* is created and in place, the deities and the building must be regularly used: the deities are treated like human beings – they are woken in the morning, put to sleep at night, they are washed and fed, and most particularly they are worshipped. Much of this is the responsibility of the *mandir pandit(s)* (or priest/s) whose function is to be a servant of the deity (Fuller 1984). But the 'lay' worshipper also plays their part: through interactions with the *mandir* deities and with other worshippers, *mandir* users may help to express a sense of religious 'ethnicity'. By placing themselves within the context of their *mandir* they help to create and maintain a sense of cultural distinctiveness.

However, from an indigenous (that is, ethnic white) British perspective, a *mandir* will appear somewhat different – in most cases it will appear strange for a number of reasons. Firstly a *mandir* is perceived (by both insiders and outsiders) as a *religious* place, a designation which occupies an anachronistic space in a society which is generally considered to be secularised. Furthermore, not only is a *mandir* a religious place, it is also the location of a 'funny' or 'other' religion. Hindu practice is not easily placed within a Christian (christocentric) framework, unlike Islam or Judaism it does not belong to the Semitic 'family' of religions, and (related to this) it is not easily recognisable as 'monotheistic', with different ideas about the nature of god, and distinct styles of worship. A religion which is hard to place in this way therefore appears to be located elsewhere – that is, not British. But a *mandir* is not only a Hindu place, it is also Indian which means it is associated with the category of 'blackness'. Hindus may be being religious like any Christian, they may be British citizens, but they are often seen as different because their skins are 'black' or 'brown' in contrast to the 'whiteness' which is considered the essence of being British. Thus the perception of a *mandir* by non-Indians is embedded within culturally constructed concepts of difference, which include (but are not determined by) categories of race (c.f. Barth 1969, Cohen 1986, Gilroy 1987, Wallman 1975) as well as place. In this sense, religion (and skin colour) are being used as a means of expressing difference (Barot 1993), which is most extremely expressed by the discourse that Hindus and Indians do not 'belong' in Britain.

Therefore, while the creation of a Hindu *mandir* may involve a substantial placing of Hindu practice for the actors/agents involved in the project, its placement may at the same time appear to be a *dis*-placement for non-Hindus and non-Indians in the nearby environment. For the majority of the population in Britain, Hinduism and Hindus do not appear to have an obvious place in British life: in fact, their presence can even appear as something of a 'blot on the landscape', which although is physically placed is not quite right. Many may have no problem with Hinduism in principle, as a disembodied idea, but the embodiment of that idea may create problems, since local non-Hindus may well object on their own principle of NIMBY (that is, Not In My Back Yard!).

This map that I am drawing of the placing of Hindu practice is – I must admit – rather stark and perhaps overstated. There are obvious exceptions to this type of negative reaction: it is still possible to find examples of the development of places of public Hindu worship where local reactions have been less hostile, and where Hindus have effectively found a place for their religious manifestations. Indeed, the *mandir* in Edinburgh where I conducted research in the late 1980s and early 1990s is one such example (Nye 1995). This *mandir* building has been owned by a group called the 'Edinburgh Hindu Mandir' since 1986, and has been used for regular worship since 1989. During these years of occupation, the building itself has undergone substantial internal reconstruction, through a project which was organised with the cooperation of the local council (then Edinburgh District Council) from the outset – in fact it was the council who offered the building (a disused church) to the Hindu group. Permission for use of the building as a place of public worship was granted with little trouble, and permission for the internal modifications was likewise unproblematic. The reaction of local residents has been generally neutral or positive, with no complaints being reported to my knowledge. There have been a few occasions of small break-ins by juveniles living near the building, and small-scale arson attacks (some old newspapers burnt in the yard behind the temple), but these incidents have not been serious and are in fact quite common in all buildings of this type. Problems of parking at the temple are greatly reduced by the existence of a decent sized parking area at the front of the building, with room for up to thirty cars. Furthermore, the building is not immediately adjacent to any residential blocks (a school – Leith Academy – is on one side, and a young men's club on the other). On the whole, the temple is well situated to serve as a place of public access for Hindus in Edinburgh. It has good facilities for the peaceful arrival and departure of worshippers, and has not as yet been noticed by local residents as a 'problematic' Hindu temple.

Likewise, the Greenwich Hindu Temple has not encountered much opposition. This former Boy Scouts' Hall in Plumstead, south east London was bought and renovated by a group of Panjabi Hindus who had formerly shared facilities with a group of Gujarati Hindus in nearby Woolwich. After constructing the main hall within the building as a large prayer area, the place was ritually dedicated as a temple in summer 1993, although use of the building began several years before that date. Unlike in Edinburgh, this temple does not have its own parking area and so visitors have to park their cars on the streets outside. Although at times of major festivals this can put severe strain on local parking facilities, this is generally tolerated – particularly because a number of Hindus (and other Indians) live in the neighbourhood, and form a substantial part of the local population. Like the Edinburgh *mandir*, though, Greenwich has also experienced break-ins to the building – on one occasion two important statues were stolen. Such activity could be interpreted as a measure of hostility toward the *mandir*, but although upsetting and inconvenient this has not prevented the general operation of the building, and there has been no concerted or collective opposition to the place.

The Leeds Hindu Temple has faced a more specific challenge over its use. When it was first constructed in the 1970s on the site of an old manor house, there were complaints from residents about street parking and the noise made as worshippers left religious meetings (Knott 1986:82). But measures were taken by the temple committee to ensure that visitors parked within the grounds attached to the temple, and meetings were scheduled so that visitors did not leave at a time that was very late. Once these measures had been taken, and local residents shown that temple worshippers were prepared to respect their views, the problem was alleviated.

However, despite these examples of tolerance which go against the grain of my earlier argument, there remains a sense among many Hindus in Britain that they do face problems in placing their religion, or creating religious places, for themselves and for future generations. The process of embodiment and interaction with a place and environment cannot be conducted without regard to certain cultural discourses in Britain, particularly the legal discourses of planning regulations. As I will discuss in the next chapter, the use of physical resources of place are very much regulated (as well as protected) by the application of local state bureaucracy through national government created planning guidelines. In practice, this means that any attempt by Hindus (or any other person or group) to create a religious place that is used in any significant way must be formally approved by the local planning authority or otherwise be subject to legal control and prosecution. Unorganised acts of racist and exclusionary hostility against Hindus by indigenous ethnic white individuals are a common part of many Hindus' lives in Britain. Despite this, there is a common perception among many such Hindus that the main obstacle in the way of placing their religion and culture within British public life is the planning system, which is the most obvious institutional means by which Hindu space, and hence the siting of Hindu religious and cultural practice, is contested and opposed.

Placing Krishna in rural Hertfordshire

Letchmore Heath: a 'typical English village'

From the time that it became dedicated as a religious site, the location of Bhaktivedanta Manor has been both an advantage and a disadvantage for ISKCON. Its situation outside of urban London is an obvious advantage: it has an immediate environment that is rural, with a large part of the perimeter of the grounds bordering onto green fields. By whatever route that worshippers approach the site of the Manor, the road takes them through relatively open countryside, whilst the interior of the grounds offer a large measure of the quietness that is associated with rural life (although the sound of the M1 motorway, which is little more than one mile away, can often be heard in the background).

These advantages also contribute to its disadvantages. The tranquillity of the village of Letchmore Heath, and its rural character mean that the other (non-ISKCON) residents of the village also see themselves as living in a 'quiet' and 'undisturbed' place. Indeed very important metaphoric and metonymic constructions of 'Englishness' derive from the physical appearance of Letchmore Heath: a small village, with a pub and a duck pond, narrow roads and lanes which snake their way between open fields and small woodlands, houses huddled together in clusters, in pretty 'cottage' gardens, festooned in the summer with roses, ivy and, perennial flowers. All these elements, many of which are deliberately produced, help to identify the village as a 'quintessentially English' place. This identity is not in itself 'quintessential' or *sui generis*, it is in fact produced and maintained in opposition to what it is not – in particular the quiet, pretty isolation of Letchmore Heath is deliberately (ferociously) maintained to keep it distinct from the sprawl, ugliness, and noise of nearby London. Furthermore, the village is made in an image that came out of a process of constructing 'Englishness' in negative relation to a number of undesirable qualities, which include modernity, industrialisation, urbanisation, and (to a certain degree) multiculturalism or diversity (c.f. Wiener 1981:45–64, Williams 1985). And of course, the high levels of wealth that make a village such as Letchmore Heath possible are themselves brought into the village by the commuters who live there (at certain times of the week), and who spend most of their time working (earning their incomes) in the urban London environment.

For example, a local newspaper wrote a special feature on Letchmore Heath in 1979, saying:

> Drive due north from Marble Arch and whether you come by A1, M1 or A41, the first village you come to worth the name – the sort with pub, pond, clustering houses and green – is Letchmore Heath.
>
> A pretty village only 14 miles from the centre of a major city is bound to have problems. On Sunday, they sweep in from Pinner, Harrow and Edgware. Fortunately for Letchmore Heath they retire by nightfall. A glance at the map must be more worrying for Letchmore folk in the long run. Watford, Bushey and Borehamwood seem to lie about it like an open pair of pincers, ready to snap shut.
>
> . . . Today most people work outside. There's been a steady influx from the young executive class in the past ten years . . . The M1, the reason the village is so popular, and its commuting homes so high priced, is only five minutes away – but as luck would have it, virtually inaudible.[7]

It is interesting to note, however, that this same feature also included a small article on the presence of Bhaktivedanta Manor in the village, as an (albeit recently arrived) part of the fabric of life in Letchmore Heath.

Two descriptions of the village, written by outsiders for legalistic (planning) documents demonstrate some of these contradictions involved in the constructions of Letchmore Heath as a timeless, unspoilt representative of a certain type of English identity, juxtaposed with a particular late twentieth century form of modernity (represented by electricity sub stations and business offices):

> The village of Letchmore Heath is . . . predominantly Victorian with some modern infill [and some sixteenth century houses]. One such modern building, currently used as offices, is located almost opposite the entrance to the Manor. The settlement has a rural village character centring on the Green and the 'Three Horse Shoes' public house. Cottages and houses and the village hall complete the village and there is an antique shop . . . Peripheral to the tightly-knit residential centre is the location of some important larger houses such as Aldenham Cottage and Aldenham Grange. The Manor grounds provide a wooded setting to the south-western part of the village.
>
> [Inspector Hanchet, based on his impressions from a planning inquiry held in 1995 (IR96:para 42–43, pp. 8–9)]
>
> The village forms a compact and well defined small settlement within an extensive area of green belt, the surrounding countryside being undulating and wooded, comprising mainly small fields, with well defined hedgerows and small woodlands. Inevitably at such a short distance from the capital there are institutional and utilitarian uses,

> including Elstree Aerodrome, Aldenham and Haberdashers Askes Schools, ... and a major CEGB [electricity] Substation about 0.6km away to the west, in full view from the Manor grounds ... The village with its houses grouped round the green, attractive old pub, duck pond and war memorial, all shaded by horse chestnut trees, has a small scale but very satisfying picturesque quality of such unspoiled surroundings are a rarity so close to London.
>
> [Inspector Russell, based on his impressions from two planning inquiries held in 1988 (IR89a:para 8.16, p. 8)]

In these descriptions one can almost imagine men in white flannels playing cricket on the village green, ending their day in the sun at the public house for a warm beer and gentle banter. Signs of encroachment of a different kind of England are noted (almost lamentingly), without mentioning here the noise that is generated by the frequent light aircrafts that fly from the nearby aerodrome, or the fact that an important factor behind the wealth (and preservation) of the village is based on its ready access to the nearby M1 motorway.

Krishna in the village

There were, therefore, a combination of factors that were likely to create some level of opposition against the placing of Krishna and Krishna conscious devotees in Letchmore Heath. As a prosperous area, where most households own at least one car, the village is poorly served by public transport facilities – the bus service is sporadic, and the nearest railway station is over two miles away in the town of Radlett. Although the village is constructed around an image of England which predates widespread car ownership (and has a road network which appears to reflect this), most visitors to Letchmore Heath do in fact come by car. Not only do they have little alternative choice, in fact for the majority of its residents car travel is the 'natural' form of transport. This means that at certain times, particularly during the morning and evening 'rush hours' of working days, the roads around the village become congested with commuter traffic (which combines with traffic taking children to and from the nearby prestigious Aldenham School).

This paradoxical juxtaposition of rural peace and quiet against commuter congestion is one of the factors that makes villages such as Letchmore Heath so sensitive to planning issues. Although the high traffic levels are themselves generated by village residents, cars (especially in large numbers) are somehow seen as not a 'real' part of the essence of village life – they lie at the boundary of the constructed notion of the quiet village, being a visible sign (or warning) of the possibility of further encroachment into the area by the 'dangers' of metropolitan London. In a similar way, Hindu visitors to the Manor have been happy to live across this ambiguity – many go there for the peace and quiet of being in the grounds of the *mandir*, and yet go at a time when there are large crowds, both within the Manor and on the roads leading to it. In this sense, both Letchmore Heath and Bhaktivedanta Manor are very ambiguous places.

When Bhaktivedanta Manor was created out of Piggott's Manor in 1973 the overall volume of traffic in the village was lower than 1990s levels, but this ambiguity of life in the village was still very much present. At that time 'London' (that is the physical boundary of urban development) seemed a little further away, but Letchmore Heath was, even then, still very much an 'island' of rural peace fearful of being consumed by metropolitan development. As a place that not only represented, but also strongly maintained, a romantic image of cosy, traditional Englishness, it was not perhaps the best of choices for the siting of a new religious group which derived from India.

It appears that the residents of Letchmore Heath suddenly discovered in 1974 (practically overnight) that what they had once thought of as their Manor had been transformed into something quite different. Whereas before it had been a quiet nurses' college, the dedication of the deities in the temple within the new theological college meant that the place became a major centre for Hindu pilgrimage in Britain, that is a place which generated large crowds. In August 1975 an average of 5,000 worshippers travelled through Letchmore Heath to the Manor over the three day Janamasthami celebrations. Gradually, over the years the numbers grew and grew – by 1980 there were an average of over 14,000 worshippers each day for the same festival (these figures are from AgHBC/A:33–34). This meant a very large number of cars and coaches, all having to squeeze into the narrow country lanes. Even worse, the devotees of ISKCON staffing the Manor were not expecting these crowds either, and so were not at all prepared for the complex arrangements required to accommodate such a volume of people. At first there was nowhere within the grounds of the Manor for people to park except for some muddy fields. Many of the visitors took the easier option and simply parked on the streets of the village – in many cases blocking the roads, whilst also causing a disturbance to the local residents.

Faced with such a dramatic change to their village, which was happening with no obvious reason – even to the surprise of the people who owned the Manor – there was a lot of justification for the complaints that were made to the local council (Hertsmere Borough Council) by local residents in the first few years of the Manor being used in such a way. The Hindu visitors were going to the temple in good faith, for profound spiritual reasons. But they were creating a nuisance through doing so. Something needed to be done to prevent this nuisance. In fact, over the first few years changes were made to alleviate the problems these crowds created. Through liaison with the local council, ISKCON made plans for a car park within the Manor grounds, and planning permission for this was granted by the council in 1977 providing space for 127 cars (AgHBC:33; AdPE:155). This relieved the problem of parking within the village, but the problems of congestion on the roads into the Manor grounds, and into the village itself, were still not resolved.

Since the opening of the Manor as a theological college there have, therefore, been a number of complaints about the use of it for public access to worship. Most of these complaints have come from residents of the village, living immediately next to the village green. By the mid 1980s these complaints had settled down into a predictable pattern, centring around the fact that villagers regularly suffered at festival times from 'diminished amenity',[8] with experiences of five mile traffic jams leading to 'congestion in country lanes'.[9] Neighbours were finding that their overall 'quality of life' was 'badly affected by life next-door to the Hare Krishna temple'.[10]

In one case, a local resident told a newspaper reporter in 1988 that:

> 'day-to-day' disturbances had forced her to speak out. Since moving to the village in 1983, Mrs Burgess says, her husband and two children, have suffered from effects of traffic at unsociable hours, jams during festivals, spotlights from the Manor that keep them awake at night, and litter, including soiled nappies, dumped in their garden. She also cited the problems of sewage leaking from overflowing drainage ... and damage caused by careless drivers at the Manor.[11]

In response ISKCON attempted to relieve those ongoing problems that could be dealt with (whilst refuting what they considered the more spurious allegations of causing sewerage overflow). On the specific level of traffic through the village, they consistently tried to take the view that they would attempt 'to ease any inconvenience that may be caused to the locality'. For many years they liaised with local traffic authorities such as the police, the council, and the AA (the Automobile Association) before any large scale event such as a festival.[12] Within Letchmore Heath, the roads were 'coned' at such times to prevent parking, and police assisted ISKCON stewards to ensure a smooth passage of cars into the Manor grounds. When these measures have failed to work there has been a great deal of congestion within the village, as happened in 1980 when the traffic police made some (unspecified) errors (AdPE:156). But even with the full traffic measures in place at peak times during festivals there could still be considerable traffic jams. For example, on the main day of Janmasthami in August 1994 at around 6pm I observed a queue of cars stretching approximately two miles back from the gate of the Manor along Aldenham Road, coming from London. Thus although Krishna is always in place at the Manor, since the

Radha-Gokulananda *murtis* remain located in their home in the temple room, their presence, and the facilities that ISKCON offer for devotees at the Manor, generates a high volume of movement, and this movement of people (people's bodies) causes disruption and disturbance to many who live in the environment of the Manor.

Krishna's place

The presence of devotees' bodies at the Manor, as well as their cars on the roads giving access to the Manor, are themselves the direct product of the embodiment of Krishna (in his manifestation as Radha-Gokulananda) at that particular place. Thus whilst the local residents see only queues of waiting cars, the occupants see something very different – that is, a highly charged location which has at its centre a powerful figure of devotion. This is the reason for visiting that ISKCON leaders themselves wish to encourage and promote, for example in promotional literature they describe the Manor as such:

> Bhaktivedanta Manor ... serves as a theological college and has a magnificent shrine for the worship of Shree Shree Radha Gokulananda and Shree Shree Sita Rama Laxaman Hanuman. In the last two decades, Bhaktivedanta Manor has become renowned as an important place of pilgrimage. People are attracted to the different facilities Bhaktivedanta Manor offers. Many come for worship, others to help on the farm or just to have a stroll in the gardens. Visitors frequently express appreciation of the Manor's enchanting atmosphere – not only its vigour and verve but the radiant calm, peace and tranquillity. According to Vedic wisdom, the temple exists for the very reason of creating a clean and soothing atmosphere that will uplift and uphold us, directing our attention towards Krishna. (JB96:52, article called 'Bhaktivedanta Manor').

In one respect, the temple room is a large space in which crowds of devotees can come together and worship: chanting, praying, dancing, and showing their devotion to the deities. However, the temple is also merely an open space adjacent (but only at certain times open) to the smaller deity room which is inhabited by Radha-Gokulananda and the other deities. This room, and particularly the deities, are considered to be the heart of the whole place, to be the reason for the existence and perpetuation of Bhaktivedanta Manor, and which give it the atmosphere that it has. The embodiment of Krishna in the deities in the temple room works to create the space around the temple, around the Manor building and grounds, as Krishna's own space – as his *dham*, or domain.

Ravinda Svarup das describes this point on a general level with respect to the embodiment of deities in ISKCON temples:

> God's descent as the *arca-murti* [as a particular *murti*] manifests not only God but God's spiritual abode as well, as the temple itself becomes the image or replica of *vaikuntha-loka*. The temple is no less than the kingdom of God on earth. Just as in *vaikuntha-loka* God is eternally served in different ways by liberated devotees in spiritual bodies (*siddha-deha*), so the presence of the *arcavatara* here below gives devotees in the material world the same opportunity to serve the Lord with their material bodies. (Deadwyler [R.S. das] 1995:84)

Although Krishna's domain (*vaikuntha-loka*) is usually considered to be beyond the material realm, accessible for spirit-souls rather than material bodies, the embodiment of Krishna in physical representations (*murtis*) and in particular places becomes an important means of communicating this transcendental reality through material forms. At a phenomenological level, this is an important motivating factor behind the presence of so many worshippers at the Manor, to experience and participate in this 'divine' embodiment and emplacement. Akhandadhi das, former president of the Manor argues that according to Hindu law 'once installed the Deities are understood to have manifested [sic.] Their "dhama", or spiritual realm, in the area of the shrine. They are considered the owner and the Lords of the dhama' (AdPE:168). Thus (providing an argument at a public inquiry that the Manor should not be relocated to a less contentious site) Akhandadhi das argued that the connection between the embodiment of Krishna and the particular place of embodiment is so great that the deities (i.e., the *murtis* Radha-Gokulananda) can not be moved from the place where they are residing. Any movement of the deities could only be within the *dham* where they are located, unless there were exceptional circumstances which justified moving them to a new temple in a difference place. As such, the development of Bhaktivedanta Manor in 1973 involved the creation of a particular, highly charged place which is considered by worshippers to be (to some degree or other) not only a place of congregation and worship, but also as a place where Krishna himself is located and manifest.

Janmasthami festival

Krishna is thus manifest at the Manor all the times (sometimes asleep, sometimes awake), but there are particular times when worshippers take the trouble to visit the temple. On most Sunday evenings throughout the year ISKCON provide a programme of worship in the temple room, combined with discussion classes and a meal, and there has gradually developed a strong core of one thousand or more regular weekly Sunday visitors. But it is at festival times that the majority of Indian Hindus go to the Manor, particularly the festivals of Ramnawmi (in spring March/April),

Diwali (October/November), and Janmasthami (August/September). And of these festivals it is Janmasthami that is by far the most popular, and it has been the crowds of visitors associated with this festival that have generated the most controversy in the history of the Manor.

Janmasthami marks the celebration of the birthday of Krishna, when it is remembered that at the stroke of midnight, in the town of Mathura in northern India, Krishna was born in a prison cell, from which he was immediately transported to the safety of a new family in the village of Vrindaban.[13] Hindus from many different backgrounds (particularly Vaishnavites) consider Janmasthami to be one of the most important festivals in the year, and will mark the occasion either by holding a special gathering in their homes, or more usually by visiting a nearby Krishna temple. For devotees of ISKCON the festival of Janmasthami is *the* most important day, and it is essential that (if it is possible) one should go to worship Krishna at his temple. It is for these reasons that the shrine to Krishna at Bhaktivedanta Manor has become a very popular location for the worship of the deity on his birthday each year, and it is worshippers making their way into the temple that cause the traffic jams.

Once a Hindu family has parked in the Manor car park they have a variety of devotional activities that they can perform at Bhaktivedanta Manor on the day of Janmasthami. Of these, the most essential is what is called *darshan* of the *murtis*. That is, the worshipper wishes to have 'sight' of the deity,[14] and to this end s/he is very keen to enter the temple to do this. However, the space within the temple is fairly limited, and as already suggested there are many Hindu worshippers visiting the place at the time of Janmasthami. To deal with this ISKCON have had to develop a system in which devotees file around the inside of the temple, and other parts of the Manor, in order that everybody has the opportunity to have darshan.

On one Janmasthami when I visited the Manor (in August 1997) I joined the *darshan* queue to experience the long wait to see the deities. A snake of devotees filed along roped off lines across the lawn, first into a space covered by an awning where they left their shoes in ordered racks, and then through another awning up into the Manor building. This line then shuffled around several rooms and corridors, past a *jhula* (swing) in which the baby Krishna was placed (ready for worship and offering), past a television set showing video footage of *darshan* of Radha-Gokulananda, and finally into the temple room itself (which was crowded with devotees singing *kirtan* before the *murtis*). Finally, as the queue brought worshippers to the front of the temple room it became possible to make *darshan* of Radha-Gokulananda and the other *murtis*. But the pressure of people in the queue behind meant that no one had more than a minute (at most) to linger at this point. Having made *darshan* the worshippers then filed back outside through another door, following the route round the side of the building to the awning where their shoes could be retrieved from the other side of the rack, and then they went into the open air to receive some *prasad* (food which is blessed because it had previously been offered to the deities).

This process of making one's way to have *darshan* of the deities is well organised even if it is rather slow. The sheer volume of numbers of devotees wishing to enter the temple on the days of Janmasthami require elaborate arrangements to accommodate them all in the temple room. It is especially slow at the most popular times on the festival days (in the evening of the main day, and at the time of midnight when Krishna is believed to have appeared) when there is great pressure to get into the temple and the queue builds up. Devotees can spend one, or indeed several hours waiting in this queue to spend no more than a few seconds in front of the deities. The worshippers' patience and devotion as they wait so long to have such a brief religious experience is a strong indication of the significance of the deities, and of the shrine.[15]

The religious experience is not, however, limited to the inside of the temple room. There are many other activities associated with Janmasthami which are considered as integral to the religious celebrations. In particular, dramas are put on in a specially erected marquee in the Manor grounds. These dramas, called Krishna-*lila*, are on the theme of Krishna's birth, acting out the story for the education and entertainment for the visiting worshippers. But such theatre is rather more than 'public entertainment', it is a profoundly religious experience, directed towards Krishna for devotional and educational purposes.[16] The drama is performed at regular intervals during the festival days, alternating between English and Gujarati. Worshippers sit and watch the drama (which usually lasts approximately an hour), as elaborately costumed devotees take on roles from the early life of Krishna, miming to words played out on a public address system, and creating tableaus of the most significant events.

Another significant event at the festival is the taking of some food in the form of a meal. Throughout the festival the residents and other volunteers at the Manor are busy in the kitchens preparing foods, particularly spiced vegetable and pulse dishes, rice, chappatis, and sweets. But this is not ordinary food: once cooked it is placed in the temple in front of the deities, as an offering to Radha-Gokulananda. Once the deities have received it, the food is then considered to be blessed, it is *prasad*, which gives grace (or 'blessings') to those who eat it. These large quantities of food are then taken from the temple to a tent in the Manor grounds, and worshippers queue to receive a plate of this food to take as a meal, called *priti bhojan*. For younger devotees in recent years there have been alternative forms of *priti bhojan* distributed: foods such as pizzas are now also prepared and offered to the deities alongside the more traditional fare. With such meals the devotees then go to sit in the peaceful surrounds of the Manor, particularly on the large lawn which stretches down towards the lake, and together they will eat and talk with each other. In the summer, when the weather is fine, this makes a very pleasant activity.

But even when *darshan* has been taken, and *prasad* eaten, there are other religious activities that many of the worshippers feel they need to do for the auspicious festival. Within the Krishna consciousness tradition (as with many other traditions within Hinduism) there is a strong emphasis put upon meditation, and particularly meditation through chanting holy phrases (or *mantras*). The Hare Krishna movement is well known for its *mahamantra*, which I mentioned in the previous chapter. Because the grounds of Bhaktivedanta Manor are the significant sacred or holy space (that is, *dham*) of the deities of Radha-Gokulananda, it is considered as a particularly good place to chant the *mahamantra* and to learn proper devotion to Krishna by so doing. Therefore devotees may use their visit to the Manor to do some chanting (*japa*), either on their own, or with one of the resident devotees. Or otherwise they may meditate on a set of 'stepping stones' that are marked out on the lawn – the devotee will say the *mahamantra* for each of the 108 steps on this 'meditational path'.

There are two other very important elements of Bhaktivedanta Manor which make it a special site for many Hindus living in Britain, above and beyond the significance of the temple deities. These are the cows that are cared for in the *goshala*, and the *tulsi* bushes that grow in a greenhouse and are worshipped within the temple. For many Hindus the cow is considered a very special creature: its milk products are the basis of life, and human dependence on its milk make the cow like a mother to humankind. Therefore the cow is considered the 'Holy Mother', who should be respected and worshipped – in contrast to the ways in which Hindus see the cow eaten and abused in British life. The reverence given to cows is also exemplified by tales of the childhood of Krishna, who grew up in close contact with the creatures in Vrindaban.

Bhaktivedanta Manor is the only *mandir* in Britain which is able to tend cows. The space within the Manor grounds includes fields for cattle grazing and cow sheds. Bullocks are harnessed and put to work pulling carts, whilst the cows are regularly milked by hand, and the products from this milk are used in the kitchen and offered to the temple deities. Such treatment of cows is well respected by the Hindu visitors, who also welcome the opportunity to do *puja* or worship to the cows when they attend the Manor. Therefore, in a corner of the main lawn there is an area in which cow *puja* can be performed, and devotees make offerings of garlands, flowers, or money to these holy creatures in a way which they are unable to do at any other British Hindu temple.

ISKCON is not only an organisation for the enablement of religious practice, it also places a strong emphasis on teaching and promoting their religious outlook. Those who are trained at the Manor (or elsewhere) have learned how to go out to others and tell them about their faith. As

I mentioned in the previous chapter, such proselytising was strongly emphasised by Prabhupada, and has played a large part in maintaining the interest of Hindus who visit the Manor out of initial curiosity. Therefore, at any festival there is an important role for those who are well involved in Krishna consciousness to be available to answer the questions of visiting worshippers, to encourage them in their religiosity, and to help them with their spiritual needs and problems. This is often done through informal conversations in the grounds or in the buildings. More formally there are also stalls and tents set up outside at which literature may be purchased, and visitors may obtain devotional items such as *japa* beads, incense sticks, religious pictures, books, tapes, and CD-ROMS. These stalls, which are set up next to the car park, allow the curious and the experienced to keep in formal contact with the events of the Manor, and to be directed to members of the training college should they have specific needs.

A visit to the Manor for the Janmasthami festival therefore involves a great many activities, fulfilling many of the visiting worshippers' spiritual needs. On a sunny August afternoon the crowds of Hindus milling around the grounds, eating food, chatting together, enjoying each others' company may give the impression of a festival that is also a significant cultural event. For most visitors their visit is a form of 'pilgrimage' to see the deities, and to gain the spiritual experiences that go alongside that. One of the attractions of Bhaktivedanta Manor at Janmasthami is that it offers Hindu worshippers a distinct set of religious experiences which are unlike any that they can find elsewhere in Britain.

Even as the devotees leave in their cars, they are given a final blessing. Traffic stewards instruct the devotees to wind down their left hand car window, and then a later steward gives a small bag of *prasad* to the exiting worshippers. Through this food grace or blessing is given by the deities to the worshippers as they make their passage back home.

Krishna's embodiment

Every year for Janmasthami, a production team at the Manor publish a large magazine cum directory containing news, developments, special features, and advertisements, which is sold or given to visitors during the festival celebrations. For the past few years, one of the features in this Janamasthami brochure has been entitled 'Bhaktivedanta Manor: The home of Lord Krishna', and has contained a picture of the Radha-Gokulananda deities next to which is written the following:

> Lord Krishna stands on the altar, the all attractive person smiling and playing His flute. Next to Him, His consort Radharani also smiles, happy to see the devotees absorbed in prayers to the Lord ... The tranquil, serene atmosphere evokes a mood of worship. Devotees

> daily come to offer their homage, respect and to thank their Lord. Their simple prayer 'please let me serve You'.
>
> Krishna, the Supreme Personality of Godhead reciprocates with His devotees. Although impartial to all living beings, He has a special loving relationship with those devoted to serving Him. This relationship is established by service to the deity ...
>
> Devotees daily bathe the Lord and adorn Him with new outfits, flowers and garlands. It's meditation. 'The Lord is kindly accepting my service,' explains Gadahar das, head pujari, 'He has kindly appeared in this form made of marble to accept our service' ...
>
> People bring flowers, fruits, vegetables or give money – an offering of love. Some come with problems looking for shelter. They submit their worries, chant the Lord's names – and return, confident that the Lord will protect them – He does. Letters are received regularly addressed to Their Lordships, describing miracles and thanks to the Lord. Devotees come for guidance or to offer the results of their practical service. 'I hope my service will please you my Lord.' Parents bring their new born to the temple ... asking the Lord for His protection and guidance. People like to have marriages performed ... before their Lordships. No matter who or for what purpose, a visit to the temple is always pleasing. It is a feeling which brings them closer to Krishna – inspiring loving service unto the Lord. (JB96:56).

As I mentioned above, Radha-Gokulananda are at the heart of Bhaktivedanta Manor. As embodiments of Krishna their presence makes the Manor grounds special, and a visit to the Manor is very often done with the intention of interacting in some way or other with that presence. This interaction between deities and devotees is well known to those who are familiar with Hindu religious practice: it is extremely common for many Hindus to take part in some sort of practice which involves having dealings with deities as embodied (rather than disembodied) entities (see, for example, Fuller 1984, Waghorne and Cutler 1995). In many respects, deities worshipped and interacted with in such ways are treated as though they are embodied as humans and thus worship of deities mirrors the veneration or worship shown to other superior humans, such as kings or distinguished guests. However, as Chris Fuller points out 'no adequate analysis can ignore the fundamental differences between gods and men (sic) ...' (Fuller 1984:14). The deities are treated as being both like and not like human beings.[17] Thus on one level:

> The presence of the deity makes the temple quite literally the house of God, and the devotees dwell with the Lord in his house as a staff of

> servants wholly dedicated to the pleasure of their resident master. The devotees worship and serve the deity in the same way that retainers, ministers, and domestics used to serve and pay homage to the king in his palace. The deity is regarded as the factual owner and proprietor of the temple. (Deadwyler [R.S. das] 1995:83)

And yet at the same time, the deity is wholly other to devotees, more so than any king or ruler could ever be, since the deity transcends not only the particularities of the place where s/he is embodied, but also the name and the form by which s/he is known.

A conceptional means of imagining this may, perhaps, be the sociological idea of *charisma*, deriving from Max Weber's (1968) writing on different types of authority. Although for Weber charisma was primarily directed to special *humans* – as significant elements within social relations by which a person is attributed as having special qualities which set her/him out as distinct – I think there is a case to be made that such a social construction can be made of an entity which is imagined as being (like) a person. Thus what I am suggesting is the idea of the *charisma* of image(s) rather than the charisma of people. The difference between the two is merely that in the latter case (to which the term charisma is usually restricted) there is a manifest human body (and person) who is obviously operating in this field of charisma (and hence power). In the case of charisma of images, however, it appears (to the western observer) that the process of attributing charisma is applied to an inert object such as a statue.

However, the difference between the two is more subtle that this suggests. Thus according to Akhandadhi das

> Hindu theology [i.e. Gaudiya Vaishnava texts] stresses that the Deities are personal and nothing should be done for Their displeasure or inconvenience. There is a tangible relationship between the Deity and the devotee. (AdPE:168)

According to Weber, and generations of scholars since, it is out of such 'tangible relations' that the dynamics of charismatic authority has been manifest. Charisma is a means by which a person can develop and use authority (and thus power) over others through the tangibility of a relationship, either directly (face-to-face) or through the manufacture of the sense of such a relationship. Thus Eileen Barker describes how members of the Unification Church can learn to recognise the power of their leader and messiah Sun Myung Moon, a process which she describes as charismatisation (Barker 1993). The endowment and manufacture of charisma towards such remote and distant figures as Moon (as even more extremely occurred with the relationships between members of The Family and their absent leader David Brant Berg for many years before his death in 1994) suggests that the production of charisma does not need to rely on immediate proximity or embodiment. Indeed, it could even be argued that the most powerful charisma is a product of a sense of distance and detachment between the charismatic leader and her/his followers.

Along with Moon and Berg, new religions scholars have very often made use of the example of Prabhupada too as a good exemplar of charisma and the processes of authority. Not only did he show how skills such as rousing oratory are not necessarily needed to be seen as a charismatic leader (in Prabhupada the special qualities of charisma were innate in other ways, although most of his followers are and were ready to attribute to him very particular skills and abilities which marked his personality out as special). But in particular, it is the redistribution of Prabhupada's authority following his death in 1977 that has most exercised sociological study of charisma in ISKCON. That is, how a movement that was initially focused around one particular man managed to routinise his considerable authority, by developing a substantial bureaucratic power structure (the GBC) as well as institutionalising and naturalising traditional lines of authority (which have in some senses been grafted, or transplanted, from the Gaudiya Math). Indeed the success (and failures) of ISKCON since Prabhupada's death has revolved around these tensions between the bureaucracy of the GBC, the tradition (for example, to what extent non-ISKCON Gaudiya Math leaders should shape the organisation's development), and the counter claims of new charismatic gurus, wishing to take on and extend the charisma of Prabhupada (see R.S. das 1994a, 1994b, T.K. Goswami 1998).

However, the embodied element of authority within ISKCON is not limited to these formal channels, nor indeed informal channels such as between men and women through the mediation of important women, such as temple presidents' wives (cf. Palmer 1994). Power and authority within ISKCON is mediated most significantly through another medium, and that medium is Krishna himself, in his embodied forms through the temple *murtis* such as Radha-Gokulananda. Just as the charisma of a leader such as Prabhupada does not completely disappear at his/her death, but is continued and maintained in his/her image beyond the physical death,[18] likewise the 'non-living' deities also have a charisma of their own which is not dependent on the existence of an organic living body.

Devotees consider that something happens when worship is made to Radha-Gokulananda at the Manor. That is, they can have a relationship with Krishna through his manifestation, his *actual* presence, as Radha-Gokulananda. This, for them, is a real relationship, something which goes 'two ways'. The significance of the deities becomes cumulative, because they are so well treated at the Manor: firstly Prabhupada installed them, secondly they are regularly tended in a very intense manner by the resident *pujaris*, and thirdly many Hindus come to worship them each year. They are certainly not neglected, and indeed all these things are considered to please Radha-Gokulananda – therefore these deities are more likely to be beneficial to those who worship them. One very obvious example of such a relationship was a story that was related to me about a couple who were finding it very difficult to conceive a child – the woman was eventually persuaded to seek the help of Radha-Gokulananda, and because of the power (and magnanimity) of the deity, she soon became pregnant and the couple immediately dedicated themselves to the service of Krishna by moving to London to be near him at his temple.

Of course, charisma is a form of authority, and as such is a means by which power operates, and is legitimated. As such, the sociological concept of charisma is a useful explanation (c.f. Wallis 1993) for how a certain field of power relations can be maintained – the power of a particular leader can appear justified (to her/his followers) because the followers attribute charismatic qualities to her/him. At its most crude level, perhaps, this gives a (rather unsatisfactory) explanation for followers who faithfully comply with an abusive or manipulative leader, or even one who asks his followers to do unthinkable actions.[19] But in cases of charisma of images – where there is no obvious agent of authority[20] – it would be expected that the field of power is going to be very different. However, in cases of human charisma the play of authority between charismatic, traditional, and bureaucratic forms of leadership often create a dynamic of power in which the person endowed with charisma is not always the only person exercising power. Thus the process of charismatisation of Revd Moon helps to retain the authority of a whole class of leaders within the Unification Church, as did the maintenance of David Berg's authority in The Family, and as Mary Maaga shows, the physical decline of Jim Jones during 1978 enabled a group of his close female friends to be largely responsible for putting forward the collective decision for mass suicide (Maaga 1998). What these quite extreme examples show is that the operation of charismatic forms of leadership can work in very different ways, and in particular the ways in which the power of charismatic authority is exercised depend on the particularities of the field of relations in which the charismatic agent and his/her followers operate. But in such a case, the charismatic leader does not necessarily have to be a person who is obviously embodied.

Thus for many devotees at Bhaktivedanta Manor, it is possible to argue that Krishna in the form of Radha-Gokulananda is a sort of charismatic leader. He is attributed with form, with an agency, and thus is a (type of) person with whom they can develop a very real (sense of) relationship. Through this relationship many different forms of empowerment can be developed, in particular through the control that ISKCON leaders (particularly gurus) can exercise over devotees. However, another very significant mobilisation of power that came about through this construction and practice of Radha-Gokulananda was the use made by ISKCON of Indian Hindu devotees within the campaign to prevent the closure of the Manor. The devotion of so many people to Radha-Gokulananda served as a power bank upon which ISKCON were to successfully draw in the campaign, as I will outline in later chapters. Thus although the problem of the Manor developed out of the physical presence of so many people at that particular place, it also came to be resolved through the mobilisation of power of the sheer weight of the numbers who were interacting with the deity who had been placed and located at that site.

Notes

1 See, for example Asad (1997), Coakely (1997), King and Carrette (1998), Sullivan (1991).

2 Lefebvre makes the following distinctions between these three categories: '(1). *Spatial practice*, which embraces production and reproduction, and the particular locations and spatial sets characteristic of each social formation. Spatial practice ensures continuity and some degree of cohesion. In terms of social space, and of each member of a given society's relationship to that space, this cohesion implies a guaranteed level of *competence* and specific level of *performance*. (2). *Representations of space*, which are tied to the relations of production and to the 'order' which those relations impose, and hence to knowledge, to signs, to codes, and to 'frontal' relations. (3). *Representational spaces*, embodying complex symbolisms, sometimes coded, sometimes not, linked to the clandestine or underground side of social life, as also to art (which may come eventually to be defined less as a code of space than as a code of representational spaces). (Lefebvre 1984:33)

3 The cultural geography/geographical anthropology of place which I discuss here is also related to questions of 'mapping', that is the ways in which place (and more generally the 'subject') are perceived through the models and constructs which are used to shape them (i.e. maps). For a discussion of the social and political uses of mapping strategies see: Friedman (1998), Gell (1985), Harvey (1989), Pile and Thrift (1995).

4 See Pile and Thrift (1995:32–33). de Certeau's reading of Bourdieu's concept of *habitus* is that it is a 'mystical reality' which finally reduces the complexities of logic and practice which he otherwise examines so scrupulously (de Certeau 1984:59).

5 Domestic spaces are another extremely important location of Hindu practice, both within India and in British contexts. For a discussion of the relationships between home and temple religious practice in Britain see Nye (1995:94–96).

6 For a general discussion of the work of ritual in creating place, see Smith (1978b).

7 *Watford Evening Echo*, A haven – 14 miles from Marble Arch (Another in our occasional series about the tiny communities which are the heartbeat of the countryside)', 1st October 1979.

8 Media Release from ISKCON communications, 2 St James Rd, Watford, 28.8.91.

9 *The Independent*, Tuesday 17th March 1992

10 *West Herts and Watford Observer*, Friday 23rd December 1988, p. 6. It should be noted, however, that not all local residents have been negative towards Bhaktivedanta Manor. On a number of occasions some residents have shown open support for ISKCON's activities, for example in 1994 four residents of Letchmore Heath wrote to Hertsmere council in support of ISKCON, whilst another 13 sent pro-forma letters of support (AgHBC:26) and these individuals

also made their positive support for ISKCON known to the Inspector of the 1995 Public Inquiry (IR96:41–42).

11 *West Herts and Watford Observer*, Friday 23rd December 1988, p. 6.

12 *Nama Hatta*, December 1986, p. 7.

13 For a discussion of Janmasthami among Edinburgh Hindus see Nye (1995:147–51).

14 The word *darshan* literally means 'sight' or 'seeing', but to 'make darshan' generally means to worship (c.f. Eck 1981).

15 Devotees' patience in this queue is remarkable. On the evening of Janmasthami day the wait in the queue can be well over an hour, even before entering the shoe area, let alone getting into the Manor building itself. My experience was that the majority of devotees were prepared to endure the tedium of this queue quite well humouredly, although examples of impatience (particularly scuffles as some individuals 'pushed in') were not always resolved amicably.

16 The term 'public entertainment' covers activities such as *bhajan* singing, dancing, and theatrical performances. All of these are, in ISKCON's view, performed for devotional and educational purposes and have been misleadingly termed public entertainment by outside authorities (See AgHBC/A3:A36S; and AdPE:84 & 134). ISKCON and non-ISKCON discourses on these activities will be a theme which I pick up later in this book on several occasions.

17 Fuller himself goes on to argue that (writing from his fieldwork in the Minakshi temple in Madurai) the practice of deity worship (particularly by male temple priests) involves a 'progressive identification of the worshipper and his god, so that the two can ultimately become one', so that before the priest 'starts any ritual, he should invoke the god within himself and then worship himself' (Fuller 1984:14). This particular observation, itself invoked from general practice among temple priests who subscribe to widespread Agamic precepts, is not however appropriate to ISKCON and other Gaudiya Vaishnava worship, for whom such monistic (*advaita*) talk of a unity between deity and human would be considered to be *mayavadi* (c.f. Deadwyler 1995:78).

18 For example, a statue of Prabhupada is worshipped in the temple room at the Manor (and most other ISKCON temples) every day, and aspects of his physical embodiment 'live on' in the taped discourses that he left, as well as his many books and papers.

19 For a discussion of the ways in which theories of charisma have been applied as explanations of Jim Jones' leadership and implication in the People's Temple mass suicide in Guyana in 1978, see Maaga (1998).

20 Krishna devotees will, of course, argue that there is an obvious agent of authority, that is Krishna himself, and in particular (in this case) Radha-Gokulananda. Although I would not like to either completely endorse or reject this claim (that is, I have no idea whether or not Krishna is real), the point that I think is worth making from this is that it illustrates quite clearly how devotees behave *as if* the object of such charismatic devotion has their own active agency.

CHAPTER THREE

Creating and Contesting Place: Planning Issues and Bhaktivedanta Manor

As I have sought to show in the previous chapter, the creation of place and the placing of religion are both political activities, since they occur within a range of political and power relationships. The processes of establishing religious sites which are undertaken by minority groups in Britain are thus framed (and resolved) within certain sets of relationships vis-à-vis these groups and state agencies, which impinge upon and are acted out within society-wide discourses on the political use and control of land as space. How space is used, and by whom, is very much controlled by the legal discourses of planning regulations, which involves the application of national government guidance through local state bureaucracies. Although practice of such planning is very often conceived of as a neutral activity, based on universalising and objectivising principles (such as 'protection of the natural environment' and allowing 'fair access and protection to all'), the construction, application, and experience of the 'planning system' highlights a number of ways through which hegemonic states and powerful groups and individuals frame and make use of planning guidelines to exercise control over minorities. In this chapter, I will be examining in particular some of the ways in which planning controls and legislation have been applied to minority religious groups, as a means of both controlling the activities of such minorities, and (on a wider level) as a place of debate about the extent to which this control should be opened up to the politics of multiculturalism.

In the case of Bhaktivedanta Manor, it is clear that many Hindus consider it to be a very significant place. Even if they only visit it on one day of the year, during the Janmasthami festival, these Hindus can conduct a number of profound religious activities which are particularly focused on the deity Krishna that is manifest in the shrine. But although there has been little debate about this religious significance, a prime question that has arisen from the use of the temple is 'is it right for this particular place to be used in this way?' That is, is the inconvenience of the disruption caused to residents of the surrounding area justified by this religious dimension? At one level this brings into conflict the separate (and possibly equally valued) rights of two groups – the Hindus and the local residents – both of whom feel they should be respected. The application and determination of planning procedures makes an explicit attempt to adjudicate the balance between these different needs. And in the case of Bhaktivedanta Manor it was unambiguously the case for a number of years that planners (and the political groups that they represented) considered that the determination of this balance should be struck in favour of the local residents, that is the planning system declared the illegality and inappropriateness of large scale public worship at the Manor.

The bases of British planning laws

Contemporary British planning laws have been continuously developed by various governments in the twentieth century, operating since 1948 on the principle that ownership of a piece of land 'carries with it nothing more than the bare right to go on using it for its existing purposes' (Heap 1978:13). Any attempt to use the land for some other purpose (that is to build upon it or to change its use) is given the generic title of 'development' (Greed 1996a:31). Such development is something for which approval is required from the state (through local planning authorities, which are part of the administration of local government or council offices), and the framework for approving an application for development is set out within government planning policy and laws (called planning policy guidance, or PPG).

Planning policies, and the laws that implement and uphold these policies, are generally concerned with the regulation of land use and development (Greed 1996a:31). But they are about more than spatial and geographical issues – planning is 'related to social, economic, environmental or cultural trends, issues and problems' (Greed 1996b:31). As Clara Greed puts it, planning is concerned 'with property and land, and therefore with money and power ... it is inevitably a highly political activity' (Greed 1996b:5). The most clearly stated objective of British planning laws was articulated in the first national planning Act of 1909, which proposed that planning procedures should have 'the general object of securing proper sanitary conditions, amenity and convenience in connection with the laying out and use of the land and of any neighbouring lands'.[1] This statement of intent focuses on the particular issue of amenity – a concept which has become of great relevance within planning procedures, particularly in recent decades (Cullingworth & Nadin 1994:165). Generally, planning laws (both in their drafting and their implementation) are intended to protect the amenity of an existing place, and so to protect and preserve 'pleasant circumstances or features, advantages' (Purdue 1977:486). But it is usually 'easier to recognise than to define' amenity, and in many disputes over planning cases 'there is considerable scope for disagreement on the degree and importance of amenities' (Cullingworth & Nadin 1994:165).

As such, the planning laws are an expression of the values that governments deem to be appropriate for protecting the rights of the individual, the general well being of society, and the preservation and appropriate development of the physical environment. For example, certain rural areas on the fringes of large urban centres are designated as 'Green Belt', and within which special planning laws restrict new buildings and limit the change of use of existing structures. Therefore, for a new development to be given planning approval (whether it is a house, a supermarket, or a place of worship) it must meet the criteria laid down within planning policy guidance issued by the government, and these criteria are even more strict for Green Belts than in other areas.

The role of planners within the implementation of planning policies, along with the institutions to which these planners are accountable, together comprise a very significant exercise of political power through what could be considered very 'everyday' or 'routine' social activities. The ways in which buildings and other spaces are structured and used are ultimately determined by the implementation (by planning officers) of planning guidance, and so at base all domestic and non-domestic space is defined by and subject to such agents of power. In an interview with Paul Rabinow, Michel Foucault rejected the suggestion that architects are directly instrumental in 'the organization, the implementation, and all the techniques of power that are exercised in a society' (1984:248). Although this point was not directly pursued in the interview, it is certainly possible to argue that it is planning officers who operate in ways similar to doctors, priests, psychiatrists, and prison wardens in Foucault's analyses: as people through whom power passes and are important in the field of power relations (1984:247). It is not architects who have power over subjects – he uses the example that 'if I want to tear down or change a house he [sic.] built for me, put up new partitions, add a chimney, the architect has no control' (ibid.:247–8). Each of the changes that are suggested by these examples would have planning implications, and any such modifications would require an exercise of control by planning authorities. The practice of place as an exercise of power is very much manifest in the activities of planning officers, and on a wider level the creation of planning policy guidance, and the adjudication by courts of significant planning disputes.

As de Certeau argues, however, the power of such (urban) planning and regulation does generate its own resistances, that is, 'the element that the urbanistic project excluded ..., contradictory movements that counterbalance and combine themselves outside the reach of panoptic power' (1984:95). These resistances are 'the microbe-like, singular and plural practices which an urbanistic system was supposed to administer or suppress; ... the swarming activity ... that, far from being regulated or eliminated by panoptic administration, have reinforced ..., developed and insinuated themselves into the networks of surveillance ...' (ibid.:96). The power that planners have is a very significant power, the decisions that they make structure the lives of the people who inhabit the environments they shape and seek to maintain, but those spaces are also lived and practised places, in which people 'walk' (to use de Certeau's grounded metaphor) and in so doing actualise some of the 'ensemble of possibilities and interdictions' of a spatial order (ibid.:98). Despite the best efforts of planning officers – and the weight of sanction and punishment that they can mobilise through enforcement orders, court rulings, imprisonment or fines – people do not necessarily live in and use spaces as they as expected to. The use-classes of planning legislation define proper and legitimate practice, whilst the people who practise within those spaces live out different codes. The disjunction and conflict usually occurs when the practice of place is so obviously different from the practice of planning, when what happens in a specific site is at odds with the determined planning status of that place, and in such cases the practitioners of place have to enter the discursive practices of the planners if they want to avoid a punishment which may even involve the loss of their place. This is what ISKCON found they had to do – to use the Manor in the way they were already doing (as a place of public worship) they had to enter the field of planning decisions and legislation. But in doing so, they were still walking in the cracks between the legislation, allowing the public worship despite a planning determination that disallowed such practice.

Religion, Planning, and Diversity

It appears that the implementation of planning policy has been practised for the large part in a way that assumes a normative heterogeneous perspective on 'British' culture and society, and thus planners have for a long time ignored both the existence of cultural diversity and the politics of multiculturalism. According to Richard Gale (n.d.) the response of planners in general, and the Royal Town Planning Institute[2] in particular, to cultural debates about cultural pluralism, and even to governmental legislation (such as the *Race Relations Act* 1976), has been both extremely slow and extremely stereotypical in relation to concepts of 'race' and diversity. Thus, writing in 1998, Gale observed that 'the terms in which the subject of "race" and planning is couched have remained largely unchanged in over eighteen years ...' (Gale n.d.:28), with a strong preponderance towards dealing with diversity (if at all) in terms of 'monolithic social entities approximating to the ascripitive terms of "colour" and "race"' (p. 21) which characterise 'black people' as 'victims rather than as agents of change' (p. 28). Although the RTPI did produce a 'seminal report' on *Planning for a Multi-Racial Britain*[3] in 1983, which 'marked a radical departure from the traditional, narrow preoccupation of the [planning] profession merely with matters physical' (Gale n.d.:19), because of the fairly weak content of this report, and particularly the overall response of planning officers to its approach, it has had a fairly minimal impact on the practice of planning policy in Britain (ibid.:28). It may only come as a surprise to planners themselves, therefore, that those planning authorities (such as Leicester, Glasgow, and Harrow) that have taken the trouble to monitor refusals of planning applications according to ethnic identity have demonstrated a clear bias against minority ethnic people (ibid.:26).

Likewise, the practice of planning policy with relation to religious diversity has been similarly ambiguous, made yet more difficult by the fact that major legislation has couched discourses on diversity in terms of 'race' rather than 'religion' (a point I will be returning to in chapter seven). Furthermore, there is very little in the way of policy guidance to planners in relation to religious issues (Edge n.d.). The practice of planning with regard to religion has had to address (in some way or other) the specific problem that planners have the power to grant or to refuse permission for the use of a particular site as a 'place of worship'. That is, the *Use Classes Order* 1987 includes the category of class D1 which, if granted by a planning authority to a particular building, allows it to be lawfully used as a place of public worship. (This category also allows its use for other non-residential purposes, as a museum, medical clinic, public hall, creche, or nursery, Greed 1996a:195.) To put this another way, if a religious group wish to make use of a building for the purposes of religious gathering and worship, for their activities to be lawful within planning regulations that building must have been formally granted 'planning permission' by the local planning authority as a class D1 property. Without such permission (that is, if its use class is for some other use, such as a residential dwelling), then the building is being used unlawfully.

Most religious groups therefore have two options in order to lawfully practise their religious activities in particular places: they can either take over a building which has previously been used for religious worship (most usually a Christian church which is no longer used) and so is already classed as a D1 property. Otherwise they can create a new building – either by constructing from scratch or by converting a building which had been used for other purposes (for example, a shop, a house, or even a stable) – in which case they are required to make an application for planning permission as a place of public religious worship to the local planning authority (that is, to change the use class of the building). The former of these two options is the more straightforward, since in the latter case the granting of permission for a new building as a D1 use class must take into account the needs of local residents and the general requirements and 'amenity' of the area.

In practice, this means that a number of religious groups in Britain have faced problems with their local planning authorities in obtaining planning permission for new places of worship. For example, the large-purpose built Swaminarayan Hindu Mission in Neasden, north west London which was opened in August 1995, took eight years to obtain planning permission from the local authority. Another purpose-built Hindu temple project in Tipton, near Birmingham is still awaiting planning permission to construct a reproduction of a Sri Venkateswara temple (based on a major temple in Tirupati, South India). In 1983, the aforementioned RTPI report on *Planning for a Multi-Racial Britain* noted that some religious groups (particularly Muslims) have been refused permission unnecessarily on the assumption of car parking requirements, when in fact the majority of visitors 'were more likely to walk than drive to a local mosque' (Gale n.d.:30).

This is therefore an area in which a religious group have to deal carefully if they want to legally practise their religion. The desire for a group to express their religion in a public way in a particular place cannot be granted automatically. They must first get permission to use that building on a regular basis, and so come under the force of the planning regulations. Should that group decide to exercise their 'right' to freely manifest their religion, by using a building as a place of public worship without the required permission, then they will be liable to criminal prosecution for breaking the law. Thus the planning system allows for the possibility of the criminalisation of an act of religious worship and as I will discuss in the next chapter, this is what eventually happened to ISKCON in 1995.

One particular area in which planning considerations often focus is the physical effect that worshippers have on the environment around a place of worship, through arriving and leaving in cars. A building which is primarily accessible by car can (and often does) create local problems of traffic levels and car parking at various times, and the resentment that this may cause among local residents or other users of the area can result in planning disputes. The idea that residents should be protected from unnecessary disturbance is most clearly articulated in planning discourses on 'amenity', as I mentioned above, since the general planning assumption is that increased traffic levels create 'diminished amenity'. Of course, such disputes are not limited to religious groups: parking and traffic are a product of nearly all public facilities in Britain, whether they are places of worship, retail superstores, public houses, or sports grounds. Complaints made against such public facilities usually occur when car-related problems are combined with other issues. For example, the construction of a retail superstore in a neighbourhood is usually welcomed because of the added convenience, but the creation of a football ground may be treated more cautiously, primarily because of the type of visitor and the behaviour associated with such a place. Therefore it is reasonable to assume that when protests are made about a particular place of worship, the substance of the complaint (that is, parking and traffic), and indeed the adjudication of the issue by a planning authority, may be an outward sign of relationships which are motivated by other issues. This does not mean that planning disputes over places of worship will always be motivated by racist or other culturally exclusionary factors: for example, in an interesting case a Roman Catholic Church was refused planning permission partly on the basis that it would be particularly busy 'at times when the residents could reasonably expect maximum peace and quiet' – that is, on Sunday mornings.[4] This case obviously discriminates against the needs of a religious majority in favour of non-church goers (since in principle the same argument could be applied to most Christian church buildings which are sited in residential areas). However, in practice the application of such discrimination is most likely to work against religious minorities since local residents, planners, and judges will be generally less disposed to tolerate infringements on amenity which fall outside of 'mainstream' cultural expectations of 'normal' behaviour.

The case of Chandra Vadivale shows some of the complexities involved in the use of houses as places of public worship. He has been using his house in north Oxfordshire (or more specifically a wooden building in the large rear garden of the house) as a *mandir* since 1986. This outhouse, which is separate from the house itself, is in Vadivale's view an integral part of his home. He uses the *mandir* on a daily basis for rituals and other forms of worship, as do his wife and children. Every week, he invites friends to worship with him, and once every month he holds a special *puja* meeting at which up to forty to fifty friends may gather. Twice a year up to 100–150 friends are invited to attend special celebrations at the *mandir*. The *mandir* is primarily dedicated to the goddess Gayathri, but it also includes many pictures and statues of other important Hindu deities and saints. One of these is Sathya Sai Baba, whose teachings Vadivale tries to follow seriously, and yet he also considers himself a traditional Hindu and sees the outhouse *mandir* as an integral part of his religious life as a Tamil. But not all the visitors to the *mandir* are Indian Hindus: a number of them are his white friends, some (but not all) of whom are Sai Baba followers.

In 1988 a neighbour made a complaint to the local authority, Cherwell District Council, about visitors parking cars in the road outside Vadivale's house. After receiving further complaints from other neighbours, and making some investigations, Cherwell council informed Vadivale that he was making improper use of his home, since the *mandir* building should not be a place of public religious worship. The basis of their decision was that the use of the *mandir* by non-family members would go 'beyond being incidental to the enjoyment of a house, to an extent that needed planning permission'.[5] He was therefore ordered to restrict use of the *mandir* to his family only.

There were various complaints arising from the use of his *mandir* by visitors, which revolved around the traffic levels, parking problems, the length of functions, and disturbance to neighbours. For the neighbours and the council these were disturbances that should not arise from the normal use of a private house, which had become too much of a public facility. For Vadivale, he was using his private house in a normal manner for a good Hindu, and furthermore the level of activity occurring was no more than that of his neighbours – it was merely different, since it was of a *religious* nature.

The problem of visitors' parking was solved by the direction of cars off the road outside the house, and through to the back garden, where there was space on a large lawn for up to twenty five vehicles. Having removed this problem, however, Vadivale was accused of turning his back garden into a *public* car park. Likewise, when he converted a part of the downstairs house into a toilet for use by visitors in the garden, he was told he had created a 'public toilet'. In the neighbours' view, he was therefore using the *mandir* as a public amenity, and providing the utilities necessary for such an amenity. Vadivale, however, merely saw these measures as a means of adapting his house for his visitors. The disturbance created by the two gatherings each year were also contestable. The presence of up to one hundred and fifty guests in his back garden obviously created a high volume of noise, as people talked together. His immediate neighbours found this noise intolerable, and it formed a strong part of their complaint. Vadivale could not see much difference between having this scale of visitors to his house for an act of worship, and having a summer 'garden party', which was a common occurrence among other households in this middle-class village. Similarly, the rituals performed at the festival involved the lighting of a special fire (*homa*), in which foods and spices were burnt as a form of sacrifice and prayer. The smells and the smoke were offensive to the neighbours, whilst in Vadivale's view he found them more wholesome than the smell his neighbours made when they 'roasted pig meat' at barbecues in their gardens. In this case, there is more than a religious/non-religious distinction being made – on the cultural level, the smell of spices and coconuts burning are not familiar in an *English* village, whereas the smell of burning animal flesh is considered (generally) appealing.

Another accusation that was made by some residents (which was not in fact taken seriously by the council) was that the use of Vadivale's *mandir* had brought an environmental threat to the area. The visitors allegedly left rubbish after them (something which is not at all apparent in Vadivale's pristine garden) and this litter had 'brought vermin to the village'. The obvious implication was that the visitors themselves were like vermin, with the use of metaphors of dirt and impurity to imply social distance (c.f. Douglas 1966; Okely 1983). Indeed Vadivale was the first Indian to live in the village, in a fairly affluent area of Oxfordshire which could be fairly accurately described as part of the 'white highlands' of south east England. On a social level, Vadivale has found little problem interacting with his neighbours, and he has not faced any outright hostility. But the complaints about the outhouse *mandir* and its (mainly Indian) visitors does reflect a level of intolerance against Vadivale's *Indian-ness* within a 'quiet English village', in many ways similar to the response of residents of Letchmore Heath to ISKCON and Bhaktivedanta Manor. At a council meeting in 1993, a councillor actually said he had no disagreement with the presence of Hindu temples in England, but such temples were more appropriate 'in the cities and towns' (such as Oxford and London), but 'not in the villages'.[6] It is certainly the case that a large majority of Hindus (and Indians) do live in urban and suburban areas (c.f. Modood et al 1997), and there are relatively few in rural areas. But this demographic separation is fluid and is likely to radically change over the next few decades. And so the suggestion that the place for Hindu temples is the cities seems to be predominantly about maintaining a concept of pure and essential English space which is defined (in part at least) against ethnic and religious diversity (c.f. Wiener 1981:46–64). Again, another councillor worried that allowing Vadivale to use his house as a *mandir* would 'open the door' to other religious groups such as Muslims to do likewise. By implication, 'the door' (an ethnic/religious boundary) should remain firmly closed.

Vadivale sees himself as something of a pioneer in this respect (in fact, he likes the term 'buccaneer'). He sees himself as one of the first of many Indians who want to move out from the cities, and of these there will be many other (particularly south) Indians who would wish to make use of the space in their homes for a *mandir* which can be used by both their families and friends. Therefore his struggle is a test case, with which he can manage to 'open the door'. He is not only fighting for a chance to worship, but also for the *right* to worship, the right to invite guests to his home, and the *right to be Hindu*. On the other hand, Vadivale may well be battling against what powerful classes of English people think of as the very 'essence' of English life, that is the countryside. That is, Hindus (and other minorities) may be accommodated into the cities because they are 'modern', industrial and alien to English life, but they could be seen as having no place within the countryside which is being actively maintained as an ahistorical and timeless representation of what Englishness really 'is'.

The conflict between Vadivale and the council was also very much located in his attempts to mix two quite different planning use categories, by allowing his home to be used as a place of public worship. The local planning authority, following planning guidance, were of the opinion that it was not appropriate for a building that is a dwelling house to be also used for public worship, and that such use without the necessary planning permission was a breach of planning laws. On this level, Vadivale did not agree, since such conceptualisations of what was and was not necessary for domestic life were at odds with his own Tamil Hindu perspective on religious worship.[7] In planning terms, he felt that the religious activity that he encouraged in his *mandir* was 'incidental' to the use of a dwellinghouse, and so he did not need to change the planning status of his house. This interpretation of planning procedures was of course at odds with those put forward by planning professionals, and so it was no real surprise that when the case was taken to a public inquiry in 1991, the Inspector judged that the use of the outhouse as a *mandir* on such as scale was not reasonable or appropriate for a domestic house. That is, use of the *mandir* lay outside of the planning determination of the house, since it could not be considered as incidental to a dwelling house. In the Inspector's view the use of the *mandir* in such as way was not a 'definite obligation' on Vadivale as a Hindu, but was in fact a matter of 'personal choice'.[8]

Following this ruling Vadivale was faced with the threat of prosecution for inviting friends to worship with him at his house. But, within a few months of the inquiry, the planning officer of Cherwell council notified Vadivale that there would be no enforcement of the council's decision, on the grounds that the number of visitors to the *mandir* had decreased. It appears that the council wished to make a legal precedent in refusing him the right to use his outhouse as a *mandir* for numerous visitors, but they did not wish him to stop his activities so long as his neighbours did not raise any further complaints. A caveat must be added, however, that although this has made it possible for Vadivale to use the *mandir* as he wishes, it is still open for the council to decide at any time to take action against him and enforce their earlier ruling.

Perhaps in contrast to this case, Leicester City Council is one of the few planning authorities in Britain to deal with contrasting cultural planning views on religious buildings in a positive and proactive way. Although, in a notorious report in 1977, Leicester council responded to a growing demand for minority religious groups in the city by seeing 'each place of worship as a potential nuisance' (Gale n.d.:29–31), by the mid 1980s they were viewing the role of religious centres as an important part of the urban infrastructure. In a 1987 report, the Council outlined a policy that recognised a potentially expanding demand for religious sites which 'was likely to continue to exceed' availability (Gale n.d.:36), but yet would be based on the unequivocal assertion that planning decisions would 'exercise a presumption in favour of proposed new places of worship, conversion of buildings to places of worship or extension of existing places of worship'.[9] To facilitate the activities of religious groups wishing to develop such facilities, the council were prepared to give practical assistance (such as requiring all major new housing developments to include land allocated for the development of places of worship) and also make clear their recognition that places of worship can in many cases 'contribute positively to the character of the city' (ibid.:36–37). Thus, rather than problematising the existence of religious and cultural diversity within the field of its planning activities, the council showed a willingness to systematically engage with the issues that were raised by the increasing demand for religious sites.

It is, of course, the case that a planning authority and council such as Leicester would find it necessary to take a rigorous look at the ways in which they deal with the application of planning decisions to minority ethnic and religious groups. After all, the city has a substantial population of people of South Asian origin, comprising a large variety of non-Christian groups (see Gale n.d., Marrett 1989). Even so, the approach that Leicester City Council have taken is quite unique, setting them apart from many urban councils with similarly diverse and multicultural populations. It is interesting to note that Leicester has for a long time had the largest number of Hindu *mandirs* within its boundaries of any city in Britain, and greatly outnumbers the ratio of *mandirs* per capita of the densely Hindu populated areas of north London. Although the positive policies of Leicester council have in recent years encouraged the development of religious sites within the city, this situation predates the 1987 report, and I would agree with Gale that the situation in Leicester is the product primarily of 'the capacity of Asians to be agents of social change' (Gale n.d.:62). There is no suggestion that all applications for development of buildings into religious sites are successful (c.f. ibid.:48–60), and the power to make decisions on the use of places still lies with the planning authorities, as delegated to them by the national government and as operated within the mechanics of local democracy. But one achievement that Leicester council have been able to produce is a political culture within the administration of planning decisions that shows a more overt recognition of cultural and religious diversity with regard to the social use of space in the city. In particular, the 'presumption in favour' of applications to develop sites as religious buildings is an approach that allows a degree of empowerment of minority religious groups, a point that I will returning to in a later chapter when I discuss the landmark case of *Manousakkis v. Greece* in the European Court of Human Rights (see chapter eight).

The planning status of the Manor

The house that is now Bhaktivedanta Manor was constructed in 1884, with the name Piggott's Manor, as a country dwelling for a family. For many years it continued in this use as a private house, until shortly after the second world war, when it was purchased by the Royal Hospital of St Bartholomew (based in central London), who converted the house into a 'residential training centre for nurses' in 1948 (AgHBC:33). The use of the Manor as a nurses' college continued for a number of years, until July 1971.

At that time a number of alternative uses for the place were considered, and applications were made for a change of planning status. As early as December 1959 an application was made to convert the Manor into a 'residential development' (AgHBC:33; IR89a:paras 9.1–9.3), but this was refused by the then local authority Watford Rural District Council

(Watford RDC). Following the closure of the nurses' college an application was made in March 1972 to change the planning permission to allow development of a country club on the site. Again this change of use was refused, on the grounds that the Manor lay within the Green Belt (and thus such development would contradict existing policy of protecting the area) and that such a country club would lead to inappropriate use and traffic levels in the small village of Letchmore Heath (ibid.). This refusal gives an indication that there were concerns about the problems of allowing a high level of public access to the Manor even before ISKCON took possession of the place. However, in June 1972 a further application to change the Manor into an old people's home was approved by Watford RDC, and it is likely that without the subsequent involvement of ISKCON and George Harrison the house would have been converted to serve this role. The planning permission for the retirement home was never implemented, and so up until 1973 the Manor retained its status as a place which was to be used as a training college.

The Manor was purchased in May 1973 by George Harrison for the use of ISKCON, and for a number of years it was formally owned by him whilst being held in a trust, until ownership was formally granted to ISKCON in 1981. It had been the expressed wish of George Harrison to find a suitable property for ISKCON near to London, to meet Prabhupada's desire to establish a substantial Krishna temple and centre near to the English capital. In many respects the semi-rural but convenient location of Letchmore Heath appeared to be the ideal location for the movement, although (as with any such building) it would require some physical modification to meet the needs of ISKCON.

As part of the negotiations for the purchase and conversion of Piggott's Manor into Bhaktivedanta Manor, ISKCON sought clarification from Watford RDC of whether an application for planning permission would be required. In February 1973 their solicitors wrote to the council:

> We are informed that since 1945 the property was until recent years used as a nurses residential college. It appears to us therefore that this is clearly the established use of the property, and that established use falls squarely within Class XII of the Town and Country Planning Use Classes Order, 'Use as a residential or boarding school or a residential college'.
>
> We are informed that our clients [ISKCON] propose to use the property as a residential education college being a theological college in connection with the promotion of the religion of Krishna Consciousness. This appears to us to fall within Class XII ... so that planning consent is not required but we should be glad to have your Council's formal confirmation on this point. From Messrs Lovell, White and Bird (Solicitors), dated 15th February 1973. (quoted in AgHBC:4)

This rather minimal outline of ISKCON's proposed use of the Manor is perhaps an indication that the Society did not expect the large scale of pilgrimage use that subsequently developed. The expectation by Prabhupada at the time was to create the type of institution as described, that is a residential educational theological college where members of the Krishna Consciousness movement would be trained to the highest standards. Furthermore, this training would be in connection with the 'promotion of the religion of Krishna Consciousness' – it would be directed not only to serving the already existing needs of the movement, but also to develop their missionary outlook and activities. It is possible that such a phrase included in the description of the college's uses could include the public worship, which ISKCON consider to be integral to the promotion of the religion. This is a point that I will return to below.

If ISKCON had at all perceived the need to use the building for public worship, then they would have had to make an application for new planning permission, since the Manor had not previously been used for such a purpose. It is perhaps a little surprising that there was no formal discussion of this option, since both Watford Council and ISKCON's solicitors must have been aware of the more appropriate Use Class XIII which was 'for public worship or religious instruction or for the social and recreational activities of the religious bodies using the building' (Purdue 1977:121). It is very likely that at that early stage the people involved in the management and construction of the Manor did not envisage the scale of public worship that was to develop, and so did not think it would be worth taking the trouble to change the Use Class of the building (especially as it was by no means certain that an application for new planning permission would be granted). At the time, and certainly in the legal disputes that ensued from this letter, it suited ISKCON's solicitors to make their description of the use of the Manor as deliberately vague as would be acceptable to the council. Moreover, it appears that it was *easier* for both ISKCON and Watford Council to treat the Manor as though it would remain an educational college, and any worship that did take place there would be ancillary to this role. Given that by this time ISKCON had created a large number of temples and other religious institutions across the world, it is quite likely that they did envisage the use of Bhaktivedanta Manor as a place of public worship (although probably not on the scale that subsequently developed), and so at some point they made a decision *not* to apply for a change of planning status to what they would have known was a more appropriate Use Class.[10]

The terms of the use of the Manor that were put forward by ISKCON were accepted by Watford RDC, who replied on 27th March 1973 that the use of the Manor was determined under Section 53 of the Town and Country Planning Act 1971 as a:

> residential educational college in connection with the promotion of Krishna Consciousness. (AgHBC:4)

In current law this is permitted under Class C2 of the 1987 Use Classes Order (AgHBC:33).

This acceptance of the use of the Manor as a theological college did not amount to formal 'planning permission', since that had already been granted to the previous occupants. But the 'Section 53' determination allowed ISKCON to use the Manor in the ways in which they had requested, and that the use 'would not constitute or involve development for which planning permission was required' (AgHBC:4). Having been given these assurances, ISKCON took over the premises and converted it into Bhaktivedanta Manor (which of course involved the installation of the deities).

As I mentioned in the previous chapter, almost as soon as worship began at the temple there were substantial numbers of Indian Hindus visiting the place to see the facilities that were available, to make *darshan* and *puja*, and to consult with the resident devotees. Complaints were received by the council from local residents regularly between the Manor's initial opening in September 1973 and June 1977. Many of these arose from the parking of visitors' cars in the village, and these were alleviated in 1977 when planning permission was given for a car park within the Manor grounds (AgHBC:33). But although this problem was alleviated, the council still remained concerned about the way in which the Manor was being used as a place of public worship, particularly because at the time the numbers of worshippers appeared to be increasing every year.

From the outset the council interpreted the planning agreement to mean that the Manor should only be used by a group of residential (and some non-residential) students and staff. There was, in their view, no allowance within this agreement for public access to the shrine and if ISKCON should wish such activities to take place then it would be necessary for them to obtain specific planning permission. Therefore the Manor was being used inappropriately for its planning status almost from the time that it became a theological college.

For ISKCON, however, the matter was more complex. In the words of Akhandadhi das, the president of the Manor, in 1991:

> We feel that Hertsmere ... have refused to recognise the character of a Hindu theological establishment. In India, a college such as ours will always involve the public. We are a missionary group and our planning determination ... recognises that the college has been set up with the aim of promoting our religion.[11]

That is, in ISKCON's reading of the law the phrase 'promotion of the religion of Krishna Consciousness' suggested that all activities connected with this promotion were legitimate for the Manor. Secondly, the role of a Hindu theological college will inevitably be very different from that such as a college in Christian traditions, and therefore some allowance should be given for this in multicultural Britain.

On the first point, ISKCON came to argue that it was very hard to judge where the boundary should lie between legitimate use of the building as a theological college and other unlawful uses. Some activities appeared to be unambiguously 'authorised', and were indeed accepted by the council as such. These included: the maintenance and worship of the deities in the shrine by the residents; the various strands of training of devotees; the teaching of the children of staff and students in the *gurukul* (school); administration of the branches of ISKCON in Britain; the educational resource group that liaises with schools and colleges throughout the country; and the 'Food for Life' programme that gives food to homeless people in north London (AdPE:51–64).

It was the activities that are associated with the shrine and particularly worship that created most of the ambiguity of interpretations. That is, the permission originally given to use Bhaktivedanta Manor as a place to 'promote Krishna Consciousness' was, in ISKCON's opinion, an obvious recognition of those activities which encouraged existing and potential devotees to come to the heart of the movement. That is, to have access for worship to the very important deities that are located at the Manor. Indeed, what better way of promoting the religion could there be than to allow these devotees to come face to face with living embodiments of Krishna? It does appear (in hindsight) to have been rather naive of Watford RDC to have accepted the phrase 'promotion of the religion' with the implications that this has for activities that could attract large numbers of people. However, as I will detail in the next chapter, on this point of interpretation of the Section 53 agreement of 1973 there has been unambiguous legal clarification throughout the British courts that 'promotion' should not extend to 'public worship' (AgHBC:5, see also chapter four).

Their second and more substantial point relies upon the different cultural understandings of what roles a 'theological college' should have. The Manor was founded as a *math*, a Bengali term which translates as 'theological college' in English, but which has rather different connotations. Such a *math* is a place where not only students learn about religious philosophy and the correct service to the temple deities, but is also a religious centre where there is open access for public worship. These places of Hindu education are centres for holy men (teachers or *acharyas*), who are given great respect for their knowledge and spiritual attainment – and as with Bhaktivedanta Manor, *maths* are also associated with high levels of good quality worship of the deity at the colleges. For these reasons, people will travel long distances in India to visit the well kept deities of a *math* (to have *darshan*), and to take the advice of the resident *acharyas*.

This model is clearly different from that envisaged by the Watford (and later) Hertsmere council, who were expecting Bhaktivedanta Manor to be used in the same way as a Christian (particularly Anglican) training college. In such a case, the predominant activity would be the teaching and instruction of a small number of trainee priests, who worship together in a small chapel which would generally not be used by people outside of the college. Of course at the time of the initial planning agreement in 1973 there would have been no cause for the council to expect otherwise – there was no attempt by ISKCON to explain that the 'theological college' that was being created would not be the same as the planners' normative expectations. But as the Manor began to develop in subsequent years ISKCON expected a degree of flexibility from the authorities, that – true to the ideals of a multicultural and multireligious society – the legal framework should allow some diversity for an alternative (non-Christian) religious group. In ISKCON's view there was clearly a great deal of legal ambiguity over what is considered appropriate for a theological college.[12] However, the planning status given to Bhaktivedanta Manor was as a theological college in the Use Class XII (now Class C2). That is, the local authority gave permission for the building to be used for teaching of residential (and a small number of non-residential) students, and for ancillary worship, but there was no scope within this permitted use for large scale public worship. Therefore, an attempt by ISKCON to argue in the law courts for flexibility over the definition of a 'theological college' has been firmly rejected, and the position made quite clear: no matter what cultural assumptions are involved, in British law a place categorised as an educational/theological college should not be used for public worship without a change in its planning determination.

Green Belt and Conservation

As there was no scope within the law to reinterpret Bhaktivedanta Manor's existing planning status, then legitimation of its use could only have been achieved by obtaining permission for development – that is, by obtaining the status of a place of public worship. Indeed, as I will show in later chapters, this was attempted in the late 1980s and was also the strategy which was eventually successful in 1994–96. In that case, the application to the Department of the Environment was to permit:

> a change of use of Bhaktivedanta Manor to a residential and non-residential theological college and religious community, together with use for public worship (including the observance of religious festival days). (AdPE:115)

Such an attempt to change the planning status was made problematic by the location of Bhaktivedanta Manor within an area which is specifically designated as Green Belt, and the village of Letchmore Heath is classified as a Conservation Area. Either of these classifications alone would make very difficult an application to change the planning status of the Manor. But the combination of the two has played a very powerful role in preventing such a change being permitted.

In 1993 a total of 1,556,000 hectares of space in England had been designated as Green Belt, which aggregated to approximately 12% of total English land space, one third of which was around London (PPG2:para 1.3). According to recent government policy guidance (PPG2, issued in January 1995) the aim of Green Belt policy has been, since 1935, 'to provide a reserve supply of public open spaces and of recreational areas and to establish a green belt or girdle of open space' (PPG2:para 1.2). This is reiterated further by the fundamental aim that:

> Green Belt policy is to prevent urban sprawl by keeping land permanently open; the most important attribute of Green Belts is their openness. (PPG2:para 1.4)

There is the additional view that:

> The essential characteristic of Green Belts is their permanence. Their protection must be maintained as far as can be seen ahead. (ibid.:para 2.1)

Quite what is meant by this governmental guidance on how 'openness' should be interpreted is not clearly set out: for whom should the land be 'kept open', and which activities and interests are served by allowing such openness? To a degree these are addressed, inasmuch as it is stated that the designation of land as Green Belt has the following purposes:

> to check the unrestricted sprawl of large built-up areas; to prevent neighbouring towns from merging into one another; to assist in safeguarding the countryside from encroachment; to preserve the setting and special character of historic towns; and to assist in urban regeneration, by encouraging the recycling of derelict and other urban land. (ibid.:para 1.5).

And so the use of land in Green Belts is to 'have a positive role in fulfilling the following objectives':

> to provide opportunities for access to the open countryside for the urban population; to provide opportunity for outdoor sport and outdoor recreation near urban areas; to retain attractive landscapes, and enhance landscapes, near where to people live ... (ibid.:para 1.6)

Thus, the ideology of Green Belt, and its implementation through the practice of planning procedures, has been a self conscious attempt by successive governments to control the indefinite physical spread of urban environments into non-urban (that is rural) locations. In doing so, non-rural 'open' spaces will be retained (or created) which serve to counter-balance the confines of claustrophobic urbanity. It is not in fact the task of the national government to determine precisely which land should be so designated as Green Belt. Instead, it is determined at a more local level by county and district councils (in consultation with national government through the Department for the Environment) to determine which land comes under this category in their structure plans. However, although the boundaries of actual land are (and should be) designated at local level, how that land should then be used through planning practice is very much under the guidance and power of national policy and policy implementors.

The philosophy underpinning Green Belt planning policy is based on a conceptualisation of space that maps two quite distinct entities (which have their own essential properties): the city and the countryside, which in this context are polarised into an evaluative dichotomy. That is, the city is dangerous and threatening, whilst the countryside is a place of peace, tranquillity and naturalness. The city is, thus, a place which is both conceived of as a totalising and rational project (as planned order) and also as a threateningly 'universal and anonymous subject' (de Certeau 1984:94), which stands as the antithesis of 'unspoilt' countryside, ready to consume vulnerable rural spaces.[13]

In planning discourses the concepts of 'encroachment' and 'urban sprawl' are manifestations of such urbanity out of place. To protect against this fearful creature, there are politically designated 'green' sites (linked together in a 'belt' around cities such as London), which Green Belt planning policies have the express purposes of keeping intact as far as possible. The current policy guidance made the clear statement that there should be 'a general presumption against development' in the Green Belt (PPG2:para 3.1), other than for purposes required for mineral extraction, agriculture, small facilities for outdoor sport and recreation, or other uses appropriate to a rural area, or for the use hospitals or similar institutions (ibid.:paras 3.4–3.12). Thus the 'presumption against development' should encourage planning officers – as well as those making higher level decisions such as planning Inspectors and even the Secretary of State for the Environment (a politician who is part of the national government)[14] – to avoid allowing 'inappropriate development' in Green Belt areas. If a proposed development can not be demonstrated to fall within the above list of categories then it should be regarded by planners as inappropriate, and is so 'by definition harmful to the Green Belt' (ibid.:para 3.2).

Even so, PPG2 still give some measure of leeway on this point, allowing such inappropriate development in cases where there are 'very special circumstances' or other advantages arising from the development (ibid.). In order to make such a decision, the planners (particularly Inspectors) are required to go through a 'balancing exercise' which weighs the harm to the Green Belt against the advantages of the special circumstances. In practice, these recommendations entail that any development that is considered inappropriate in a Green Belt area is unlikely to be allowed, unless a case can be made powerfully enough in its favour. This may, in some cases rely on the social or moral power of the case that is made – such as the religious or cultural need of a particular group to be considered as special circumstances – but most usually depends on more pragmatic and tangible political and economic arguments.[15]

As I discussed above, the foundation of the Manor in 1973 as a theological college was only possible because the council did not consider such an institution to be much different from the previous nurses' home – any suggestion of the uses that subsequently developed would have led to refusal on the grounds of inappropriateness in the protected Green Belt site. Throughout the subsequent years of conflict between Hertsmere council and ISKCON, the council argued that to allow the Manor to be used for anything more than this, particularly for public worship, would be inappropriate in such a sensitive Green Belt site. This was most clearly summed up in a statement they made in 1994 that:

> the intensity of the use which attracts large numbers of people and their vehicles to the Manor on a regular basis throughout the year and very large numbers at festival times ... materially impinges on the character, appearance and openness of the surrounding Green Belt and is detrimental to the character of the surrounding, essentially rural, countryside. (AgHBC:Recommendations, p.1)

And so any suggestion of development of the Manor as a place of public worship 'conflicts with Green Belt policies both at national and at local levels' (AgHBC:1).

Linked to this attempt to protect the immediate Green Belt environment of Letchmore Heath and Hertfordshire, the council also considered the use of the Manor for large-scale worship as against the interests of the wider national and global environment. Allowing the Manor to be developed as a place of public worship would, according to Hertsmere council, encourage even more visitors, thus bringing larger numbers of cars into the Green Belt area, creating 'additional travel by private motor vehicles and cause an increase in CO2 emissions' (AgHBC:Recommendations, p.2). Such a view was considered by the council to be in line with the recent international planning idea of 'sustainability' which 'aims to meet the needs of the present without compromising the ability of future generations to meet their own needs' (AgHBC:Report, p.6). This was outlined in PPG13 (Planning Policy Guidance) issued in March 1994 which have the key aims:

> that local authorities carry out their land use policies and transport programmes in ways which help to reduce growth in the length and number of motorised journeys; encourage alternative means of travel

> which have less environmental impact; and hence reduce reliance on the private car. (AgHBC:6)

The implication was that in the interest of the Green Belt, Hindus should be discouraged from travelling to the area in their cars, and that the principles of 'sustainability' could be achieved by making Hindus worship at *mandirs* closer to their homes.

The status of Letchmore Heath as a Conservation Area further amplified the council's position that the creation of a place of large scale public worship in the village would be an inappropriate development. The village became a Conservation Area in 1969 and is 'regarded as one of [Hertsmere's] most attractive areas' for which 'special attention shall be paid to the desirability of preserving or enhancing the character or appearance of that area' (AgHBC:11). To a large extent this status derives from the image of Letchmore Heath as a particularly picturesque place. The designation as a Conservation Area is intended to preserve and enhance these physical characteristics which fit in with this image, and to downplay, prevent, and remove those which do not fit in. Within this framework, Bhaktivedanta Manor is an integral part of this Conservation Area, and it was itself listed as a Grade II building in 1985. However, this could be considered a factor in favour of the public use of the building, since as the council report states:

> The use of listed buildings is generally welcomed provided that the uses to which they are put are compatible with their conservation. The use of the Manor for public worship enables public access to an historic building ... While the use could in general be supported as being an appropriate one for a listed building some concern has to be expressed about the intensive nature of the use and the effect that this could have on the buildings and its grounds. (AgHBC:12)

Overall, the council felt that:

> One of the particular characteristics of the village is its quiet ambience and it is considered that this would be adversely affected by large attendances at festivals in the grounds of the Manor. ... It is the use for public worship and the observance of festival days which causes harm to the character of the village by the amount of activity generated. (AgHBC:11–12)

Therefore:

> the use of Bhaktivedanta Manor for the purposes of public worship and the observance of public festivals would, especially by virtue of the scale of the numbers of people attracted to such events: (a) be detrimental to the character of the Conservation Area by reason of the

> intensity of the use; (b) be detrimental to the appearance of the Conservation Area by reason of vehicular parking and the erection of temporary structures within the grounds of the Manor... In the light of the above the proposal ... fails to preserve or enhance the character or appearance of the Conservation Area. (AgHBC:Recommendations, p.3)

The level of traffic making its way to the Manor on festival days was, therefore, considered by the council to be contrary to both the Green Belt and Conservation Area status of the area, in which any development should discourage rather than encourage a high volume of traffic in the area.

Thus, in planning terms, ISKCON were facing a very much uphill struggle to change what they had first registered as a theological college into a place of public worship. There were strong arguments coming from within the planning system to prevent such development, even though the Manor was for many years (from 1973 onwards) a very popular place of worship. If the Manor had been outside of the Green Belt then their case might have been looked on a little more sympathetically, but even then the experiences of other religious groups has shown that planning approval can be difficult to obtain even in less sensitive areas. It is worth remarking here that the Leicester City Council policy of presuming in favour of applications for religious sites would have given ISKCON a strong advantage in this respect since. If they had had to make such an application in Leicester on a site that was not classed as Green Belt, then the onus would have been on showing the reasons *against* the development of the temple, rather than (as they had to) having to work hard to show the reasons for the proposal.

In this brief overview of the planning considerations surrounding the Manor dispute I have condensed into a relatively synchronic perspective a series of perspectives and arguments that were in fact developed over a period of twenty years. The period between the initial planning determination of the Manor as a 'theological college' in 1973, and the eventual granting of permission for its use as a place of public worship in 1996 saw a continuous development of debate which emerged from the planning conflict. Although the eventual outcome was achieved within the mechanics of the planning systems, the conflict and the outcome extended far beyond any 'pure planning' issues and were bound up very strongly with contested ideas about multicultural Britain and the place and placing of religiosity (particularly alternative and minority religious groups) within this context. In the next chapters I will examine how the conflict between ISKCON, their neighbours, and Hertsmere council gradually unfolded and developed as a test case for how the needs of a particular minority group should be considered within a planning system that for the large part fails to recognise the political control that it wields over the use of space in contemporary Britain.

Notes

1 The Housing, Town Planning, Etc. Act 1909, quoted in Heap (1978: 5).

2 The RTPI is the national representative body of the town planning profession in Britain.

3 This report was a (delayed) response to the implementation of the *Race Relations Act* 1976, section 71 of which required local authorities (and hence planners) to 'eliminate racial disadvantage' and 'to promote equality of opportunity, and good race relations between persons of different racial groups' (Gale n.d.: 18).

4 *South Cambridgeshire District Council v East Anglian Roman Catholic Diocese* (1986) I P.A.D. 498, quoted in Edge (n.d.).

5 *Oxford Times*, Friday 19th April 1991.

6 Quotes in this paragraph are Mr Vadivale's renditions of the councillors' statements.

7 An earlier planning case in 1987 had involved the dilemma of a Sikh family who were subject to an enforcement notice, following an extended visit to their home of a religious leader (*sant*). During his stay, groups of around forty Sikhs had come to the house to pay their respects to the *sant* and to chant prayers, which prompted the local council to assume that the use of the house had changed to mixed residential and religious use – hence the enforcement notice. However, following the departure of the *sant* the enforcement notice remained, and even when the Sikh house owner applied for the notice to be quashed the judge refused to do so since the law was quite clear that there is a boundary between public worship and activities that are incidental to the enjoyment of a dwelling house. Quite where this boundary lies, and what types of religious activity are and are not incident to residential use, was not made specific. See *ex parte Sarvan Singh Seera* [1986] 53 P. & C.R. 281 (Queen's Bench Division), and Edge (n.d.).

8 *Cherwell District Council v. Vadivale* (1991) 6 P.A.D. 433, quoted in Edge (n.d.).

9 *Places of Worship in Leicester, 1987*. Planning Department, Leicester City Council, 1987, quoted in Gale (n.d.: 35).

10 It is also worth noting that at around this time (as I will discuss in chapter five), ISKCON were already facing a similar problem of planning permission for worship at their central London temple in a flat in Bury Place.

11 Media Release from ISKCON communications, 28.8.91.

12 *West Herts and Watford Observer*, Friday 20th March 1992, p. 7.

13 There is undoubtedly a gendered element to the conceptualisations underpinning this representation, which plays upon the concepts of control and licentiousness explored by Elizabeth Wilson (1991). The rapaciousness of urban development is both feared by men as an expression of uncontrolled and chaotic female sexuality, and at the same time can be seen as a threateningly male sexuality which seeks to devour the prim propriety of the ordered (feminised) locations of countryside in the 'virgin' Green Belt. Indeed the location of the Green Belt on the borderlands and margins between the city and the countryside places them within the heart of these contradictory constructions of gendered sexual identity.

14 A governmental reorganisation of ministries in 1998 led to the creation of a new administrative Department of Transport, the Environment, and the Regions, with a single Secretary of State, under whom various ministers have responsibility for particular areas.

15 The case of the mobile phone company Vodafone in Newbury is an obvious example of how economic arguments can be used as an effective lever to allow

'inappropriate development' on Green Belt land. In April 1999 Vodafone were granted permission by the local planning authority to build a large office complex for their administrative headquarters after they threatened to move the complex to another town, thus depriving the local area (and economy) of a substantial number of jobs. Because the granting of this permission violated local planning policy, as well as national Green Belt policy, the decision has been referred to the Secretary of State (currently John Prescott), and thus will require a public inquiry (*Guardian*, April 29th 1999).

PART TWO

CHAPTER FOUR

The Battle over Public Worship: Attempts to Enforce

Early problems

By the end of the 1970s, Bhaktivedanta Manor had become a very popular religious centre for a number of Hindus living in Britain. A pattern had been established that at Janmasthami particularly, but also at other smaller festivals, there would be thousands of visitors arriving at the Manor, and thus causing some traffic disturbance to the neighbouring village of Letchmore Heath.

Complaints were made by local residents on a number of occasions during the 1970s about the level of traffic associated with the festivals, and with other disturbances that they felt these religious activities caused. In response to these complaints Hertsmere Borough Council had numerous consultations with the Manor authorities. One result of these consultations was the permission given for the car park within the Manor grounds in 1977, and for a short time following this development the complaints appeared to diminish.

However, the relationship between the council and ISKCON deteriorated again in 1980. At the Janmasthami festival in August that year the council found that the scale of attendance was far greater than they had been led to expect, with an average of 14,000 visitors per day instead of the forecasted 6,000 (quoted in AgHBC/A1:33). Furthermore, although the council had been notified that Janmasthami would take place on a Sunday and Monday, in fact the festivities began earlier with large scale worship on the Saturday (IR89a: para 18.10, p.46). A further gathering on the Tuesday (the actual day of Janmasthami) was attended by 15,000 worshippers, when traffic congestion caused the village to be 'sealed off for some hours' (IR89a: para 18.10, p.46).[1] According to ISKCON, this congestion was the result of 'an error by the police supervising the traffic in the village' (AdPE:156). It seems, therefore, that a combination of factors over the Janmasthami weekend led to a large number of complaints from the local residents, and a feeling on the part of the council that some action needed to be taken.

Within a few months, in November 1980, a planning sub-committee of Hertsmere council decided to issue an Enforcement Notice against ISKCON, which was formally issued in March 1981. This notice, prompted by the failure to control the volume of visitors to the Manor, tried to stop public festivals being held at the Manor[2] by limiting attendance to no more than 1,000 visitors on any day.[3] The purpose of this notice was to ensure that within three months ISKCON should:

> discontinue the use of the [Manor] for public worship and public entertainment involving visits by more than 1,000 persons during any one day except with the prior written approval of the local planning authority and in compliance with any condition subject to which such approval was given.[4]

ISKCON objected to this notice and made an appeal. A Public Inquiry was opened to hear this appeal on 8th June 1982. However, at this point there was clearly no wish by either party to fight the issue out at this level. On the first morning of the inquiry negotiations took place between the parties leading to ISKCON agreeing to enter an agreement that would restrict the number of worshippers at the Manor. In response, Hertsmere agreed to withdraw the enforcement notice, and so the inquiry closed (IR89a: para 9.9, p.10).

The Section 52 Agreement

It was with some reluctance that ISKCON decided to enter a binding agreement with Hertsmere which would 'limit the numbers of visitors to not exceed 1,000 persons on more than 6 occasions per year, and that not more than 50 persons be accommodated for residential purposes' (AgHBC/A1:34). Some years later a subsequent temple president said that he felt they 'had to some extent been bullied into signing' the agreement.[5] But after several months delay – in which efforts were made to find a 'suitable arbitrator' – the two parties signed a Section 52 legal agreement under seal voluntarily[6] on 25th January 1983.

The main clause of this section 52 agreement stated:

> The Society . . . shall not arrange, or cause or permit to be arranged at the Manor any event involving visits to the Manor or any part thereof by more than 1,000 persons on any one day except with the consent of the Council. (IR89a: para 9.10, p.11)

However, ISKCON were also given consent to hold events involving more than 1,000 people on up to six days each year, so long as they notified to the council at the beginning of the year which days these would be. According to Hertsmere this was intended to provide for the three major festivals of Ramnavami, Janmasthami, and Diwali (IR89a: para 9.10, p.11).

According to ISKCON:

> The Section 52 Agreement regulated the six festival days when there were major attendances at the Manor, by imposing specific arrangements to cope with traffic, parking, noise, sanitation, etc. It further stipulated that ISKCON should 'not arrange ... any event involving more than 1,000 persons on any day'. Thus, ISKCON was not to organise festivals on other than the six days. (AdPE:157)

To a large extent this agreement did make clear and fairly unambiguous provision for public worship at the Manor. Although it was limiting in the sense that it restricted large scale worship to six days each year, it showed recognition by the council of Hindus' needs to worship at the Manor at these festivals. By permitting such worship it did appear to show a concession by Hertsmere council that Bhaktivedanta Manor could at last be used as a place of public worship, even though its planning determination as agreed in 1973 remained unchanged. That is, the section 52 agreement gave permission for public worship, even though the formal planning determination of the Manor remained as a *residential theological college* (i.e. to be used as a class XII type building).[7]

In fact the council showed some foresight in this respect by inserting a clause into the agreement which permitted them to take further action if they felt that ISKCON had not abided by the agreement. The section 52 agreement was issued 'without prejudice to its right to serve such further enforcement notice as may hereafter appear expedient' (IR89a: para 9.10, p. 11). That is, although there was a tacit agreement that ISKCON could use the Manor for public worship within agreed limits, the agreement should only hold so long as ISKCON kept within the terms of the agreement. If they did not, then Hertsmere would take more enforcement action.

For a number of years the compromise appeared to work, and the Manor continued to be used as a place of public worship on this provisional basis. In the mid 1980s the anthropologist Sean Carey wrote in an academic article on ISKCON in Britain that he was confident that any problems that may have existed between the council and ISKCON had been resolved, particularly because the costs of a legal battle appeared to discourage both parties from taking the matter any further (Carey 1987:98). Unfortunately this prediction proved to be unfounded, and the use of the Manor was in fact to be debated in a number of different courts, committees, and inquiries in Britain and Europe for many more years.

Breakdown in 1985

The accord that the section 52 agreement had brought between the parties in the dispute was broken in late 1985. A series of events led Hertsmere council to issue a writ against ISKCON seeking an injunction to prevent the organisation of any gathering which involved more than a thousand people in any single day,[8] thus attempting to prevent public festival worship. It appears that the celebration of Janmasthami that summer (1985) had not, in the council's view, been in accordance with the section 52 agreement. In particular, complaints were received from local residents that traffic arrangements were 'inadequate' and the Manor's tannoy system caused 'disturbance' (IR89a: para 18.22, p.48). Furthermore a drain which reportedly originated from the Manor overflowed that day, causing sewage to discharge into the village pond (ibid.).

The Diwali festival two months later in November gave rise to further complaints. Although the day of Diwali was one of the six agreed days large numbers of worshippers attended at the Manor on two days during this festival. The 'agreed' day was Sunday 10th November when several thousand attended. But then a few days later on Wednesday 13th November – which was the first day of the Hindu New Year – a survey showed that 3,119 visitors came to the Manor even though it 'was *not* one of the previously agreed festival days where 1,000 visitors could be exceeded' (AgHBC/A1:34, emphasis in original). ISKCON felt, however, that there was overestimation by the council of the number of visitors on this day since they included 'all the comings and going of residents, as well as students and staff living locally' (AdPE:158). This notwithstanding, the council decided that the way in which the Manor was being used by ISKCON needed to be made subject to further controls, and therefore they initiated legal proceedings again.

Factors behind the breakdown

For ISKCON, however, the change that occurred in 1985 was not interpreted as the result of any breach of the agreement on their part. For example, they say that none of the complaints 'raised about the Janmasthami festival ... were substantiated' (AdPE:157). ISKCON's interpretation of the real factor for change in this 'watershed year' was the purchase in May by a Hare Krishna devotee of a house in the village of Letchmore Heath (ibid.:159). This was soon followed by the purchase of the local village shop by two (Indian) Hindu women who began to sell items for use by Krishna devotees. The presence of ISKCON in the village beyond the confines of the Manor began to cause alarm among the white non-Hindu residents. One villager described the situation as

> [ISKCON] taking over the village shop as 'Krishna Food and Gifts' ... and excessive numbers of people living in 'Krishna Kirtan House' in Grange Lane [as] an annexe to the Manor, where the residents caused some disturbance to their neighbours.[9]

Another resident wrote a letter to the council in September 1985 describing the activities in this house and shop as 'an extension to the freaky goings on at the Manor'.[10]

The residents of the village worried that these purchases were the first stage of a plan by ISKCON to buy more and more properties and so eventually 'take over' the whole of the village, and that Letchmore Heath as the residents knew it would 'disappear'.[11] A campaign was begun by some leading residents, involving 'a number of letters and petitions which went to Hertsmere', the majority of which 'referred to their concern that devotees were purchasing homes in the village and that something should be done about it' (AdPE:159). Whether or not it was ever ISKCON's intention to 'take over' the village is highly debatable. Of course, if ISKCON supporters had ever managed to purchase a large number of local properties then they would have significantly reduced the local opposition to the activities at the Manor. But the high property prices for most of the houses in the village made such an option extremely impractical and unlikely.

A parallel could be (and probably was) drawn with the stories that were coming out of Rajneeshpuram, Oregon in north west USA in 1985. At Rajneeshpuram the unrelated Rajneesh movement – led by the charismatic Indian Shree Bhagwan Rajneesh – were in the process of taking over a whole town in the vicinity of their rural commune. Unlike Letchmore Heath, however, the Rajneesh movement had an obvious policy of expansion and involvement in local politics, and the site of Rajneeshpuram was in extremely isolated mountain country, not in the heart of commuter Green Belt.[12] It was highly unlikely, therefore, that there was ever any serious intention to convert Letchmore Heath into a 'Krishna Village'.

ISKCON did, however, try to respond to the local residents' fears by making it clear that they had no intention of taking over the village. In a meeting with Hertsmere representatives two years later, in June 1987, ISKCON gave assurances that 'members would not buy any more properties in the village' and they would:

> exert influence on members to relinquish properties already bought and on the owners of the erstwhile village shop ... to return it to its former function as a village general store rather than catering mainly for devotees. (IR89a: para 9.17, p.13)

But the villagers also feared that events happening among ISKCON elsewhere would effect the use of the Manor. In particular, the closure in 1984 of a property called Chaitanya College (Croome Court) in Pershore, Worcestershire, would result in an upsurge of use of Bhaktivedanta Manor. When it was purchased in 1980 it had been intended that Chaitanya College, which was a much larger building than the Manor, would become a major centre for ISKCON, particularly in the West Midlands (c.f. Knott 1987). Many of the activities and indeed the devotees that were based at the Manor could easily be accommodated at Chaitanya College instead, although the popularity of the Manor as a place of large scale public worship and pilgrimage would not be significantly affected. However, the building proved too costly to maintain and so it was sold in 1984. In fact, the sale of Chaitanya College happened more quickly than ISKCON had anticipated, and so accommodation for the former residents needed to be found quickly at the Manor. For a few subsequent months some devotees from this college were temporarily housed at the Manor. A council officer noted in July 1984 'several caravans parked on land at the rear of the Manor' (AgHBC/A1:34) which ISKCON agreed to remove soon after (AdPE:157). Temporary planning permission was given for them to use caravans and portacabins as short-term sleeping and office accommodation, but by July 1985 all the caravans and temporary buildings were removed (IR89a: paras 18.19–20, p. 48; para 30, p.107).

But the experience of this 'caravan site'[13] arriving in the Manor grounds was a source of complaint by the local villagers. According to one resident whose house was on the village green

> Since Croome Court was sold in 1984, there had been a great increase in traffic and numbers of visitors, with resulting pollution from exhaust fumes, and irritation from constant requests for directions to the Manor . . . The level of traffic (in 1988) had never gone down to what it was before 1984 . . .[14]

It is likely, therefore, that the influx of temporary residents to the Manor in 1984 following the closure of Chaitanya College was a contributory factor towards the breakdown of the agreement between ISKCON and the council the following year. When the house and the shop were purchased in 1985 there was a feeling among local residents that the new accommodation was being bought as a replacement for the recently removed caravans, and that some of the devotees from Chaitanya College would now crowd into houses in the village. Complaints and allegations made by villagers resulted in council officers visiting the Hindu house to investigate 'overcrowding', although it must be noted that 'nothing untoward was found and the investigation was abandoned' (AdPE:160).

Ethnic monitoring

Whether or not the council were motivated to take action in 1985 because of the arrival of devotees and Indians in Letchmore Heath, they did make concerted efforts to monitor attendance at the Manor that year. A private investigator was hired to stand near the gates of the Manor 'on a number of days in October and November' to monitor the arrival and departure of visitors.[15] However, it is clear that elements within the council were not only interested in the *number* of visitors, but also these visitors' *skin* colour. Frank Ward, a local Labour (opposition) councillor in Hertsmere, disclosed late in 1985 that these investigators were recording figures for 'coloured' and 'white' visitors separately (AdPE:158).

Given the nature of the dispute, the motivation behind monitoring overall attendance levels was quite obvious: the section 52 agreement relied on ISKCON having only six occasions in the year when over one thousand visitors attended, and therefore the council *would* be interested in whether this figure was exceeded. But the attempt to keep a separate record according the visitors' skin colour does encourage the conclusion that the Indian-ness of the worshippers was considered to be problematic in some way. The motivation may well have come from the fear of the 'Indianisation' of Letchmore Heath with the arrival of some Hindus, but this is no real justification. However, the council acted very quickly to distance themselves from the implications of racism arising from the disclosure of this monitoring: the private investigators were instructed to immediately stop making a count of visitors according to their 'race'. Council officers have also made it clear that the instructions to monitor according to race had not come from the planning authority, indeed it had been the investigators' own initiative.[16]

The decision by the council to re-open legal action against ISKCON therefore came against a backdrop of heightened tension between the groups throughout much of 1985. Another precipatory factor may have been the presence of a local resident in a key area of Hertsmere council. Councillor Michael Jefferis – an elected Conservative member of the council – was the Chairman of the Development Services Committee from 1981–1988, and it was this group that took the decision to begin legal proceedings in November 1985 (AgHBC/A1:34). In fact, Councillor Jefferis had a family connection with the Manor. His grandfather had been the owner of the house until its sale to St Bartholomew's Hospital in 1949 (ibid.). As the local representative of the villagers, however, Michael Jefferis took a leading role in many of the negotiations between ISKCON and Hertsmere during the period of his Chairmanship of the committee. He had been closely involved in the drawing up of the section 52 agreement, and was insistent that the Manor should conform to its planning determination.[17] The presence of such a figure at the head of such an important committee in Hertsmere council most probably acted as a strong influence on the decision to take further legal action in late 1985.

The High Court decision in 1986

The action that Hertsmere took was to issue a High Court writ against ISKCON in January 1986 to obtain an injunction 'due to ISKCON's breach of the Section 52 Agreement' (AgHBC/A1:34). If successful, the injunction would prevent ISKCON organising any event which might involve more than a thousand people in any single day[18] – that is, the section 52 agreement was revoked (since in the council's view it had been broken by ISKCON's failure to comply with it). The primary aim of the injunction was to reinforce the planning determination of the Manor as a purely theological college and to prevent the public access for worship which had been permitted under the section 52 agreement for the past few years.

The writ referred to the Diwali festival on 13th November 1985, alleging that ISKCON 'had arranged, caused or permitted to be arranged an event . . . which was attended by more than 1,000 persons without prior consent' (IR89a: para 9.11, p.12). In their defence ISKCON argued that the section 52 agreement required ISKCON to notify Hertsmere of any event which was likely to attract more than 1,000 visitors. But in the case of this particular day, ISKCON had 'no reason to suppose that more than 1,000 would in fact attend' (ibid.) and so could not be said to be in breach of the agreement.

The writ failed at a High Court hearing in April 1986. The judge, Mr Justice Leggatt, refused the application for an injunction agreeing with the case argued by ISKCON. He decided that the wording of the section 52 agreement 'provided for some element of foreseeability' and so 'the only elements prohibited were those which ISKCON expected would attract more than 1,000 visitors' (IR89a: para 9.13, p.12). In other words, his interpretation of the section 52 agreement was that ISKCON were expected to notify Hertsmere of any events at which they *expected* more than one thousand visitors, but they could not be held responsible if more than one thousand arrived at any other time if they did not have good reason to foresee such numbers.

Furthermore, Judge Leggatt felt that he could not grant an injunction under the section 52 agreement, even if he had agreed with Hertsmere's interpretation of it. This was because he did not 'believe that a local planning authority can sensibly restrict the number of persons attending and being admitted on any one day' (AgHBC/A1:35). This important point recognised that ISKCON and the council would be unable to set a limit to the attendance of worship at the Manor, and therefore it would be impossible to stipulate that no more than a certain figure (i.e. one thousand) should be allowed to worship at any one time. Thus the injunction that Hertsmere were seeking – and indeed the section 52 agreement too – were both impossible to enforce.

However, Judge Leggatt recognised that his decision would by no means be the end of the matter. He advised Hertsmere that it was their duty to 'enforce restrictions which were expedient and clearly understood by both parties' (IR89a: para 9.14, p. 12), and so they should find some way in which a revised form of the section 52 agreement could be negotiated with ISKCON. But if a new agreement was not possible, then ISKCON's success with this court case would only be a 'pyrrhic victory' since the council would be left with no alternative but to take more 'draconian enforcement action under the Planning Acts' (AgHBC/A1:35; IR89a: para 9.14, p.12). In fact, despite his ruling in favour of ISKCON he remarked that Hertsmere had been 'almost unbelievably reasonable' in its dealings with ISKCON.

With such further action in mind, the council continued to monitor the use of the temple, and found that the numbers of visitors on Sundays (that is, non-festival days) were 'rising steadily' each week (IR89a: para 18.24, p. 49), and were often 'well in excess of one thousand' (AgHBC/A1:35). Given the recognised impossibility of preventing such high attendance the council decided at a meeting of the Development Services Committee in June 1986 that there could be no means by which the present section 52 agreement could be modified, and an appeal against Judge Leggatt's ruling would probably be pointless. It was clear from the judge's ruling that 'that the agreement did not in fact mean what the planning authority thought it meant'[19] and that it was 'unenforceable' (IR89a: para 21.9, p. 65). Instead, the committee decided that a new Enforcement Notice was necessary, which would prevent all public worship at the Manor and limit its use to a 'residential theological college'.

Having reached this decision a period of further consultation between the parties ensued. Representations were made by ISKCON 'requesting an understanding of the situation' and suggesting 'measures for alleviating the sort of problems the council alleged' (AdPE:158), whilst the council's monitoring of attendance by worshippers continued. On six consecutive Sundays in May-June 1986 traffic monitoring showed that 'well over one thousand visitors in and out of the Manor had been counted' (IR89a: para 18.28, p. 50). At Janmasthami that year they recorded 4,631 worshippers on the Sunday of the festival, 2,339 the following day, and 8,781 two days later (on the main day of the festival) (IR89a: para 33/D/15, p. 111). According to a nearby resident the festival seemed 'to go on all the week' allowing them 'only two and a half hours sleep on one night' (ibid. para 27.23, p. 82). In the meantime the threat to the Manor was beginning to receive media attention at both the local and national level for the first time.

The 1,000 limit

The breakdown of the section 52 agreement followed by the action taken by the council were by no means inevitable, although in retrospect it is very difficult to see any other outcome. There was a strong sense among a number of villagers that ISKCON were causing a problem, whilst at the same time there was a sense by ISKCON that the section 52 agreement gave them the right to use the Manor as a place of public worship. The point at which these two conflicting perceptions met and came into conflict was the issue of the numbers attending for worship at the Manor – particularly the numbers who attended on days other than the six days permitted under the section 52 agreement. The agreement clearly stated that there should be a limit of 1,000 visitors at the Manor on any one day and, as noted, the agreement broke down – and the writ issued – because on 13th November 1985 there were clearly many more worshippers than this. In the recriminations that followed it became clear that this was not an isolated occurrence, and that on most Sundays during the year the number of worshippers regularly exceeded the limit of one thousand.

The point made by Judge Leggatt in April 1986 was that an agreement based on limiting numbers was unworkable. Even if it was possible to count every person entering the Manor grounds each week, it was highly unrealistic to expect ISKCON to turn away the 1,001st worshipper. Hertsmere planning authority did suggest a possible solution to this, which unsurprisingly was not taken up by ISKCON:

> Any limitation on numbers could perhaps be related to vehicles rather than people. A limitation of 1,000 persons would result in movements in and out of 576 vehicles per day. Any condition or clause in an agreement limiting numbers could only be effective if there was some positive control, as in a National Car Park where a light went on and the barrier stayed down when the premises were full. (IR89a: para 24.13, p. 75)

The matter was made even more complex by ISKCON's submission that the counting of visitors needed to take into account who the visitors actually were. In their understanding of the section 52 agreement, the figure of one thousand related to visitors who attended for public worship, and not those who entered the Manor for other reasons (i.e. on business related to the use of the Manor as a residential theological college). Thus according to their calculations

> a total of 220 people resident and non-resident came and went on a regular basis. These regular visitors . . . should be excluded from any count of visitors, since their comings and goings were a normal element of the use as a residential, educational, and theological college. (IR89a: para 12.20, p. 25)

For Hertsmere this interpretation only showed further that the section 52 agreement was useless. As their chief planning officer commented, if the Agreement could only be enforced by monitoring daily visits to the Manor to see who was using the building and for what purposes, then 'it would involve continued checks on every person going in and out of the Manor virtually every day, including weekends' (IR89a: para 21.24, p. 68). This clearly was impossible.

Several years earlier, however, in 1980 the situation had appeared somewhat different. In their response to the complaints from local residents after the Janmasthami festival that year, the council's barrister Michael Rich QC made the suggestion that they might allow the Manor to be used for 'something beyond' its planning determination as a residential theological college (IR89a: para 18.41, p. 52). Thus, public worship could be allowed 'in consideration of an agreement limiting the numbers to 1,000–1,500' (ibid.). He did indicate, though, that in his opinion an institution with a planning determination as a residential college (Class XII Use) whose population was 53 adults and children should not expect to have attendances of between 563–1119 people (ibid.).

This advice, therefore, was the source of the figure of 1,000 visitors that was later to be so contested. It did not take long for the planning authority to make use of the figure as a base line for their attempts to restrict the use of the Manor to what they considered a more reasonable proportion. In the early 1980s, Hertsmere had felt that it was:

> expedient to under-enforce, and took the view that attendances of less than 1,000 visitors could be tolerated without undue damage to amenity. Their attitude at that stage was that there was a problem with gatherings of less than 1,000 visitors, but they would strike a compromise, and consider at what level it was appropriate to take enforcement action. They were distinguishing between that which was merely prejudicial to amenity, and that which was seriously prejudicial to the comfort of residents in the village.[20]

More strongly Michael Jefferis, the local resident who chaired the Hertsmere Development Services Committee took the attitude in 1988 that:

> The figure of 1,000 was set well beyond the expected number of visitors on an 'ordinary' day. It was not intended to be a licence to have one thousand visitors every day. It was a backstop, not expected to be approached, and certainly not exceeded. If the villagers had been consulted they would have said a limit of 200 was appropriate ... (IR89a: para 18.63, p.55)

This figure of 1,000 was first suggested to ISKCON in a letter from Hertsmere on 6th January 1981 (ibid.: para 9.6, p. 10). It was nearly a year later before ISKCON responded to the suggested figure, when a letter was sent by their solicitors to Hertsmere saying that they 'would be prepared to agree to the restriction of 1,000 visitors for all other occasions except the festivals' (ibid.: para 18.13, p.47).

This led to further discussion between the parties, and so at a meeting of Hertsmere's Development Services committee in February 1981 the then temple presidents Ian Cheverton and Stephen Davies 'indicated that they could and would control numbers'(ibid.: para 18.82, p.59). According to Michael Jefferis, who chaired this meeting:

> It could be that Mr Cheverton and Mr Davies thought they were not giving away anything by offering to reduce numbers on ordinary Sundays to below 1,000, but from his counts he was under the clear impression they were in fact doing so. The agreement was intended as a restriction, not an opening up for further activity. (ibid.: para 18.82, p.59)

Therefore, in Jefferis' view in 1981, ISKCON 'had been prepared to acknowledge that there was a problem and that they would do their best to co-operate in resolving it' (ibid.: para 18.73, p.57).

The situation obviously changed over the next few years, so that by the time the case was discussed in the High Court, ISKCON were arguing that they could not – and indeed need not – control the numbers of visitors. For Jefferis, and others in Hertsmere council, the lengthy legal dispute that followed was created by this change of approach by ISKCON. According to Jefferis 'it was [ISKCON]'s subsequent change of stance in this respect which had provoked the service of the [enforcement] notice [in 1987]' (ibid.: para 18.65, p.56).

In contradiction to this, however, ISKCON claimed that the creation of the figure of 1,000 visitors emerged as a recognition by Hertsmere of public worship. The traffic counts at the Manor which Jefferis had taken in September and October 1980 – i.e. before the section 52 agreement was signed – showed that even at that time there were regularly *more* than 1,000 visitors on 'ordinary' Sundays. According to Jefferis there were over 1,100 visitors on more than one occasion during this period, and as many as 1,500 on one evening (ibid.: para 18.61, p.55). This does indicate that the 'planning authority were clearly aware before they entered into the agreement that more than 1,000 people were entering the Manor on non-festival days'[21] It does also rather contradict Michael Jefferis' view expressed in 1988 (quoted above) that the figure of 1,000 was a 'backstop' which was 'not expected to be approached' (ibid.: para 18.63, p.55).

By 1986, however, it was clear that there were more than 1,000 visitors attending the temple regularly each week. The monitor of traffic levels made by the council between 1986 and 1988 showed an average of 1,640 visitors per week, with the lowest figure at 960 (ibid.: para 24.1, pp.72–3). Not only was this somewhat higher than the levels of attendance monitored in 1980, it was also well in excess of the agreed limit of 1,000.

In this sense, therefore, it is possible to argue that the enforcement notice and the years of conflict which were to ensue from it were all framed because of Hertsmere council's feelings of frustration with ISKCON. In 1981, it had appeared a compromise could be reached which relied on the setting of a numerical limit on visitors. By 1986 such a limit had become intangible, and at the same time use of the Manor seemed in the council's eyes to be getting greater and greater. On the other hand ISKCON were feeling victimised and frustrated for their own reasons – particularly because of a sense of racism from the incidents of racial monitoring, and also the backlash from the villagers when ISKCON had purchased properties outside of the Manor. From 1986 onwards both sides began to retreat into their separate camps, and all attempts to find compromises proved futile because of the failure of the earlier compromise agreement.

The Enforcement Notice

Having failed in the High Court to control activities at the Manor, Hertsmere decided they would have to take some other course of action, as Judge Leggatt had himself suggested. The action they took was the serving of an Enforcement Notice on ISKCON on 8th January 1987. The notice required ISKCON to:

> 1) Discontinue the use of the said land for public worship, save and except for worship which is ancillary to the primary use of the premises as a residential educational college in connection with the religion of Krishna Consciousness; and
> 2) Discontinue the use of the said land for public entertainment in connection with religious festivals. (AgHBC/A3: p.36D)

Commenting (in 1994) on the notice, the European Commission on Human Rights noted that council had made the claim that:

> by using the land for 'the purposes of a residential educational college and a religious community and public worship and public entertainment in connection with religious festivals' ISKCON had materially changed the use of the land, and that this material change of use amounted to a breach of planning control. In the annex to the enforcement notice the local authority referred to the section 52 agreement, and alleged that, following repeated complaints from the local residents, the local authority had been made aware that the number of persons attending on non-festival days was increasing and had exceeded the 1,000 person limit. (EHRR:2)

The primary purpose of the notice was to stop 'the unauthorised use [of the Manor] for public worship/religious community and public entertainment' (AgHBC:35). That is, it 'was designed to curtail all visits on any day for any type of public worship or festival' (AdPE:158). Within the terms of the notice, ISKCON were given six months to comply.

ISKCON appealed almost immediately against the notice, thus requiring the need for the planning determination of the Manor – and thus ISKCON's use of the site – to be examined at a level of authority higher than that of Hertsmere council. The appeal meant that a Public Inquiry would be held, to be presided over by an independent Inspector who would write a report to assist the Secretary of State for the Environment to make a judgement on the local authority's decision. Such an inquiry would be a rather lengthy process and would involve barristers and consultancies, and would therefore be of great expense to both parties. If some solution could be found before this process began then it would be preferable – especially as it was by no means clear which party the Secretary of State would choose to favour.

In 1987, ISKCON presented an idea which they had been considering for a while – that is to build a road which provided access to the Manor without the need to pass through the village of Letchmore Heath.[22] This proved to be a complicated solution, as I will detail in chapter six. The council, however, did not appear to be keen on this idea and so preparations continued for the appeal to be heard at the public inquiry – with a date set for November. But the situation changed only a week before the inquiry was due to begin, when Hertsmere suggested an alternative solution – they would assist ISKCON in 'finding and developing an alternative site' (AdPE:161). The issues involved in such a solution were, again, very complex, and these will be discussed more fully in chapter six. But the central idea was that the problems both of access to and the improper use of Bhaktivedanta Manor could be best solved (in the council's opinion) if ISKCON relocated their deities and the temple to a large purpose built site, that is to create a new Hare Krishna temple – either within the borough or elsewhere.

Coming only a week before the inquiry opening it was considered that a postponement of the formal proceedings would be necessary to explore the idea more fully. Therefore on 9th November 1987 the inquiry was opened and immediately adjourned, following a joint statement made by Hertsmere and ISKCON (IR89a: para 9.10, p.13; AdPE:162). Over the coming months the parties consulted over the practicalities of this idea, and negotiations soon started to falter again. The reopening of the inquiry in May 1988 needed to be rescheduled – this time the Department of the Environment decided that further time was needed to investigate the possibility of the alternative site.[23]

The Public Inquiry in December 1988

Eventually the inquiry opened on 21st November 1988, continuing until 21st December. It was followed soon after by a second inquiry in February 1989 which looked at the specific issue of the alternative site (which by this time had been rejected by Hertsmere). The first inquiry was concerned specifically with ISKCON's appeal against the enforcement notice, although contained within the appeal was an application by the Society to change the planning determination of the Manor to allow public worship.

Under the planning laws (Town and Country Planning Act 1971), it is possible to appeal to the Secretary of State against an enforcement notice on the following grounds:

(a) that planning permission ought to be granted for the development to which the notice relates or, as the case may be, that a condition or limitation alleged in the enforcement notice not to have been complied with ought to be discharged;

> (b) that the matters alleged in the notice do not constitute a breach of planning control;
> (c) that the breach of planning control alleged in the notice has not taken place;
> ... (g) that the steps required by the notice be taken exceed what is necessary to remedy any breach of planning control ...
> (h) that the period specified in the notice as the period within which any step is to be taken falls short of what should reasonably be allowed. (EHRR:11)

ISKCON used all of these grounds as the bases for their appeal, but the inquiry and subsequent decisions particularly focused on grounds (a), that is, that permission ought to be given for the Manor to be used as a place of public worship. At the heart of this appeal was the argument that the prevention of public worship at the temple was an attack on Hindus' basic human rights. According to their counsel, David Altaras, in his opening address to the inquiry:

> This local authority [Hertsmere] in its actions appears to be striking at the very roots and foundation of the most fundamental of human rights, to worship at the temple of his choice and to the God of his choice.[24]

In support of their case ISKCON asked Dr Kim Knott, of the Department of Theology and Religious Studies, University of Leeds to give expert witness on their behalf. From her previous research conducted on ISKCON in Britain[25] Kim Knott argued for the importance of the Manor as a Hindu shrine, and as a very significant place of worship within Britain. She confirmed the religious significance of the Manor as a shrine for ISKCON devotees and other Hindus, and argued that the need to provide a place of worship for the Hindu population was a factor of such weight that the balance should come down in favour of ISKCON. That is, Bhaktivedanta Manor should be allowed to provide public worship and its planning determination should be changed in line with this.

On grounds (b), ISKCON also argued that the phrase in their planning determination 'promotion of Krishna Consciousness' allowed them to admit the public to the Manor for worship, as this was a very important part of the propagation of the religion (see chapter three). They also argued festival activities such as drama, dancing, and feasting were erroneously labelled 'public entertainment' in the enforcement notice, and as they were a valid form of religious devotion they came within the overall religious activities of the Manor. Further to these grounds, ISKCON felt that the earlier section 52 agreement had been tantamount to granting permission for the Manor to be used for public worship – that is the allowance of festivals on six days in the year, and up to one thousand worshippers at other times had given de facto planning permission (see above).

ISKCON also made it clear that they desired some compromise with the local authority, and put forward the possibility of a new section 52 agreement being signed along the lines of the previous agreement that had worked between 1983 and 1985 (EHRR:10; IR89a: para 41.1, p.124). In fact, in their closing submission they also argued that the original section 52 agreement still held, despite subsequent events, arguing that it was 'valid and subsisting, binding upon the parties according to the law of contract' (IR89a: para 30.13, p.94) and it 'could only be brought to an end consensually' (ibid.: para 30.20, p.95).

In their appeal, therefore, ISKCON tried to regularise the pattern of worship that they felt had been established at the Manor – six days of large scale festival worship, and regular Sunday worship throughout the year of less than one thousand visitors. Hertsmere had already rejected the possibility of such an agreement, considering that the only means by which ISKCON would comply with their planning status was through the force of legal action (i.e. the enforcement notice).

It has already been noted above that the dispute between the Manor and Hertsmere went to a public inquiry in June 1982, following the issue of the first enforcement notice. The 1988 inquiry was in this sense a re-run of the earlier process, but unlike the 1982 inquiry, this one continued beyond the first day since no compromise could be found between the parties. It is interesting to contrast the fact that in 1982 it was relatively easy for Hertsmere and ISKCON to agree on the section 52 agreement, whilst in 1988 the situation was quite different. No compromise could be found and, once the inquiry had begun, the dispute began to gather momentum so that no resolution could be reached, even after the inspector reported and the decision was announced by the Secretary of State. In fact, during the 1988 Inquiry one of the representatives for Hertsmere, Michael Jefferis, commented on the fact that in 1981 'there had not been any of the same determination [by ISKCON] to rally support' and contest the enforcement notice (IR89a: para 18.73, p.57).

The change of attitude perhaps came about because of a change in presidency of the temple during the interim years (with the arrival of Akhandadhi das), but was probably also a result of other factors. The enforcement notice that was being challenged at the inquiry in 1988 was far more harsh on ISKCON than the one issued in 1981 – in 1988 ISKCON were fighting to keep the temple open to public worship, whilst in 1981 they had only been required to limit numbers to 1,000. This indicated a change of attitude not so much by ISKCON than by Hertsmere council. But at the same time ISKCON were probably given comfort by the ruling at the High Court in 1986, when Judge Leggatt ruled that there was no way in which a limit on numbers worshipping could be enforced, and that ISKCON should not be held responsible for the people who came to visit the Manor to worship. It is also likely that the change was the result of the increasing support that

ISKCON were finding that it could rely on from Indian Hindus. The issue of ethnic monitoring had caused a great deal of upset, and the high media profile that the case was now obtaining helped ISKCON to find a willing bank of support from the Hindu population. Thus, many Hindus were now becoming active in the fight to keep the temple open (see chapter five). Altogether, attitudes had developed so much from 1985 onwards that by 1988 both sides were well and truly ready to fight a battle over the status of the Manor, far more so than at any time previously.

The Inspector's Report

Following the conclusion of the inquiry in December, Inspector Russell provided a report which was then passed to the Secretary of State for the Environment, to assist him making a decision on the Manor. The Inspector, after hearing the evidence and the arguments from both sides, concluded in favour of Hertsmere council. He recommended that the Enforcement Notice should be upheld and that six months was 'adequate' time' for the Society [ISKCON] to comply with the Enforcement Notice. At the same time, following a public inquiry in February 1989, the Inspector recommended that ISKCON's appeal against refusal of permission for the alternative temple site also be turned down (see chapter six).

On the use of the Manor, the Inspector felt that there was a fine balance between the needs of the various parties, but:

> ... it still seems to me that the combination of policy and clearly identifiable physical disadvantages to the use of Letchmore Heath constitutes specific and convincing planning objections of such force that they amply outweigh and displace the arguments on the grounds of need. (IR89a: para 37.23, p.120)

The appeal on ground (b), that is that no breach of planning controls had been made, was dismissed, since the primary use of the Manor was fundamentally different in many ways from a residential theological college and because there had been a material change of use. (IR89a: para 36.5, p. 114). Furthermore, the appeal that the section 52 agreement gave de facto permission was also rejected, since within that earlier agreement was a clause to allow further enforcement 'if it was deemed expedient' (see above). Indeed, the existence of the section 52 agreement did not 'estop' the planning authority from serving the enforcement notice and the section 52 agreement had no bearing on the ground b. appeal, which failed (ibid.: para 36.8, p. 115).

The more substantial grounds for appeal, that is ground (a), to grant permission for a change of use, were dealt with at length. The Inspector summarised some of the most important issues of this part of ISKCON's appeal as such:

> vi. Does the importance of the Manor as a shrine and the need to provide places of worship for the Hindu population:
> a. constitute those very special circumstances which justify development in the Green Belt in any event;
> b. outweigh any specific and convincing planning objections on any of the grounds noted above and justify an exception to Green Belt and other Development Plan policies?
> vii. Whether, given the long history, the presumption in favour of development and the previous decisions by the planning authority, any injury to amenity can be met by suitable and enforceable conditions. (IR89a: para 37.1, p.115)

In response to these issues, the Inspector's conclusions were fairly balanced, but came down on the side of the villagers. To quote:[26]

> 37.13 I turn next to issue (vi), very special circumstances. I accept that the Manor has become a special place of worship and pilgrimage for the Hindu community in this country, and that there appear to be very few Hindu places of worship in North London and nearby counties. The Manor is of special importance as the home of ISKCON's founder. I do not doubt that the traditional religious rites and ceremonies, in sylvan surroundings, bring inspiration and spiritual comfort to many who visit. No one could ignore the national and international concern, and the social issue posed by the possibility of restricting participation in the worship at the Manor and the celebration of the Hindu festivals ... [p.118]

In the Inspector's view 'the appeal of Krishna Consciousness and the Hindu population have both increased substantially in the past 15 years', and so 'regular attendances at the Manor over and above those at festival times have also increased significantly in recent years' (para 37.14). Hence

> ... The Manor has become an important place of worship and pilgrimage. This is unfortunate in view of the fact that it is situated in one of the most vulnerable areas of Green Belt, so very close to London, in a village of high amenity value, with poor access, where every planning policy aims to restrict high profile public activities ... [p.118]

He noted (para 37.15) that 'the Manor has been allowed to be used for public worship and public entertainment at festivals for many years'. But he did not consider that this implied any 'toleration of the status quo' on the part of the council, but rather that 'the planning authority have been doing everything they can to avoid the confrontation which the present enforcement notice has provoked'. Even though some local residents had accepted that there had been less to 'complain about from noise and disturbance in recent years', he thought 'it is in the nature of things that uses which have caused conflict are toned down when there are enforcement proceedings pending' [p.118].

As far as suitable numbers were concerned:

> 37.16 The appellants maintain that because the earlier enforcement notice and the [section] 52 Agreement provided for a tolerance of up to 1,000 visitors on non-festival days, this figure at any rate should be regarded as accepted. I do not consider this should necessarily be so. A figure of 1,000 visitors ... is in my view too large a crowd to bring into the village in any event on a Sunday ... [p.119]

For the Inspector, the problem was not one specifically caused through the temple being a Hindu shrine. Rather:

> 37.17 I am in no doubt that any church of any faith or denomination in a small village, or indeed in any closely built residential area, which regularly attracted 1,000–1,500 people for late evening services on Sundays, and crowds of up to 12,000 for festivals 3 times a year, would encounter objections from the host community. The intimate small scale closely built character of a home counties village simply cannot accommodate the crowds attracted to a tirtha in the Indian sub-continent, especially when most of the worshippers or pilgrims have to come in their own private transport or in coaches. When religious meetings of this scale are held in the United Kingdom, such as those by Billy Graham and other evangelists, Earls Court or Wembley Stadium are booked ... [p.119]

He also felt it important to stress that this was not a problem of racism, a point which ISKCON had conceded:

> 37.20 In his submissions Counsel for [ISKCON] expressly withdrew any allegations of religious or racial prejudice which had been made against the planning authority. In this, as in very many other planning decisions it is necessary to weigh the needs of one group or interest against others, and the needs of religious or ethnic minorities, however important, cannot necessarily be allowed to override those constraints which have to apply to everyone, in planning as in other matters, in the interests of a tolerant and free society in a small and crowded country. [p.119]

Despite his attempts to be balanced, Inspector Russell does show a lack of patience with ISKCON themselves over the regular activities that take place at the Manor:

> 37.18 It also seems to me that the fact that the tenets of Krishna Consciousness prescribe that there must be devotions virtually 24 hours a day, with comings and goings very late at night, are particularly

> intrusive in a small village. The appellants are not prepared to even consider curbing their night time activities, and maintain that it would be contrary to their faith to do so. I understand what they say, but this inevitably makes the use very difficult to fit into a residential village where most people travel some distance to work, and come home expecting a measure of peace and quiet, especially at weekends when use of the Manor is at its most active. [p.119]

What is rather surprising about these comments is that he is referring to activities which were already accepted as authorised uses of the Manor, since they were included within its planning determination (and hence within the enforcement notice) as a 'residential theological college'.

On the subject of support for the Manor, Inspector Russell shows a fair degree of impatience with the tone of many of the letters he and others had received.

> 37.19 I take due note of the very large number of letters and petitions, addressed to HM the Queen, the Prime Minister, and members of HM Government, members of Parliament, the planning authority and myself relating to this matter. Unfortunately many of these are based on the premise that there is some antipathy to the Hindu religion, which is not the case. Inevitably many of these letters come from people far away from Letchmore Heath who are not aware of the full circumstances and the problems posed by the attraction of crowds into a small English village. I take particular note however that there are also some letters from local residents supporting the appellants ... [p.119]

It is also interesting to note the juxtaposition he makes between Letchmore Heath and the distance of the worshippers/supporters – that is, 'people far away' from 'a small English village' and as quoted earlier he had spoken of 'crowds attracted to a tirtha in the Indian sub-continent' not being appropriate in the 'intimate small scale closely built character of a home counties village' (para 37.17).

Leading up to his conclusion Inspector Russell outlined the main question to decide upon, and his views upon it.

> ... 37.22 It was suggested that need justified an exception to, or setting aside Green Belt policy altogether in this particular case. However, when I weigh on one side the need of the appellants and their congregation and on the other not just the Green Belt policy, but the actual disquiet and inconvenience to residents, and add to that the positive duty which Conservation Area status imposes on the decision maker, not just to preserve but also to enhance the character of Letchmore Heath, I consider that the interests of the village and its

> residents should prevail, and that there is insufficient justification for setting aside that weight of policy as well as other specific and convincing planning objections. [p.120]

Hence in his view the religious needs of Hindus were not sufficient to 'set aside' the policy of environmental protection.

> . . . 37.24 . . . the planning authority have shown themselves willing for at least 10 years to devise some machinery whereby the religious aspirations of the appellants and their devotees can be equated with the interests of the residents. Whilst it is not for me to disagree with the legal interpretation of the [Section] 52 Agreement, it does seem to me that the appellants have chosen to disregard the spirit if not the letter of it, and I can only conclude that they are unwilling on principle to restrict the number of people attending their premises in the interests of the neighbouring residents. [p.120]

In particular, he stressed the problem of the volume of visitors which could not be accommodated satisfactorily on the site.

> 37.25 It seems to me that a condition limiting numbers would be the only basis on which the damage to amenity caused by the scale of the public worship and public entertainment [sic.] activities could be remedied. Given the past history however I have the gravest doubts as to whether such a condition should be enforced, and the very fact that such a condition is necessary points to the fundamental unsuitability of the premises for activities of this kind on anything but a purely local scale. I have to agree with the planning authority that restrictions on numbers have already been proved not to work. I can think of no other form of condition which would remedy the damage to the amenities of the village caused by the present activities, and I do not consider therefore that a conditional permission is appropriate in this case. *I conclude therefore that the appeal on Ground (a) should fail.* [p.120, emphasis added]

Much of this statement from the Inspector's report shows a balanced approach towards the needs of both parties. However, the final decision is clearly to favour the needs of the local residents at the expense of the needs of the Hindu worshippers. The decision was, therefore, grounded in the opinion that, although the Manor was of great significance to the many Hindus in this country, it was basically in the wrong place, and that its significance could not be judged to be sufficient justification for allowing public worship at the site. The diminished amenity that public worship would entail for local residents could not be countenanced. The obvious implication was that either Hindus should stop worshipping at the site, or otherwise find/build an alternative temple.

Secretary of State's decision

The 136 page Inspector's report was then passed onto the Secretary of State for the Environment, Chris Patten, for a decisive ruling. Bearing the report in mind, the Secretary of State announced his decision on 20th March 1990. The Inspector's conclusions formed the basis of this decision, which upheld the enforcement notice and dismissed the grounds of ISKCON's appeal. At the same time he agreed with the ruling to not allow planning permission for the alternative temple site.

But the Secretary of State did make what an ISKCON representative described as a 'minor amendment ... to the use to which the Manor and the land could be put' (EHRR:10). That is, without commenting on the change, he altered the planning determination of the Manor, which had hitherto been a 'residential educational college in connection with the promotion of the religion of Krishna consciousness'. The change omitted the words 'the promotion of', thus making it a 'residential educational college in connection with the religion of Krishna Consciousness'.[27] Although this appears a very slight change, it did remove a possible ambiguity (which ISKCON had pointed out) that suggested the Manor could be used as a place of public worship in 'promoting' the religion.

He also extended the period of compliance required for the enforcement notice. Hertsmere and the Inspector had set a limit of six months for ISKCON to make alternative arrangements before public worship ceased, but Chris Patten extended this to two years[28] – intending that this should provide a long enough period for a new site to be found and prepared. He justified this decision by saying

> ... it is physically possible for the use to cease within the six month compliance period specified [by Hertsmere]. However ... in the special circumstances of this case ... ISKCON should be given an appropriately extended period in which to identify a suitable alternative site. (DoE90: para 16, p.5)

Appeals in the British Courts

ISKCON still felt that it might be possible to overturn this negative decision through the courts. Their immediate response was that they would appeal, and they would take their case 'through the Appeal Courts, House of Lords and right up to the European Court of Human Rights if necessary'.[29]

Therefore an appeal was made to the High Court against the Secretary of State's decision under the Town and Country Planning Act 1971.[30] The appeal was heard in October 1991, at a time which happened to coincide with the Hindu festival of Dusehra – when the defeat of the evil demon Ravana by Lord Rama (an incarnation of Krishna) is celebrated. The evil

Ravana is a figure whom one ISKCON devotee described as 'the epitome of attempted abuse of the Lord's property'.[31]

The main bases for ISKCON's appeal to the High Court were:

> (i) that the Inspector and the Secretary of State had failed to have proper regard to [their] willingness ... to enter into a new Section 52 Agreement
> and (ii) that the Secretary of State had been wrong to accept the Inspector's conclusion that the planning objections outweighed [ISKCON's] arguments ... on grounds of need. (EHRR:10)

The case made on behalf of the Secretary of State was that even if ISKCON were willing to make a new agreement, this was not now possible since the other party had no interest in doing so. They described the position as being 'like one hand clapping. There was nothing ... to take into account' (EHRR:10). On the other point, ISKCON pointed to a few misapprehensions on the part of the Inspector regarding their religious needs and use of the Manor, which in their opinion demonstrated that the basis of the Secretary of State decision had been flawed. In response, however, counsel for Hertsmere pointed to passages in the Inspector's report (particularly paragraph 37.22 quoted above) in which Inspector Russell had shown consideration for the needs of ISKCON and Hindus to worship at the Manor (even though he decided these needs were outweighed by other needs).[32]

Amongst several other small points of objection raised by counsel for ISKCON was a point concerning the enforcement notice which had been upheld by the Secretary of State. ISKCON argued that the notice was defective because it allowed for 'public worship which was ancillary to the primary use [of the Manor] as a residential educational college, but contained no similar saving for public entertainment'.[33] This small and rather technical point was dismissed. But it is rather surprising that ISKCON allowed it to be raised, bearing in mind their strongly felt position that the Krishna-*lila* and other such dramatic events at the Manor are *not* 'public entertainment'.

Despite the auspiciousness of the date for this hearing, judgement went against ISKCON. On 31st October 1991 the High Court judge Mr Justice Kennedy said that the enforcement notice (and the Secretary of State's decision) were valid, 'the Secretary of State was entitled to regard the Inspector's conclusions as firmly founded' (EHRR:11), and all the 'points which had been argued in support of the appeal' had 'no substance'.[34]

Having lost this appeal, ISKCON then applied for leave to appeal to the Court of Appeal, which is the highest court in British law, again challenging the basis of the decision made by the Secretary of State. This appeal was considered by Lord Justice Glidewell on 16th March 1992, who 'agreed largely with the decision of Mr Justice Kennedy' in the High Court, that there were no legal flaws in the earlier ruling, and thus leave to appeal was refused.[35]

This ruling meant that not only was the legal challenge in the British courts lost, but also from that date the two year period of compliance with the enforcement notice would begin to run. That is, on 16th March 1994 ISKCON would be required to comply with the full terms of the enforcement notice – and particularly to not allow any public worship at the Manor.

The European Commission on Human Rights

With no further redress possible in British courts, ISKCON appealed to the European Commission of Human Rights to have their case heard by the court in Strasbourg. As Akhandadhi das commented:

> At first we discussed the case in planning terms, Green Belt issues for example, and then at the High Court we talked in legal terms ... But there are human issues. We are being denied religious rights.[36]

An application was made to the Commission on 24th April 1992 by ISKCON and eight others, alleging a violation of Article 9 of the European Convention on Human Rights.

The Commission communicated the appeal to the British government in February 1993 in order to hear their responses to ISKCON's case, and these were received in June that year. ISKCON then were invited to give their own responses to the government's position, and which were received by the Commission in September 1993. The Commission was then able to give full consideration to ISKCON's appeal, and the First Chamber of the Commission sat to discuss the case on 8th March 1994.

The central argument of ISKCON's appeal was that the enforcement notice to prevent public worship at the Manor 'interfered in an unjustified way with their freedom of religion' (EHRR:13), and was therefore in violation of Article 9 of the Convention on Human Rights which states:

> 1. Everyone has the right to freedom of thought, conscience and religion; this right includes freedom to change his religion or belief and freedom, either alone or in community with others and in public or private, to manifest his religion or belief, in worship, teaching, practice and observance.
> 2. Freedom to manifest one's religion or beliefs should be subject only to such limitations as are prescribed by law and are necessary in a democratic society in the interests of public safety, for the protection of public order, health or morals, or for the protection of the rights and freedoms of others. (EHRR:13)

For ISKCON, the particular application of the planning laws in this case amounted to an unjustified interference with Hindus' rights under this article which went beyond that which was 'necessary in a democratic society'. They did not claim the relevant planning laws were in violation of their rights, but that in the consideration of this case by the planning authorities and by the government 'inadequate weight was given to their freedom of religion in the proceedings' (ibid.:14–5).

In giving consideration to this appeal, the Commission did say that the attempt through the enforcement notice to limit ISKCON's use of the Manor to a residential educational college may be considered 'an interference with ISKCON's freedom of religion, including the freedom to manifest that religion in worship, teaching, practice and observance' (ibid.:14). Furthermore, they considered that the local planning laws did prescribe limitations on 'ISKCON's freedom to manifest its religion' (ibid.).

But the important point for the Commission to evaluate was whether or not such limitations were 'necessary in a democratic society'. That is, was it necessary to limit ISKCON's activities in order to protect the rights of others?[37] The Commission found that there was justification to impose such limits: 'the interference with ISKCON's right to freedom of religion under Article 9 of the Convention can be regarded as "necessary in a democratic society"' (ibid.:15). Furthermore, ISKCON's claim that the planning proceedings in Britain had given inadequate weight to their freedom of religion was also rejected, on the basis that the Inspector and the Secretary of State had considered the 'special circumstances' – that is, the possibility that planning laws could be put aside for the needs of the Hindu worshippers (ibid.)

ISKCON also argued that there was a violation of their freedom to use their property (i.e. Bhaktivedanta Manor), as protected under Article 1 of Protocol No. 1 to the Convention on Human Rights. According to the Commission:

> Although the effect of the enforcement notice is radically to alter the use to which Bhaktivedanta Manor has been put in recent years, the Commission finds that it does not amount to a deprivation of possessions, but a control of property. (ibid.:15)

Therefore, although ISKCON were being forced to use their property in a manner which was restrictive, the restriction was in accordance with their planning status, and the Commission found that 'a proper balance has been struck between ISKCON's interests and the general interest' (ibid.). This appeal was also rejected.

A further grounds of ISKCON's appeal was based on their claim that the interference with their freedom of religion had not been adequately considered within the British courts, and therefore was in violation of Article 6 of the Convention (paragraph 1), which states:

> 1. In the determination of his civil rights and obligations . . ., everyone is entitled to a fair and public hearing within a reasonable time by an independent and impartial tribunal established by law . . . (ibid.:17)

This again depended on the crucial claim of restriction of freedom of religion, insofar as the civil right to religious freedom had not be given a fair hearing in the British judicial system. On this point the Commission noted: 'as ISKCON submit, that freedom of religion has no formal status as a right which is guaranteed in United Kingdom domestic law' (ibid.:17).

But this meant that such religious freedom does not constitute a civil right in the United Kingdom, and so did not come within the meaning of Article 6 of the Convention (ibid.). In a rather paradoxical way, the Commission said that the issue of freedom of religion in Britain was not a matter for them to consider, since there was nothing to guarantee such rights in British laws, and indeed freedom of religion does not exist as a civil right within this country.

On the more specific claim by ISKCON that their case was only considered in terms of '"pure" planning issues' (ibid.), the Commission resolved that ISKCON had been given the opportunity within the High Court to contend the accuracy of findings of the Inspector and/or the Secretary of State. The High Court would have been able to interfere with the Department of Environment's and Hertsmere council's decision 'if those decisions had been irrational having regard to the facts established ...' (ibid.:18).

The eight individual applicants who also submitted appeals to the Commission made fairly similar points concerning violation of Articles 9 and 6 of the Convention. They asked the Commission:

> to construe Article 9 of the Convention according to international standards and developments, with particular reference to the United Nations Declaration on the elimination of all forms of intolerance and discrimination based on religion or belief, 1981. (ibid.:12)

Some of these applicants, who were parents, also claimed that their rights under Article 2 of Protocol no.1 of the Convention were being violated. That is, they were 'not able to ensure education and teaching in conformity with their religious convictions, and that they are no longer able to ensure this because of the enforcement notice' (ibid.:13).

In February 1994, only a few weeks before the case was heard by the Commission, one of the individual applicants (Chatrabhuj Vasanji Majithia) had died, and so his appeal was withdrawn (ibid.). In response to the remaining seven individual appeals the Commission accepted 'that each of them is sufficiently affected ... to be able to claim to be a victim of an alleged violation of the Convention' (ibid.:19). However, they considered that the reasoning applied to ISKCON also applied *mutatis mutandis* to these individuals. That is,

> In the same way as ISKCON cannot derive from the Convention a right to exemption from the ordinary planning controls (provided due

> attention is paid to their interests), the individual applicants must accept that the enforcement of those planning controls affects the modalities of their worship and, so far as relevant, the education of their children. (ibid.:19)

In sum, the Commission decided that ISKCON's and the individuals' applications were 'manifestly ill-founded', and therefore declared the applications 'inadmissible' (ibid.:19). Therefore, ISKCON's final legal challenge to the enforcement notice was lost and some other solution to the dispute would be required.

The Enforcement in 1994

In fact, alternative solutions were already being seriously considered at the time of Commission's decision in early 1994. In late 1993 negotiations for the construction of an access driveway to the Manor, which would bypass Letchmore Heath, were well advanced and an application for planning permission for this road had already been submitted to Hertsmere council. The history of this proposal, and how the consideration of the application proceeded, will be discussed in the next chapter.

But in March 1994 ISKCON faced the immediate prospect of the enforcement notice coming into effect. This was because 16th March 1994 was the date two years after the rejection of ISKCON's appeal by the British Court of Appeal, and therefore marked the end of the two year 'grace period' which ISKCON had been allowed to find an alternative site for worship. The decision by the Commission would not have a direct bearing on the enforcement notice, since the judgements made by the European Court are not legally binding. Rather, if the case had been admitted by the Commission to the court, then a decision in ISKCON's favour would have exerted moral pressure on the government to rethink the enforcement.

Therefore, during the months before the March deadline worshippers at the Manor were regularly warned about the impending change. Announcements were made regularly at events at the Manor, and messages were put in newsletters saying that after the deadline there would be:

> No Darshan No Worship No Festivals[38]

Worshippers were left in no doubt that the date would be significant and that every action should be taken to prevent the closure occurring. During the preceding months the political campaign to save the Manor gathered momentum (as I will describe in chapter five), and strenuous efforts were pursued by ISKCON to solve the issue by promoting the access road. On the day before the enforcement notice came into action the Manor was 'packed with worshippers because they believed that was their last chance to see the shrine'.[39]

But on that same day, 15th March 1994, Hertsmere issued an information sheet in which they stated:

> in a statement today the Managing Director of Hertsmere Borough Council, Philip Copeland, said the Council were not minded to take legal action on any breach of the order until a planning application concerning the Manor had been considered by Hertsmere. 'Although we are legally entitled to prosecute anyone publicly worshipping at the temple from Wednesday [16th], we shall for the moment simply be monitoring the situation', he said. 'Whichever way one looks at the situation those who publicly worship at Bhaktivedanta Manor after Wednesday are breaking the law. Our officers will be monitoring the situation, and as long as there is no significant increase in numbers worshipping there, we shall not take action.' (Quoted in AdPE:172–3; see also AgHBC/Ac)

Therefore, full implementation of the enforcement notice was delayed further, to give the possibility of the access road a full chance. What was quite clear from Hertsmere's statement was, however, their readiness to take action to prevent public worship (or to punish worship that did take place) if the numbers attending the Manor 'significantly increased'.[40] Hertsmere did not specify, though, what level of increase would prompt them into further action.

It is worth noting, in passing, that the legal position as stated by the Hertsmere leader was incorrect. According to Judge Daniel Rodwell, reviewing the case in court a year later (see below), Hertsmere 'have not got the right to prosecute worshippers. They have got the right to prosecute the owners of the land. So that was a nonsense' (Judge Rodwell in LCC: summing up). In his opinion, to say the worshippers would be breaking the law was 'complete rubbish' (ibid.) since it was the landowners who were causing the breach of the enforcement notice.

During the following months, worship continued at the Manor almost as normal. ISKCON felt that strict compliance with the enforcement notice would only be possible if they physically barred entrance of worshippers to the Manor grounds and with, regard to the council's stated position regarding the enforcement, it appeared that such action would not be necessary so long as the council were kept informed of and allowed to monitor the situation. According to the temple president, it had been the intention 'to shut the gates on 20th March to stop members of the public coming in', but because of the council's letter 'we did not close the gates' (Akhandadhi das in LCC). At the end of March, and then in April, there were festivals held for Holi and Ramnawmi respectively, which went uncommented upon by the council, and worshippers continued to visit regularly on Sundays (AdPE:173).

The new planning application that helped to delay the implementation of the enforcement was not only concerned with the possibility of an access road. ISKCON put forward the case that the established use of the Manor over the previous twenty years should be regularised, especially if a solution could be found for allowing worshippers to get access to the site (by the driveway) which took the traffic completely away from the village. Therefore, part of the application was for permission to be granted for a change of use of the Manor:

> ... to a residential and non-residential theological college and religious community, together with use for public worship (including the observance) of religious festival days. (AgHBC/A3: p. A36E)

This would create a *sui generis* combination of uses from Classes C2 and D1 of the Use Classes Order 1987 (AgHBC/A3: p. A36E). It would obviously require the council, and the local residents, to accept the Manor as a place of public worship – something which had proved to be extremely contentious for so long.

A meeting of the local planning sub-board of the council (the Bushey and Aldenham Area Planning Sub-Board) met on 12th July 1994 to consider this application. By this stage it was clear that there was considerable local and political opposition to the application, and the sub-board decided that they could not make a decision on the issue. Instead they referred the application to a full meeting of the Council to determine.

This application was not to be considered until October of that year, when the next convenient meeting was held. At that meeting, the council voted to recommend rejection of the application for the access road. But by this time the matter was in the hands of the Department of the Environment, because ISKCON had made an appeal over non-determination (this will be discussed further in chapter six). In the meantime – before the October meeting – there were still arrangements that needed to be made concerning the Janmasthami festival in August, which is of course the most well attended festival in the year.

On 20th July, the temple president and his planning advisor Peter Trevelyan met council officials to discuss what would happen at this festival. According to the council's chief planning officer it was made clear that a prosecution would be likely if the festival went ahead in the way it had in past years. The temple president claimed that this was not made clear at the meeting, although his advisor Mr Trevelyan contradicted this. Furthermore, Trevelyan was of the strong opinion that even if the council had decided not to act on the enforcement notice they could have been legally compelled by local residents to prosecute for a breach of the notice. In Trevelyan's words, 'no one can licence anyone to commit a criminal offence' (LCC), and so he gave ISKCON the advice to close the gates of the Manor on certain occasions (particularly Janmasthami).

Despite the apparent ambiguity of the position following the 20th July meeting, the council's position was made clear in a letter sent to

Akhandadhi das by the council's chief planning officer on 28th July. In this letter ISKCON were warned that they would face prosecution if they allowed public worship at the Manor on Janmasthami. Thus:

> As the Managing Director Philip Copeland advised at our meeting on 20th July, if you celebrate Janmasthami this year in a similar fashion to the way it has been celebrated in previous years ... the council may have no option but to prosecute for breach of the enforcement notice. I would therefore strongly urge you to make alternative arrangements for the celebration of Janmasthami this year. (LCC)

But ISKCON still felt that the council's previously stated position would hold, that is there would be no legal action until the planning application had been considered, and this had obviously not yet been resolved. Worshippers had been going to the Manor every Sunday throughout the spring and summer as usual, and they would be doing so on Sundays following Janmasthami. Therefore it 'seemed inappropriate [to ISKCON] to expect them not to attend on the actual holy day Janmasthami' (AdPE:175). In response to the 28th July letter, Akhandadhi das wrote back to the council on 3rd August making it clear that ISKCON would not take 'any action to prevent public worship at the Manor' (LCC).

Janmasthami 1994

To prevent worshippers using the Manor for the festival would require some measure of physical prevention, since many Hindus may arrive at the place unsure of whether it would be possible to worship at the temple or not. The only effective prevention would entail a closing of the gates to the Manor, and posting stewards at the gates to stop the passing through of pedestrians who had parked outside the grounds. Although this solution would be in compliance with the Enforcement Notice, it would clearly not be in anybody's interest. The worshippers would be frustrated, devotees at the temple would find it very difficult to bar people from genuine devotion, and furthermore the local villagers of Letchmore Heath would have a situation of pandamonium to face as thousands of cars choked the roads, unable to go anywhere. ISKCON did not feel that it was right 'to create inordinate difficulties' (AdPE:175) for the villagers in this way, and the council recognised that this was no real solution. In an interview given after the event, the Managing Director Philip Copeland said:

> I indicated to the [temple president] very clearly that if they proceeded with Janmasthami then that was leaving himself and others open to prosecution. It was not however open to me to guide and advise him. The decision must be his. And equally I had had representations from some of the villagers that they were concerned if the gates were

> locked, and of course devotees would come into the village and would pay homage to the shrine on the roadside. And clearly that would have created difficulties for the police.
>
> But as things stand technically the very holding of the festival is a breach of the enforcement notice and we would need to determine the attitude and likely response of the courts to the bringing of a prosecution.[41]

Therefore, the Janmasthami festival went ahead on Sunday 28th and Monday 29th August, which happened to coincide with the late Summer Bank Holiday weekend in England. No publicity for activities at the Manor were sent out, and the brochure that ISKCON produce each year at Janmasthami did not contain the usual programme for the festival. Instead they simply said:

> At the time of going to print, it was not possible to know how Janmasthami would be observed at Bhaktivedanta Manor... We hope that we will be able to celebrate Janmasthami at Bhaktivedanta Manor just as in previous years. But, if not, please accept our assurance that the Society will continue to fight for your right to attend Bhaktivedanta Manor for worship and festivals. Please read the current Campaign newsletter for full information on the situation. (JB94:4)

However, ISKCON anticipated correctly that there would be many visitors worshipping at the temple on the festival days. Clearly there was a worry that large numbers of worshippers would cause great inconvenience if the Manor gates were closed during Janmasthami. But there were several weeks before the festival when ISKCON (if they had wished to) could have put out publicity giving notice that the festival would *not* take place. As will be discussed in the next chapter, ISKCON have been very successful in their use of the media to promote support for the Manor, especially among British Hindus. It is likely therefore that they could have successfully prevented many worshippers visiting the Manor at Janmasthami – simply by putting out the message that the place would be closed.

Even if such a message was tried and failed, ISKCON still prepared a great deal for the festival as though they anticipated it to take place. Facilities were provided for worshippers such as an awning over the entrance to the temple room, a marquee for the performance of the Krishna-*lila* dramas, a tent in which *priti-bhojan* (*prasad*, that is consecrated food) was served, and a number of small tents containing stalls (selling small items, and providing information and advice). Many of the facilities, such as the marquee, were similar to those provided in previous years. However, there was one difference in that no public address tannoy system was used. This was intended to make the activities less intrusive for the local residents, and ISKCON themselves found it a change that would be worth retaining in future years (AdPE:87). But overall preparations were made for the festival which required detailed organisation. In other words, there was no real evidence that ISKCON made any effort to stop the breach of the enforcement notice (Judge D. Rodwell's comments in LCC: summing up). One may, of course, conclude that ISKCON had no wish to avoid such a breach (since in their opinion the enforcement notice was unjustified, and much less important than allowing worshippers show their devotion to Krishna).

On the two days of Janmasthami that year over 15,000 worshippers attended the Manor (LCC), and there was a constant traffic flow through the village of Letchmore Heath for several hours in the evening of the festival day. Two months later, at a full council meeting on 19th October the council members decided that Hertsmere would attempt to prosecute ISKCON over this breach of the enforcement notice.

This decision to prosecute was held back for several months as discussions took place between ISKCON and villagers over other issues prior to the beginning of the Public Inquiry beginning in January 1995 (see chapter six). But when these talks broke down a writ was issued against the temple president Akhandadhi das (under his birth name of William Martin Fleming) and ISKCON. An ISKCON representative, Atmanidevan Swami, and Akhandadhi das appeared before the local Watford Magistrates Court on 14th February 1995, where they both pleaded 'not guilty' to charges of breaching the enforcement notice. They also both elected to have the trial heard at a crown court, rather than at a magistrates court.[42] In doing so they risked a higher fine if found guilty (since in a magistrates court there was a maximum fine of £20,000). But by going to a crown court they would have their case decided by a jury.

After discussion it was decided to hold the trial at Luton Crown Court, since ISKCON felt that venue would be more distant (and hence less partisan) from the ongoing conflict. The trial, which was held between 30th October and 6th November 1995, was the culmination of the legal process that began in 1986 with the decision by Hertsmere to issue an enforcement notice.

The trial at Luton Crown Court

The temple president and ISKCON were both being charged with failing to comply with this enforcement notice, which after 16th March 1994 had become legally binding. Two other charges were also brought relating to the notice, that both Akhandadhi das and ISKCON permitted the Manor to be used for 'public entertainment in connection with the religious festivals' (LCC).

The beginning of the trial saw demonstrations by thousands of Hindu worshippers both outside the court building in Luton, and also at Bhaktivedanta Manor.[43] Many were aggrieved by the nature of the prosecution, since ISKCON were being dealt with under criminal law: the perpetration of worship at the Manor was now being treated as a crime. Of course, it was a rather unusual sort of crime, as the counsel for the prosecution admitted in his opening speech:

> This is not a crime in the same league as robbery or worse, but nevertheless it is a crime to commit an offence contrary to the provisions of an enforcement notice.[44]

Throughout the trial itself all concerned stressed that the temple president and Atmanidevan Swami, the representative for ISKCON, were both people of good character (LCC). The criminal prosecution was being brought against them purely because of this breach of the enforcement notice, and for no other misdemeanours.

The trial was fairly straightforward: it was the prosecution's case (i.e. the Crown, acting for Hertsmere Borough Council) to prove that a breach of the enforcement notice had taken place insofar as public worship had been organised and allowed by ISKCON at the Manor on Janmasthami in 1994. Although ISKCON and the temple president had pleaded not guilty, they made no effort to deny the public worship at the festival, but instead stressed the importance of the worship as an integral part of the Manor's activities. Indeed, according to Bhasker Ghorpade, (counsel for ISKCON and the temple president) the Manor 'was always designed for public worship, and it just happened by chance to be a theological college' (LCC). As the judge, Daniel Rodwell, pointed out in his summing up, this statement was legally in error (ibid.). In all the time the Manor had been used by ISKCON it had *not* had planning permission for public worship, and the challenges in the Public Inquiry and the courts had made it quite clear that the planning determination was as a 'residential educational college' and no more.

A further defence by ISKCON which did not impress Judge Rodwell was the argument that Britain is a 'free country' in which 'the Government and Parliament are committed to a multiracial society' (ibid.). This argument returned to a point frequently made throughout the long running dispute, that British authorities and laws should allow more diversity, and act tolerantly and fairly in the interest of minority cultural and religious groups. Judge Rodwell was of the opinion that even in a multicultural society the law should not 'allow Hindus to overturn our democratic institutions like the council. ... If it did ... that would lead to anarchy, because any group would feel it could do just the same thing' (ibid.: summing up).

It is quite likely that ISKCON were aware that they did not have much chance of winning the case. The weight of the law, through the enforcement notice, was quite firmly against them, albeit they felt the law was being used unjustly against them. Their main hope was that the jury (and perhaps the judge) might share the view that ISKCON were the victims rather than the perpetrators. It was also fairly reasonable to assume that the publicity that the case would generate would be useful for ISKCON in the long term, even (or perhaps especially) if they were found guilty. The case was being heard in November 1995, within months of the expected decision by the Secretary of State on their application for the access road and new planning permission.

So it is not altogether surprising that their defence counsel presented a case which was founded more on moral grounds (i.e. Hindus' need for the temple to be open) than on any sustained effort to demonstrate that the enforcement notice was not breached. Even so, it is still rather surprising that counsel for ISKCON introduced a degree of mitigation into his closing speech, when he pleaded that this whole affair was a 'storm in a tea cup' and asked the judge to deal with the matter with 'utmost leniency'.[45] Even though as a criminal prosecution the case did seem rather bizarre and unfortunate, it was pushing the matter a little to suggest that it was unimportant. For both ISKCON and the council, as well as for local residents, the status of the Manor was clearly something of great importance.

Under fairly strong direction from Judge Rodwell the jury did not take long to find both the temple president and ISKCON guilty. That is, both were guilty of failing to comply with the enforcement notice by allowing public worship. However, at the same time the jury found both Akhandadhi das and ISKCON not guilty of the other charges: of allowing a breach of the notice through organising public entertainment.

These latter verdicts were a significant decision in their own right. For years ISKCON had challenged the description of Krishna-*lila* as 'public entertainment', and were therefore unhappy that it was still included within the enforcement notice. The argument at Luton Crown Court by ISKCON was the familiar one that the dramas were inaccurately described as 'entertainment' since they were an integral part of the public worship. As an expert witness called by the prosecution, I had myself also made a similar argument during the case. The verdict of not guilty on this charge therefore clarified this position. Judge Rodwell himself argued

> I rule that as a matter of law if what was going on was an integral part of religious worship then it cannot by law be public entertainment. I am of the opinion that it is impertinent for an ordinary layperson to try and tell members of a different religion from his own what is or is not an integral part of that other person's religion. (LCC: sentence)

It is interesting that in recent years, perhaps under the direction of Gill Gowing, who had been the chief planning officer for Hertsmere since 1993, the phrase 'public entertainment' had not been used so much by the council in their consideration of activities at the Manor. It was something of a surprise to most concerned that the issue had been included in the charges brought against ISKCON. The arguments made in the courts, and particularly the verdict of not guilty, made it clear that the phrase – and the debate about whether the dramas were worship or entertainment – were an irrelevance to the main issues. The main issue was of course the large scale public *worship* at the Manor, for which there was no planning permission. With regard to this the Krishna-*lila* dramas were considered illegal as *forms of public worship*, and so were included in the debate (and prosecution) over public worship in breach of the enforcement notice.

Having received the verdicts, the Judge's sentences were extremely severe. The temple president, as an individual, was given a conditional discharge for two years – which meant no fine, but if he were to break the law again within that time (particularly breaking the enforcement notice) then he would be liable to be resentenced for this offence. But the sentence on ISKCON was very heavy – the Society were fined £30,000 and made to pay half (£7,184) of the prosecution's costs. Judge Rodwell made it clear that it had been ISKCON's choice to be tried in the crown court rather than the magistrate's court. As noted above, if they had chosen the latter then the fine would have been £20,000 at most. So for Judge Rodwell 'they must expect a heavier penalty than they might have faced in the Magistrate's court' (ibid.: sentence).

His evaluation of ISKCON's actions was by this time quite harsh. According to Judge Rodwell 'ISKCON decided that it would . . . push its luck . . . and just try and see if it could get away with not complying'. Therefore, for him it was 'quite clear that a deliberate decision was taken to flout the law' (ibid.). It was for this reason that the judge imposed such a heavy fine:

> I have to pass a sentence that makes it quite clear that however devoted, however religious people may be and however sincerely their feelings are held, everybody in this small and crowded country has to comply with the law otherwise it becomes impossible for the community to live in peace together. (ibid.)

The reaction to the verdict and the fine from ISKCON was one of shock. The temple president, Akhandadhi das told the local press outside the court house that they had been 'expecting something in the region of £1,000 to £2,000 at the most' (ibid.).[46] He was particularly surprised that a fine of such proportions could be imposed for an event which was 'purely religious' (ibid.). ISKCON decided almost immediately to launch an appeal to the High Court. This appeal would not be against the conviction since according to ISKCON's UK director of communications 'we couldn't really argue that there wasn't public worship going on for Janmasthami'.[47]

There was certainly some justification for ISKCON's sense of harsh treatment and their wish to have the fine reduced. Judge Rodwell had at times shown a degree of impatience with ISKCON over the affair, perhaps because he felt that ISKCON's challenge against the prosecution was half-hearted. (As the director of communication indicated in his remarks, ISKCON probably did not ever believe that they would win the case.) In his summing up Judge Rodwell found very little to say in support of ISKCON's case, and strongly directed the jury into finding guilty verdicts for the charges of public worship. His talk of possible 'anarchy' if ISKCON were allowed to 'get away' with 'flouting the law' clearly showed a lack of sympathy for their position. But, most interestingly, he commented that in his view concerning the Manor

> it is perfectly clear [they] would never be granted planning permission for public worship ... It simply is not a suitable area. That is the reality of the matter. (LCC: sentence)

This opinion was probably based on the previous findings of Inspector Russell and Secretary of State Chris Patten in 1990, when such planning permission had been turned down. But in making this comment he was also pre-empting the decision that was yet to be made in 1996 by Inspector Hanchet and Secretary of State John Gummer over the most recent and outstanding application for planning permission (for public worship and the access drive). In fact, Judge Rodwell was proved wrong just over six months later, when the planning permission was granted. After such a radical change in the status and position of the Manor in 1996, with public worship finally allowed, ISKCON were somewhat relieved when in summer 1996 the fine was reduced by the high court to £5,000 (even though the conviction remained).

Notes

1 That is, all the roads into the village were blocked by cars of devotees travelling to the Manor.
2 *Nama Hatta*, December 1986, p. 7.
3 AdPE:156; *Journal of Planning Law*, 1st October 1992, p. 963.
4 Enforcement notice, dated 3 March 1981, quoted in IR89a: para 9.7, p. 10.
5 Akhandadhi das, giving evidence to the 1988 Public Inquiry, reported in IR89a: para 12.41, p. 29.
6 That is, an agreement under section 52 of the Town and Country Planning Act 1971 (*Journal of Planning Law*, 1st October 1992, p. 963). See also EHRR:10.
7 This legal interpretation by Hertsmere Borough Council was upheld in the British courts and also by the European Commission. See EHRR:6.
8 HBC:34; NH, December 1986, p. 7.
9 Michael Jefferis, giving evidence to the 1988 Public Inquiry (in IR89a: para 18.70, p. 57).
10 Philip Marsh, letter to HBC Planning Authority, 24th September 1985 (quoted in IR89a: para 29.10, p. 87).
11 Philip Marsh (in IR89a: para 29.10, p. 87).
12 For a discussion of the rise and fall of Rajneeshpuram see Carter (1987). Rajneesh's city of Rajneeshpuram was disbanded in 1985, and Rajneesh himself eventually returned to India. In the late 1980s he changed his name to Osho, and he died in 1990. The Osho Foundation has continued after his death, based in Pune in India.

13 Mrs J Burgess, speaking for the Letchmore Heath Village Trust at the Public Inquiry in 1988 (IR89a: para 27.21, p. 81). Three other local residents at the inquiry also drew attention to the experience of the arrival of the temporary accommodation (see IR89a: paras 18.79, p. 58; 27.10, p. 79; & 29.16, p. 88).
14 Mrs M Rogers (quoted in IR89a: paras 29.17–17, pp. 88–89).
15 ADPE:160; Media Release from ISKCON communications, 28.8.91.
16 Gill Gowing, Chief Planning Officer, Hertsmere Borough Council, personal communication, January 1995.
17 Michael Jefferis' testimony to the 1988 Public Inquiry on behalf of Hertsmere council is reported in IR89a: paras 18.56–86, pp. 54–60.
18 AgHBC/A1:34; *Nama Hatta* Dec. 1986, p. 7.
19 Mr R Smith, Chief Planning Officer, Hertsmere Borough Council, speaking at 1988 Public Inquiry, in IR89a: para 21.6, p. 65.
20 Mr R Smith, chief planning officer, Hertsmere Borough Council, at the 1988 Public Inquiry (in IR89a: para 18.41, p. 52).
21 David Altaras, council for ISKCON at the 1988 Public Inquiry, Inspector Russell (in IR89a: para 30.24, p. 96).
22 AdPE:160; *Hare Krishna*, Summer 1988, p. 3.
23 *Hare Krishna*, Summer 1988, p. 3.
24 *West Herts and Watford Observer*, Friday 9th December 1988, p. 7.
25 *My Sweet Lord*, published in 1987, and *Hinduism in Leeds*, published in 1986.
26 Quotations taken from IR89a: paras 37.13–25, pp. 118–20.
27 Secretary of State's decision letter (DoE90a: para 17.1), noted in *Journal of Planning Law* 1st Oct 1992, p. 965.
28 *WHWO* Friday 23rd March 1990, p. 5.
29 Akhandadhi Das, quoted in *West Herts and Watford Observer*, Friday 23rd March 1990, p. 5.
30 International Society for Krishna Consciousness v. Secretary of State for the Environment and Hertsmere Borough Council (Queen's Bench Division, Kennedy J., October 31 1991). See *Journal of Planning Law*, 1st October 1992, pp. 962–972; also EHRR:10.
31 *MYF*, Issue 4, Autumn 1991, p. 21.
32 *Journal of Planning Law* 1st Oct 1992, p. 972
33 Ibid., p. 970
34 EHRR:11; *The Independent*, Friday 1st November 1991.
35 EHRR:11; *The Independent*, Tuesday 17th March 1992.
36 Akhadadhi Das quoted in WHWO, Friday 20th March 1992, p. 7.
37 As will be discussed in chapter eight, this clause on article 9 of the convention does strongly limit the protection that the convention gives to the general principle of 'freedom of religion'.
38 *Temple Campaign Newsletter*, no. 10, 1993, p. 1.
39 Comment made by Akhandadhi das to Luton Crown Court (reported in LCC).
40 *Today* programme, BBC Radio 4, 16th March 1994.
41 Philip Copeland, Managing Director of Hertsmere Borough Council speaking on *Everyman*, 'The Road to Hare Krishna', BBC TV, 2nd October 1994.
42 *RBA*, Wednesday 22nd March 1995, p. 1.
43 *The Times*, Tuesday October 31st 1995, p. 9; *WHWO*, Friday November 3rd 1995, p. 13.
44 Richard Humphries, quoted in *WHWO*, 3rd Nov 1995, p. 13.
45 *WHWO*, Friday November 10th 1995, p. 12.
46 *WHWO*, Friday November 10th 1995, p. 12.
47 Bhagavat Dharma das, in *IWR*, vol. 14 no. 4, Nov/December 1995.

CHAPTER FIVE

The Political Campaign

In 1975 ISKCON made a strong effort to mobilise support from Indian Hindus living in London to help save their temple, which was under threat of closure from the local planning authority. A leaflet was circulated which said:

> **Return Religious and Racial Tolerance to Britain**
>
> Save this place of worship now!
>
> Since 1969 the Radha Krishna temple ... has been serving as a place of worship for thousands, particularly among Britain's Hindu Asian community. Its location provides easy access for thousands of worshippers working in central London. The Temple, an international book publisher, like many others in the area, is a cultural asset to the neighbourhood. The ancient Vedic culture of Indian is on display in many Western language texts, a large number of which are unavailable elsewhere in England.
>
> ... This is a heartfelt appeal to all intelligent, thoughtful and compassionate persons, especially to the government bodies involved, to SAVE THIS PLACE OF WORSHIP. Anyone, irrespective of faith, race, nationality, or age, who wishes to see rectified this violation of religious freedom, and abuse of racial tolerance, is earnestly requested to contact: Mr Ian Cheverton, The Society for the Protection of the Religious Rights of Asians in Britain, c/o the Radha Krishna temple, 7 Bury Place, London.[1]

At this time the temple in question was not Bhaktivedanta Manor. It was, instead, another temple which had been dedicated by Prabhupada in late 1969 in a flat in Bury Place, a central London residential street. Access to this location had been very poor and, as the leaflet states, despite 'extensive soundproofing' of the temple 'some residents have complained to Camden council about noise; others have complained about visitors' with the result that an enforcement notice was served on ISKCON requiring them to turn 'the whole Temple premises ... into offices' (ibid.). ISKCON attempted to challenge this notice but were unsuccessful, and so in 1979 decided to relocate the temple (including the deities which had been installed by Prabhupada) to a more suitable site nearby in Soho Street, where they have remained since.

A year earlier, in July 1974, the main Gujarati newspaper in Britain, *Gujarat Samachar*, carried an article (in English) entitled '100,000 Hindus to protest in Trafalgar Square', which called on Gujarati Hindus to protest against the decision made by the government refusing permission for ISKCON to stage the annual Rathayatra festival in London that year, which would involve the pulling of a large decorated chariot through the centre of the city followed by large crowds of worshippers.[2] Since that time, the Rathayatra procession has occurred regularly in London, usually bringing local traffic to a standstill as the large numbers make their way through the streets between Hyde Park and Battersea Park.

Around this same time ISKCON were beginning to experience for the first time the problems that would bedevil them for over twenty years at Bhaktivedanta Manor, problems associated with large scale Hindu worship at the temple that Prabhupada had installed. And in all three of these cases, one of the major planned bases for support in their attempts to fight unfavourable official decisions was to mobilise the political support of a substantial constituency of interest for them, that is from people of Indian ancestry who identified themselves as Hindus. In many ways this was an ambiguous strategy, particularly because in the early to mid 1970s it was by no means clear how much Krishna conscious devotees wished to align themselves (theologically or culturally) with the various forms of Hindu religious culture that were accessible in Britain. But it was eventually to prove successful for ISKCON, not only because it was through the 'Hindu campaign' that a decision was made to safeguard the temple, but also because the relatively successful development of the UK *yatra* of ISKCON has been greatly aided – financially and in many other ways – through the support and participation of large numbers of devotees of Hindu Indian backgrounds.

Thus the campaign for the Manor was not only fought through the courts and the planning structures: although attempts to redefine the planning status of the Manor as a place of public worship were a vital strategy. Another very significant arena for the conflict was the public domain. And within this arena a very important audience for ISKCON was the 'Hindu community' in Britain, that is the 500,000 British Hindus of Indian ancestry,[3] who were targeted and mobilised through a number of media to create a support base for ISKCON'S campaign. The campaign was, however, also directed at this constituency as a means of reaching a wider audience, that is the section of liberal white British society that would respond to calls for 'tolerance' and 'religious freedom'.

Although, as the above examples show, there was obviously considerable support from some Indians for ISKCON, it could not be taken for granted that the 'Hindu community' could be mobilised in sufficient force to make any significant difference to the legal deliberations over the status of the Manor. One very significant strategy for ISKCON, therefore, was to make sure that large numbers of Hindus did care enough to make their voices heard, and to ensure that the people who were making decisions about the Manor were actually able to hear these voices. It was this strategy, which developed particularly in the late 1980s and early 1990s, that above all led to the successful conclusion of the campaign in 1996. As it turned out, the strategy was powerfully multifocused, soliciting support from a number of important and well placed sources across a broad band of British cultural life. It required a delicate balance being achieved between generating visible mass support from Hindu devotees whilst making significant friends in the social and political establishment.

The Hindu campaign

Attempts by ISKCON to mobilise support from Hindus for their temples (particularly those under legal threat of closure) began in the 1970s, and have been a long running strategy, not only in Britain, but also in India (such as the case in Mumbai discussed in chapter one, see Brzezinski 1998:42). What is different about the Manor, however, is the intense level at which the campaign was maintained for a number of years, and the way in which the Manor became such an important symbol for many Hindus, indicated by the fact that for a while it was frequently referred to as 'the most important Hindu temple in the UK'. ISKCON's campaign for Hindu support was successful insofar as they did not only *ask* for help to fight to keep the temple open, they were *given* such support in large quantity.

Interaction between ISKCON and the wider Hindu population needs to be contextualised within the range of relationships that have developed in the past two decades. On the one hand, ISKCON have been actively involved in reaching as many people as possible in Britain who would identify themselves (in some way or other) as 'Hindu', whilst at the same time they have also very intensively developed institutional links with the organisations that have been formed to represent and organise Hindu interests (and thus British Hindus). The sustained nature of both these levels of engagement have helped to develop what is known as the 'Indianisation' of ISKCON (c.f. Carey 1987), particularly through the recruitment of both devotees and also leaders who were Hindus of Indian ancestry. As I discussed in the first chapter, however, this process has been as much about the 'Hinduisation' of the organisation as its 'Indianisation', since the development has primarily created a closer alignment with a broad 'Hindu' identity, whilst the Indian-ness of ISKCON was from its origins always a very important element.

On the other hand, alongside this shift by many Krishna consciousness followers towards placing ISKCON within a general 'Hindu' umbrella identity (as well as an engagement with significant number of people who bring a Hindu identity and practice *into* the movement), there has been a development the other way. That is, ISKCON leadership have used their contacts and influences among a range of Indian and Hindu groups to stamp their imprint onto the development of Hindu identities and practices in Britain, to shape the ways in which Hinduism should be practised in British contexts in future generations. These processes I have broadly labelled the 'Iskconisation' of the various forms of Hinduism in Britain (see Nye 2000).

An example of this can be seen in the ways in which ISKCON have developed relationships with the NCHT and the HCUK, the two main national organisations for Hindus in Britain. Until the mid 1990s, the National Council of Hindu Temples (NCHT) was the Hindu representative group in the country. It has a membership of around ninety temples in England, Wales, Scotland, and Northern Ireland, and was founded in the 1970s by several Hindu temple groups including Bhaktivedanta Manor. Thus ISKCON, and particularly the Manor leaders, have been involved with this national organisation right from the start, and so have in a sense been one of the key players shaping not only the development of the NCHT, but also through it the overall direction of Hindu organisations.

The role of the NCHT has predominantly been as an advisory body, providing a great deal of help and advice to local groups of Hindus – not only on how to organise, build, and set up temples, but also on the provision of Hinduism through education and worship. At the same time, however, the NCHT have occasionally taken a more political/pressure-group type role, such as in March 1983 when the nightly television news programme *Nationwide* showed a negative story on the Hare Krishna movement, making comparisons between the movement and groups such as the Unification Church (the 'Moonies') and alleging that ISKCON use techniques of mind-control to gain followers. This programme drew strong complaints not only from ISKCON themselves, but also from the NCHT.[4] The NCHT president, P. Bhardwaj, forwarded a statement made by their executive council to the Director-General of the BBC, which said that:

> The NCHT is outraged at the insult to and attack on the Hindu religion shown on BBC's Nationwide . . . How dare you call the Hare Krishna temple, which is a centre for all Hindus and a member of our Council, an extremist religious cult . . . By doing so you have slandered our Hindu religion. The Hare Krishna Society is a bona fide Hindu group and well respected amongst all Hindus. Indeed, we praise their efforts in spreading knowledge of Hindu religion and culture. The philosophy and the practices they follow are exactly in accord with

> proper Hinduism and we are proud that they are setting such a good example in this country. (Bhardwaj n.d.)

The NCHT also issued a press release which made it clear that they:

> fully support the work of the Hare Krishna Movement, whose temples are important places of worship accepted by all Hindus ... Any slight on them is an insult to all Hindus in Britain ...[5]

In December 1992, it was the NCHT who took the responsibility of entering discussions with Muslim organisations on behalf of Hindus, to try to resolve Hindu-Muslim tensions in Britain following the destruction of the Babri Mosque in Ayodhya, India. This lobbying role was, however, superseded in November 1994 by the creation of the Hindu Council of the UK (HCUK).

Both the NCHT and the HCUK are federal umbrella groups, which try to be balanced and represent the needs of all those who consider themselves as Hindus in Britain without regard to their religious affiliation, or any other factor. Of the ninety temple members of the NCHT only two are ISKCON temples, whilst the majority are non-sectarian – being 'ecumenical' in approach.[6] However, the administrative facilities of ISKCON, and the presence of efficient personnel within their movement, are useful resources upon which the NCHT can draw – since they have no offices of their own, and usually tend to be based at the local temple of the Council's president. Because of their organisational skills, ISKCON have been effective in providing key support (and hence a high degree of input) into the NCHT. For example, it has been the practice for a number of years for a member of ISKCON to hold an important administrative (if not leadership) role within the NCHT, and in 1992 a Krishna consciousness devotee called Bimal Krishna das (who is also known as Vipin Aery) was appointed the secretary of the NCHT. Bimal Krishna has played an important role for both organisations, and was energetic in promoting the issue of the Manor within the Hindu population (for several years this was his primary role as an ISKCON devotee). Speaking on behalf of the NCHT, he said in 1993 that:

> No other Hindu temple offers such facilities as Bhaktivedanta Manor to practise our Sanatan Dharma. It is vital that the British government recognise how important the Hare Krishna Mandir [temple] is to the Hindu community throughout the United Kingdom, before it is too late. The NCHT pledges to do all in its power to help save the temple for all our community. We beg all Hindu organisations to support the campaign now at this vital stage.[7]

Of course the NCHT has other concerns as well as Bhaktivedanta Manor, and so only had limited resources to put into assisting the campaign. Furthermore, the president of the NCHT in 1994, Om Prakash Sharma, was keen to stress that there have been other cases in Britain of Hindu temples experiencing difficulties in obtaining planning permission. These include temple projects in Wolverhampton, Dudley, Crawley, Leicester, and Tipton, and also the Swaminarayan Hindu Mission in Neasden, north west London. On a television documentary on Bhaktivedanta Manor he was quoted as saying:

> It is not easy to get planning permission in this country for our Hindu temples. We are having a lot of troubles. More or less in every temple whichever we try to set up here, some sort of obstacles are put in our way by the planning authorities.[8]

This notwithstanding, the NCHT gave great support to the issue because they perceived the threat to the Manor as a direct threat to the interests of all Hindus in Britain.

As with the NCHT, ISKCON was also a founding member of the HCUK in 1994, and have also provided some very useful personnel to help in the organisation and running of the group. In the few years since its foundation the HCUK have been trying to develop its role as a mouthpiece for all Hindus in Britain, modelling itself to a degree along the lines of the British Board of Deputies for the Jewish population. Therefore, the HCUK has the potential to become a strong lobbying organisation for the 500,000 Hindu population of Britain, and the corollary of this is that ISKCON is a strong force within this political representation. If the HCUK succeeds – and to a certain extent this relies on the support they get from groups such as ISKCON – then it may have a strong influence on the future development of Hinduism in the UK, particularly through bringing some measure of cohesion to a population characterised by strong divisions. At the same time, though, such a success for the HCUK would also be a success for ISKCON, since they would be providing a large measure of input into this body.

It is important, however, to bear in mind that there is a great deal of heterogeneity within British Hindu groups, and that ISKCON is playing against other powerful groups who are also seeking to shape the future direction of national movements such as the NCHT and the HCUK. There are several large non-sectarian temples, such as the Geeta Bhawan in Birmingham, and the Ram Mandir and the Vishwa Hindu Mandir which are both in Southall, all of which have a high measure of public support from both local and wider communities. There are other sectarian groups with very different approaches to ISKCON, in particular the Swaminarayan groups – the International Swaminarayan Satsang Organisation (ISSO) and the Swaminarayan Hindu Mission. There are also regional groups such as the Hindu Council of the North and the Hindu Council of Brent, and caste based groups such as the Patidar Samaj. Each of these groups has a different agenda to ISKCON, and so, of course, will be wanting to take the national organisations in different directions to those proposed by ISKCON. But in some cases there may be some overlap – for example, the Patidar Samaj has a considerable number of members who are supporters of ISKCON.

Another very important organisation within this political milieu is the Vishwa Hindu Parishad (VHP), an international organisation, with its main centre in India, who more than any other group are actively seeking to shape the direction of Hindu identities (see, for example Bhatt 1997). Although the philosophies of ISKCON and the VHP are very different, as well as their political agendas (since in particular the VHP are strongly involved in national politics in India, as a militant Hindu revivalist organisation with close links to the right wing Hindu nationalist Bharatiya Janata Party), the VHP have been supportive of ISKCON on a number of occasions, including during the campaign. For example, the VHP issued a statement from Bombay in 1981 in which they gave formal recognition to ISKCON as an authentic Hindu tradition. In the statement the president of the VHP, Maharani B.S. Mewar said:

> We Hindus consider the activities of ISKCON to be an integral part of our life to preserve and propagate the pure Vedic culture and thought for the preservation of mankind ... The religious tradition that ISKCON represents is the oldest and purest in its approach to life in the world, and all respect should be shown to this great and noble work, which is preventing the misguidance and misuse of youth.[9]

In sum, the VHP considered that ISKCON were 'a great modern representative of' Vaisnavism who were playing an important role in the 'Vedic Renaissance'.

In 1988, a VHP conference in Nepal passed several resolutions to create an International Campaign Committee to save Bhaktivedanta Manor, whose remit was to 'arouse awareness of this matter worldwide and bring pressure to bear on each country's respective government to urge the British government to intervene and save the temple at Bhaktivedanta Manor', a measure which ISKCON warmly welcomed.[10] Although the immediate effect of these resolutions were not successful – since at the governmental level the Secretary of State for the Environment decided shortly afterwards to uphold the enforcement notice and refuse permission for the Dagger Lane temple – in the longer term the VHP were of great assistance in the campaign. Thus the secretary of the British branch of the VHP worked with ISKCON for a number of years to help to raise awareness of the issue within this country, particularly through the temple defence movement (see below).

One of the main strengths of the NCHT and the VHP is that they are effective lobby groups, with considerable power as national representatives of the British Hindu population. Until late 1994 there was no official group that represented all Hindus in Britain (this changed when the HCUK was launched), and so when the government needed to know the 'mind' of the Hindu population they would turn to the NCHT or the VHP. For example, a source within ISKCON told me that before the Department of the Environment made their judgement in March 1990 there was considerable fear that the Hindu population would react violently, in the same way that some Muslims had done over the Salman Rushdie novel *The Satanic Verses* only a few months before. Therefore the government consulted through these bodies with a representative of British Hindus, asking whether a ruling against ISKCON would lead to Hindus rioting on the streets in favour of their temple and their religion. The response was an accurate prediction that the Hindus would be upset, but they would not riot.

The international dimension of both ISKCON and the VHP have also created some political pressure on the British government in the international arena. Representatives of the campaign lobbied in India as well as in Britain over the issue – for example, contacts were made with the Indian Home Affairs Minister in January 1993 to coincide with a visit made to the country by the British Prime Minister John Major.[11] In 1994 there were reports that the Indian Environment Minister, Kamal Nath, had warned on a visit to Britain that 'many Anglo Indian trade arrangements could be jeopardised' if the Manor was closed to the public.[12]

The HKTDM and mass action

In some respects, support for the Manor was not only produced by ISKCON's active efforts with groups and liaisons across the political spectrum of British Hindu organisations, but also through its own Indian devotees who used the temple on a regular basis. In 1990, following the Secretary of State's decision, a group of prominent devotees decided to form an organisation called the Hare Krishna Temple Defence Movement (HKTDM). The founding Chairman of this group was a businessman called Naresh Chadha, who went on to take a high profile role in his defence of the temple. Also involved within the group were Shantoo Ruparell (a prominent solicitor who has given free legal representation to ISKCON), Venilal Vaghela (the vice-chairman of the Hindu Council of Brent), Kishore Ruperalia (the secretary of the VHP (UK)), and Frank Ward (a Labour local councillor) (JB93:77; JB94:88).

This movement worked to create support for the campaign, to raise funds for their efforts, and to encourage people to make the pledge:

> to continue to fight to defend the temple until justice is obtained and all the devotees can visit the shrine without further intimidation and persecution.[13]

Those who joined the HKTDM were encouraged to manifest their support by (i) writing to the (then) Prime Minister John Major 'demanding the right to worship at your temple', (ii) by 'offering a prayer every day to Lord Krishna that He protect His temple so that His devotees can worship Him without harassment', and (iii) by 'taking part in all the rallies and events organised by the temple and the HKTDM' (ibid.).

Such rallies occurred regularly, taking various forms. Perhaps the largest one happening in central London on Wednesday 16th March 1994, having been planned to coincide with the end of the two year 'grace period' of the enforcement notice. This march was attended by several thousand Hindus coming from many parts of Britain, including both Indians and white devotees, following a bullock cart whilst they carried plaques showing their support for the Manor.[14] Before the rally leaflets were distributed in temples around London advertising the march saying:

> Because the Government supports persecution, they ignore our needs and rights, they refuse to listen to reasoning. We must NOW take action. We will show our outrage at this minority injustice. We will show our defiance at the ban.[15]

According to ISKCON the attendance at the rally was 36,000, whilst a more conservative estimate by the Daily Telegraph was 'more that 20,000' (JB94:79&98). This was the largest ever gathering of Indian Hindus in Britain, making a clear demonstration of the strength of feeling that the issue had generated – the figure of 36,000 represents between 5–10% of the total Hindu population of Britain, which is a very significant proportion to become mobilised to attend a weekday rally in London. It is no surprise, therefore, that the scale of support for the rally was considered to be a great success for the campaign. According to the ISKCON report the demonstrators 'were heralding the dawn of a new era for this awakening [Hindu] community' (JB94:79).

In some cases ISKCON have organised protest marches which also have a strong devotional dimension. For example in July 1987 the Rathayatra, the annual parade of deities through the streets at the front of a procession of devotees (mentioned briefly in another context at the beginning of this chapter), was promoted as a 'procession against the unjust closure of the shrine'.[16] The Rathyatra is a traditional form of deity worship among many Hindu groups, and was introduced as an important event for Krishna consciousness devotees by Prabhupada soon after the foundation of ISKCON, with a procession of deities through the streets around the temple in San Francisco. The first such Rathyatra in London was held in 1970, and it usually attracts thousands of Indian Hindu worshippers each year. As a very obvious display of support for the Hare Krishna movement it obviously lends itself strongly to the use of the procession as a political demonstration *as well as* a devotional event.

A smaller scale event called Padayatra makes use of the oxen that are kept at the Manor. This 'walking pilgrimage' (or 'walking festival')[17] involves two oxen pulling a wooden cart on which are installed movable deities (called Nitai-Gaurasundar), slowly covering distances of over one hundred miles in the space of several weeks. Devotees follow the cart singing *bhajans* and chanting, and at various points the cart is stopped to allow the distribution of *prasad*, and for dancing, dramas, or preaching to be performed by devotees. Such Padayatras are made fairly regularly through London, as well as in other parts of Britain, and also in continental Europe. A one hundred mile Padayatra made its way through London in April and May 1993, stopping each night at Hindu temples on the route, with the purpose 'to increase the awareness of the Campaign to Save Bhaktivedanta Manor' (JB93:78). With the obvious support of the seventeen temples which gave the pilgrims hospitality, ISKCON made it clear that such displays were needed if the Manor was to be saved:

> It is essential that every member of the Hindu community is made aware of the plight of the largest Hindu shrine in the UK. This is not the temple of a few, but of each and every member of the community. We therefore want each person to recognise their responsibility and step forward and join us in our campaign. Time is running out for us, and it is very much required that we join hands and hold back the threat to our culture. (JB93:78)

As with the Rathayatras, the Padayatras were also sometimes used as large scale processions to make a very visible demonstration of support for ISKCON. Indeed, ISKCON were sometimes keen to encourage this. For example a one day Padayatra in September 1991, which made its way from Wembley to the Manor, was publicised by ISKCON Communications through a press release. The release, sent out several days before, was headed: 'Hindus demand access to the shrine: three thousand to take part in non-violent protest'.[18] This theme of non-violent protest was further stressed by drawing parallels with Mahatma Gandhi's use of 'walking pilgrimage' as a 'method of opposition to injustice' in his protest 'against British rule in India' (ibid.).

ISKCON, the Indian population, and the Manor

These public processions demonstrated that a large number of Indian Hindus were behind ISKCON in the campaign to keep the Manor as a place of public worship. They gave backing to the claim that the closure of the Manor would alienate not only white Hare Krishna devotees, but also a large number of Hindus of Indian background. As mass lobbies of the political process they were probably very effective, and are likely to have played a key role in the support given to ISKCON by party politicians (which I discuss below), and indeed probably helped to produce a climate in which the Secretary of State finally made a decision in favour of ISKCON.

At the same time, however, the use of mass action gave ISKCON an opportunity to raise awareness and support from the many Hindu groups in Britain. This support did not come automatically – it needed to be worked at – and so leafleting temples and other groups about forthcoming processions, and the visits made by Padayatras to local temples, along with other activities, all helped to keep Hindus informed about ISKCON's campaign. Many Hindus did already feel a great deal of sympathy for ISKCON, but this sympathy did not necessarily entail the large scale politicisation among British Hindus over the issue that actually occurred.

It does appear that ISKCON were extremely successful in mobilising this support. The rally in London in March 1994 clearly showed that a very significant proportion of the Hindu population were prepared to make a strong show of outrage at the threat to the Manor. ISKCON themselves would have argued that this was because of the quality of the worship performed at the Manor, and because these Hindus were Vaishnavas, close to the heart of the Krishna consciousness message. This not withstanding, much of the support from the Hindu population came from people who did not have any attachment to Krishna consciousness as propagated by ISKCON. That is, there was a great deal of sympathy with ISKCON and the Manor as a branch of Hinduism, and as centre for Hindu worship, but this did not usually translate into membership of the organisation.

It appears, therefore, that many Hindus in Britain took to heart the message that the Manor was a crucial national centre of Hinduism, and that the threat to the Manor was also a threat to them as Hindus. This helped to raise the profile – and indeed the public image – of ISKCON in Britain among the general British Hindu population, and indeed it may well have significant long term consequences. It is indeed ironic that support from British Hindus for ISKCON probably grew a great deal because of the dispute. That is, although the actual attendance at the Manor (on days such as Janmasthami) stabilised in the late 1970s/early 80s, the awareness of the presence and significance of the Manor significantly increased from the late 1980s onwards as a result of the coverage of the dispute in the national media, and through the various campaigns. This point was not lost on Hertsmere council, who (as I will discuss in the next chapter) later used it as an argument for not allowing worship at the temple.

Hindu Youth Movement

Over the years ISKCON have made a strong effort to develop the needs of their younger followers and potential supporters. In 1979, Akhandadhi das (who later became the temple president) was given the responsibility of forming a number of youth clubs, first in Southall and then later in other areas associated with South Asian residence – such as Wembley, Forest Gate, and Thornton Heath. In 1982 he was reported as saying:

> I began to realise more and more that young people wanted to take shelter with us, that they were actually having a lot of difficulty

> coping with western life and how they should understand their religion in the context of day-to-day life. They weren't clear about what their parents were trying to explain. There were so many difficulties. So I thought: the interest and enthusiasm is there. Let's try youth clubs! (quoted in ICAP)

This strategy had been partly initiated because of a fear that 'People had warned the devotees that after the older generation had passed on, the youngsters would never be interested' (ibid.). As ISKCON were by that time beginning to realise the great benefits of large-scale support for the organisation from wealthy and enthusiastic Indian benefactors, the worry obviously began to develop that such support could begin to dry up if the current generation of British born and educated Hindus became progressively more secularised, westernised, and de-Hinduised. More importantly, however, as a movement with a fundamental missionary aim, ISKCON were more than ready to take on a challenge of promoting Krishna consciousness to a group of people who it was feared might even lose the Vaisnavite religious culture of their parents. It was clear that future relationships between ISKCON and British Hindus would depend to a large extent on how well ISKCON managed to introduce both the distinctiveness and authenticity of what they were doing.

During the 1980s and early 1990s several different Krishna youth groups have been formalised out of these efforts, most notably the 'Manor Youth Forum' in the mid 80s and 'Pandava Sena' in the mid 90s. As well as the local youth clubs, these more centralised groups have focused on the Manor, and have worked closely with devotees living and working there. The groups have provided youth-club type activities for teenage Hindus from London, as well as religious educative classes. One of the functions of these groups has been to provide young Hindus with a viable Hindu alternative to the problems they perceive in British 'materialistic' society without completely renouncing that society. Of course the young devotee will be encouraged to avoid drugs, alcohol, meat, and pre-marital sex, and also to try to live a life directed to Krishna. But at the same time this does not mean that they cannot live Krishna consciousness out in the world – practically all of the members of the current Pandava Sena are heading for university education, professional careers, and (most likely) comfortable lifestyles. On another level, Pandava Sena has given its members a means by which they can be Hindu and still enjoy some of the aspects of the wider society – the group like to wear black tee-shirts and trousers, with black baseball caps, all marked with red borders and insignia (an emblem of the deity Hanuman, and the words 'Pandava Sena'). One member of the group told me that this is part of the appeal of Pandava Sena (apart from its religious appeal), one can 'look good' if you belong, and that *part* of the popularity of the group is that 'people like the clothes'.

One of the successes of the Manor Youth Forum was that a number of the youths initially involved through it have been working their way up through to significant leadership roles within the UK *yatra* of ISKCON. Indeed Vipin Aery, who on initiation took the name of Bimal Krishna das, was one such recruit, who as well as becoming the secretary for the NCHT also went on to devote several years to coordinating the political campaign for the Manor. Indeed, many of the youths who were involved through these groups became actively involved in fighting in some way or other for the temple cause. In the late 1980s the Manor Youth Forum became transformed into an active group called 'Hindu Youth Saving Our Temple' (HYSOT), roughly at the same time that the HKTDM came into being. Young women and men in this group were active campaigners, particularly making up numbers on public demonstrations, as well as lobbying ISKCON devotees to take firm action to ensure eventual success for the cause.

As events unfolded in 1994, particularly with the implementation of the enforcement notice in March of that year, the group HYSOT began to reconstitute itself with an emerging new set of personnel, and decided on the identity of Pandava Sena – referring to the army of the righteous Pandava brothers who fought a war that is told of in the classic *Mahabharat* epic. The war that Pandava Sena wished to fight was on behalf of Krishna consciousness and Bhaktivedanta Manor, but they stressed their means would be a non-violent militancy. On several occasions they organised vigils on behalf of the Manor, in the village of Letchmore Heath (outside its gates), outside the offices of Hertsmere council in nearby Borehamwood, and also alongside the large demonstrations in central London. They were easily identifiable, particularly because of their black clothing and caps, but also because of the dynamism and noise that they were prepared to generate to get their message heard.

Two years later in early 1996, as the frustrations of the campaign began to show, and before the decision was made in favour of the temple and access road, I was at a conference organised by ISKCON Communications on the issues generated by the Bhaktivedanta Manor case. During a final discussion session, some members of Pandava Sena joined the debate to ask what could and should be done if permission for the road was refused. One young man made clear his strongly felt impatience with the British government, and British society in general, and suggested that tactics of non-violent militancy had not really got them very far. He went as far as suggesting that perhaps Pandava Sena, and the campaign, should consider going beyond non-violence, without specifying how (and to what extent) violent means could be used to forward the case for the Manor. The conference organiser, Shaunika rishi das (ISKCON's European director of communications), took immediate steps to dissociate ISKCON from such a suggestion, pointing out there was no place for the use of violence in Krishna consciousness, and the campaign had always, and would always be fought on the principles of *ahimsa* (that is, non-violence).[19] Within just a few weeks, the Secretary of State's decision was announced and the campaign was resolved, so this call for direct and possibly violent action on behalf of Krishna was never put to the test. But the suggestion made a clear demonstration of some of the difficult tensions that ISKCON were faced with, insofar that the support of activist groups such as Pandava Sena helped to keep the issue public, and yet also threatened to undermine some of their more subtle tactics.

Indeed ISKCON played a careful game with Pandava Sena throughout the last years of the campaign. Although the group had emerged out of a Manor Youth Forum, and they were, of course, very much affiliated to the aims of Krishna consciousness and the need to 'save the temple', ISKCON tried to make it clear that Pandava Sena were an independent group over whom they could not exercise control. It is quite probable that while many of the older (and white male) leaders were happy with the Pandava Sena youths' enthusiasm and fighting spirit, they were also rather worried that the group would unbalance their strategic political campaign which was based more on quietly influencing the right people with a persuasive argument, based on the size of the Hindu community rather than on the noise that it could generate. In particular the worry was that 'the Hindus' (in general) might come to be seen as political activists who did not fully respect or uphold 'British law', and thus become bracketed as similar to 'the Muslims'. If this happened, the goodwill of the campaign could be seriously undermined. On the other hand, however, the activism of Pandava Sena could be politically advantageous: so long as it was polite and manifestly non-violent it invoked the political and cultural capital of Mahatma Gandhi, suggesting a nobility and patience of suffering which had become familiar to white British audiences through Richard Attenborough's film. At the same time, the loud activism of the young Hindus of Pandava Sena also helped to encourage and generate the quiet activism of the larger and more sedate older generations, whose physical support behind ISKCON was crucial for making the case of the Manor as a place of Hindu worship.

The political campaign

In September 1990, six months after Secretary of State of the Environment Chris Patten had turned down ISKCON's appeal against the enforcement notice, and plans for an alternative temple site, the national Council of Management of ISKCON in Britain held an extraordinary general meeting to discuss 'the way forward for the Manor campaign'.[20] At this meeting various strategies for continuing the campaign were discussed, with much of the discussion showing quite a strong ambivalence towards the directions being taken by the HKTDM. Instead of, or as well as, the mass public demonstrations advocated by leading members of the 'Hindu community' is was felt that a quieter strategy should be pursued of making agreements with important and influential people, and winning friends within the establishment. In particular this would involve lobbying behind the scenes, finding potential allies among the intelligent and thoughtful people with influence who might support the general cause for a place of public worship for Hindus. This would require direct fact to face meetings with church leaders and politicians, who might give a sympathetic ear. This approach was strongly contrasted, in some of the discussion, with the unsubtlety of the HKTDM campaigning strategies so far.

In the circumstances, this was probably a wise decision for ISKCON to have made. The mobilisation of the Hindu population behind them had by this stage been established. Thus in 1988 at the public inquiry, the counsel for Hertsmere accepted the scale of support for the Manor:

> The fact it is of national importance; that three or four million Hindus [sic.] do not have sufficient amenities; that many of them live in north west London; and the fact that the Manor takes a special place in their heart cannot possibly justify planning permission being granted, and the consequent effect it will have on the village. (Elizabeth Appleby QC, counsel for Hertsmere)[21]

And Inspector Russell concluded in his report for this inquiry that 'the Manor has become a special place of worship and pilgrimage for the Hindu community in this country . . .' (IR90a:para 37.13, see chapter four). Most particularly this was also remarked upon in the Secretary of State's decision letter in March 1990, who said 'it is abundantly clear that the Manor is regarded by the Hindu community as a place of very special religious significance' (DoE90a:4).

With this case now well established, and indeed well reported in the national media, ISKCON needed to go beyond flexing their Hindu support if they were ever going to create the right conditions for salvaging some solution to their quandary. By this stage, all the legal possibilities of challenging the enforcement notice in English courts looked fairly hopeless, and the bid to the European court was always going to be a lottery. So they were faced with the prospect of trying to keep the Manor open for as long as possible until another alternative presented itself, and then with having to mobilise their political muscle to actually realise that possibility. This might have taken the form of an alternative site or (as eventually happened) the chance to remain at the Manor under alternative circumstances.

Thus, the period between 1990 and 1996 was marked by a developing campaign which still relied, although to a slightly lesser extent, on mass demonstrations, but was fundamentally based on the strategy of winning friends and influence in the establishment. The arguments that were put forward in the courts (particularly the European Commission of Human Rights) were particularly favourable to this approach, since it emphasised the point of multicultural tolerance and fundamental human rights to religious freedom, which is of such great importance as a discourse of liberal democracy in contemporary Britain. On the other hand, the case of Hindu support was not to be marginalised, even if some Hindu campaign tactics were considered rather distasteful by ISKCON's leaders. With the Hindu population of Britain numbering approximately 500,000, in political terms this constitutes a large and fairly prosperous constituency, whose views and feelings could not be easily ignored. If the majority of this population began to consider one particular political party to be unsympathetic to them – for example, if a party was seen as supporting moves to close an important temple – then this could have important electoral consequences for that party. On the other hand, a party supporting the Manor could well find some benefit from being seen as helping Hindus. Hindu leaders in Britain were indeed aware of this political leverage that they could exert, and there was considerable lobbying on this temple issue. Such lobbying was also supported by sustained media coverage at national level, which meant that the issue continued to be debated and did not go 'off the boil'. At times, this political campaign took place blatantly in public view, particularly during and close to elections, when political capital could be gathered by politicians displaying their interest in the case. But for the most part this campaign relied on a very sophisticated political lobbying process, pursued by Akhandadhi das in particular.

At the level of local politics (that is, within Hertsmere council) ISKCON for a number of years were only able to gain support from a minority of councillors. Generally, the large majority of Conservative councillors sided with the residents of Letchmore Heath against the case put by ISKCON, and it was these Conservative councillors who had a large majority in the council chamber until 1994. Whatever support ISKCON could get from the council was mainly from the Labour councillors, who formed a minority group until 1995.

However, at the national level the situation was more complicated, and indeed ISKCON found that received a sympathetic ear from many politicians. For example, in March 1992, during the General Election campaign, there were visits to the Manor by prominent figures from the major political parties, including Glenys Kinnock (the wife of the then leader of the Labour party), Zerbanoo Gifford (ethnic minorities adviser to the Liberal Democrats), and James Clappison (the prospective Conservative parliamentary candidate for the area).[22] In 1994, as Hertsmere were deliberating about the access driveway, twenty six Members of Parliament – from all political parties and including the Chancellor of the Exchequer – wrote to the council over the issue, mainly to seek 'additional information and a sympathetic hearing of the application' (AgHBC/A:30).

In particular Keith Vaz, the Labour MP for Leicester East (and the only Asian Labour MP in the 1992 Parliament) took up the cause of

Bhaktivedanta Manor in 1994.[23] Vaz had already established a reputation as a successful campaigner in his fight to protect investors (mainly of South Asian backgrounds) who had lost money in the collapse of the Bank of Credit and Commerce International (BCCI). He took the opportunity in March 1994 to put down an early day motion in the House of Commons in support of the Manor 'to encourage suspension of the Enforcement Notice' (JB94:83) until the application for the access driveway had been considered. This motion was signed by 117 MPs, which is a relatively high number to give their support to such an issue. Keith Vaz also played a prominent role in demonstrations and rallies in support of the Manor through 1994. Later in the year Vaz was given the brief of opposition spokesman on planning issues within the shadow environment team, a position which he described as 'fortuitous'.[24]

In their lobbying, however, ISKCON did not only seek the support of mainstream party politicians. A number of pressure and lobby groups also became involved, especially those actively involved in promoting and producing liberal multicultural values. Thus support for ISKCON at the 1995 public inquiry came from a number of senior Christian leaders, from the Interfaith Network, and from the Commission for Racial Equality. The particular strength of the case that ISKCON made was the emphasis they placed on the point that the implementation of the council's enforcement actions would have entailed the closure of a *Hindu* temple. That is, the prevention of large scale public worship at the Manor would not only have affected a small 'religious sect', it would have curtailed the religious freedom of a very large number of British Hindus. The root cause of the conflict was of course the fact that many thousands of Indian Hindus considered the deities in the temple at the Manor to be of great religious significance, and therefore chose to visit the place on a regular basis. This gave a serious foundation to the claim that the actions against the Manor were principally against a Hindu place of worship, and were in fact against one of the most important Hindu temples in the country. Once ISKCON began taking this message to directly to politicians they found they received quite a lot of personal support, sometimes from the most surprising people.

The Media Campaign

As part of a political struggle to produce support for free access to Bhaktivedanta Manor, and eventually for the specific option of an access road to safeguard the future of the place, ISKCON also needed to help generate a favourable public opinion of their organisation and their efforts. To ensure this, they also realised that they needed to influence the various forms of national media – particularly the television, radio, and newspapers. As I discussed in the first chapter, Knott (1999) has shown that from the mid 1980s onwards ISKCON in Britain developed a sophisticated communications focus, and in fact there are now two communications (or public relations) departments working in the country (in Watford for the UK, and in Belfast for Europe). These departments were created to deal with problems created by representations of ISKCON as cultish and dangerous, with a communications officer monitoring media references to ISKCON, trying to inform journalists about misperceptions and stereotypes, and directly challenging any obviously false or outrageous reports.

Thus by the early 1990s when ISKCON decided to seriously lobby for public support for the Manor, they had a fairly sophisticated outfit who were well experienced in producing news releases and generating news items which were favourable to them. The most probable strength of such news management was not so much the production of a particularly favourable image of ISKCON as a Hindu religious group, but rather the prevention of the typically unfavourable images that beset them in earlier years. That is, in most media reports of the Manor campaign ISKCON were rarely presented as a 'cult' or as sinister, and any negative reportage usually concentrated on more 'neutral' problems such as the traffic problems in Letchmore Heath and the inconvenience this caused for the local residents. Indeed, it is remarkable how much of the media coverage of the Manor conflict presented the Hindu rather than the 'new religion' side of ISKCON.

Alongside this, there were also several quite crucial interventions in the media which, without doubt, helped to create the climate in which ISKCON were ultimately successful. One of these came in 1994, as the events around the enforcement notice began to gather momentum and the prospect of the access road became a serious possibility. During the summer of that year, the BBC TV religious affairs department put together a documentary on the Manor for the *Everyman* programme (which has for many years been broadcast late on Sunday nights, dealing with serious 'religious' issues). This programme on the Manor, given the title 'The Road to Hare Krishna' was finally shown in October 1994, just three months before the public inquiry on the access road began, and indeed was used by the Inspector in the inquiry as evidence to consider. The programme makers tried to give a balanced consideration of the various arguments in the dispute, featuring not only Akhandadhi das putting the case for ISKCON, but also Philip Marsh, one of the most vocal of the opponents in Letchmore Heath.

However, the overall direction of the documentary was most favourable to ISKCON and towards toleration of the Manor as an important site of Hindu worship, which was only really balanced by closing shots of the volume of traffic entering and leaving the temple during the Janmasthami festival.[25] There are a number of possible reasons for this general bias towards ISKCON in the programme: the programme researcher, Amanda Sealy, was herself from a British Indian background and, although she did not identify herself as Hindu, she had a strong familiarity with contemporary Hindu issues in Britain and India. However, as researcher she was not responsible for the final editing of the programme, and so it is probably correct to assume that the decision to put together the material so that it gave most attention to ISKCON was based on a collectively favourable response by the production team. This may be due to the fact that they simply found more sympathy for the way ISKCON leaders and devotees put their case, or otherwise because they made use of various religious studies scholars (including myself and Kim Knott) as consultants on the background of the conflict. In short, the production of the *Everyman* programme occurred in a climate in which the team found expert opinion to be generally favourable to ISKCON, and thus those who were opposing the Manor appeared marginalised and reactionary. And it was this impression that the programme generated, and so helped to develop (as well as possibly reflect) a general public acceptance of Hindus' rights to use the Manor for worship.

The other significant public intervention in the media was an editorial written by a former editor of the London *Times*, William Rees-Mogg (Lord Rees-Mogg) in that newspaper in summer 1994. The *Times* is the newspaper which is probably most identified with the English establishment, and Rees-Mogg is himself very much an establishment figure (generally identified with right wing opinions). However, he chose to use an editorial slot to write in favour of the general principles that ISKCON were campaigning for, and thus produced a commentary on the conflict that delighted ISKCON leaders. The significance of such a figure choosing such a forum to make this point is worth taking the trouble to quote his leader at in full:

> **Let Hindus share all our freedoms**
>
> Last Thursday I was walking past the Liberal Democrat head office in Cowley Street, a quiet Queen Anne street just behind Westminster Abbey. There were two Hindu monks standing outside the office, and some yellow posters placed against the railings. I stopped to talk to them, to find out they were conducting a hunger strike outside the Liberal Democrat's building. The protest was held not with any hostile intent but in the hope that the Liberal Democrats on Hertsmere Borough Council would support Bhaktivedanta Manor's planning problems. There was a larger demonstration of Hindus outside Parliament earlier in the week.
>
> As we talked, one of the monks continued to pray, while the other acted as spokesman. The scene was a peaceful one; the spokesman argued his case with gentleness and moderation, showing understanding for those who are opposed to the Hindus. The planning question now has a 20 year history. There are always practical problems to be worked out, although British planning rules tend to be

> stifling and obstructive. The principle, however, is clear. Freedom of worship is part of the tolerance which is a core belief of British life. The Hindus are one of the largest non-Christian communities in Britain. Their freedom to worship demands not only our tolerance, but our active support. It would be an outrage if Canterbury Cathedral were to be closed to worship because it caused congestion in the narrow medieval streets of that city. It will not be less of any outrage if Bhaktivedanta Manor is closed to worship and it will incidentally do particular damage to Britain's reputation in India.[26]

It is very contestable whether or not this leader, or indeed the *Everyman* programme actually caused the final decision to come out in ISKCON's favour. As I will discuss in a later chapter, the political situation in which the Secretary of State for the Environment found himself in spring 1996 was probably the most crucial element in the resolution of the conflict. However, the production of these two very favourable representations of ISKCON were in themselves a measure of the success that ISKCON had had with their campaign of quiet diplomacy and making influential friends, and thus also indicated in an overt way, the power and influence that they had managed to produce in the establishment which made their success much more likely.

Notes

1 Campaign leaflet produced by ISKCON, titled 'Return Religious and Racial Tolerance to Britain', c.1976, in archive of the Oxford Centre for Vaishnava and Hindu Studies, Oxford.
2 Report in *Gujarat Samachar*, 26th July 1974.
3 Estimates of the size of the Hindu population various quite considerably, from 370,000 (Knott 1991: 91), to 400–550,00 (Weller et al 1997), to over a million. Akhandadhi das (AdPE:15) estimates the population to be somewhere in the range between 500–850,000.
4 Press releases from National Council of Hindu Temples, 14th March 1983 and 25th March 1983.
5 Press release from NCHT, 14th March 1983.
6 See Williams (1988) for a discussion of the notion of ecumenical Hinduism, and Nye (1995) for a description of such inclusive Hinduism in the context of a temple in the Scottish capital
7 Quoted as Vipin Aery, Secretary of the NCHT, in *Temple Campaign Newsletter*, no. 10, 1993, p. 3.
8 Om Prakash Sharma, President of the NCHT, speaking on *Everyman*, 'The Road to Hare Krishna', BBC TV, 2nd October 1994.
9 *ISKCON World Recorder*, vol. 2, no. 6 (no date, approx 1982).
10 *Hare Krishna*, Summer 1988, p. 3.
11 *Temple Campaign Newsletter*, no. 10, 1993, p. 2.
12 *Temple Campaign Newsletter*, no. 11, 1994, p. 2
13 *Temple Campaign Newsletter*, no. 10, 1993, p. 4.

14 *West Herts and Watford Observer*, Friday 18th March 1994, p. 3
15 Leaflet produced by Hare Krishna Temple Defence Movement, for Rally on 16th March 1994, (emphasis in original).
16 *Hare Krishna*, June 1987, no. 2, p. 1
17 JB93:78, also Media Release from ISKCON communications, 2 St James Rd, Watford, 28.8.91, p. 1.
18 Media Release from ISKCON communications, 2 St James Rd, Watford, 28.8.91, p. 1.
19 However, for a re-evaluation of some of the violent connations of conceptualisations of *ahimsa* see Jennifer Reid (1998).
20 My discussion of this meeting is based on minutes of 'A special meeting to discuss the way forward for the Manor campaign', held at Bhaktivedanta Manor, 8th September 1990. These minutes are kept in the archive of the Oxford Centre for Vaishnava and Hindu Studies, Oxford.
21 Quoted in *West Herts and Watford Observer*, Friday 9th December 1988, p. 7.
22 *West Herts and Watford Observer*, Friday 20th March 1992, p. 7.
23 *Today* programme, BBC Radio 4, 16th March 1994.
24 A remark given in a speech to the launch of the Hindu Council of the UK, Kenton, London, 27th November 1994.
25 This was the same festival that ISKCON were later prosecuted for organising, in breach of the enforcement notice. This festival was, in fact, attended by a number of interested 'spectators' – including myself and (unknown to me at the time) another anthropologist of religion, with an interest in pilgrimage – all of whom had been warned through the media by the Managing Director of Hertsmere council (albeit erroneously) that such attendance was a breach of the law.
26 Lord Rees-Mogg, Leader comment, The London *Times*, 11th July 1994, p. 16.

CHAPTER SIX

Alternatives and Solutions

Alternative solutions

One perspective on ISKCON's problems over the Manor is that they were almost literally trying to fit a square peg into a round hole. That is, the location of the Manor in a place of such poor physical access would inevitably lead to problems, and made it quite unlikely that they would ever gain planning permission to use the temple for large scale public access. An easier solution to this dispute was only likely, therefore, if the problem of access could be bypassed in some way: either by taking temple traffic away from the narrow roads of the village of Letchmore Heath, or otherwise relocating the temple in a site which was more suited to the volume of traffic required to bring devotees to worship at festival times. ISKCON was prepared to pursue both of these options, preferring the former rather than the latter since it would allow them to remain at the Manor, but for a few years the possibility of a purpose built new temple on a larger site was an extremely exciting prospect. It was, however, the successful proposal by ISKCON to construct a new access driveway that linked the Manor almost directly to a major road that eventually led to a resolution of the conflict in 1996. In this chapter I will be examining the histories of the main alternative solutions, beginning with the possibility of ISKCON creating a large purpose built complex in nearby Elstree, and then discussing the issue that eventually 'saved' the Manor – that is the access road.

An alternative site

As I discussed earlier (chapter two), the site of Bhaktivedanta Manor has very special associations for devotees of Krishna Consciousness. It was founded by Srila Prabhupada, he installed the main deities in 1973, and he spent much time in the place in the last few years of his life. Indeed, on his last visit to the west before his death in 1977 it was at the Manor that he chose to stay. The rooms where he worked and slept are now dedicated to him as a place of study and meditation, a life size statue of Prabhupada sits at his desk, which has itself been preserved to appear as he used it when living. As the founder *acharya* of ISKCON, Prabhupada is also given honour and veneration in the temple room, where another large statue of him is installed and is the focus of worship (*guru puja*) for devotees. The very significant historical and personal connection between the founder of ISKCON and the Manor means that it is highly unlikely that the movement would wish to move out of the site. As Akhandadhi das states:

> Bhaktivedanta Manor will not be relinquished by the Society ... Neither the local devotees nor the Society's international governing body would countenance the sale of the Manor. (AdPE: 167)

The location of the Radha-Gokulananda deities within the shrine at the Manor make the significance of the place even greater. Ideally, therefore, ISKCON have always been in favour of remaining where they are, with public worship allowed in the shrine. But for several years the movement were prepared to seriously consider the option of moving many of the activities from the Manor to a nearby site, where they would create a purpose built temple with superior facilities. This option eventually fell through, but if it had been allowed to proceed then it would have created the largest and best equipped Hindu temple in Britain (and Europe).

The idea of a large temple complex in the London area had been considered by ISKCON for many years. As mentioned in the last chapter, a Krishna consciousness temple was founded in central London in 1969, first in Bury Place, which was then moved to a nearby site in Soho Street. The purchase of Croome Court in Worcester, which was converted into Chaitanya College for training of devotees in 1980, provided further facilities for the movement (although at quite a distance from London) for a few years before it closed in 1984. Elsewhere in Britain ISKCON have facilities in many towns and cities – in 1999 they had twelve major centres.[1]

The felt need for a major centre in London was particularly strong, because of the combination of several important factors. The significance of London as a major national capital combined with the location of a congregation of thousands of ISKCON devotees[2] (as well as a larger population of other Hindus who could make use of such a temple) provided a large incentive for creating such a centre. According to Akhandadhi das, writing in 1994:

> It was always ISKCON's intention that this project [a major cultural centre] – a very ambitious one – would be undertaken in London in place of the present Soho centre ... Although there is some newly-rekindled desire within the Society to explore the viability of this project, it is not something ISKCON foresees becoming a reality for many, many years. (AdPE: 109)

In August 1984 ISKCON were asked by Hertsmere council to give an indication of their long term objectives. According to the council:

> These were to secure a large additional property in easy reach of London (not necessarily in Hertfordshire) which could accommodate not only a substantial number of the Society's members and students, but also much of the activities presently housed at the Manor, possibly even the temple. The Manor would then be used as a spiritual retreat with a select staff, housed on the grounds ... (AgHBC/A1: 34)

However, the relocation of deities – and the new location of a temple – depended to a large extent on the location of the previous temples. As discussed in chapter two, at the time of installation the deities in a temple are placed within a certain 'sacred space' or *dham*. This *dham* is specific to the site where the deity is – for example, the *dham* of Radha-Gokulananda is the grounds of Bhaktivedanta Manor. But the *dham* also extends to cover a certain (less defined) area. The deities now present in the Soho Street temple are installed within the *dham* of central London – their names are Radha Krishna Londoniswara. Therefore, if there is for some reason a relocation of the deities of a temple (and this is by no means a simple operation, as will be discussed below) then the deities should be relocated within (or at least close to) their *dham* or domain. In short, this means that the temples at Bhaktivedanta Manor and Soho Street are placed in two separate domains, and any intention to create a new religious centre in central London would be related to the London temple and not necessarily the Hertfordshire one.

It is against this background that the attempts by ISKCON to 'relocate' the facilities at the Manor should be understood. According to ISKCON:

> The idea of an alternative site [i.e. for the temple] was not ISKCON's. It originated with the Council as a way to resolve the dispute. ISKCON was willing to explore the proposal subject to three agreed principles:
>
> a) That the aim of the project would be to fulfil ISKCON's previously stated long-term objective to develop a major Temple and cultural centre for London, and not just as a one-for-one replacement of Bhaktivedanta Manor.
>
> b) Hertsmere would help to identify a site which the Society could afford, and that might well be a green field site within the Green Belt.
>
> c) Hertsmere would provide the required planning permission. (AdPE: 102–3)

It was in the midst of the actions surrounding the 1987 Enforcement Notice that the idea of relocation to an alternative site emerged. One week before the first Public Inquiry on this notice was scheduled to begin – in November

1987 – Hertsmere proposed the idea, saying that they would assist ISKCON in finding and developing an appropriate site (AdPE: 161, see also chapter four). ISKCON agreed to this proposal on the three conditions mentioned above, and a search was begun to find such a site which would suit ISKCON's needs and be acceptable to Hertsmere (and local residents). To assist Hertsmere in this search ISKCON:

> did its best to make [the council] aware what a temple was, how it functioned, the role of the Deities, the need for the residential and teaching facilities that went with the shrine and the needs of the Hindu community. The Society tried to explain all the requirements of a purpose-built Hindu temple. (AdPE: 162)[3]

In response, Hertsmere set out the criteria that they would require for the site, which included the need for 'ease of access and parking provision for Janmasthami' (AdPE: 162). After only a short while, in early 1988 a piece of land fortuitously became available. This was a site of 41 acres in the Green Belt area about two miles from Bhaktivedanta Manor in Dagger Lane, Elstree on a greenfield site owned by London Regional Transport (LRT). It was in fact Hertsmere council who first initiated the idea of the use of this site – making the first contact with LRT, and making the suggestion that it should be sold to ISKCON (AdPE: 162). The purchase involved a complex deal: ISKCON would buy the land from LRT for a nominal sum of £1, on the condition that ISKCON covenant an agreement that the land be used 'solely for religious purposes'; in return Hertsmere would give planning permission to LRT to build a business park on adjacent land.[4] Once this was agreed by the parties, ISKCON and LRT presented their applications for planning permission to Hertsmere. ISKCON proposed to build a large temple with ancillary accommodation, and also a hall, plant area, cow barn, and a 'hostel' (*ashram*) for devotees. It was envisaged that this arrangement would be ideal for all concerned – ISKCON would be able to purchase a large site for development for practically nothing, LRT would be able to make commercial use of presently unused land, and the village of Letchmore Heath would be relieved of the pressures of mass public worship at the Manor.

But after the submission of ISKCON's planning permission, Hertsmere decided on their conditions for the use of the Dagger Lane site. The council were concerned about the suggestion that the new temple would be used as a large residential centre, which they felt would be a duplication of the Manor's role as a residential theological college. To prevent this, Hertsmere proposed to limit the number of residents (when it was completed) to no more than 20 residents (AdPE: 163), or otherwise to limit the area within the new buildings for residential use to no more than 185 sq.m. (IR89b: para 21.38). Otherwise, if ISKCON wished to create a training college of the same size as the Manor on the Dagger Lane site, Hertsmere suggested that

Bhaktivedanta Manor itself be sold (to the council for example) and then permission would be given for up to 50 residents at the new temple/college (IR89b: para 21.33). As noted already, ISKCON had no intention of selling the Manor. The insistence by the council on limiting the number of residents demonstrated, in ISKCON's view, that they had no 'understanding of what is required to provide for the maintenance of the shrine' (AdPE: 163). The temple deities (either at the Manor, or at the new temple) would require a number of *pujaris* living in close proximity to provide the high level of ritual and devotional service that is required. It would not be possible to achieve this if only a small number were resident next to the temple.

A further condition by Hertsmere was that the new temple should be completed in two years. The intention was to ensure that the residents of Letchmore Heath were relieved of the volume of worshippers at the Manor within a fairly short time-scale. For ISKCON this was impossible. Their estimate was that it would take at least four years to complete a purpose built marble temple in the Rajasthan style of north India (IR89b: para 21.31). Hertsmere suggested that the temple could perhaps be completed more quickly using more modern construction methods, such as a 'simplified form of modular construction' like that used for offices and warehouses (IR89b: para 21.31), but, in ISKCON's view, this was completely inappropriate for the type of building envisaged. This timescale condition again indicated that Hertsmere did not fully appreciate the requirements of the temple that ISKCON were trying to build.

The most important condition, however, that Hertsmere put forward in May 1988 related to the proceedings surrounding the enforcement notice on Bhaktivedanta Manor. The Public Inquiry on the notice was scheduled to reopen that month, after the earlier postponement to give the parties the opportunity to examine the alternative site (see chapter four). Hertsmere put forward the requirement that it would only give planning permission for the Dagger Lane site if ISKCON withdrew its appeal against the enforcement notice, and therefore cancelled the Public Inquiry. In doing so, the great expense and inconvenience of the inquiry would be prevented, but more importantly the council would ensure that they did not find themselves with public worship at two Krishna Consciousness temples – that is, at the new one in Dagger Lane, and also at Bhaktivedanta Manor (AdPE: 163).

ISKCON did not feel that they could accept this condition. They felt that they were being asked to 'abandon their only legal defence against the enforcement notice' (AdPE: 164), when it was not even clear if permission would be given for the Dagger Lane site. At that stage the details of the new application had not been fully negotiated and, furthermore, the Secretary of State for Environment had instructed Hertsmere to send their decision on the planning permission to him for 'final determination' (AdPE: 164). He could override any such permission, leaving ISKCON with nothing – 'having given up their defence of the Manor, they could be left with a refusal at

Elstree [Dagger Lane]' (AdPE: 164). ISKCON decided that this was not a risk worth taking.

Instead they made an offer to Hertsmere that they thought would prevent the possibility of a 'two temple' situation, ensuring that the 'public would attend only the new site at Elstree' (AdPE: 163). The central deities at the Manor, Radha-Gokulananda, would be transferred to the new temple as soon as it was ready, 'thus removing the reasons or need for the Hindu community to continue visiting the Manor' (AdPE: 163). This relocation would not be a straightforward process: it would require complex rituals to remove and reinstall the living deities and, according to Vedic teachings (*shastra*), such a move was only permissible in 'extreme circumstances' (AdPE). But ISKCON resolved that they could justify a transfer of the deities to a new purpose built temple with good facilities, and where the public could obtain easy access for worship.

This assurance was not enough for Hertsmere, who decided to refuse the application for permission for the temple in Dagger Lane. They gave the justification that if the appeal against the enforcement notice was still in place, then 'there could be no "exceptional circumstances" which would warrant the council being minded to grant planning permission' (quoted by Akhandadhi das [AdPE: 164]).

With permission for the site refused, ISKCON found themselves having to appeal against that decision also, and therefore a second public inquiry was scheduled for February 1989 – to begin soon after the inquiry into the enforcement notice ended.

Public Inquiry into the Dagger Lane site

The Public Inquiry began in February 1989, its purpose being to consider ISKCON's appeal against Hertsmere's decision to refuse planning permission for the Dagger Lane site. ISKCON made this appeal together with the landowners London Regional Transport, who were challenging the refusal to grant them permission to develop the adjacent site into a business park. The basis of ISKCON's case was again that there was a pressing religious and cultural need for this site to be developed into a temple, and that this need gave overwhelming justification for such a development, even though the land did form part of the Green Belt.

However, the Inspector's conclusions found in favour of Hertsmere's decision, and recommended a rejection of ISKCON's appeal. The Inspector, Mr Russell, listed the following as the primary issues in the appeal:

> a. will the proposed temple and ancillary development, including the Ashram, Community Hall and parking facilities, cause demonstrable harm to an interest of public importance, namely the appearance, character and integrity of the Metropolitan Green Belt;

> b. will the proposed result in the likelihood of significant additional congestion and danger on the nearby highway network;
>
> c. if there are such objections, are they overridden by very special circumstances arising from:–
>
> i). the need to provide a suitable site for a temple form public worship by the Hindu Community;
>
> ii). the need to relocate the existing public worship facility at Letchmore Heath in the interests of the comfort and quality of life for residents of that village;
>
> iii). the absence of any other suitable site;
>
> iv). the provisions of any proposed conditions or Section 52 agreement, and the undertaking given on behalf of the applicants in respect of the moving of the deities. (IR89b: para 21.1)

The main consideration of the Inspector and Hertsmere council was the effect that the development would have on a greenfield site in a designated Green Belt area. The issue of possible traffic congestion was considered, but the Inspector decided that any strain put on the local road network would not 'justify refusing permission for the temple on its own' (IR89b: para 21.15). However, the large volume of traffic created by worshippers at times of important worship would require a large parking area within the temple grounds, and this would involve hard surfacing substantial areas thus adding 'to the urbanisation of a greenfield Green Belt site' (IR89b: para 21.14).

The creation of this car park, together with the temple, residential block, community hall, and other buildings would all be 'intrusions' into the Green Belt. The Inspector considered that the Dagger Lane area marked a clear space of open countryside between the towns of Bushey and Elstree:

> Travellers along the M1 [motorway], the A41 and the A411 [major roads] have a clear view of open countryside and of a break between settlements at this point. For the northbound traveller the site is within an area which represents the first clearly defined break after leaving the London conurbation ... (IR89b: para 21.6)
>
> However much is achieved in fitting this highly novel proposal into the landscape, it will still be a major new built development, occupying one of the few wholly agricultural sites in this most vulnerable area of Green Belt. The effect will not just be visual ... [it] will generate substantial movements of vehicles and people ... This will also tend further to blur the distinction between town and country at this point, and detract from the remaining open character which is clearly much valued by the residents of the immediate area. (IR89b: para 21.9)

The Inspector also seemed to imply that ISKCON's development of the site would go beyond the planning application submitted to the inquiry. He described the project as 'amorphous and highly ambitious' (IR89b: para 21.8) and pointed out the fact that the new site was three times larger than that presently used at the Manor:

> It seems clear from a comparison between the appeal site, with its total area of 17 ha [41 acres] and the Manor with 7 ha [17 acres], and the proposed buildings with a floorspace of 4500 sq.m., and the Manor with 1650 sq.m., that what is proposed cannot be described as a replacement. This is conceded by ISKCON, and they give their reasons, based on long term aspirations not just for a place of worship, but for a cultural complex, similar to those in India, America, and South Africa. (IR89b: para 21.20)

His query about the appropriateness of the temple within the Green Belt also focused on the number of residents that ISKCON anticipated living in the new complex (as Hertsmere had done during the earlier negotiations, as described above):

> It seems to me firstly that the need for up to 50 people to live on the site substantially increases the objections to the development on Green Belt grounds. Institutional uses on the Green Belt do not normally involve a provision for 50 residents. (IR89b: para 21.32)
>
> I accept that a permanent presence is required on the site, for religious and for security reasons. However I consider that Hertsmere Borough Council are being entirely reasonable in seeking to ensure that the temple does not in future duplicate the residential use at the Manor. If permission is to be granted for an Ashram this would be a permission for a residential use ... I am left to conclude that this requirement for a substantial residential use ... only goes to show once again that this ... is an unsuitable place for ISKCON's project ... (IR89b: para 21.33)

As this last quote shows, the Inspector felt strongly that the development of the site would be intrusive into the Green Belt, and that the exceptional circumstances did not justify this intrusion. He did, however, acknowledge that there was a strong need for such a temple complex:

> I accept Dr Knott's evidence, that there are only very limited facilities for the mainstream Sanatan Panth of the Hindu religion in the North London area, and at present the needs of the Hindu community are being met largely at Bhaktivedanta Manor ... If my conclusions in respect of the previous inquiry are accepted [i.e. to uphold the enforcement notice], then ISKCON clearly have a need to relocate their public worship activities and festivals from the Manor. (IR89b: paras 21.16 & 21.18)

But such a relocation should be made to another site which was not so vulnerable, and which perhaps was more appropriate for the needs of ISKCON. For example, he pointed out the excessive traffic noise at Dagger Lane from the nearby M1 motorway (IR89b: para 21.10). The large size of the site was probably not necessary for ISKCON's requirements and 'by insisting on such a large site, and imposing such very restrictive criteria as to what is acceptable' – particularly that the site should be within the *dham* of the Manor deities, and therefore be close to Letchmore Heath – 'ISKCON have limited their choice to a point which seems to me to verge on the unreasonable' (IR89b: para 21.21):

> The worship practised at the Manor has attracted visitors on such a scale as to swamp the village [i.e. Letchmore Heath], giving rise to unfortunate resentments. However, this has arisen largely on account of ISKCON's seeming inability to control their activities in a way to make them acceptable to their neighbours. This does not in my view entitle them to demand as a replacement a prominent Green Belt site in a most vulnerable part of the Green Belt. It seems to me that before any planning permission is granted which involves such a substantial exception to Green Belt policy every opportunity should be taken to explore the re-use of existing developed sites. (IR89b: para 21.22)
>
> I am not convinced that this prominent sensitive site . . . is the only one for the new temple. (IR89b: para 21.25)

The Inspector's overall conclusion was:

> there is a need for a temple for the Hindu community, there is also a pressing need to relocate the present uses for public worship, and public entertainment in connection with religious festivals, from Letchmore Heath. It has not however been shewn that there is no other suitable site, and none of the very special circumstances advanced outweigh what I regard as specific and convincing planning objections to a new temple and ancillary development on this particular Green Belt site. (IR89b: para 21.30)

This report was passed onto the Secretary of State for Environment, along with the report from the inquiry into the enforcement notice. The Secretary of State gave his decision on both appeals together on 20th March 1990. Both decisions were negative for ISKCON, confirming the Inspector's judgement by upholding the notice (see chapter four) and refusing planning permission for the Dagger Lane site. The Secretary of State's findings closely followed the Inspector's recommendations: that is, the proposal would cause demonstrable harm to the Green Belt and that the special considerations in the case did not provide sufficient grounds to override the planning objections and justify the development. That is, although there was a clear need to find somewhere to transfer the public worship away from the Manor, the particular site at Dagger Lane was not appropriate:

> [The Secretary of State] considers that it has not been demonstrated that the uses to be relocated from Bhaktivedanta Manor could not be satisfactorily accommodated on an existing site elsewhere. He also considers that a major religious and cultural centre for members of the Hindu community on the scale proposed does not necessarily require such close proximity to the Manor . . . (DoE90b: para 8)

Indeed, the extension of the period of compliance with the enforcement notice (from six months to two years, see chapter four) was a concession to allow a further search for such an alternative temple site. He recommended that the search for a new site:

> should take into account both the need for good transport access and adequate car parking arrangements for public worship and festivals, as well as those requirements which derive from the pursuit of ISKCON's religious activities in themselves. It will be necessary to identify a site that minimises the risk of unacceptable intrusion and disruption to any nearby residents at the times of public worship and religious festivals. While this combination of requirements is unusual, the Secretary of State has no reason to conclude that it cannot be satisfied. He does not rule out the possibility that a site located elsewhere within an area designated as Green Belt could prove acceptable. (DoE90b: para 9)

These decisions were obviously very disappointing for ISKCON and worshippers at the Manor. In the words of the temple president, Akhandadhi das:

> The Hindu community was left with neither securing access to Bhaktivedanta Manor, nor the opportunity to develop an alternative temple . . . (AdPE: 165)

Other parties were less sanguine. For example, a representative of residents living close to the Dagger Lane site was quoted as saying:

> We are over the moon. It was not a question of racism, it was a question of sensibility. We, the little people, have won our case. (Leslie Winters, chairman of Bushey and Elstree Green Belt Association, March 1990[5])

Despite the encouragement that the Inspector and the Secretary of State had given for the relocation of the temple to a different site, the collapse of the Dagger Lane proposal made ISKCON's search very difficult. ISKCON pointed out that the day after the announcement by the DoE:

> Hertsmere's chief planning officer, Mr Robin Smith, wrote to the Society saying that the Council knew of no other sites within Hertsmere suitable as an alternative site for the temple. (AdPE: 166)

Despite this, ISKCON had meetings with other local authorities, including Hertfordshire County Council, and various boroughs (AdPE: 169). But they faced several problems in securing agreements, particularly the high cost of property in the region and the unwillingness of landowners to sell to ISKCON when planning permission might not be granted.

Any other attempt to find a site would involve considerably more expense than the £1 purchase fee for the Dagger Lane site. Assistance from Hertsmere council may have helped to arrange a similar low cost deal, but no such help was forthcoming. Therefore ISKCON 'was left to compete with commercial developers for sites with price tags far in excess of what could be expected of a religious charity' (AdPE: 171). This search also coincided with the aftermath of the collapse of the Bank of Credit and Commerce International in which many Asian Hindus (some of ISKCON's major benefactors) lost a great deal of money (ibid.).

The issue of planning permission had obviously been made very public by the two inquiries – and to seriously consider a new site ISKCON would have to be very certain that they could obtain permission for the type of development they envisaged.

> Not surprisingly, there are no sites or buildings with existing planning permission for the type of temple required. ISKCON contacted several boroughs. The nearby London boroughs were sympathetic, but did not have any sites known to them large enough to accommodate all of the Manor's activities. The boroughs outside London were not at all sympathetic. (AdPE: 170)

> No vendor ISKCON contacted was willing to sell . . . They and their agents knew that such a planning application would be contentious and that the site could be tied up by a lengthy planning inquiry. They were also aware that the DoE had already turned it down at Elstree. (AdPE: 171)

It appears that ISKCON had gained something of a 'reputation' through the exposure that the inquiries had given them, that even extended further than the London area. For example, when the ISKCON group in Scotland applied for permission to develop a site in Lammermuir near Edinburgh they were turned down, presumably because of the public fears of 'swamping' that had come out of the use of the Manor.

The search for an alternative site in the area continued until the end of 1991, when it appears that ISKCON decided that it was fruitless to continue since they were 'utterly convinced that this was not a practical way forward' (AdPE: 170).

This resignation was clear from statements made during the autumn of 1991. For instance, the ISKCON youth magazine told its readers in an article entitled '"Alternative temple" option is abandoned' that:

> it would be a sad illusion for [ISKCON's] members and friends to believe that there was going to be an alternative venue. The only real hope of continuity of public worship seems to rest on access to the Manor – and the campaign to achieve that is far from over.[6]

Likewise Akhandadhi das told reporters in September 1991:

> Our community has decided to stay put, we are happy here and we believe that the idea supported by some politicians and half the village residents for a new access road to the temple is the right solution.[7]

By this time, what had once seemed an exciting possibility for ISKCON was now no longer practical. The construction of a new temple would be expensive (even if the land was obtained at a nominal sum), and would require a redefinition of the role of Bhaktivedanta Manor. However, the decision to remain at the Manor and to pursue the access road would still leave some long term problems for ISKCON – in particular, the fact that they wanted (and needed) to develop the physical facilities that could be offered to worshippers at the temple. The Dagger Lane temple would have been far larger, for there would have been room for nine hundred devotees in the main temple room, which was on a far greater scale to anything that could be achieved at the Manor. Alongside the temple, there would also have been another large *kirtan* hall which could accommodate even larger gatherings. Again this was in excess of the relatively cramped facilities that the Manor offers.

It is worth noting that Prabhupada once made a prediction that a field adjacent to the Manor (owned by another farmer) would one day be the site of a large hall for Krishna Consciousness.[8] At the time that he said this it must have been seen as a dream for his followers, and later events would show that it was difficult enough to keep the temple that they had open, without trying to get planning permission for another large building. During the negotiations in the mid 1990s concerning the access road, however, ISKCON also managed to purchase the field that Prabhupada had made this prediction about. Thus they now own the land, which is used as a pasture for their cows, and at festivals as an overflow for car parking. It is probably the worst kept secret in Hertsmere, therefore, that in remaining at the Manor, ISKCON would like to create new buildings to improve on the facilities that they can offer, and perhaps even eventually create a temple complex on the scale of that proposed for the Dagger Lane site. Given the extreme planning sensitivity of the site, however, this dream (of both ISKCON and Prabhupada) is not likely to be realised in the foreseeable future – but Prabhupada's own prophecy was that the hall would be there 'in a hundred years' or so.

The access driveway

The popularity of ISKCON and the Radha Gokulananda temple has meant that any site on which ISKCON have a temple (whether it be at Dagger Lane, the Manor, or anywhere else) would require suitable access for the arrival of large numbers of vehicles in cars. Even if there were good public transport links to the site, many Hindus would prefer the convenience of travelling to the temple in their own cars, so that they can come and go when they like and travel as a whole family together. As noted above, the traffic consideration formed part of the public inquiry into the Dagger Lane site, and of course residents of Letchmore Heath have primarily focused on the disturbance that worshippers cause to the peace and quiet of their village. ISKCON therefore decided that if there was any chance of them remaining at the Manor, then they would have to find some practical means of getting worshippers to the Manor without them having to travel through the village.

As had been noted already, the Manor is located in an area which is very close to a major network of trunk roads. Both the M1 motorway and the A41 trunk road pass within a mile of the grounds of the Manor. A simple solution was proposed in 1987 to construct a small driveway over some fields at the back of the Manor, which would provide a connection with existing roads which lead onto the A41. A visitor to the Manor would therefore turn off the A41, down Sandy Lane, left into Hilfield Lane, and then right into the access driveway leading directly into the grounds of Bhaktivedanta Manor. The distinct advantage of this route is that it goes direct from a major road through countryside to the Manor without going through any residential area, and so does not cause any disturbance to the residents of Letchmore Heath.

Although supposedly a simple solution, implementation of this idea proved to be very contentious, and it took over ten years to translate the suggestion into reality. As early as July/August 1984 Akhandadhi das (the newly arrived temple president) unsuccessfully attempted to buy or lease a strip of land at the back of the Manor from his neighbour Michael Jefferis to use as an alternative access road into the temple. Later, in 1987, considering such a road to be 'a more constructive way of dealing with the issue' (AdPE: 160), ISKCON entered into negotiations with the two owners of the land over which the road would pass and, following a positive response, they asked the consultancy group Ove Arup and partners to design the plans (AdPE: 101). An application for planning permission was duly submitted in August 1987 (AgHBC/A1: 35).

But Hertsmere were not enthusiastic about this idea. At the time they were already unhappy about the unauthorised use of the Manor, and did not wish to change its planning status. Therefore, the construction of an access road would be of no benefit, since it would only encourage worshippers to go to the temple when in fact they should not be doing so. Furthermore, the land on which the road would be built was also Green Belt land, and they did not wish to countenance the loss of this land (i.e. through tarmacing). Previously, the landowners had made quite separate applications to use the land for other purposes – in 1981 permission had been refused for an industrial/warehouse development, whilst more recently in 1986 there was an unsuccessful application to build a sports complex (AgHBC/A1: 36).

It was unlikely, therefore, that permission would be given by the council for the proposal of the road. Unsurprisingly, at a meeting in July 1988 the council refused ISKCON's application on the grounds that:

> Traffic generated by the existing unauthorised use of Bhaktivedanta Manor would make the road unacceptable in the Green Belt and it would not be permitted while the unauthorised use remains. (AgHBC/A2: 36)

ISKCON appealed against this decision, and consultations were made. In November 1988 the council decided that these grounds were 'somewhat ambiguous', and obviously worried that the appeal might go against them they altered their stated reasons to:

> The proposed road is totally unacceptable in highway and environmental terms for the amount of traffic generated by the present uses at the manor whether authorised or unauthorised uses. (AgHBC/A2: 36)

The decision came at the time when ISKCON were appealing against both the enforcement notice and the refusal of permission for the Dagger Lane site. The appeal against the decision concerning the road therefore was added to these other appeals, to be included in the public inquiry in December 1988. But following this refusal, one of the landowners – St Bartholomew's Hospital in London – decided that they no longer wanted to sell.[9] This meant that the prospect of the road would be impossible, and in late 1988 ISKCON withdrew their appeal.

At that time all prospects for resolving the conflict through this proposal had ground to a halt. The land was not available, and the council did not want to give planning permission. For several years ISKCON's efforts were spent attempting to challenge the enforcement notice and to pursue the idea of an alternative site. But the option of the road was not completely forgotten and, as the quotes given above show in 1991 it still appeared that the future of the Manor would be secured if the road could be made possible.

However, in 1993 – as the date for the implementation of the enforcement notice drew near – ISKCON finally managed to resume negotiations with St Bartholomew's Hospital over the land, and to persuade them to consider selling. It is possible that one factor behind the change of mind by the hospital was their changed situation – St Bartholomew's Hospital itself was under threat of closure, and therefore facing a costly battle to remain open, and so may have been persuaded by the opportunity to make some money on the land (ibid.). The owner of the other piece of land that was needed, a local farmer, was also willing to sell. Therefore by autumn 1993 ISKCON had secured an option-to-buy on both pieces of land, subject to contract, and had put down deposits. Planning consultants ABT Planning and Highways were then asked to draw up the planning application for the road, and this was submitted to Hertsmere council on 16th December 1993 (AgHBC: Recommendations, p.1).

The application included detailed plans of the path of a 840m long driveway with a width of 4.8m, which (like in the previous application in 1988) would provide access to the car park in the rear of the Manor to Hilfield Lane, and thus from there to the A41 trunk road. The specific wording of the application was for:

> a change of use of Bhaktivedanta Manor to a residential and non-residential theological college and religious community, together with use for public worship (including the observance of religious festival days) and construction of a driveway and access to Hilfield Lane. (AdPE: 115)

As discussed above (in chapter four), part of this application was directed towards changing the planning status of the Manor, to regularise and authorise its use as a place of public worship. ISKCON thought that this would be possible because the construction of the access driveway – if permitted – would substantially alter the exterior use of the Manor. That is, visitors to the Manor (even several thousand) would not disturb the residents of the village, and so could legitimately attend to worship.

But this would only be possible if the driveway was allowed to be constructed. It was also possible that the council would agree to the driveway, but still rule against the authorisation of public worship at the Manor. The council was further left with the option of refusing the application, but allowing permission for a road and/or public worship whilst attaching their own specific conditions.

The Council's resolutions

Another alternative

As I have mentioned already (chapter four) the application was first considered by a meeting of the Bushey and Aldenham Area Planning Sub-Board of the council on 12th July 1994. In preparation for this meeting, the council officers – Gill Gowing, Head of Planning and Mike Peters, Area

Planning Officer – prepared a detailed report and recommendations on the application, which had at their core the recommendation that

> planning permission should not be granted for the development proposed . . .; as the observance of religious festival days with all the ancillary activity that has become associated with such events will continue to cause demonstrable harm to local residents and the character and appearance of the Conservation Area and Green Belt. (AgHBC: Recommendations, p. 1)

But they also made the recommendation that

> the applicant be advised that the local planning authority is minded to grant conditional permission for:
>
> a) the change of use to a residential theological college, together with the use of the existing Manor buildings for public worship. (This excludes worship and the observance of the religious festival days outside the existing Manor buildings).
>
> b) the proposed new driveway and access to Hilfield Lane; subject to the officers agreeing with the applicants satisfactory alternative arrangements to accommodate the car parking requirements and those additional activities and associated temporary and other structures connected with the observance of religious festival days. This envisages 'off-site' provision with a 'park and ride' facility to facilitate worship of the deities only in the Manor on those days.
>
> . . . Furthermore, if such an agreement were to be reached between the council and ISKCON it would need to be referred to the Secretary of State for the Environment as it was a departure from established Green Belt policy. (AgHBC: Recommendations, p. 1)

What the council officers envisaged was to allow construction of the driveway, and also limited public worship at the Manor, but only on condition that large scale public worship (particularly at festivals) took place primarily on another site. This 'park and ride' idea would involve worshippers at Janmasthami travelling in the first instance to a large open site, such as Aldenham Country Park, where they would park their cars and be 'entertained' by activities such as distribution of *prasad* meals (*priti bhojan*), the dramas, dances, stalls, etc. which form a large part of the outside activities during the festivals. There would also be a coach shuttle service from the park to the Manor, giving access for devotees to the temple deities. The council officers felt that this arrangement would be 'thereby acknowledging the importance of the Manor to the Hindu community', whilst also preventing 'the volume of cars/coaches etc. historically gaining access to and parking within the grounds of the Manor' (AgHBC: Recommendations, p.1).

ISKCON, however, did not think that this 'park and ride' would be any solution to their needs. In August 1994 their campaign newsletter reported that these would be 'unreasonable conditions'[10] and that:

> Hertsmere's landscape officer is not objecting [to the plans for the access driveway] and the planning officers have recommended its approval, (although they suggest the impractical situation of the festivals happening elsewhere and pilgrims being 'bussed' in for darshan). (ibid.: 2–3)

On a more formal level, the temple president Akhandadhi das gave the following reasons against the idea:

> What would be gained, so it was argued, was the avoidance of the noise of outdoor activities and a reduction of the 'dwell time' of devotees ... Weighed against that minor gain would be:
>
> a) diminution of the overall religious experience
>
> b) the logistical problem for ISKCON in separating the functions, and
>
> c) the new amenity issues created elsewhere. (AdPE: 112)

As described above in chapter two, the celebration of Janmasthami involves a number of activities which have religious significance because they take place within the sacred area surrounding the deities at the Manor. To move these activities to some other site might have been a convenient solution in planning and traffic terms, but would not necessarily be spiritually or culturally satisfying for those practising them.

The consideration of the driveway

The proposal for the access driveway was to create a narrow lane of approximately 840m length across open countryside which would be 'gently undulating ... and interspersed by traditional hedgerows and field boundaries' (AgHBC: Report, p.3). The driveway would follow the existing boundaries of fields, and would be landscaped to blend into the environment, with grass verges on either side and trees planted along its route (AgHBC/A3: p.A36F). The driveway would also incorporate traffic calming measures such as speed humps and cattle grids, to encourage moderate speeds, with particular concern for the safety of a local badger population (AdPE: 137 & 141; AgHBC: Report, p.14). An important condition of the construction of the driveway would be the permanent closure to traffic of the main gates to the Manor from Letchmore Heath, thus preventing stray cars ('rat runners') making their way to the temple through the village (AgHBC/A3: p.A36J).

Despite a number of measures in the application to enhance the environment around the driveway, the council officers still considered that the road would be 'contrary to Green Belt policy, firstly by paving over open fields, and secondly by encouraging the use of the Manor' (AgHBC: Report, pp.7–8). Although the closure of the main entrance of the Manor would substantially reduce the traffic disruption within the village, the driveway may merely 'shift' or 'transfer' such disturbance to a neighbouring area (AgHBC: Report, p.13). Furthermore, the council conservation officer commented that:

> the effective separation of the Manor, as that is what the new road would achieve, would break a historic link between the house and its predecessors, and the village. A moderate amount of 'coming and going' is an important component of village life and the proposal would appear to mitigate against that, creating an enclave divorced from the village. (AgHBC: Report, p.11)

In this sense, there appeared to be a feeling that the complete displacement of traffic away from Letchmore Heath would be too disruptive a solution, since it would radically alter the relationship between the Manor and the village.

But a major fear was that worshippers would not actually use the access route in the way that ISKCON envisaged. Thus cars and coaches would continue to make their way to Letchmore Heath, and either park on the street or at least unload their passengers there, and so worshippers would then enter the Manor through the pedestrianised main gate. In ISKCON's view, both of these possibilities were unlikely because policing arrangements would prevent such parking in the street – as indeed had happened at Janmasthami for many years (AdPE: 133).

An even greater concern was that visiting worshippers would find their way to the access driveway along another route than the one along Sandy Lane from the A41. In particular, the village of Patchetts Green lies a short distance along Hilfield Lane, and visitors might drive through there on their way to (or on leaving) the Manor. The fear was, therefore, that the result of the new access driveway would be that the traffic problems of Letchmore Heath would be 'shifted' to Patchetts Green (AgHBC: Report, pp.13–14).

ISKCON had given this possibility some consideration already, and had built into their plans the intention to construct the junction between the new driveway and Hilfield Lane so that the car driver would find it easiest to turn in the direction of Sandy Lane/A41 as intended. A very sharp corner and a large traffic island would make it extremely difficult to turn in the opposite direction and drive through Patchetts Green. This would also make the incomer find the junction very difficult if s/he was coming from the wrong direction (i.e. had come through Patchetts Green), and therefore such an approach would be discouraged. Additionally, the route from the A41 down Sandy Lane would be clearly signposted, so that visitors to the Manor would be directed along the correct route (AdPE: 14; AgHBC/A3:

p.A36J). Furthermore, they pointed out that the route would involve substantial traffic flows on only a small number of days each year (i.e. six), for most of the year the use of the Manor is of a moderate level and most would probably follow the correct route, and indeed much of the traffic from the temple prior to the access road already passed through Patchetts Green on its way to the A41 (AdPE: 131–2).

The local Director of Transportation, from the county authority Hertsfordshire Country Council, gave these questions detailed consideration and produced a report for Hertsmere. The conclusion of their report was that:

> I consider that the proposal would bring relief to some local roads currently affected by the consented use. There would be an unavoidable impact on a short stretch of Hilfield Lane ... There could also be some residual traffic which is not persuaded to reach and leave the site via Sandy Lane and A41, which may remain on the local roads and it is suggested that this is addressed by measures to introduce temporary traffic regulation orders [for example by closing much of Hilfield Road on festival days]; and there is a further possibility that a permanent order, or orders, could be made ...
>
> ... I have concluded that, excepting major festival occasions, technical issues can be addressed and whilst there could be an impact on local roads this should not cause harm such as to amount to grounds for refusal, in my view. Regarding festival occasions, there are a number of disbenefits, including the need for traffic management, and a police presence. Without the prospect of such measures I would have to recommend refusal, but I believe that it should be possible by means of a planning agreement to introduce the necessary safeguards. (AgHBC/A7: 6)

Hertsmere planning officers appeared to concur with these conclusions in their report.

The officers remained concerned, however, with the activities that took place *within* the Manor. ISKCON's application had sought not only permission for the access driveway, but also for authorisation of the established uses of the temple. It was not clear to Hertsmere whether such authorisation was desirable, since public use of the Manor may still cause disturbance to residents of Letchmore Heath. Thus although the traffic problems in the village would be solved (or displaced) there would still remain other problems such as excessive noise levels coming from worshippers in the grounds of the Manor. The large festivals at the Manor:

> involve outdoor activities in the vicinity of the Manor itself which inevitably impact upon residents living close by. Such festivals include

> the erecting of tents/marquees in the ground, flood lighting, amplified sound systems and extensive open parking so that the large numbers can be accommodated ... (AgHBC: Report, pp. 8–9)

They considered that these problems had already been examined by the Inspector in the December 1988 inquiry (AgHBC: Report, p. 9). They also noted that:

> the strength of feeling among the Hindu population about the future of the Manor is indicative of the numbers that could come to the temple were it to become authorised. (AgHBC: Report, p. 9)

In other words, the scale of use could in fact increase (and thus become more intrusive) once planning permission was given, and that the evangelisation by ISKCON's priests 'to a wider audience' would further potentially increase the number of worshippers who would come to the Manor (AgHBC: Report, p.9). Indeed greater use could also be encouraged by the new easier access (ibid.: p.13).

The officers' overall view of the road was therefore that it was a potential solution to a number of the existing problems, but that it could add further problems of its own. In particular 'in straight policy terms' the application was contrary to local and national Green Belt policies (AgHBC: Report, p.19), and for these reasons they recommended that planning permission should not be granted (ibid.: 1). But they did also recognise that ISKCON had a case to argue concerning the special nature of the Manor as a significant religious centre, and that

> these represent the basis of the 'very special circumstances' which warrant overriding normal Green Belt policies ..., [particularly] since the environmental harms are considered to be significantly reduced by the construction of the proposed access road and consequent removal of traffic from Letchmore Heath. (AgHBC: Report, p.20)

For this reason they put forward what they considered to be the compromise solution which, as described above, gave permission for the road and for use of the Manor for some public worship, but which stipulated some 'park and ride' arrangements for festivals such as Janmasthami. As I have noted already, this relocation of parts of the festivals to an alternative site was not considered practical by ISKCON.

It is possible to interpret the officers' conclusions as a partial endorsement of the access driveway as a practical solution to the dispute over the temple. In effect they were saying that there were no justifiable reasons for not allowing worship at the Manor on most occasions, even though the large scale festivals did need some special arrangements. In this sense they had met ISKCON's needs 'half way' and, if their recommendations had been implemented, the access driveway would have been built and many of the causes of the dispute would have been diffused. But it is unlikely that the 'park and ride' arrangement would have worked, since the idea did not take into account the ways in which the Manor and the temple were actually used by worshippers. It is possible, therefore, that if the officers' recommendations had been accepted then the road would have been built and any 'park and ride' arrangement would have broken down (perhaps even within a year). In that case, worshippers may have gone directly to the Manor to use it in an unauthorised way, and thus new enforcement proceedings would have begun.

The Council's decision

At the sub-board meeting in July 1994 at which this report was first discussed the recommendation was framed as:

> ... planning permission should not be granted for the development proposed ... as the observance of religious festivals days with all the ancillary activity that has become associated with such events will continue to cause demonstrable harm to local residents and the character and appearance of Conservation Area and Green Belt. (AgHBC: Recommendations, p.4)

That is, the sub-board were asked to make a straightforward decision on whether to grant permission for the driveway and public worship at the temple, with the council recommending refusing such permission. The council officers' recommended compromise plan was not considered.

The sub-board meeting were not able to reach a decision on the issue, and therefore referred the application to the council to resolve. This occurred at the beginning of the summer holiday period, which meant that it would be impossible to schedule a discussion of the issue at a full council meeting until September at the earliest. For ISKCON, it was beginning to appear that they would not get a favourable result at such a meeting – the voting at the sub-board had been according to political factions (with Conservatives and Liberal Democrats against granting permission, and Labour for it), and if this was reproduced at the full meeting then the application would be refused. ISKCON were also worried that the option agreements on the land may lapse, since they were only valid until December 1996. If Hertsmere did reject their plan, then an appeal would be necessary and if action was not taken soon this might not be able to reach any conclusion until after that deadline. ISKCON did not want to be in a position again where they lost the chance to purchase the land. Therefore in August 1994 ISKCON submitted an appeal to the Department of Environment 'against the council's non-determination of the application' (AdPE: 175).

This meant that the council were no longer in a position to reach a decision on the planning application. The decision would be made by the

Secretary of State for the Environment after a public inquiry and the Inspector's report. Hertsmere were therefore left with the opportunity to discuss the application at the full meeting, but any decision that they reached would only form the basis of their position at the public inquiry.

The council finally sat to discuss the application at a meeting on 19th October 1994. The planning officers' report for the July sub-meeting formed the basis of the assessment of the application, along with some other submissions that had been received more recently. As had been the case with the earlier meeting, the council did not propose the officers' recommendations, but instead made their own recommendation that:

> had the Council been in a position to do so the application for the change of use to a residential and non-residential theological college and religious community, together with use for public worship (including the observance of religious festival days) and construction of a driveway and access to Hilfield Lane as proposed ... would have been *refused* ... (AgHBC: Recommendations, p.1, emphasis in original)

The political nature of the issue meant that the vote on these recommendations did generally follow party political lines, and therefore the council's recommendation was passed and the decision was made that (if they had been in a position to do so) they would refuse ISKCON's application. What this meant was that the public inquiry would be necessary to resolve the issue, and that at the inquiry the Secretary of State would be asked to decide between ISKCON's proposal to build the road and hold public worship, and Hertsmere's wish to prevent both options.

However, immediately after this decision was made a last minute motion was introduced to the meeting's agenda which proposed that ISKCON enter into negotiations with the managing director of the council, and then subsequently with local residents' groups, to find a compromise solution which could keep the Manor open without creating inconvenience for the residents of Letchmore Heath. This motion was brought forward in response to a letter from Akhandadhi das, the temple president, who had written to the managing director several days before indicating that:

> ... I felt that it might be helpful to mention that the Society remains open to considering a solution to the temple issue which may not include provision for new access ... Although the inquiry ... is due to commence on 17th January 1995, we would be willing in the meantime to participate in discussions to explore a possible compromise solution which may obviate the need for the public inquiry ... I would be happy for any individual to contact me directly to discuss the issues on a 'without prejudice' basis. In order that there be free and frank exchange of views, none of the discussions that may

arise should be referred to in any way at the inquiry. (AgHBC: additional material relating to item 10a)

The opportunity, and the motion, were welcomed by members on both sides of the council chamber, although the idea was rejected as unworkable by the leader of the Conservative group. Several other speakers more positively used the rhetoric of peace in support of the motion, comparing the situation with the very recent ceasefire in Northern Ireland, and other hopeful developments in Israel and South Africa. It was felt that if these insoluble international problems could be resolved, then so could the Bhaktivedanta Manor issue. However, as mentioned in chapter four, at a private session of the same meeting the council went on to decide to prosecute ISKCON for failing to comply with the enforcement notice.

The Decision and Resolution

Public Inquiry

Discussions went on between ISKCON and Hertsmere over the next weeks, whilst at the same time both parties prepared for the upcoming Public Inquiry. At the beginning of January 1995 there was a meeting between the council leader Philip Copeland, ISKCON, and local residents to try to find an 'eleventh hour' solution. The discussion centred around issues related to ISKCON's freedom to worship at the temple and on the prospect of the new access driveway.[11] But like earlier discussions no solution could be reached, and these negotiations failed to prevent the public inquiry.

The inquiry began on 17th January 1995, running until 10th February. Initially it was intended to last three weeks, but the weight of the proceedings led to it being extended for a further week, and then adjourned for three months to reopen for three more weeks. Thus the inquiry resumed on 16th May and concluded on 11th June, lasting seven weeks altogether.

In the inquiry, Hertsmere Borough Council maintained their position of contesting ISKCON's argument that the road would solve the problem. This case was supported by a local group called the Patchetts Green, Round Bush and Aldenham Conservation Society whose main interest was to contest the road in order to protect the village of Patchetts Green. On the other hand, the main argument that ISKCON sought to put forward was – as before – to demonstrate the significance of the Manor to local Hindus, and again they called on evidence from Dr Kim Knott in support of this position.

Alongside this evidence, though, ISKCON also put forward detailed evidence to show the possible effects to the environment and the local roads network if the access driveway was permitted, arguing that the drive would be to a large extent in harmony with the surrounding countryside. They also attempted to address the concerns of the Patchetts Green residents, by outlining their plans to ensure that all traffic to the Manor (particularly at festival times) would drive directly from the A41 trunk road to the Manor, and so would avoid the local villages altogether. Thus for ISKCON, the driveway would not displace the traffic problem from one village to another (i.e. Letchmore Heath to Patchetts Green), but would remove the problem altogether. The corollary of this, according to ISKCON, was that the provision of a 'quick and direct connection' to the Manor from the national primary road network would reduce both journey times, and the time spent by cars in traffic queues – the combination of which would reduce carbon dioxide emissions (IR96: para. 136, p. 22).

Hertsmere refuted these claims, continuing to make the argument that the site was not suitable for a temple of this scale, that 'it was in the wrong location' (IR96: para. 160, p. 25), and that the building of the road would be directly against government Green Belt policy. In her evidence to the inquiry, Hertsmere's chief planning officer Gill Gowing expressed a reservation that the granting of planning permission for both the road and public worship at the temple would create a situation in which 'almost anything would go',[12] since it would then be nearly impossible to enforce any further breaches by ISKCON of the Manor's planning status.

The council also remained unconvinced about ISKCON's optimism over the traffic benefits of the road. Instead they argued that a decision in ISKCON's favour would allow a large volume of traffic, which would have a negative impact traffic on the roads around Sandy Lane and Patchetts Green. Likewise, Dr Alan Goodlen of the Patchetts Green, Round Bush and Aldenham Conservation Society argued in his evidence that the road would create problems for the preservation of the Green Belt area whilst 'overloading the road network in the Patchetts Green area' and destroying the 'rural character' of Hilfield Lane (ibid.).

From another perspective, however, what was being proposed by ISKCON was not at all dealing with local issues. Instead the access driveway and the temple in general was an issue coming from the needs of people living elsewhere, quite removed from Letchmore Heath and the local vicinity. Hertsmere's counsel at the inquiry, Elizabeth Appleby QC, argued that:

> The Manor does not serve a local need, it serves a very much wider need, catering for the Hindu community throughout London and the Home Counties, and to some extent throughout the country. (ibid.)

The place of this Hindu community, and particularly its size (real and potential) played an important role in the debates going on at the inquiry. Hertsmere's planning officers looked to demographic circumstances as part of their argument for declining planning permission for the temple. They argued that the current (i.e. 1995) use of the temple for public worship was already too much – there were too many people wanting to visit the place –

but that in future there may be even more coming to the site and placing overwhelming demands on its rather inadequate resources and relatively poor amenity. It was clear according to population statistics that there was a growing Hindu population in north London, and that over the next few decades it would be ageing considerably. This meant there would in the future be more elderly Hindus, who (according to the theory that people become more religious as they age) would be wishing to use the temple more. ISKCON interpreted this argument in a rather negative light, feeling that there was a sinister basis for such interpretations of population statistics. For example, one witness for ISKCON at the inquiry, Asmita Haria, a long serving devotee, was cross-examined on the significance of bringing her children to the Manor to worship. She felt that the implication of the questioning was if all Hindu worshippers 'took their children' then this would create problems because of an increase in the numbers using the Manor.[13]

The argument on statistics had in fact been made before – Michael Jefferis had warned at the 1988 public inquiry 'there was no reason to think that attendances [at the Manor] had reached a plateau, particularly in view of the growing Hindu community in the country' (IR89a: para 18.71 p. 57). At an obvious level it was a clever way of refuting ISKCON's own argument that the weight of numbers of Hindus needing the Manor was justification enough for the temple – Hertsmere and others preferred to point out that things would get worse and not better, and so Bhaktivedanta Manor was not a solution, either in the short or the long term.

However, this line of argument raised substantial fears among ISKCON and their followers that there was some racist thinking underlining the use of these demographics. Indeed in their internal literature on the public inquiry (in a newsletter for devotees published in the summer of that year), ISKCON compared the use of such statistics by Hertsmere to the Demographic Profiling used in Nazi Germany in the 1930s.[14] Likewise, a local newspaper reported that:

> Allegations of racism have been hurled at Hertsmere planners after their use of population statistics in the temple inquiry ... [ISKCON] believes Hertsmere's head of planning, Gill Gowing, will claim the area would be overrun as the current generation of young Hindus in Harrow, Barnet, and Brent become more religious as they grow older, and swarm to Letchmore Heath.[15]

In response to such accusations Hertsmere argued that such use of population statistics 'was standard practice in planning applications for community facilities – to assess potential demand' (ibid.). They pointed out that Kim Knott's evidence in support of ISKCON 'referred to the census statistics of the Indian ethnic population' (ibid.). In her evidence the Hertsmere council head of planning Gill Gowing said:

> ISKCON's repeated endeavours to taint what is solely a planning issue with racist connotations do them no credit and are grossly unjustified and irresponsible. (ibid.)

In Hertsmere's view they were merely looking at people, regardless of colour, race, or ethnicity – they were dealing with a planning issue purely on planning terms. Although it may be the case that no sinister or racist intent was behind their use of population projections, the suggestion that there can be such a thing as 'pure planning' is highly contentious. All planning decisions – particularly high profile disputes such as this one – take place in a wider social and political context that goes beyond any 'pure' application of the technicalities of planning policy.

Between February and May 1995 the inquiry adjourned, partly to consider new government planning policy documents which had recently been released, and also because of the pressures of work of the barristers involved in the proceedings. During this adjournment local elections were held in Hertsmere which changed the political make up of the borough. The national political swing away from the Conservative party (at that time the national government) was manifest in Hertsmere, with the result that five Conservative councillors lost their seats to Labour candidates. This left a completely hung council – with 19 Labour, 14 Conservative, and 5 Liberal Democrats – and so no party was able to take overall control of Hertsmere council, the Conservatives lost the power which they had exercised for many years, and Labour looked poised to take control.[16] Immediately following this election the Labour group felt confident that in further elections scheduled for the next year (i.e. 1996) they would win more seats from the Conservatives, and so this Labour group began to prepare for power. Although the question of Bhaktivedanta Manor was not the only important issue facing Hertsmere council, it was still an issue of national renown which could not be easily ignored at the local or the national level. Therefore, the Hertsmere Labour group leader, Bryan Stanley, gave evidence to the public inquiry following its resumption to the effect that:

> he would see that there was proper justice for the temple. If it was up to his group ... the proposal [for the road] would have been approved. (JB95: 81)

However, the lack of overall control meant that the Labour group were powerless to act in 1995, and even if they could command a majority vote in the council, the planning determination of the Manor – and the access driveway – was out of their hands, since the appeal and the public inquiry meant that any decision would now have to be taken by the Secretary of State for the Environment at national government level.

At the time, though, there was considerable conjecture on what might happen if the Secretary of State refused to grant permission for the temple.

There were a few possible options that the Labour group could pursue if they took power in 1996. One idea was that, even if it proved impossible to grant full planning permission to the Manor for public worship, it would be possible for the council to allow ISKCON to organise a large 'car boot sale' in the grounds of the Manor – which would effectively be a cover for Hindus attending the place for worship. Perhaps more seriously, and holding out more possibilities for long term settlement of the issue, it might be possible for ISKCON to submit an altered version of their planning application which a Labour majority could then ratify in the council chamber. All this indicated an edging towards a resolution for ISKCON, but a lot still depended on the conclusions reached by Inspector Hanchet in his report, and to what political decision the Secretary of State would come.

The inquiry finally concluded in June 1995, and the parties were told that a decision would be made within a matter of months. This was clearly an important political matter that would need to be carefully considered by the Secretary of State, but ISKCON were concerned that they had put down deposits on the land for the driveway, and a time limit was set on these deposits. To further complicate the matter, the criminal proceedings over the breach of the enforcement notice finally took place in November 1995, in the run up to the inspector's report (see chapter four). Although the trial had no direct bearing on the planning decision it could perhaps have given some indication of how the decision might go, and it came as a shock to ISKCON that the fine for the breach was so high. What also made this so disheartening in their eyes was the judge's comments that he did not expect ISKCON to ever be granted planning permission for the temple (LCC: sentence, see chapter 4). Justice Rodwell was not of course directly involved in the details of the public inquiry, the evidence that he considered in Luton Crown Court was of a rather different nature, and less detailed than that presented to Inspector Hanchet. For whatever reason, as it turned out, Hanchet came to a very different conclusion.

Inspector Hanchet's report

Nearly a year after the end of the public inquiry, at the beginning of May 1996 there had still been no announcement from the Department of the Environment about the Manor – the matter was obviously being given a great deal of consideration either by the inspector, or by the secretary of state. On 2nd May further local elections were held in Hertsmere, which showed the predicted swing away from the Conservatives, and put the Labour group in overall control of the council. They were now in a position to take positive action with regard to the Manor, although they could not make any decision until the Secretary of State had announced his judgement. What was clear from the Hertsmere result – as well as in many other parts of England – was that the political map of the country was changing considerably. Areas such as Hertsmere were traditional key Conservative controlled councils, and yet now Labour groups were being elected to control them – Conservative support was obviously ebbing away at a national level. A general election was scheduled to happen sometime before June 1997, it was only a year away at most, and the Conservative government – who had been in power for 17 years – were acutely aware that they would need to play for every vote that they could find if they wanted to keep in office. Any decision that was made by Conservative politicians during this time had to be made with these considerations, especially sensitive decisions which had been publicly debated (such as the Manor had been).

Finally, on 10th May 1996, John Gummer, the Secretary of State for the Environment released his decision, along with the report produced by Inspector Hanchet. The two were in agreement that permission should be granted to ISKCON for the access driveway and public worship at the Manor, although there was a measure of disagreement between them over how to interpret the national planning policies.

For Inspector Hanchet, although this was a very complicated case which required the consideration of a number of factors, including Green Belt policy, the religious significance of the Manor to Hindus, as well as traffic levels, controls and manoeuvres, landscaping, and so on, the final decision needed to look at the whole picture. To quote his conclusions:

> In my opinion the proposed development, embracing both a material change of use and the carrying out of 'works' – namely the construction of the driveway – should be seen 'in the round'. They cannot be divorced. They should be considered together, as they are indeed, in the way the application was made to the Council. (IR96: para 392, p. 59).

Looking at it from this perspective, the decision would require weighing up Green Belt considerations (that is planning policies designed to protect vulnerable Green Belt areas) against the special circumstances of the religious significance of the Manor. As far as the appropriateness of the road and the allowing of public worship at the temple was concerned he concluded:

> I consider the driveway would represent an example of encroachment into the countryside threatening the openness and permanence of the Green Belt ... The change of use similarly would regularise, if not intensify, the religious activities at the Manor and with it the level of car parking. Particularly on Festival days ... such parking and the erection of temporary structures and tents in the grounds of the Manor would be visible from the local footpath system and would undermine the purpose of including the land in the Green Belt ...

> It follows that there should be a general presumption against this proposal which, in my opinion, would represent inappropriate development in the Metropolitan Green Belt. (IR96: paras 393–394, pp. 59–60).

Taken on its own, this would have led to a rejection of the application, but David Hanchet pointed out that Planning Policy Guidance (PPG2 at paragraph 3.1) states that inappropriate development in the Green Belt 'should not be approved, except in very special circumstances' (IR96: para 395, p. 60; see also chapter three).

> In dealing with the weight which I conclude should be attached to the very special circumstances in this case, I return to a matter which I believe, irrespective of its Green Belt location, is a relevant material consideration in this case – namely the extent to which it is reasonable for a significant group of the community to be able to worship according to their religious beliefs and tenets. (ibid.: para 396).

He pointed out the 'undisputed fact' that the Manor had a great significance to 'the Hindu community' and 'is without rival or comparability elsewhere in the UK' (ibid.). It was important to recognise that 'one attribute of the project referred to by virtually all who have spoken or written – including those opposed to it on other grounds – is its important religious significance and the contribution it makes to religious choice' (ibid.: para 397). On this basis, Inspector Hanchet noted that 'This in my judgement underlines the continuing importance attached to religious tolerance and freedom in society' (ibid.: para 398).

On giving consideration of a particular planning consideration suggested by Hertsmere council, the inspector also sought to differentiate the activities of the Manor from what planning policies (Structure Plan policy 16) defined as 'leisure use'.

> The activities at the Manor – both internal and external – are associated with its religious nature. Religious activities, including those where it is the custom of the religion to celebrate and intensify the religious and spiritual significance of the event by rehearsing religious plays and dramas, are not leisure activities. (ibid.: para 410, p. 62)

This perspective not only discarded the old argument that the religious dramas were somehow different from the other religious activities (previously referred to as 'public entertainment'), but also, and more significantly, planning policies designed to control leisure activities should not 'be applied to an established religion and its practice at a temple of undoubted national significance' (ibid.: para 411). On a different, but related, point he made the rather controversial statement that:

> I have difficulty in accepting that either local or national Green Belt policy is, or indeed should be, concerned with the impact of people (as opposed to the cars they arrive in and park, or the buildings or structures they attend) in terms of assessing openness. (ibid.: 412)

In relation to the Manor issue, the argument he was presenting was that the problem for Green Belt policy was not the volume of *people* – as bodies physically present on Green Belt land. Green Belt policies were not in his opinion designed to regulate access of these people (or bodies) to land – the regulation was intended to limit other (non-organic) physical entities, such as cars and buildings. After all, Green Belt policies were not designed to prevent people having access to land, but to allow people to have full and proper use of that land without spoiling it for others or for later generations. This view – although it may seem uncontentious – was in fact picked up by the Secretary of State who refuted it, as I will discuss below.

David Hanchet's overall view of Green Belt policy was, however, based upon his interpretation of policy guidelines, as set out in PPG2. As noted above, he felt that the temple along with the driveway would be an inappropriate development in the Green Belt, but yet there were special circumstances that could (potentially) allow Green Belt considerations to be set aside:

> In reaching the overall Green Belt conclusion that the project should be allowed I have taken the view that the combined effect of firstly (and most significantly), the public interest served by making provision for public worship in this very special and religious place and, secondly, the degree of harm to the Green Belt which would result, together tell in favour of the proposal.
>
> In saying so I should confirm, lest there be doubt, that the very special circumstances in this case are the application of the principle that the Town and Country Planning system is designed to regulate the development and use of land in the public interest (PPG1 paragraph 2).
>
> In applying and considering the proposal in Green Belt terms I conclude that the religious, spiritual and customary needs of the Hindu community are both so fundamental and relevant to so many people that they should be considered as representing a public interest. As such they are a material consideration in this case of such weight that they represent the very special circumstances for allowing, exceptionally, a form of development which is inappropriate in Green Belt terms. (IR96: paras 416–418, p. 63).

This understanding of 'use of the land in the public interest', therefore, played a crucial part in Inspector Hanchet's conclusions. Rather than taking a majoritarian perspective[17] on what he considered to be the 'public interest', he accepted that in this particular instance the 'customary needs' of a large section of the population (that is, the Hindu community) were 'so fundamental and relevant to so many people' that this particular minority's needs counted as part of the general 'public interest'. This point was made by distinguishing a *groups'* or a community's needs from those of individuals or organisations: an individual or a single organisation (such as ISKCON) could not in itself constitute a public interest, and this could only be argued on behalf of a sizeable population group (such as the Hindu community) whose needs were obvious and manifest. Hence:

> the combination of religious importance and the scale of benefits to the Hindu community differentiate this case from one of benefits to a private interest, say to a single householder, group or organisation, to that of a type and scale of use which serves a public interest. (ibid.: para 460, p. 70).

In arguing this case, David Hanchet was taking an innovative and rather controversial approach to the application of planning policy, and he was in fact making explicit some of the manifest problems of implementing such policy in a multicultural environment. As I will discuss below, the Secretary of State disagreed with Hanchet's interpretation of planning philosophy (i.e. his use of PPG1), but what Hanchet was trying to do was articulate an understanding of the purpose of planning laws which defined the concept of 'public interest' to allow minority groups to have such a public interest, if that minority group was substantial enough. In this sense, the planning laws are not implemented for 'everyone's' interest, in which case the general (usually discursive) needs and interests of the majority are most likely to take precedence over the more specific needs of minorities. Instead, he took the view that there could be a substantial public interest for a minority, if there was no clearly articulated majoritarian public interest. In sum, the general public interest of needing to preserve Green Belts from inappropriate and intrusive development was weighed against the more particular – and pressing – interest of the 'Hindu community', who in themselves constituted what he felt was a public interest.

Overall, therefore, Inspector Hanchet came to the conclusion that the balance between the two main factors of this case – that is, between Hindus' religious needs and the need to protect the Green Belt – came down in favour of Hindus and the development of the temple. He concluded thus:

> My final conclusion is that very special circumstances exist to allow this development in the Metropolitan Green Belt. There is no other identified harm which suggests a different conclusion should be reached. At the time of the Enforcement Inquiry [in 1988] and the decision on it, ... the current planning advice in PPG2 [was not] ...

> available to be applied. The decision in that appeal was made without the considerable advantages of the proposed new access drive which, I consider, would substantially overcome many of the issues upon which Ground (a) of the Enforcement appeal failed. (ibid.: para 471, p. 71)

His recommendation was, therefore, that planning permission should be granted by the Secretary of State 'for the change of use of Bhaktivedanta Manor ... to a residential and non-residential theological college and religious community, together with use for public worship (including the observance of religious festival days), and the construction of a new driveway and access to Hilfield Lane ...' (ibid.: para 477, p. 72).

The Secretary of State's decision

As indicated above, John Gummer, Secretary of State for the Environment announced his decision on the planning appeal on 10th May 1996. In a letter signed by one of his administrators to ISKCON's solicitors, the Secretary of State outlined his Department's reasons for allowing the development of Bhaktivedanta Manor, as well as examining Inspector Hanchet's conclusions, and setting out some planning conditions with which ISKCON would have to comply.

The letter outlined the fact that current Planning Policy Guidance on Green Belts (PPG2) had been issued just after the opening of the inquiry, and that this guidance states 'there is a general presumption against inappropriate development in the Green Belt' and that such development should not be approved except in very special circumstance (DoE96: para 12, p. 3). Under the terms of this guidance, 'it is for the applicant to show why permission for such development should be granted' (ibid.). Therefore, the Secretary of State had given consideration to the case being made by ISKCON for a development which could be considered inappropriate for the Green Belt area, and indeed he agreed with Inspector Hanchet's view that the change of use of the Manor and the construction of the driveway would be inappropriate (ibid.: para 16, p. 4). Therefore, he considered that 'the main issue in [the] ... appeal is whether there are very special circumstance which would justify allowing the proposed developed in the Green Belt' (ibid.: para 17, p. 5).

In examining the Green Belt policy implications of the proposed development, he returned to the conclusions that Inspector Hanchet has reached about the issues of leisure activity and people in the Green Belt, highlighting his disagreement with both of the points that were noted earlier:

> The Inspector concluded that Structure Plan policy 16, which seeks to limit leisure activities depending on the intensity of leisure use and its

> location, was not applicable to the appeal proposal. The Secretary of Sate does not entirely share the Inspector's view. He is of the opinion that there is an element of entertainment in some of the activities associated with Bhaktivedanta Manor, especially at the major festivals, which would conflict with the spirit of the ... policy. He considers, however, that the religious background and significance of these activities mean that one cannot apply Structure Plan policy 16 rigorously to them. (DoE96: para 21, p. 6)

As far as the overall case was concerned, this partial refutation of Inspector Hanchet's judgement is insignificant. The Secretary of State declined to apply this particular policy to ISKCON's use of the Manor, and even if he had it is very questionable whether it would have made much overall difference to his conclusions. But what this statement did seem to be saying was that even if an action is religious it should not (in planning terms) be seen as that alone. Inspector Hanchet had argued strongly that 'religious activities, including [dramas] ... are not leisure activities' (IR96.: para 410, p. 62, see above), and so should not be considered in terms of planning policies which are explicitly framed for controlling and directing leisure. The Secretary of State seemed to be going back to the old argument that the religious dramas could be classed as a form of 'public entertainment', even though their performance as religious dramas made them somewhat different from other forms of leisure. In planning terms (as well as in wider public discourses) this disagreement could have some significant implications. It is generally accurate to assume that most religious practitioners would not consider their religious activities and manifestations to be of the same category as 'leisure', even though it could be argued that there are structural similarities between. It would seem clear, however, from the ongoing debate that has centred around this question of 'public entertainment' that more explicit provision should be made in planning policy for religious activities. Planning policy guidance notes could give some outline of what criteria distinguish religious from other activities, so that such activities could be considered more in terms of how they are seen by those who practice them, rather than requiring planners, civil servants, and government ministers to conjecture on whether particular religious activities should be described as 'leisure' or not.

On the point about Green Belt and people, again the Secretary of State outlined his disagreement with David Hanchet:

> The Inspector could not accept that ... Green Belt policy is, or should be, concerned with the impact of numbers of people in terms of assessing openness. In the Secretary of State's view the question of whether people can affect the openness of the Green Belt is a matter of fact and degree. He can conceive situations where large crowds, or

> intense human activity, could adversely affect the openness and accessibility of the Green Belt. However, in this instance, he shares the Inspector's conclusion that the festivals to which crowds will be attracted are limited in number and are capable of being controlled. (DoE96: para 22, p. 6)

As with the previous point, the Secretary of State was wishing to clarify the Department of Environment's view on this policy matter, rather than directly address any specific issue in the determination of this application. However, his point is remarkably vague in asserting that he could 'conceive situations' without giving any particular example of how people (i.e. as bodies) could have such an effect, when those bodies are distinguished from non-organic accessories such as cars and buildings. On a theoretical level it is perhaps possible to conceive of such a situation, where the presence of large numbers of people (thousands or perhaps hundreds of thousands) on a regular basis could be destructive to Green Belt, in terms of the damage caused by trampling of feet and the congestion so many bodies may create. What this perspective seems to refute, however, is the argument that Inspector Hanchet made about the implementation of planning policies with regard to public interest. Surely if there was some theoretical situation in which thousands of individuals did wish to regularly use a Green Belt site, and the main planning issue was the weight of numbers of bodies – rather than traffic related issues arising from vehicular access – then a strong public interest case could be made. Or to put it another way, it would be necessary to make a public interest case *against* allowing access for such a significant number of people.

This question of public interest was discussed in detail by the Secretary of State, who took up the inspector's comments in a critical manner without making any satisfactory recommendations of his own on how such public interest should be interpreted. Instead, he choose to refer the issue back to the implementation of 'special circumstances'.

> The Inspector was of the opinion that there was a wider public interest in the outcome of the appeal which was a material consideration in its own right. He also considered that the extent to which it was reasonable for a significant group of the community to be able to worship according to their religious beliefs and tenets also constituted a material consideration. At paragraph 417 of his report, he referred to the principle that the Town and Country Planning System was designed to regulate the development and use of land in the public interest. (ibid.: para 36, p. 10)

The Secretary of State did not make clear the extent to which he agreed with this perspective, but he does critique the way in which the inspector approached his decision:

> Paragraph 3.2 of PPG2 states that very special circumstances to justify inappropriate development in Green Belts will not exist unless the harm by reason of inappropriateness, and any other harm, is clearly outweighed by other considerations. The Secretary of State does not consider that the Inspector approached the question of whether very special circumstances existed in the correct way. (ibid.: para 37, p. 11)

The problem was that Hanchet 'gave overriding weight to the religious and spiritual needs' of Hindus who used the Manor, 'without undertaking the balancing exercise which is necessary when considering whether very special circumstances exist or not' (ibid.). Although Inspector Hanchet had made it very clear in his report that he was weighing up the issues in terms of the harm to the Green Belt against the special circumstances, for the Secretary of State this was not enough: 'It is necessary to look at all the objections to a proposal, not just those relating to the Green Belt' (ibid.), and he left no doubt that he had 'examined the various impacts of the proposal', although he had 'attached substantial weight to the harm that would be caused to the Green Belt' (ibid.).

My interpretation of what the Secretary of State was arguing at this point is that – although he avoids an open discussion of the question of 'public interest' – he was picking up on Hanchet's argument and criticising him for not following it through consistently. The Secretary of State did not deny the conclusion that Hindus' needs for worshipping at the temple constituted a 'public interest' and therefore should play a significant role in the determination of this planning decision. However, as my discussion of this issue of public interest above touched upon, there can rarely be any clearly defined single 'public interest', especially if one recognises social and cultural diversity (such as multiculturalism). Therefore, although the Hindus' needs did (and still do) in themselves constitute a public interest, in any planning decision there will be other groups' needs to also consider – some of which will be substantial enough to be *also* considered a public interest. The role of the inspector and secretary of state is therefore to balance these competing public interests, to determine which group's interest should be given priority for the overall 'public good', whilst also bearing in mind that governments have created planning policies which define the protection of Green Belt and other vulnerable sites as a high priority and as a significant public interest. In this respect, the Secretary of State remarked:

> Freedom of worship, and the spiritual needs of religious groups, are matters of great importance; but they can only become material planning considerations to the extent that they are directly related to the physical impacts of a proposed development in a particular case. The religious needs of one section of the community are not in

> themselves of such paramount importance that they can automatically override national and local planning policies. [The Secretary of State] concludes that the spiritual and religious needs of the Hindu community, when considered in the planning context of this case are material to his decision; but they must be weighed against the harm the development would cause to the Green Belt and to other interests of acknowledged importance. (ibid.: para 37, p. 11)

In this particular case, although this is not clearly stated by the Secretary of State, the 'other interests' he refers to are fairly diverse, some of which are obvious but others are less so. The particular interests of local residents – in Letchmore Heath and Patchetts Green – who may suffer a diminished amenity if the road and development proceeded probably counted as the strongest 'other interest' to balance the decision against (and indeed following the Public Inquiry in 1988 a previous Secretary of State Chris Patten had concluded that the interests of the local residents should prevail over ISKCON and Hindu devotees, see chapter four). But other more specific interests came to play within the decision, particularly the problem highlighted by Hertsmere with the junction of Sandy Lane and the A41, which would be used by all of the traffic going to and from temple. This junction was already considered dangerous, having been the site of a number of accidents in recent years, and it was arguably in the public interest to prevent greater use of that junction (and so it was against the public interest to encourage the development of the temple). However, ISKCON submitted to the public inquiry that it would undertake road improvements around the junction which would make it safer, and so hopefully reduce the number of accidents, and in doing so this would mitigate any increase in traffic at the junction during temple festivals. This submission was accepted in large part by the Inspector (IR96: para 433, p. 65), and the Secretary of State did not consider this to be a sustainable objection (DoE96: para 27, p. 7). Therefore, there was no strong public interest case to be made on behalf of the general population of road users who could be put at greater risk at this junction by the development of the temple. But this was one of a number of interests which the Secretary of State felt should be weighed against those of Hindus' religious needs to worship at the temple.

In agreement with the inspector, the Secretary of State accepted that the Manor does 'make a special contribution' to these religious and spiritual needs of Hindus, and so accepted that that they 'should be given considerable weight' (ibid.). Although this fundamental conclusion was the same as the inspector's, he was outlining in his decision letter what he considered to be the necessary procedures for evaluating and balancing out the special circumstances in what was a very difficult case. Indeed a number of factors made this quite an extraordinary planning application, and so meant that any decision that the Secretary of State made would be significant. Because of this one can also read in his report a large measure of caution: it is clear that the Secretary of State and his officials were studiously attempting to avoid setting any significant precedents in this case.

Following this deliberation, the Secretary of State's conclusion was that:

> the religious and spiritual importance of the Manor to the Hindu community clearly outweighs the harm that the proposed development would cause to the Green Belt and to other interests of acknowledged importance, and that therefore very special circumstances exist to justify inappropriate development in this particular Green Belt site. (ibid.: para 39, p. 12)

His decision was therefore to grant planning permission for the construction of the new driveway and for change of use of the Manor to a 'residential and non-residential theological college and religious community, together with use for public worship (including the observance of religious festival days' (ibid.: para 46, p. 13). This permission was granted subject to a list of conditions (thirty three in total) which related to the design and construction of the driveway, but which also imposed certain restrictions on activities at the Manor (such as regulating the use of fireworks and public address systems). However, most of these were fairly minor and did not detract in any substantial way from the fact that the long awaited permission had finally been granted.

Dharm Hinduja Marg

ISKCON and their supporters were obviously delighted by this announcement. It was the result that they had dreamt about, although many were surprised that they had finally won. The recent change of council in Hertsmere was an added bonus to the celebration, as the Labour control of the council meant that there was not even a possibility of an appeal by the 'loser' in this planning decision (that is, Hertsmere council). It is quite certain that if the Conservative group had still been in office at the time they would have challenged the Secretary of State's decision in the High Court (just as ISKCON had challenged the previous decision in 1991). Without this appeal, ISKCON could now consider the future of the Manor to be secure – they had won the victory. All that needed to be done was to build the road.

One of the most substantial conditions attached to the Secretary of State's decision was that permission for change of use of the Manor would not come into effect until the access road had been completed and was available for use by vehicular traffic. This meant that the Manor could not (legally) be used for public worship (and particularly large scale worship at festival times) until the driveway had been built and opened. The decision was announced in early May, so the next significant festival would be Janmasthami – which would be occurring in the first week of September that year. The announcement of the successful decision for ISKCON was well reported amongst the Hindu population, so by Janmasthami there would be a large number of Hindus who were fully aware of the change to the Manor, and the fact that worship at the temple would now be legal (and indeed validated by a governmental decision). It would be rather difficult for ISKCON, therefore, if the road was not ready by that time, which would put them in a position where they had to tell devotees not to come to the Manor – or otherwise to allow devotees to come in large numbers and cause the usual (or worse) traffic disruption along the roads around Letchmore Heath.

It was clear that, if possible, the road should be built as soon as possible, and preferably by the time of Janmasthami. Direct appeals were made to many of the wealthy (mainly British Indian) individuals who had financially supported ISKCON in the past – and ISKCON were delighted to find that the money for both the materials and labour for the construction project was found almost immediately. Within very little time the 840m road was laid out and built, so that by the end of August it was possible for cars to drive over it. On the weekend before the Janmasthami festival, a special opening ceremony was held at the Manor to mark the inauguration of the new road, and indeed a new era for Bhaktivedanta Manor. Although the road was not completely ready for public use – it still required a final surface material to be laid on it to comply with highway regulations – its physical presence was enough. Through the building of the road the Manor itself was being literally turned around – once it was opened all visitors would be entering the grounds from what was once the 'back' of the estate, and the old narrow entrance from the village was to be closed off for all except pedestrian access.

And so on the evening of Saturday 31st August 1996 several thousand visitors – many of whom had been specially invited (including the politician Sir Rhodes Boyson, and Om Prakash Sharma, the president of the National Council of Hindu Temples) – arrived at the Manor through the gates from Letchmore Heath, parked their cars in the grounds, and walked the half mile distance across open countryside to the point where the Manor estate met Hilfield Lane. As the light began to fade ceremonies and speeches were made by Krishna devotees and priests to bless the auspicious occasion of the dedication of the new road, and then, led by Akhandadhi das, the large party walked back to the Manor on the newly tarmaced surface of the road, many carrying lit torches to show the way in the growing darkness. Victory celebrations were then held in a large marquee which had been specially erected next to the Manor. Figures such as Sivarama Swami, the guru with responsibility for British Krishna devotees, spoke in praise of Akhandadhi das' phenomenal achievement in leading ISKCON to victory, and on a number of occasions Akhandadhi das (who had recently retired from his position as president of the Manor) was called by the name of Arjun, the Pandava warrior whose service to Krishna is told of in the *Mahabharat* and the *Bhagavad Gita*. Akhandadhi das then himself gave a long speech of thanks to all the people who had helped ISKCON in their ten year battle (from the enforcement notice in 1986) to keep the temple open, and certificates were given out to those who were considered to have played a significant role in the campaign.[18] At this presentation it was also announced that the new road would be named 'Dharm Hinduja Marg': it would be a memorial to Dharm Hinduja, the son of the wealthy Indian magnate S.P. Hinduja who had died in a road accident a few years earlier. This naming was in itself a recognition of the great support, particularly financial, that ISKCON had received from the Hindujas during their long campaign to save the temple – the Hindujas' wealth is legendary, and they are also well known for their generosity in donations to religious, social, and educational organisations that they consider to be worthy.[19]

By the following Wednesday the road was as ready as it could be for the influx of worshippers arriving for the Janmasthami celebrations. It was estimated that up to 35,000 visited the Manor over the two main days of the festival, which also included a celebration of the centennial of Prabhupada's birth (in 1896). The centennial year had itself been planned for quite a while as a time to celebrate Prabhupada's achievements and to give devotees a chance to show their service to him, and through him to Krishna. For all concerned the most fitting 'present' that could be given to Prabhupada was the gift that Krishna had himself bestowed (after so many years) – that was the permission for the driveway and the securement of the long term security of the temple.

Notes

1 There are centres at: Bhaktivedanta Manor; Soho Street, central London; South Norwood, south London; Manchester; Birmingham; Coventry; Liverpool; Leicester; Newcastle; Lesmahagow, in Lanarkshire; Belfast; and Inish Rath, in Co Fermanagh.

2 Indeed, it was around this time that ISKCON were beginning to recognise the need for temples to cater for non-residential devotees (the congregation) as well as the core resident devotees who lived in or close to the temples (c.f. chapter one and Rasmandala das 1996).

3 It should be noted that at this time, the Swaminarayan Hindu Mission temple in Neasden temple had not been constructed. The Neasden Hindu temple, which was opened in 1995, may have given the Hertsmere planning authority a better idea of what to expect of such a large-scale purpose-built temple.

4 *West Herts and Watford Observer*, Friday 25th November 1988, p. 7.

5 Quoted in *West Herts and Watford Observer*, Friday 23rd March 1990, p. 5.

6 *Manor Youth Forum*, Issue 4, Autumn 1991, p. 21.

7 *West Herts and Watford Observer*, Friday 13th September 1991, p. 7.

8 According to a senior temple devotee, writing during the height of the campaign, 'Although Prabhupada personally installed the Deities downstairs in our temple room, at the same time he was eager to establish a thirty storey temple on the grounds. Later, in 1974, when it was clear that the Council was opposing our presence here, Srila Prabhupada wrote to us that there are so many lands nearby, and that we could get another site and tell the Council that it's okay because we're building our temple on another spot. And it's clear that Srila Prabhupada intended that Radha-Gokulananda could be residents at that site, rather than at the Manor' (document in OCVHS archive, Oxford).
9 *Temple Campaign Newsletter*, no. 10, 1993, p. 3.
10 *Temple Campaign Newsletter*, no. 11, Janmasthami 1994, p. 1
11 *Borehamwood Times*, Thursday January 5th 1995, p. 3.
12 *WHWO*, Friday June 2nd 1995, p. 12.
13 Asmita Haria, personal communication.
14 *Temple Campaign Newsletter*, no. 12, Janmasthami 1995, p. 3.
15 *Borehamwood Times*, Thursday May 18th, 1995, p. 5.
16 *Radlett and Borehamwood Advertiser*, May 10th 1995, p. 3.
17 That is, he did not appeal to any demographic or cultural 'majority' as a normative guide for considering what the 'public interest' should be. He rightly assumed that although Hindus constitute a minority of the overall British population, their particular identifiable interests (especially as a sizeable population) can be considered as publically significant, even if these are different from the general interests of those who belong to a non-Hindu cultural majority.
18 Three British scholars of religion were recognised in this way: Kim Knott (whose contributions to the public inquiries has been mentioned above), Rohit Barot, of University of Bristol, and myself. Although I was present at this ceremony I did not collect my certificate at the time: my name was read out rather late, by which time the sheer weight of numbers had led to people declining to go up to the stage to collect. The certificate was posted onto me instead, arriving several weeks later.
19 Among the beneficiaries of the Hinduja Foundation (UK) is the Dharam Hinduja Institute of Indic Research which is an academic research centre, based in the Faculty of Divinity at the University of Cambridge.

PART THREE

CHAPTER SEVEN

Rights, Power, and Religion: Articulating Freedom of Religion

Rights and political discourses

In this chapter I will be moving away from the specific detail of ISKCON and Bhaktivedanta Manor to examine and discuss a key part of ISKCON's discourse and campaign. That is, I will be widening the discussion to more general and theoretical questions on how and why it may be possible to talk about 'freedom of religion' in social and political contexts. Much of the rhetoric of ISKCON's campaign was that it was their (that is, ISKCON's and more generally Hindus') *right* to exercise free practice of their religion – a right which they argued most explicitly in their application to the European Court of Human Rights. Indeed, the final resolution of the case was achieved through parties in the British state (that is, Inspector Hanchet and the Department of the Environment) accepting this as a strong argument, even though such a freedom was in direct conflict with other social needs (such as the need to protect vulnerable areas of countryside from development). Thus there was a certain taken-for-grantedness about claims of religious freedom, even though the application and consideration of such claims was an area of considerable public and political debate. This 'naturalisation' of religious freedom discourses (that is, they are made to seem natural and routine) had been further strengthened by the inclusion of rights to religious liberty within international rights conventions, particularly the European Convention on Human Rights. Indeed, the ECHR was directly invoked in the ISKCON dispute, and has subsequently developed a wider relevance to British public discourses following the incorporation of the ECHR into the British legal systems by the Labour government in the *Human Rights Act 1998*.

What is worth asking, therefore, is what is implicit within these discourses on religion liberty? Why are the discourses being framed in these ways, and what sorts of political factors construct and create such debates? Moreover, with reference to the ISKCON conflict, how well do rights discourses express the political and social needs of minority groups, such as religious minorities, within the context of a broadly multicultural Britain? Do rights discourses help or hinder the power relations between religious minorities and the state?

One problem arising from the application of rights discourses in a multicultural context is that rights cannot in fact be detached from ideas that are implicit in western (predominantly European) political philosophies. In this respect, rights tend to express the needs and expectations of western individuals, and are not particularly suited to the alternative cultural perspectives that are now present in the west following migration from non-European countries. The adoption by the United Nations countries of the Universal Declaration on Human Rights (UDHR) in 1948 glosses over the fact that such rights discourses are not universal, in the sense that the term (and the concept) can not be found univocally across cultures. In fact, the articulation of concepts of rights developed out of particular cultural and historical processes in western Europe and north America over a period of roughly three hundred years up to the present. Thus, according to Ziauddin Sardar:

> The western liberal notion of human rights ... reduces the issues of the rights of human beings simply to preserving the civil liberties of individuals and provides a moral high ground for these rights to be imposed, by coercion if necessary, on all non-western, by definition illiberal people. (Sardar 1998:67)

The UDHR, the ECHR, and other international statutes such as the ICCPR (the International Covenant on Civil and Political Rights) were all created and framed in reaction to the abuses and atrocities carried out by nation states in the first half of the twentieth century – most notably by the National Socialists in Germany and the Japanese imperial state. The human rights statutes, drafted and accepted within just a few years of the defeat of these two powers, relied on certain assumptions about distributions of power within state contexts, and on projected notions of relations between individuals and the hegemonies that govern them. Within this, the concept of rights sets out the space for an individual person to claim 'freedom' from interference from others: from other individuals, or from the power of state structures and organisations. As conceived, this makes the practice of rights an individual matter – through a discourse on rights it is possible that each person can claim his or her own private space where s/he should not be interfered with.[1] Thus, conventions on rights were designed to set out the basic standards of society, stating that each individual should have the right to practise free speech, to education, to liberty (or at least a fair trial if s/he contravenes state laws), etc. Exactly what composed an 'individual' was not made altogether clear, since it was held to be self-evident to those who drew up the human rights agendas, but it has been argued that what lies behind this is the assumption that 'the individual is seen as absolute, irreducible, separate and ontologically prior to society' (Sardar 1998:69). This notwithstanding, in contemporary international politics most governments and states have accepted this predominantly western-derived rights discourse as a most practical and effective means of ensuring a reasonable balance between the powers controlled by states/ruling elites and the people they govern. Indeed, for those living in a western country it is hard to imagine any other ways of perceiving these relationships which are not dependent of conceptualisations of 'human rights'.

An important part of rights is that they are a strong articulation of the frameworks for certain relationships, that is relationships between *individuals* and *hegemonic* power groups (most usually 'the state'). Rights discourses, and in Europe the ECHR in particular, allow a particular mechanism for *negotiations* between individual people and ruling powers. By stating what rights an individual person may (and may not) have, it becomes possible to challenge the state (or other hegemonies) when they consider that such rights have not been allowed, or have been violated. It should be noted, of course, that although this framework for challenging hegemonic power structures appears to empower individuals, the mechanism for making any challenge is still very much controlled by the existing power structures, in particular by the courts and the judiciary.

Furthermore, the wording of the ECHR is sufficiently broad enough to allow a substantial margin of appreciation on the part of national governments, as I will show in the case of article 9 below. Many rights (such as the rights of free expression, freedom of religion, and freedom of association) are hedged by the necessities of law, and any other limitations that are considered to be necessary in a democratic society.[2] Rights can often be simultaneously an expression of individuals people's needs within contemporary social and political contexts, and also a means by which ruling groups maintain and justify their exercise of power for and on behalf of 'the people'. Thus rights can be a means of challenging the power of states, but only through the controlled channels that are legitimated by that state.

One significant problem with the articulation of such discourses is the strong element of individualism and atomism that runs through the conceptualisation of the relationship of individuals and the state. The wording of rights conventions and declarations place the stress on the needs of people as individuals, albeit acting in association with others, but there has often been a deliberate vagueness about the articulation of the rights of people acting together in groups. Some post-colonial critics of contemporary world politics point out that 'the person and the individual are not the same thing', and that every person is embodied within a particular social community so that 'violence inflicted on a person equally damages the whole community' (Sardar 1998:69).

Much of the discussion of this debate over the balance between individual and group (or collective) rights has focused on the idea of 'minority rights' – that specific provision needs to be made to protect individuals who differ from the prevailing norms of the cultural or political majority within a state (see, for example, Evans 1997:370–74, Poulter 1998:68–119). Given the limitations that are built into human rights conventions for states to curtail individuals' actions (and rights) in the interests of the general needs of law and of a democratic society, it is argued that this approach makes it possible for the collective needs of substantial subsections within national societies to be ignored or abused because they remain minorities within the wider social group.

This argument has been particularly articulated by cultural or national minority groups, as nations within nations – such as Scots and Welsh in the UK, Bretons in France, Basques in Spain, Quebecois in Canada, etc. – who can claim an obvious difference from the needs of the wider national society, and if effectively mobilised can pose a substantial and sometimes disruptive challenge to the power of the national state. Indeed it was fear of the pulls of these national minorities creating fragmentation of European (and non-European) nation states in the wake of the Second World War that was a contributing factor to the avoidance of the articulation of collective rights in the UDHR and the ECHR (Evans 1997:179–83, Poulter 1998:77–78). Instead it was felt by Eleanor Roosevelt and other key figures involved in the framing of the United Nations declaration that the best interests of all individuals would be to have their rights protected as *individuals*, whether they be suffering at the hands of the state because of their individual circumstances or because of their cultural, national, or political identity and affiliation. In the 1990s the issue of minority rights has still not been resolved at any substantial political level: the Council of Europe is still debating whether to include a protocol on minority rights within the ECHR, whilst the main international document that addresses the rights of cultural minorities is the ICCPR, which in article 27 vaguely refers to everyone's (i.e. individuals') right to 'enjoy their own culture, to profess and practise their own religion, or to use their own language' (quoted in Poulter 1998:79).

The main arguments for minority rights have come from large cultural and national minorities, particularly in European countries and, thus, the discourse on extending the interpretations of individual rights to groups and collectives has tended to focus on the role of substantial political minorities, and their relations with large nation states. However, this debate has not significantly addressed the wider issues of smaller and less well defined minority groups, such as religious and cultural minorities (whether newly formed by migration or conversion or historically present), or other minorities such as those defined by sexuality (gays and lesbians), politics, or any other criteria. In this respect, the question of the extent to which a person as an individual and a person as a member of a particular social or cultural location (or community) has largely been left unresolved. The assumption is that the rights to freedom given to all people by rights conventions will address such people's needs directly, and that indeed the articulation of individuals' rights is intended primarily for those who do differ (or are treated differently) by the state, whether that be because of their own individual circumstances or because of their membership of a particular minority group.

The choice, therefore, appears to be between two strong perspectives. On the one hand there is a universalist/libertarian viewpoint that assumes every person should have the same individual rights, and thus the same protections from the powers of the state in which they live. And on the other there is the view that seeks to qualify and extend these rights to protect significant cultural and national minorities (who are large, or politically active enough to make their case heard), who as members of such large minorities are particularly vulnerable from the state. Between these two there appears to be little attempt to articulate a wider multicultural rights discourse, in which it is recognised that individuals within many contemporary states can belong to a particular minority group, and experience particular problems because of their group membership and identity, and so may wish to articulate their viewpoint in a way that reflects not only their needs as individuals but also as a group. Furthermore, it needs to be recognised that members of these minority groups may in themselves conceptualise notions of the 'individual' and the 'collective' in quite different ways. Thus, as an example, Sardar suggests that Islamic perspectives (such as the 'Universal Declaration of Islamic Human Rights') provide a wider agenda of rights based on Islamic teachings and tradition, which formulates more clearly individual people's rights and responsibilities vis-à-vis the communities and states in which they live. For Sardar 'the main difference between western and non-western perspectives is that while the former focuses exclusively on individual rights, the latter emphasises the rights of *humanity* – including the humanity of the individual – and combines these rights with responsibilities' (1998:73, emphasis in original).

Clearly, therefore, the concept of rights depends on a particular western perspective, and is articulated as a particular way of describing (either as a critique or as a means of maintaining) the set of relationships between individual people (as individuals and groups) and the power structures under which they live. The rhetoric of rights is extremely grandiose, expecting a universalistic applicability (despite the cultural location of the origins of such a discourse) and framing the bases of rights in terms of certain possible freedoms. In particular, rights granted through the ECHR talk of freedom of religion, freedom of expression, and freedom of association (as well as certain other freedoms). What these freedoms amount to is not so clear – in one sense they are merely a rehearsing of the old enlightenment (and eighteenth century revolutionary) discourses of liberty and equality. Are such freedoms 'absolute rights', or merely a permission or leave granted by a benevolent state?

In practical terms the right to freedom in the ECHR articulates a discourse that from one perspective *challenges* the balance of power. It speaks of a libertarian world in which 'the citizen' should be free from the constraints of the state. The challenge is, however, nowhere near as radical as it appears – this is, in fact, a 'higher level' discourse which is practised and controlled by a professional class, including lawyers, judges, politician, and lobbyists. The ECHR holds its status as a legal text, which is implemented through court procedures and, although in principle is open to all, freedom to claim such freedom is of course subject to financial access. It is true that below this legalistic discourse there is another more popular discourse (or many such discourses, to be more accurate), in which concepts of freedom operate as a means of framing individuals' (and groups') sense of how a modern nation should be – even if the reality is quite different. The articulation of freedom talks of a normative *equality*, which is in fact far removed from any actuality, as though humans are 'naturally' in a Rousseau-ian state of freedom which needs to be protected rather than constructed from the complex power structures of social relations. Despite these strong limitations, however, discourses on rights do still give some mechanisms by which power imbalances can be challenged. They can serve as a framework through which minority individuals and groups can at least attempt to articulate an alternative perspective from the dominant hegemony of those in power.

It must be remembered, however, that rights discourses do not stop minorities being minorities, despite the rhetoric of equality, and all minorities are subject to the power of the majority (the ruling elite and/or the democratic majority on whose behalf the elite claim to exercise their power). Neither do rights discourses give minorities any more political power, although they can be used as a forum for *exerting* what power they have: such as the power to mobilise an effective legal force (i.e. to pay for barristers to fight a rights case), or to mobilise public opinion (through lobbying, and the use of media, etc.). In this sense, the use of rights discourses is not limited to the legalistic level, and it is probably more important as a popular discourse which is used by various groups as a political rhetoric, for exerting political pressure as a minority group. The limitations and strengths of this approach are quite obvious: an argument can only be as strong as a group's ability to make its case beyond the 'pure' application of the question of rights, those groups who are successful at political lobbying will be able to apply rights discourses far more effectively than those without such power. On the other hand the rhetoric of freedom, equality, and fairness can raise strong expectations: minorities who find that their treatment by the state is motivated by other factors such as cultural intolerance, apathy, or racism can be easily disappointed and disillusioned by the ways in which rights do not always deliver what they appear to promise.

Religion and human rights

One of the important elements of contemporary human rights discourses is the placing of the concept of religious liberty within such a framework. That is, according to rights discourses, 'freedom of religion' is one of the basic needs of individuals. However, whether or not religion should be privileged in this way, and what indeed it means to talk of 'freedom of religion' as a 'human right' is not clear. It is worth asking on what basis is it possible to claim that religious freedom is being prevented and such rights are being violated? In what sorts of contexts is it sensible and useful to talk in this way – or engage in these discourses? How do these discourses work? And perhaps most importantly, are there other ways of framing these questions, of dealing with conflicts such as Bhaktivedanta Manor, which do not get implicated in some of the tricky issues that 'freedom of religion' as a 'human right' creates?

In some sense, discourses on religious freedom are a way of thinking about what types of action and identity are acceptable within a particular political culture and to what extent the behaviour and actions of others (cultural/religious minorities) should be determined and adjudicated in relation to their manifestations of religion. Much of this depends on what is actually understood by the term religion: certain actions and identities are thus described (and marked out as religious), because such religion (however it may be defined) is considered to be beneficial to individuals, and to some extent to the wider society as a whole. Although the question of what is (or is not) a religion or a religious manifestation is a very important part of the articulation and discussion of issues on religious freedom, what remains of central importance are who are the various agents within these discourses: that is, who it is that is articulating conceptualisations of liberty (for themselves or for others), and who it is that makes the decisions and arbitrations when such articulations are contested. The process of defining religious freedom as a right places such agents within a political arena (since rights are a political sphere) in which the balance between groups (their actions and intentions) can be contested, most usually through the courts or through formal (and informal) public political processes.

The issue I want to highlight from this is the question of *power*, which I think plays a crucial role in determining the working out of these considerations of 'rights' and 'religious freedom'. It is not simply a matter of process *who* decides these issues. The procedures, the decision makers, and the discourses on making decisions (implementing rights) all need to be contextualised to show how power is exercised, and how minority groups operate against and within the controlling hegemony of a dominant majority. The argument I would like to put forward follows that of Stephen Feldman (1997), who argues that we should examine not only the discourses of how claims of religious freedom are made and (sometimes) resolved, but rather how issues of power are manifest in the application of these discourses.

When applied to areas of life which are conceived as religion, there is one obvious problem with the rights perspective. That is, how is it possible to reconcile a concept of individual rights with religious practice? Or, to put this another way, is religious practice something that can easily fit into conceptualisations of individual rights? Is religion always going to be a matter of individual action (and belief)? There is strong evidence to suggest (Feldman 1997) that this view privileges *certain* perspectives on religiosity – those that assume religion is a private and individual matter – and that furthermore such perspectives come from certain religious (and cultural, and political) contexts. The assumption that religion is a matter of individual choice – that a person should be free to choose his or her own religiosity and to practise that religion in whatever way s/he sees fit – is an assumption that comes out of liberal western Protestant Christianity. This is one cultural and political perspective on what religion is (and should be), which when framed and transformed into a universal human right becomes a political strategy for defining how others should be practising their religiosities, and of course leaves those who have alternative conceptualisations (and religions) at a political disadvantage.

Thus, in discourses on rights to religious liberty there is a strong ambivalence about how, and in what ways, religious groups which do not fit into a Protestant Christian derived framework should be dealt with. Indeed, commentators on the ECHR have made great stress of the fact that the Convention was framed by and embodies Christian values (see chapter eight), not only in its guarantees of religious freedom, but in its delineation of basic human rights. The weakness of applying such legislation (or any other Christian derived legislation) to non-Christian manifestations of religion are quite obvious, for it calls into question how much tolerance should be given for groups that do not 'fit in' with the normative expectations of the (culturally) christocentric judges and politicians who are asked to decide on the implementation of these rights.

There is a strong tradition in rights discourses, therefore, that upholds the idea that the basis of religious liberty is inviolable and quite easily granted, since such a basis is freedom of *belief* – for individuals to *believe* in any or no gods, as they so choose. As I will discuss below, this perspective depends on certain Christian-derived definitions of religion that privilege belief over practice. But it has also become very much a contested idea, particularly following the 'brainwashing' debates of the 1970s onwards in the US, Europe, and elsewhere, in which a counter-discourse emerged that the 'inner space' of individual's beliefs could in fact be violated by others. Allegations of brainwashing, or mind control, therefore relied on and contested this view of absolute freedom to believe. On the one hand, those making the allegations argued that individuals' rights to believe what they chose were being taken away from them through hostile psychological techniques of coercion. On the other hand, however, the act of making such allegations was also in direct opposition to the idea that individuals are free to believe what they like, since if a belief was in an 'erroneous doctrine' (for example, that Sun Myung Moon is the Lord of the Second Coming), then this belief could not possibly have been freely chosen.[3]

The place of religious practice in rights discourses is, however, even more complicated. Most rights discourses include a recognition of the importance of religious *manifestation* (a word which implies a strongly embodied and performative element of conceptualising religion which appears to go beyond most normative expectations of what religion is). But the right to manifest religion is rarely as clear cut as the right to 'believe'- when it comes to the determination of legal judgements, governments and courts rarely feel it is necessary to consider rights to manifest religion as absolute, over and above other rights. Thus a person's or a group's right to practise their religion freely is only admissible if it does not infringe too severely on the rights of others. An extreme example of this is that few would argue for the right of a *hypothetical* religious group to practise ritual murder or child abuse, simply on the basis of the principle of the 'freedom of religion'. In practice this means that a balance needs to be struck – which and whose rights should be considered more important when a person or group comes into conflict when they practise their religion? When is a manifestation (or a belief) properly qualified to be classed as 'religious'? And who should arbitrate such a decision? This brings the debate back firmly into the political arena, since decisions on these matters are always made through political processes, most usually by those in power on behalf of minorities.

Defining religions: including and excluding

The framing of discourses on religion and freedom, as well as the operation of religious groups within a social and political context, depends to a very large extent on the 'basic' question of what constitutes a 'religion' – or to put it another way, which groups should be seen as legitimate (by the state) and so should be allowed respect and toleration as *religions*. Similarly, what does it mean to frame certain rights as 'religious', that is to talk of 'freedom of religion'? Such an articulation depends on a notion that there are certain actions (and thoughts) which can be classified or designated as 'religious', and so rely either explicitly or implicitly on a definition of religion. Thus although public discourses may not necessarily be put in these terms, a basic premise of many of these discussions is the problem of defining religion and religions. In other words, what is meant when something is described as 'religious' or as a 'religion', and how does one distinguish something which is 'religious' (or 'a religion') from something which is not?

There are, in fact, two different sets of questions being asked here, and two different ways in which definitions of religion and religions can be used. That is:

(i) what sort of definition can be found which will include particular groups (which are generally agreed on to be *bona fide* 'religions' or religious groups) and exclude groups which are not religious (either because they themselves dissociate themselves from the term, or because they do not fit the category); and
(ii) what sorts of action can be legitimately claimed to be 'religious'?

In some senses, the first question is dependent on the second, since only groups performing those actions which are accepted as 'religious' can confidently expect to be classified as 'religions'. But it is worth keeping the two types of question separate, if only because most of the debates based on definition within legal and political discourses have come down predominantly in terms of either one or the other.

However, it needs to be recognised that the question of defining either religion or religiosity is in fact by no means simple: academic studies of religion are strewn with attempts to reach a working definition (some of more use than others),[4] and there has been a tendency amongst contemporary academics in recent years to attempt to move on to ask more useful questions.[5] One particular question that does need to be asked is who is making a particular definition and for what reason (c.f. Asad 1993a). Definitions of religion are useful ways of helping people think and act, they are a means of categorising, and can help facilitate political action (such as the application of legislation and taxation), but what needs to be avoided is an assumption that there can be a 'neutral' definition of religion – definitions serve political purposes. That is, the process of defining – or even trying to define religion – is a *political* strategy, even when it is done by academics. Whatever definition may be used needs to contextualised, and recognised as being the product of a particular social discursive context.

Here it may be helpful to look in more depth at the work of Talal Asad: following his argument, there is certainly a case for challenging the widely held assumption that religions are primarily about beliefs (or religious thinking) and that action is secondary (Asad 1993a:43–44, see also Bell 1992:30–54, 79–80). Most of what is called 'religion' is as much about practice as thought, and so it is fallacious to reduce religiosities to simple elaborations of statements such as 'the Xs believe in Y', or to wider metastatements such as 'religion is about belief in Z' (whether this be a single [male] deity, or a more abstract concept such as a 'Supreme Being' or supernatural force). Religion is done as much as thought, and the two are not separate, but in a sense thought and practice produce each other.[6]

More particularly, though, Asad argues for a recognition that all attempts to set out parameters or definitions of religion are products of the social contexts in which they are embedded:

> there cannot be a universal definition of religion, not only because its constituent elements and relationships are historically specific, but because that definition is itself the historical product of discursive processes. (Asad 1993a:29).

Thus he asks 'how does theoretical discourse actually define religion?' (p. 44), and what sorts of power/knowledge relations construct situations (and relationships) so that a particular definition and classification can seem reasonable? There cannot be an objective and universal definition of religion: the process of making and using a definition is a political strategy which cannot be separated out from the particular power relations of the context in which the groups defining and being defined are acting. The questions to ask, therefore, are not so much whether a particular definition 'works' or is applicable to a certain group, but rather why is a group or action being defined as 'religious' in such a way, and by whom, and for what purposes? In fact the juxtaposition of Asad's approach with questions of religious rights is fortuitous, since human rights are – if anything – also part of the same sorts of political processes. If rights are part of the negotiations between individuals and hegemonic power groups, then the construction of certain of these rights as 'religious' becomes a strategy for the contestation of certain aspects (and manifestations) of these power relations.

Following this line of argument, therefore, the definition of certain activities as religious is relational: there are no absolute standards for separating out some actions as distinctly religious. Indeed, on this basis, it is worth asking the obvious question of 'so why stress religion anyway?' Could not the same protections of minority groups interests and actions be achieved by stressing categories such as 'culture' or 'ethnic identity' (or something similar), which would help not only to avoid the need for a definition of religion, but also avoid the tendency to essentialise religion as a category? In one sense, this is what British laws have been doing: principles of multicultural equality in Britain were enshrined within the *Race Relations Act 1976*, which makes provision for preventing cultural or racial discrimination, but does not explicitly deal with discrimination directed at religious groups qua religions (see Menski 2000). Although this may perhaps be a robust means of avoiding the problems of defining religion, it runs into a number of other problems. In particular, the complaint has been from some minority groups that the *Race Relations Act* has not been effective in dealing with their grievances. For example, some religious groups, such as Sikhs and Jews, have succeeded in court in arguing that they have been discriminated against as *religious* groups, since their religion has been accepted as being the same as their racial/ethnic identity.[7] Other religious groups have not been so successful, primarily because courts have taken the view that groups such as Rastafarians and Muslims could not be described as 'racial' groups.[8]

The operation of the *Race Relations Act 1976* has therefore been selective, working with rather fixed categories of race and culture,[9] whilst also avoiding (as far as possible) questions of religious definition. It needs to be recognised that in fact *all* of these categories – culture, 'race', ethnic identity, and religion – are constructed notions which have ambiguous and nuanced meanings coming from particular cultural and political discourses which are constituted and maintained through hegemonic principles. In this respect the problem of definition cannot be avoided – discourses on religion are too much a part of British popular and legal cultures, and indeed are similarly recognised and used by minority groups as well as those administering state power. After all, ISKCON considered their main problem to be a violation of their right to practise their *religion* freely. Therefore, if there is a sense in a political state that legislation is necessary to allow free manifestation of religious and cultural practices, then there does have to be some relatively clear exposition of why free manifestation of religiosity is desirable, and what sorts of manifestations could be reasonably accepted as 'legitimate'. Built into that, at some level, it is also necessary to recognise the fact that there is no 'absoluteness' or neutrality about these discourses on what is 'religion'.

Applications of definitions

Great Britain

A generalisation could be made that in Britain (until the end of the twentieth century) the question of defining a group as a *religion* has not played a very significant role in legal discourses. The reason for this is that the lack of provision for religious freedom in British laws has meant that there has been relatively little to gain in terms of privileges as a religion, over and above those given to other social, humanitarian, or charitable institutions. The absence of reference to religion in the *Race Relations Act 1976* has made it difficult for individuals and groups to seek protection against discrimination on religious grounds. Unlike in many other countries, a religious organisation cannot claim any distinct tax advantages as a religious organisation. The main tax concessions that are available to religious groups come to them as 'registered charities', working for the public benefit (c.f. Beckford 1993:136), and are also available to non-religious charities. Further to this, buildings used for public religious worship are given exemption from local taxes (council tax, formerly rates), although this exemption is at the discretion of the local authority (see Wilson 1990a:73).

It is primarily these two issues that have created most legal debate about the extent of definitions of religion in British courts, particularly as new and alternative religious groups have sought to challenge certain British normative perspectives of what is or should be a religion or a place of religious worship.[10] One such normative requirement has been the expectation that a religion should be monotheistic – that is, there should be some exposition of a concept of a single deity or god. Not only does this mirror very strongly basic assumptions which are transferred from Christian theology onto religious groups which may be distinctly non-Christian (such as Hindus and Buddhists), but it also falls very much into the trap of emphasising the 'belief' aspect of religion at the expense (and even the exclusion) of practice. Even when this assumption of monotheism has been widened out to a (marginally less christocentric) concept of theism (i.e. including monotheism, polytheism, and pantheism), the absurdity of this approach was revealed by the requirement by a Buddhism group to swear an affidavit to a court saying that although there is an no explicit concept of theism in Buddhist doctrines, most Buddhists do in fact believe in some notion of theism. This development was especially bizarre since for many Buddhists there is no expectation to 'believe in' anything.

Likewise some Pagan groups have experienced problems with the Charity Commission in being recognised as charitable organisations on the basis of the fact that the Commission did not consider 'Paganism' to be a religion. In May 1996 the Charity Commission would not allow the Pagan Federation status as an educational charity on the grounds that 'Paganism does not have a sufficiently certain meaning in ordinary English speech for its promotion to be charitable'. In a related decision shortly after this the Pagan Hospice and Funeral Trust had their charitable status revoked because 'Paganism has not been recognised as a religion by the courts, and does not fall within the criteria they have accepted to define a religion'.[11] These decisions have been subsequently revoked, and both organisations now are granted charitable status under British law.

The Church of Scientology has in Britain, as elsewhere, also been excluded from such privileges. This organisation, founded in the US in 1954 by L Ron Hubbard as a religious foundation coming out his psychotherapy of Dianetics, has continually been dogged by accusations that it is more like a 'business' than a 'religion'.[12] The reputation that has been built up around Scientology has led the group into a number of legal wrangles across the globe, some of which will be discussed in more detail below. In Britain the group have been refused the status of a charity, on the grounds – according to Lord Denning – that there is no veneration of a Supreme Being and it is 'more of a philosophy of the existence of man [sic.] rather than a religion'.[13] Likewise, their religious buildings cannot be registered as 'places of worship'.

ISKCON in Britain, however, have faced no real problems in this respect – for a number of years there has been little challenge to its status as a *religious* organisation. Some may argue over what sort of religion it is: whether it is a 'new' religion, or a part of 'the Hindu religion'. But with respect to its relations with the state (over issues of charitable status, and also within all the discourses related to the dispute over the Manor), it has been taken as fundamental that ISKCON are a 'bona fide' religion.

In recent British parliamentary discussions of human rights (as part of the scrutiny of the *Human Rights Act 1998*, which I will be discussing in more depth in chapter eight), the question of definition of religion was debated by the House of Lords with particular reference to whether any such definition was useful or possible. During the third reading of the Human Rights Bill, an amendment was presented (and subsequently defeated) which would give certain religious groups ('principal religions') a degree of immunity from the statutes of the European Convention on Human Rights.[14] The main proponents of the bill were unsure about the consequences of allowing such immunities, since it would inevitably lead to a difficult debate about which groups could quality as 'principal religions' and which should not. Thus according to Lord Lester of Herne Hill, speaking in support of the Bill and against the proposed amendment:

> The Moonies, the Scientologists and other sects would no doubt claim that they are religious bodies and that, therefore, they are entitled to the protection of this kind of immunity under the convention. I would not like to see our courts, as has happened with other countries, having to decide claims of discrimination between, say, the Scientologists and the Moonies on the one hand and Christians or Jews on the other ... Some of us may think that the Moslems are a principal religious tradition represented in Great Britain, while others may think that they are not ...[15]
>
> The last time that the amendment was put forward it sought to give the Minister the power to define what was a religion. This time the aim is to give courts the power to define what is and what is not a religious body. That would simply transfer the problem of divisiveness ... it is not for us to decide what is and what is not a proper religion. (ibid., columns 753–4)

In respect of defining what religion is, and what is (or is not) a principal religious body, Lord Lester felt that it was not the duty of either the courts or of government to make any such decision. His colleague Earl Russell observed that in his consideration 'I imagine that Hinduism and Islam will be recognised as principal religions' but he was not sure how other groups such as 'Sikhs, Zoroastrians or Baha'is' might be categorised (ibid., column 779). Using a sporting analogy to rather mischievous effect, he suggested that this approach would place some religions in a first division and others in the second division, and that the considerable jealousies between religious groups that would be produced by this 'would need a system of promotion and relegation' (ibid.). More seriously, he concluded that if he was a judge then the question of defining religions 'is not a question that I should be particularly happy to have come before me because it is not a question in which the authority of the law is particularly well placed' (ibid.).

Speaking for the amendment, however, Baroness Young argued that the problem was nowhere near as difficult as suggested by these speakers, since in fact the question of defining religions had already been examined by parliament a few years previously:

> On an earlier amendment Lord Lester raised the question of how to keep out crank religions. This amendment uses wording taken directly from the Education Acts which define what is taught in religious education in state schools. Section 375(3) of the *Education Act 1996* refers to the Christian and other principal religions. That was first introduced in the *Education Reform Act 1988*. That has been widely interpreted to mean the big six: Christianity, Judaism, Islam, Hinduism, Buddhism and Sikhism. The phrase 'teaching and practices' is also found in legislation. I believe that if religion is respectable enough to be taught in schools it is respectable enough to be covered by this amendment and defined in that way. (ibid., column 771)

The debate could be broadly expressed, therefore, as dividing religious groups (or bodies) into two different types – principal (or respectable) and 'crank'. Another supporter of the amendment suggested that the application of the *Education Reform Act 1988* had not produced any problems in this respect, nor should the amendment. According to the Lord Bishop of Ripon 'it is clear, with reference to the examples given by Lord Lester, that Moslems are within and Moonies are without' (ibid., column 775).

One problem with this approach, which was not touched on in the Hansard debate, was the considerable difference between teaching *about religions* in schools, and legislating for *religious organisations*. Moonie theology may not be considered to be a principal religion to be taught by necessity as part of the English National Curriculum, but it is another matter altogether on how the state should deal with the organisation of the Unification Church. For another example, the claim was made that Islam should be recognised as a 'principal religion' and, indeed, what are considered as the basic elements of Islam are taught in British schools. But it is a far more difficult matter to decide *which* Islamic groups could qualify as Islamic in this sense. The courts and the state may choose to consider *all Islamic* groups (of a certain size perhaps) to qualify, but groups such as the Ahmaddiyas and the Ismailis (or even the Nation of Islam) may seek to qualify – all of which would be refuted as non-Islamic by other (perhaps more mainstream) Muslims groups in Britain (c.f. Lewis 1994). On what basis would the courts make such a decision? It would not be enough to say that Muslims are within and Moonies without. Instead there would be an extremely difficult task of deciding what makes a group qualify for the recognised status as a Muslim religious organisation.

The case of ISKCON would likewise need some consideration. Following the successful resolution of the Manor dispute a strong argument could be made that ISKCON should be granted this principal religious organisation status as a *Hindu* organisation. However, there would still be some who would argue that ISKCON are a 'crank religion' (as a 'new religion') and so should be without. The long standing membership by ISKCON of the National Council of Hindu Temples, its role within the formation of the Hindu Council of the UK, and its obvious large scale support by Hindus would all be strong evidence against this argument, and it is hard to envisage ISKCON not succeeding in this hypothetical application. However, if such a case was being argued (theoretically) under the same laws twenty years previously, in the late 1970s, then I am certain that ISKCON would have been excluded as a 'crank religion'. Fundamentally, ISKCON are not a different organisation now compared with twenty years ago, and certainly their basic (religious) principles have not changed. What has changed is mainly the way they have *presented* themselves, and the extent to which they have been able to convince observers that they are 'genuinely Hindu'. Thus, temporal, historical developments have created an extremely significant change in the ways in which ISKCON are viewed in British cultural and religious discourses, and this change shows the fluidity of any attempt to place a religious organisation into the static and highly politicised categories of 'principal' and 'non-principal' (or crank).

The USA

At the international level this issue has been debated in rather different ways. In many cases the debates have again focused around the issue of definition, which usually comes down to the application of a definition of 'religion' from some standard dictionary or other authoritative source. But the debate has been more sharp – and in some cases more clearly argued – where state governments give substantial advantages for a group to be registered or recognised as a religion over and above any other form of charitable status. Thus when the law gives a guarantee of religious freedom – such as in the case of the USA – then one barrier for a group to overcome in order to claim this right is to be recognised as being a religion. Likewise in the USA (as in many countries) there are distinct tax advantages in having the status of 'religion' and so a number of groups (including Scientology) have fought extremely hard to be so recognised.[16] However, in the case of the USA there has been a studious avoidance by the courts of clearly delimiting or defining religion. The closest that has been attempted is the statement by the Supreme Court Judges in 1970 that: 'the central consideration in determining whether the registrant's beliefs are religious is whether these beliefs play the role of a religion and function as a religion in the registrant's life'.[17] Although this 'definition' does not seem to be all that prescriptive (since it does not invoke any concepts of 'monotheism' or 'theism') it still places a great emphasis on the concept of beliefs as the prior element of religiosity (thus again downplaying practice), and more importantly it leaves it to the 'common sense' of the judiciary to decide whether something 'plays the role and function' of a 'religion'. It even leaves the possibility that a judge will *expect* a person's belief to be theistic/monotheistic, but does not even need to articulate this in his/her judgement. Indeed, Stephen Feldman's analysis of religious freedom discourses in the USA concludes that 'even in decisions that seem to protect religious outgroups, the justices typically understand and present religion in predominantly Christian terms' (1997:271).

Australia

In Australia, the much quoted decision by the Australian High Court has been more bold, and certainly more explicit, than most other countries. In 1983 judges Acting Chief Justice Mason and Justice Brennen when considering a tax exemption case involving the Church of Scientology, stated that:

> The chief function in the law of a definition of religion is to mark out an area within which a person subject to the law is free to believe and to act in accordance with his [sic.] belief without legal restraint ... A definition cannot be adopted merely because it would satisfy the majority of the community or because it corresponds with a concept currently accepted by that majority ...[18]

The judges therefore outlined the definition of religion which they thought most applicable for purposes of law in Australia:

> the criteria of religions are twofold: first belief in a supernatural Being, Thing, or Principle; and second the acceptance of canons of conduct in order to give effect to that belief ... (ibid.)

On this basis the judges ruled that the Church of Scientology should be considered as a religion, and so given the tax concessions which are due to religious organisations. But, they did provide the caveat that 'charlatanism is a necessary price of religious freedom', and it is possible for followers to belong to a religion even if the leader is lacking in 'sincerity or integrity' (ibid.).

However, the case was examined by five judges in total and, although the majority (unanimous) decision was to recognise the Church of Scientology as a religion, the other three judges disagreed with Mason and Brennan's viewpoint on definition. As a result of this, along with this particular definition a further two approaches to the definition of religion were provided, and the outcome of the case was that three quite different criteria were set out for Australian law to deal with. According to Lynne Hume (1995:138 fn16) none of these three contrasting viewpoints has achieved ascendancy since the case was decided, and 'so exactly what constitutes a legal definition remains uncertain'.

Justices Wilson and Deane made it clear that they did not agree with Mason and Brennan's twofold definition, considering that it was too restrictive and unnecessary to define religion primarily in terms of a supernatural being (or entity or thing). Instead, they proposed their own criteria:

> One of the more important indicia of 'religion' is that the particular collection of ideas and/or practices involves belief in the supernatural, that is to say, belief that reality extends beyond that which is capable of perception by the senses. If that be absent, it is unlikely that one has 'a religion'. Another is that the ideas relate to man's [sic.] nature and place in the universe and his [sic.] relation to things supernatural. A third is that the ideas are accepted by adherents as requiring or encouraging them to observe particular standards or codes of conduct or to participate in specific practices having supernatural significance. A fourth is that, however loosely knit and varying in beliefs and practices adherents may be, they constitute an identifiable group or identifiable groups. A fifth ... is that the adherents themselves see the collection of ideas and/or practices as constituting a religion ... All of these indicia are satisfied by most or all of the leading religions: it is unlikely that a collection of ideas and/or practices would properly be characterized as a religion if it lacked all or most of them ... (quoted in Wilson 1990a:78)

On the face of it this is the most all encompassing and inclusive definition of religion suggested by any court, and would probably include most manifestations that would normally be labelled as 'religions' by academic scholars. Its main weakness is that it places a great deal of emphasis on the concept of 'supernatural', which is an idea that comes out of European Enlightenment ideas of religiosity, and so does not sit all that easily with many non-western concepts of religiosity in which religious manifestations can be considered as being part of the 'natural' (or non-supernatural) sphere (see Sadurski 1993). And, of course, there is again the emphasis placed on belief, with notions of practice ('codes of conduct' and participation in 'specific practices') coming rather low down on the list of indicia. In fact, the judgement of Mason and Brennan made this point more explicitly, saying that 'religion encompasses conduct no less than belief' (quoted in Hume 1995:139). When considered for what it is, however, Wilson and Deane provided a useful attempt to extend the politics of legal definitions of religion, and showed a willingness by the judges to open up the privileges available to religious groups to a wider range than are often considered. As such it is a good attempt to create a workable legal definition of 'religion' within a multicultural context.

The remaining judge, Justice Murphy, argued against any attempts by the courts to define religion, which he interpreted as making a judgement on the truth or validity of the claims made by a particular religion. In a statement which makes explicit the implicit theological dimension of trying to legally define religion, he argued that 'the truth or falsity of religions is not the business of officials or the courts' and 'if each purported religion had to show that its doctrines were true, then all might fail' (quoted in Hume 1995:139). Questions such as the absurdity, morality, fraudulence, or novelty or a group should not determine whether or not a particular group is considered a religion, instead 'in the eyes of the law, religions are equal' (1995:139).

The problem still remained, however, about whether a group – such as the Church of Scientology – should be granted tax exemption. But for Murphy what was necessary was for each applicant to prove 'on the civil standard' that it was entitled to such exemption (1995:139). This suggests an approach which removes the process of evaluating a religion in broadly 'theological' terms (often in terms of whether a group deserves to be in the 'big league' of recognised or proper religions). Instead it places the emphasis on the more obvious political level of whether the state wishes to, or has the obligation to, treat the religious group in an equitable way with other groups (such as mainstream churches) which already enjoy charitable status on the basis of their (recognised) claims to be religious. In a sense he was offering a critique of legislation that grants tax exemptions to groups on the basis of a vague and contested concept such as religion, which does so without making explicit how (or why) the status of being categorised as a religion should be determined.

Murphy's suggestion was that 'any body (i.e. organization) which claims to be religious, whose beliefs of practices are a revival of, or resemble earlier cults, ... [or] offers to find meaning and purpose in life, is religious' (1995:140). I think this could be interpreted as saying that *most* groups that make a claim of being 'a religion' should be accepted as such,[19] unless there are very clear indicators that the group is not religious in any accepted way.

He further added that his own list of criteria was 'not exhaustive' and there was certainly scope for accepting new and different 'categories of religion' (1995:140). This point is an important one to make, especially in a multicultural social context where there is often the possibility of non-western religious groups acting in ways that do not 'look obviously' (i.e. christocentrically) like religions.

Italy

A decision made in October 1997 by the Italian Court of Cassation (which for jurisdictional purposes is the Supreme Court in Italy) put forward a rather different definition which actually recognised the socially constructed nature of defining.[20] The case again involved the Church of Scientology, and was brought through legal action to examine the question of whether Scientology could be categorised as a religion or not. The Italian Supreme Court had been asked to consider a judgement by a lower court – the Court of Appeal in Milan – in December 1996. The Milan court had held that there were no grounds for categorising the Church of Scientology a religion since, although there was 'no legislative definition of religion' in Italian law and no 'useful element in order to distinguish a religious organization from other social groups', it was still possible for the courts to reach a conclusion on such a matter (ibid.). In the absence of any clearly stated definition, the Milan court had relied on a definition through which they viewed religions as 'a system of doctrines centered on the presupposition of the existence of a Supreme Being, who has a relation with humans, the latter towards him a duty of obedience and reverence' (ibid.). This definition was not all that dissimilar from Mason and Brennan's position in the Australian judgement quoted above, although it did narrow that perspective by interpreting the phrase 'Supreme Being' in a theistic sense. It was in regard to this view, therefore, that the Milan court of appeal had rejected Scientology's claim to being a religion, since Scientology theology is generally non-theistic.

The Supreme Court, however, took a very different view on the matter. On 9th October 1997 they annulled the Milan decision and asked the Milan court to re-examine the facts of the case. They strongly criticised the lower court's definition, on the basis that it was 'based only on the paradigm of Biblical religions', and used as an example the recognition by Italian authorities of a Buddhist organisation as a 'religious denomination', which (like Scientology) does not postulate the concept of a Supreme Being. Therefore, taking a more consistent approach than British courts had done to the exemptions (such as Buddhism) to christocentric assumptions, the Italian Supreme Court suggested other ways of trying to delimit the boundaries of religion. One possible approach would be to accept all self-definitions of groups, so if a group claimed to be 'a religion' then the courts could be expected to accept this at face value. However, the Supreme Court felt that such a self-definition was 'not enough in order to recognize it as a genuine religion' (ibid.). Instead the court followed the Milan court's use of case law in the Italian Constitutional Court, which relied on a concept of 'common opinion', but which the Supreme Court felt should be understood as the 'opinion of scholars' rather than the 'public opinion' (ibid.). Echoing the Australian judgement, they felt that public opinion would be extremely difficult to determine, and in fact tends to be hostile to religious minorities. Scholars, on the other hand, tend to follow definitions which are more robust and reflect the received wisdom of society. Commenting on this judgement Massimo Introvigne argued that

> The Italian Supreme Court 1997 decision on Scientology includes one of the most important discussions – so far and at an international scale – of how courts may apply existing laws apparently requiring them to decide whether a specific group is, or is not, a religion. It argues that the non-existence of a legal definition of religion in Italy (and elsewhere) 'is not coincidental'. Any definition would rapidly become obsolete and, in fact, limit, religious liberty. It is much better, according to the Italian Supreme Court, 'not to limit with a definition, always by its very nature restrictive, the broader field of religious liberty'. 'Religion' is an ever-evolving concept, and courts may only interpret it within the frame of a specific historical and geographic context, taking into account the opinions of scholars.[21]

To a large extent, I agree that this approach has many advantages and is certainly more innovative and pragmatic than many of the narrow definitions that have been suggested in other countries (as well as in the Milan court). I think Introvigne's own comments can be further unpacked, especially his remark about the 'ever-evolving concept' of religion. It needs to be recognised that the changes are happening in two different ways. On the one hand, it is clear that religious groups and manifestations do change and develop according to social and cultural (and historical and geographical) contexts. But on the other hand there are also evolving social and cultural responses and perspectives on religious manifestations. The judges' argument is that the assumptions on what is perceived as 'religion' and 'religions' can and do tend to change over time, and this is reflected by scholars' own ideas about definition.

As Introvigne himself would admit, the prospect of involving scholars directly in the production of definitions and perspectives can be problematic. In most countries there are competing scholarly views on this matter, the judgement reached on a particular religious group will depend to a large extent on which scholars are consulted, and it may well be extremely hard to find any particular 'common opinion' among scholars. In some cases the academic scholarship may show enough consensus to make it fairly easy for judges to find a 'common opinion', but the field of understanding and categorising minority religions (especially what are commonly perceived as 'new religions') can be highly contentious, and a judge in many countries may find a 'common' scholarly opinion which argues that Scientology is not a religion, just as the Italian judges found the other way. This can be especially the case when the academic study of religion is predominantly influenced by (Christian) theological discourses, which tend to have their own political (and theological) perspectives on what is religion, or not.[22]

I would agree with Introvigne that overall, the avoidance by the Italian court of a definition of religion is a useful approach to make. However, I am not altogether sure if a definition can be avoided, since definitions often work in implicit as well as explicit ways within these legal (and other) judgements. But, unlike in the USA, the absence of a definition could be a useful basis for legal discussion if the non-definition is made explicitly inclusive, that is if it is made clear that narrow implicit definitions should be avoided.

United Nations perspectives

A similarly relaxed attitude to definitions has been suggested through the implementation of the United Nations' Declarations on Human Rights, and on the Elimination of All Forms of Intolerance and Discrimination Based on Religion or Belief. The organisation has come to the conclusion that a number of 'new religious movements' come within the mandate of these declarations, including ISKCON and indeed Scientology (Evans 1997:250). Acting as a UN Special Rapporteur on religious intolerance, Angelo d'Almeida Ribeiro wrote in his annual report in 1988:

> freedom of religion and belief is indivisible and all religious or belief-based movements, regardless of their length of existence, geographical origin or ideological foundations, must benefit from all the guarantees attaching to respect for the right to freedom of thought, conscience, religion or belief.[23]

This inclusive attitude is perhaps possible when providing mechanisms for protection, rather than the more national concerns of dealing with social or financial advantages for such religious groups. But as a United Nations interpretation of an internationally accepted exposition of religious human rights the way in which the 'field' of religion is delineated it is worth considering. Therefore, in a report in 1990, Special Rapporteur Ribeiro commented that:

> aspects having to do with the antiquity of a religion, its revealed character and the existence of a scripture, while important, are not sufficient to make a distinction. Even belief in the existence of a

> Supreme Being, a particular ritual, or a set of ethnic and social rules are not exclusive to religions but can also be found in political ideologies.[24]

In fact, in the same report he proposed that this protection should be given to 'theistic, non-theistic, and atheistic beliefs' (Evans 1997:251) – a phrase which was included in an initial draft of the declaration (Sullivan 1988:491 fn16) – and hence drew a very wide definition of religion which probably goes far further than any state would be prepared to consider. However, the intention behind the wording of the UN Declaration was to include more than is normally associated with the term religion. Hence the phrase used in the title is 'elimination of intolerance and discrimination based on *religion or belief*'. This term 'religion or belief' may, therefore, be used to refer to manifestations that are 'obviously' assumed to be religious (such as are associated with well recognised religions such as Christian or Islamic groups), but is also held to cover non-theistic and non-'religious' world views. However, it still needs to be observed that despite this wide ranging approach (or perhaps because of it) the:

> application of the Declaration is most straightforward when the belief or practice under consideration corresponds to a typically Western model of religion, in which religious institutions and authority are structurally separable from political and other social institutions. (Sullivan 1988:490)

In the absence of any explicit definition, another Special Rapporteur, Elizabeth Odio Benito proposed a working definition of religion as 'an explanation of the meaning of life and how to live accordingly', which she further sought to clarify by saying 'every religion has at least a creed, a code of action and a cult'.[25] However, this has only remained at the level of a suggestion. For the main part the Declaration is used and discussed without any particular attempt to define what is meant by the phrase 'religion or belief'.

The operation of this UN Declaration in an international and intercultural domain – and particularly its political application – shows something of the problems associated with attempting to place non-western cultural and religious forms into a western discourse in which it is held possible to delimit and map religion, separating it from what are considered to be other spheres of life, such as politics. It may be (just about) possible for national governments, legislators, and judiciaries to put forward a set of normative criteria which mark out what in legal discourses can be accepted as 'religion', since to a large extent the power to make such assertions is a function of the power of a state. In the case of the United Nations the power relations are less clearly determined, and it is (to a large degree) discursively expected that the western nations (particularly the USA and western

European states) should not exert ideological or political hegemony over other member countries. To this extent, the setting out of what is meant by 'religion or belief' cannot be too explicitly stated – if it is, then the western bias in the concept will become evident – and so it has been avoided as much as possible.

Donna Sullivan, in fact, argues that 'the omission of definitions of religion and belief from the Declaration may prove more conducive to the protection of freedom of religion and belief than would any definitions that could be agree upon' (1988:491), since it allows the UN Special Rapporteurs a large measure of freedom in investigating and reporting allegations of religious intolerance and discrimination across the world. However, I would argue that the ambiguity of the delineation of the concept – although helpful in itself – is primarily conducive to the work of the UN Special Rapporteurs and their implementation of the Declaration, rather than directly 'protecting religious freedoms'. That is, by avoiding a clear definition of religion or belief, UN Rapporteurs can more easily report on (and so bring to international attention) activities relating to religious intolerance or discrimination, without necessarily having to impose a western concept of what constitutes religion.

Self-definitions and religious action

To conclude this discussion of judicial and other definitions of religion, I would like to reiterate the perspective that all definitions need to be located in social and political contexts and discourses. There can be no universal and definitive definition of religion which can be applied in all cases, and so although attempts at definitions which move away from christocentric concepts of monotheism (or even theism) may give some benefits to minority groups, they can still cause as many problems as they are intended to resolve. A deliberate avoidance of definition, on the other hand, may (or may not) help provide a more inclusive basis for state and governmental dealings with minority religious groups. But, even so, an absent definition may carry within its own discourse an implicit assumption or definition of where the dividing line between the status of 'religion' and non-religion should be. Thus it seems that many states in Europe and elsewhere have been working on the problem of how to categorise the Church of Scientology, and the implicit assumptions of many politicians, judges, and state officials working in a number of these states is that Scientology should be 'without'. For varying reasons it appears that the categorisation (or designation) of a group as a 'religion' gives status and credibility to that group, as well as (varying) material and legal benefits. The boundaries between religion and non-religion have therefore been strongly contested, and the intense legal debates about which definitions (if any) should be applied through courts and legislation have often helped to hide the political relations between minority groups and hegemonic states behind quasi-objectivist terminology.

To clarify, I am not arguing that attempts to define religion should not be attempted by the courts – although I agree with Earl Russell (in the British House of Lords) that trying to make and then judge upon such a definition is not something at which most judges would be particularly effective. Instead, I am arguing that the processes of setting and implementing definitions need to be understood as discursive procedures that come out of certain power relations, and that these processes can either help to legitimate and maintain the power relations or in some way challenge and redefine them. On the one hand, attempts by certain British politicians to define groups within and without of the status of religion is an obvious exercise of political marginalisation of minority religious groups. But even the more seemingly liberal approaches of the Australian judges (both Mason and Brennan *and* Wilson and Deane) still perpetuate a set of relations in which it is assumed that there can be 'indicia' or characteristics that a judge can 'tot up' to help decide whether a particular minority group fits into the category of religion. In doing so, the indicia can be set widely enough for most groups to qualify, but the act of setting the criteria, and the goal of achieving the status of religion, both in themselves create the opportunity that some groups should *not* qualify and so be excluded. To a large degree this is lessened by Justice Murphy's approach that sets very wide criteria and then refuses to fix those criteria, thus allowing for re-evaluation and a continuing flexibility in the application of the term 'religion'. Again, the question of power is still very much relevant to this since exactly who decides how the criteria should be re-evaluated is not clear: Murphy appears to assume that it is the judges who should make this decision, whilst the Italian judges in the Court of Cassation allowed for this political control to be shared with academics. Very few would argue explicitly that the issue of definition should lie with the minority group themselves – the Italian judges decided that this was not enough to decide if the group was a 'genuine religion', as any group (minority or otherwise) can seek to empower itself through claiming the status of religion, but there also (it appears) needs to be a recognition of this self-empowerment by state authorities.

If Sullivan is correct in her argument that one of the strengths of the UN Declaration on the Elimination of All Forms of Intolerance and Discrimination Based on Religion or Belief is its absence of a definition, then this in itself does perhaps offer one way in which religious diversity could and should operate at the level of multicultural nation states. Although the work of the UN Rapporteurs has been primarily concerned with reporting on cases of violations of the principles of the declaration (and hence on intolerance and discrimination against groups and individuals because of their religion *or* belief), the inclusive assumptions of the declaration and the rapporteurs could also be applied in legal discourses and the application of states laws to minority groups. By this I mean the rapporteurs have tried to avoid any eurocentric or christocentric impositions of definition (or assumption) onto non-western cultural groups for whom the boundaries between religion and non-religion are not so clearly defined, if at all. In doing so, the hegemonic and controlling power of the dominant groups in the United Nations (particularly the USA) are not exactly avoided but are at least contested, and the role of the declaration on rights as a vehicle for (and a challenge against) that hegemony becomes a little more transparent. If applied at the level of nation states, I would argue, the operation of any legal discourses on definitions of religion should rely on an assumption that the boundaries between religion and non-religion cannot be set (and certainly not fixed), and that the emphasis should be on the state (most usually through the judiciary) to show how and why discourses (and protections) on religiosity should *not* apply to certain groups that claim to be included in such discourses. To put this another way, the self-definition claims of minority groups as religious groups should be accepted at face value, unless state agencies can articulate clearly any compelling political or social reasons for not so doing.

Behind much of this discussion of defining religion lurks the mainly unasked question of why 'religion' should be marked out as something separate from other human activities. Here again I think it is worth coming back to the distinction I made earlier between 'religion' (or religions) as entities or groups, and what could be called the practice of 'religiosity' (or religioning). The claim to 'be a religion' is a group claim that gives a certain social and political status to the collection of people making such a claim. When there is an obvious social benefit (such as tax exemption) involved in being recognised by the state as a religion, as a corporation, then the claim by a group to be a religion becomes even more important (and open to contestation). Many legal discourses on religion seek to make this distinction – that is, to give some criteria by which a group that claims to be a religion can be distinguished as being somehow different from other (non-religious) groups. Justice Murphy's criticism in Australia of the theological work of definitions raises the intriguing question of whether it is worthwhile attempting to talk and act in these terms. By granting a special status to a group/organisation on the basis that it is 'a religion' there is recognition by the state at some level that the 'religious' practices and assumptions of that group are (hypothetically) valid and worthwhile. I am not advocating here a rationalist secularist viewpoint that such religions should not be accepted on this basis. Instead I argue again that the processes of making these judgements is bound up with wider political processes, and that in a sense the theological is political (and vice versa). Any attempt to place some groups within the category of religion relies on a set of political and theological assumptions, which come out of Christian cultural and religious traditions. And a process of putting some groups within the category also entails the possibility of excluding other groups because they do not match up with such assumptions (because these groups are not 'genuine' or 'principal' religions). Hence it is possible for perspectives on some groups to mutate over time, such as ISKCON, which I argued has moved (hypothetically) over twenty years from the status of crank to principal religion.

An alternative to this approach (which is equally problematic) is to shift the emphasis away from collective groups and organisations to actions and descriptive qualities. Hence my mention of *religiosity* or *religioning*. At one level, this strategy might appear to be rooted strongly in eurocentric notions of liberal individualism, taking the focus away from groups and instead placing it on what individuals do in groups. However, I would not like my argument to be read in such a way: religiosity and the practice of religion can be as much something that is done by groups of people as it is done by individuals as individuals. What I would wish to emphasise with this concept is that the types of practice and assumptions that are marked out by the category of religiosity are considered to be (in some way) qualitatively different (to a greater or lesser extent) from practices which are not 'religious'. Thus, for example, it allows a debate over the extent to which religious practice is in some way different from what is classed as 'leisure activity' – a point about which Inspector Hanchet and Secretary of State John Gummer disagreed in the ISKCON case (see chapter six). ISKCON argued that when Krishna-*lila* dramas are performed, the activity is religious, and so is not the same as other forms of drama (considered by the state to be 'public entertainment'). Although there is a theological element to such a viewpoint, by shifting from the notion of 'a religion' to religiosity or religious practice, the assumption becomes more dependent on performative self-descriptions than on any rigid concept of the validity of a 'truth claim'. The ISKCON example shows how the concept of self-description of a certain activity as religious can be highly contested, but it does at least side-step the problems of assigning status to a group in terms of being a 'religion' or not.

By placing the emphasis on *religiosity*, rather than on *religion*, I would argue that there can be a point in marking out some measure of protection for certain (religious) groups and individuals. In terms of rights discourses, the 'freedom of religion' is better expressed as protection of the freedom of *religiosity*, or the manifestation of *religiosity*. Such protection is best promoted as relating to people who are practising their religiosity (through action or through their thinking about religious assumptions), as well as groups which collectively (as well as individually) practise such religiosity. Therefore, tax exemptions (if any) should be granted as a recognition of such practised religiosity by groups such as the Church of Scientology, rather than for much more nebulous debates on whether Scientology are a 'religion' or not.

Returning to Justice Murphy's comments, this does, I believe, involve the 'civil standard' that he invoked, since if the particular group does not act in a way that its religiosity can be considered to be in line with the public benefit then tax exemption could be revoked. The decision would still be a political decision, but it would be obviously political, rather than being dressed up in a technical discussion of definitions. And it would not be a matter of denying any tax exemption on the basis that Scientology (or any other group) are not a 'genuine religion', nor on the basis that the group are not acting religiously. Rather it can be accepted that the group generally do consider themselves to be acting religiously, but their activities (whether religious or not) are not of a standard that justifies their tax exemption. Such a claim would, of course, be for state authorities to prove, and there would need to be compelling grounds to make such a case, for example if there was firm evidence that the group (as an organisation) were promoting behaviour that was illegal or strongly anti-social.

This, therefore, does salvage something from the inclusion of religion (or religiosity) within rights discourses. There does not necessarily have to be any attempt (by judges or legislators) to define the boundaries of religiosity (since it can and should be used as a descriptor of any person or group that wishes to claim that their activities are religious). Morevoer, rather than having to make a quasi (or overtly) theological decision on whether a group's activities measure up to some standard on what religion 'should be' about, this approach locates religious activities within the domain of other social and cultural activities. In doing so, it recognises that questions of religiosity (and relations between religious groups) are not apolitical, but are bound up with power relations between groups.

The issue of whether it is necessary to distinguish religious human rights is also (possibly) dealt with here. Although the practice of religiosity may perhaps be protected by other specific rights (such as freedom of assembly and freedom of expression), by also highlighting religiosity some recognition is made of two important perspectives. One is that, generally, most states tend to expect some (socially, culturally, or individually) positive element to be associated with the practice of religiosity (whether or not this is the case is of course debatable), and so in most cases (it is felt) free practice of religiosity is in the public interest. The second, more important, perspective is that many groups wish to describe themselves as religions, and their practices as religious manifestations. Unless there are compelling reasons to deny such self-descriptions, it seems unnecessary for legislators and judges to do so. Tax exemption could still be denied to a group that does consider its activities to be religious, if there were political reasons to say that overall the group's activities were against the public interest, or benefit. Otherwise, the view that a definition by state authorities on whether a particular groups is 'religious' or not is primarily a means of using seemingly objective criteria for overtly political purposes.

Notes

1 There are a number of ways in which such a view on rights can be challenged, without necessarily rejecting rights discourses. For example, Partha Chatterjee argues that the assertion of rights by a minority group (rather than an individual) is in fact a group assertion of 'the right not to offer a reason for being different' (Chatterjee 1998:371). From a different perspective, Upendra Baxi argues that human rights discourses should also include human *needs*, particularly basic needs such as food, shelter, clothing, health, and education, and that universal declarations on human rights are severely limited because they do not include such basic needs along with those that are articulated around issues of freedom (Baxi 1989).

2 Each of the three relevant clauses differ on exactly how the freedoms and rights should be restricted by what is necessary in democratic society, as such:

Article 9 (2). Freedom to manifest one's religion or beliefs shall be subject only to such limitations as are prescribed by law and are necessary in a democratic society in the interests of public safety, for the protection of public order, health or morals, or for the protection of the rights and freedoms of others.

Article 10 (2). The exercise of these freedoms [of expression], since it carries with it duties and responsibilities, may be subject to such formalities, conditions, restrictions or penalties as are prescribed by law and are necessary in a democratic society, in the interests of national security, territorial integrity or public safety, for the protection of health or morals, for the protection of the reputation or rights of others, for preventing the disclosure of information received in confidence, or for maintaining the authority and impartiality of the judiciary.

Article 11 (2). No restrictions shall be placed on the exercise of these rights [of assembly and association] other than such as are prescribed by law and are necessary in a democratic society in the interests of national security or public safety, for the prevention of disorder or crime, for the protection of the rights and freedoms of others. This article shall not prevent the imposition of lawful restrictions on the exercise of these rights by members of the armed forces, of the police or of the administration of the State.

(Quoted from the ECHR, Council of Europe 1968).

3 Generally, brainwashing allegations are treated with scepticism by most social scientists – for discussions of this issue see Barker (1984), Robbins (1988: 63–99), Zablocki (1997, 1998), Bromley (1998). This is not to say that change and manipulation of religious beliefs is not possible, but it is nowhere near as widespread (or demonstrable) as is commonly assumed in popular discourses on brainwashing.

4 For a general taste see: Clarke and Byrne (1983), Geertz (1973).

5 In particular see Asad (1993a), Chidester (1996), Arnal (1999), see also Nye (n.d.1).

6 I have argued elsewhere that for these reasons it is perhaps more appropriate to talk about religion as religioning – emphasising the active element involved in all religious manifestations (Nye n.d.1).

7 The watershed case in respect of the application of the *Race Relations Act 1976* to religious groups is *Mandla v Dowell Lee* ([1983] 1 All ER 1062), which is discussed by Menski (2000) and Poulter (1986: 185–87). In this case a Sikh successfully argued that his son was being racially discriminated against as a Sikh because a headmaster refused to admit the boy to a public school unless the boy removed his turban and long uncut hair.

8 A Rastafarian, Trevor Dawkins, brought a similar case to Mandla on the basis of discrimination over his employers' requirement that he remove his dreadlocks. The Court of Appeal found, however, that the criteria for defining a racial group, set out in the *Mandla v Dowell Lee* case, did not apply to Rastafarians. See *Dawkins v Dept of the Environment* [1993] IRLR 284, discussed in Menski (2000), Cumper (1996: 230), and Poulter (1998).

9 In his submission to the *Mandla v Dowell Lee* judgement, Lord Fraser in the House of Lords argued that ethnic identity should not be construed on purely 'biological' or 'racial' identity, but should depend on a number of criteria, of which he set out two essential characteristics and five further elements which might be relevant. The two essential characteristics of an ethnic group were 'a long shared history, of which the group is conscious as distinguishing it from other groups, and the memory of which keeps it alive' and 'a cultural tradition of its own, including family and social customs and manners, often but not necessarily associated with religious observance'. The five minor elements were a common geographic origin, a common language, a common literature, a common religion, and having the status of being a minority group. ([1983] All ER at 1066–67, quoted in Poulter 1986: 185–86).

10 For a discussion of the problems faced by English courts in defining what is and is not a religion, see Wilson (1990a: 75–83).

11 Quoted in an email sent by Michael York, of Bath Spa University College to the Nurel-l discussion group, 13th May 1996 (see <http://www.ucalgary.ca/~hexham/nrm/nurel-l.html> for Nurel-l archives).

12 Bryan Wilson (1990b) gives a useful, but fairly controversial discussion of ways in which the Church of Scientology could be defined sociologically as a religion. Members of the Church of Scientology are themselves keen to put forward an inclusive definition of religion, through which they themselves may find it easier to receive recognition by and protection from certain states in Europe and elsewhere (for example, see Weightman n.d.).

13 [1970] 2 QB 697, quoted in Cumper (1996: 221).

14 The purpose of the HRA 1998 was to incorporate the ECHR into the British legal systems, see chapter eight.

15 Third Reading of the Human Rights Bill, House of Lords, 5th February 1998. Reported in Hansard, column 753 (available at <http://www.parliament.the-stationery-office.co.uk/pa/ld/ldhome.htm>).

16 The US Internal Revenue Service (IRS) has a list of criteria as to what is considered to be a 'religion', out of which a particular group must satisfy several, but not necessarily all. These criteria are: (i) a distinct legal existence; (ii) a recognised creed and form of worship; (iii) a definite and distinct ecclesiastical government; (iv) a formal code of doctrine and discipline; (v) a distinct religious history; (vi) a membership not associated with any other church or denomination; (vii) an organization of ordained ministers; (viii) ordained ministers selected after completing prescribed studies; (ix) a literature of its own; (x) established places of worship; (xi) regular congregations; (xii) regular religious services; (xiii) Sunday schools for religious instruction of the young; and (xiv) schools for the preparation of its ministers.

17 *Welsh v. United States*, 398 US 333 (1970), quoted in Sheraton and Kiss (1996: 571).

18 *Church of the New Faith v Commissioner for Payroll Tax* (1983), AJLR 785, quoted in Wilson (1990a: 77).

19 It is worth noting that not all groups that 'look like' religions actually make this claim. Neither Transcendental Meditation or the Brahma Kumari World Spiritual University wish to be considered as 'religions'.

20 This discussion is based on a report by Massimo Introvigne, Director of CESNUR (the Center for Studies on New Religions), which is available on the CESNUR web site at <http://www.cesnur.org> (document 'The Italian Supreme Court Decision on Scientology', <http://www.cesnur.org/testi.htm>). The full copy of the Court of Cassation's judgement (in Italian) is also available at that site. All quotes are of Introvigne's translations of court judgements, except where it is stated that the quote is of Introvigne's own comments and interpretations (see next note).

21 Massimo Introvigne, 'The Italian Supreme Court Decision on Scientology', (<http://www.cesnur.org/testi.htm>), CESNUR web site.

22 See for example Martin Baumann (1998) on academic and non-academic perspectives on Scientology and other minority religions in Germany.

23 UN Special Rapporteur Ribeiro, in UN document E/CN.4/1988/45, para 17 (quoted in Evans 1997: 250).

24 UN document E/CN.4/1990/46, para 110 (quoted in Evans 1997: 251).

25 UN Special Rapporteur Odi Benito, in UN document E/CN.4/Sub.2/1987/26, para 4 (quoted in Sullivan 1988: 491 fn16).

CHAPTER EIGHT

The ECHR, HRA, and 'Freedom of Religion' in Britain

The ECHR

In the time since I started writing this book, a very significant shift has occurred in British legal discourses on religious liberty as a human right. A year after the campaign for the Manor was finally resolved, the British general election resulted in a landslide victory for Tony Blair and his new Labour party, putting them into government with a very substantial majority. One of several constitutional reforms which this new government effected[1] was legislation to incorporate the European Convention on Human Rights (ECHR) into the British legal systems. Thus, the Human Rights Bill was published in October 1997,[2] and this became the *Human Rights Act* 1998 (HRA) in November the following year.[3] The implementation of the HRA was not immediate, however, since it was decided that the judicial systems of Britain needed some time to prepare for the substantial changes that incorporation of the ECHR would involve. Full implementation is expected to be brought about sometime during the second half of 2000, and so at the time of writing (as indeed during the whole period of the Manor campaign) the status of the ECHR within the British legal systems is fairly anomalous.[4]

In fact, the European Convention on Human Rights has been part of British law since 1951, when it was accepted and ratified by the British government. But, until 1997, subsequent governments chose not to incorporate the convention, and so its implication through the courts was fairly ambiguous. Without the passing of a statute through the British Parliament to transform the provisions of the Convention into domestic law, the Convention was 'no more than an aid' for the judiciary 'to statutory interpretation' (Bradney 1993:4, Hamilton 1995:18). When there was a direct conflict between the provisions of the Convention and domestic legislation, a test case in the House of Lords (acting as the supreme court) ruled that the provisions of the Convention should *not* take precedence, otherwise that would mean the incorporation of the Convention 'into English law by the back door' (Hamilton 1995:18).

Thus, access for citizens to any legal protections that are offered by the ECHR has been fairly restricted with the British context. There has been no direct course through the British legal systems through which a claim could be made of a violation of the rights set out in the ECHR. Indeed, if, prior to 1998, any party in Britain felt that their rights under the ECHR were being violated and they felt this violation was not been properly addressed in the British courts, then their only redress would be to take the matter to the European Commission of Human Rights in Strasbourg, who would decide whether the case should be heard by the European Court of Human Rights.[5] Even here, if a judgment was made that a violation of the Convention had occurred, the judgment was not legally enforceable in Britain. It merely created moral pressure on the British government to make legislative changes to redress the violation. Furthermore, the processing of applications to the European Court of Human Rights has been notoriously slow, with waiting times of five years or more being normal, and the average cost to applicants being around £30,000 (RBH:para.1.14).

For these reasons, the place of the European Convention within British law has been rather tenuous, and so, in a number of respects, it has not made all that much difference in practice to the way British laws operated. Indeed, it has been argued that the lack of incorporation and the need to go to Europe for redress has meant that the rights which were 'originally developed with major help from the United Kingdom Government are no longer actually seen as British rights' (RBH:para.1.14). But the legislation introduced by the Labour government has created a substantial change in the ways in which discourses on human rights are dealt with within the British legal systems. For the director of the London-based civil rights group Liberty:

> The Human Rights Act 1998 will have a momentous impact on our legal system. It is the most important piece of constitutional legislation in Britain for many years ... The Human Rights Act 1998 is unique: no other jurisdiction has ever adopted the same approach to giving effect to an international human rights instrument in domestic law. (Wadham and Mountfield 1999:xi).

Thus the Human Rights Act 'will radically alter the interpretation and use of all other legislation' (Wadham and Mountfield 1999:22).

By incorporating the ECHR into British law, the *Human Rights Act* 1998 has made it the preserve of judges in British courts to decide over whether or not a public authority (such as government, a local authority, the police, etc.) have violated an individual's or a group's rights as set out in the Convention. Thus, a party that considers their rights to have been violated will be able to make a case against the public authority through normal court procedures, and redress to the European Court will only be necessary when the British government fails to take action on a law which has been judged to be in violation of the Convention. In all other instances, the treatment of human rights will be a matter for British courts to decide. Thus, 'the overriding objective is to weave the Convention into the existing legal system, so that all courts will consider Convention arguments, and rights which could have been obtained in Strasbourg can be secured in national courts, whilst minimising disruption to the existing legal system' (Wadham and Mountfield 1999:22). Furthermore, the HRA also requires that all future legislation that is passed by Parliament will not contravene the Convention (RBH:chapters 2 & 3). The status of the European Court will, however, remain important: British judges will have to take note of recent decisions by the European Court for guidance on how the Convention should be interpreted, although decisions made there will not be legally binding in Britain.

Article 9

I have noted in previous chapters that one particular clause of the European Convention on Human Rights is concerned with articulating explicit provision for the protection of religious freedom. Although I have quoted this already in chapter four, I think that it is worth repeating the text of Article 9(1) of the ECHR, which states that:

> Everyone has the right to freedom of expression, conscience, and religion; this right includes freedom to change his [sic.] religion or belief and freedom, either alone or in community with others, and in public or private, to manifest his religion or belief, in worship, teaching, practice and observance. (Council of Europe 1968).

However, this is significantly limited by Article 9(2), which states:

> Freedom to manifest one's religions or beliefs shall be subject only to such limitations as are prescribed by law and are necessary in a democratic society in the interests of public safety, for the protection of public order, health, or morals, or for the protection of the rights and freedom of others. (ibid.)

Alongside this, there is a further article which sets out clearly that religious identity (along with other identities) should not be the basis of discrimination, particularly any contravention of the rights set out in the Convention. Thus Article 14 states:

> The enjoyment of the rights and freedoms set forth in this Convention shall be secured without discrimination on any ground such as sex, race, colour, language, religion, political or other opinion, national or social origin, association with a national minority, property, birth or other status. (ibid.)

Overall, therefore, it is possible to read the ECHR as making explicit provision for actual religious freedom through its implementation, both in those European states where the Convention is incorporated, and most particularly through the European Commission and Court in Strasbourg.

However, the ways in which these centralised judicial organisations have interpreted this part of the ECHR has been significantly questioned by the sociologist James Richardson, who has pointed out the very small number of cases that have been declared admissible by the Commission, and the even smaller number where the Court have ruled on a violation of Article 9 (Richardson 1995). Writing in 1995, he noted that there had only be one case which had been successfully upheld on the basis of Article 9 by the Court (*Kokkinakis v. Greece*, decided in 1993) – although since that date there have been two further successful cases (*Manoussakis v. Greece* in 1996, and *Larissis v. Greece* in 1998). With reference to the details of each of these cases (and some of those which the Court has recently turned down), the articulation of religious freedom through the provisions of the ECHR have been interpreted extremely conservatively by the majority of the judges sitting in the Court. In doing so, Richardson argues, rather than upholding and protecting the needs and rights of religious minorities in Europe, the decisions made at the level of the pan-European institutions may actually have helped to stifle them.

The main problem is that, although the Convention does set out rather clearly that 'freedom of expression, conscience, and religion' is a universal human right for all, this does not give a guarantee that all claims to religious freedom can or should be upheld. Regardless of whether an individual applies to a British court or the European court against a violation of the Convention, Article 9 does not declare freedom to manifest religion as an absolute principle. Rather, the limitation imposed by Article 9(2) on 9(1) means that the interpretation (and implementation) of such freedom is subject to limitations 'as are necessary in a democratic society'. And, thus, in the case of the European Court of Human Rights, this limitation has been interpreted quite widely. As one judgement by the Court has made clear:

> the Court has consistently left the Contracting States a certain margin of appreciation in assessing the existence and extent of the necessity of an interference [with rights defined under the Convention], but this margin is subject to European supervision ... The Court's task is to determine whether the measures taken at national level were justified in principle and proportionate.[6]

Therefore, on several occasions the Court has ruled that it is necessary to restrict individuals' religious freedom for reasons of public safety and public order, and they have also ruled that limitations on freedom of religion should be imposed where otherwise there would be an infringement of the fundamental rights and freedoms of others (Hamilton 1995:25, 29). But even in the cases where the Court has ruled that a violation of Article 9 has occurred, the rulings failed to establish clearly the degree to which the balance should be struck between protection of freedom of religion and other human rights (such as freedom of privacy).[7]

Furthermore, it is also possible to argue that the wording of Article 9(2) is framed in such a way that can cause problems for minority religious groups since, as Richardson suggests:

> . . . it could be argued that Article 9 ends up being used as a way to limit religious freedom, especially for minority religions, not to protect or expand such freedoms . . . [T]he focus of Article 9 is on individualized and privatized religion . . . [and] such a conceptualization of religion can be turned against minority religions, in the interest of the greater society. A majoritarian approach to religion is easily justified under Article 9 . . . (Richardson 1995:44, emphasis in original)

In this respect, the implication and reading of the European Convention does not give any absolute freedoms (if such is indeed possible), but rather makes the free practice of religion subject to the will of the democratic majority.

Alongside this, it is almost too obvious to be mentioned that the writing of the Convention was made by people with Christian values which they took to be normative. Thus, according to Lord Lester, the main proponent of the incorporation of the ECHR into British law

> the founders of the European Convention on Human Rights were men and women imbued with religious values as well as with the secular values of the Enlightenment. I was reminded of that fact by one of the Vatican's most senior lawyers when I was a rapporteur at an international gathering and referred to the Enlightenment. The Vatican lawyer pointed out, quite rightly, that the convention is steeped in Christian values. Indeed, it is part of our Christian and Judeo-Christian tradition. That is why, as my noble friend pointed out, the guarantee of religious freedom is so ample in the convention.[8]

The creation and implementation of a legal document will obviously be the product of a certain discursive context, and will thus embody the particular expectations of those who put it together. This in itself is not altogether surprising, but what does need to be noted is that by universalising such a (eurocentric and christocentric) voice into a rights discourse the practice of such a discourse may implicitly work for the benefit of some people and groups over others without this bias being recognised explicitly. Thus if the ECHR is 'steeped in Christian values', as Lord Lester suggests, then either this is to the exclusion of other (minority) religious groups, or otherwise is an exercise of benign paternalism which extends the hegemonic privileges of Christian toleration to such minorities.

The ECHR in the European Court of Human Rights

As I outlined in the previous section, in the 1990s there have been a number of cases considered by the European Commission and the European Court which have dealt specifically with Article 9, in some form or other. Indeed, it is quite remarkable that from 1948 to 1993 there had not been a successful appeal to the Court on the basis of this article, and then over the space of five years the judges adjudicated violations on three separate occasions. At one level, it appears, that the Court have collectively been reticent to come to a positive ruling on Article 9, perhaps because it is the most nebulous (and controversial) of the rights set out in the ECHR. The responses by the Court judges to the issues involved have been mixed and show that they do not wish to set any substantial precedents with regard to this article. In doing so, however, they have put forward fairly widely different perspectives on the same issues – and it is hard to build up a consistent picture of how Article 9 could and should be interpreted. In most cases, the judges have opted for fairly conservative interpretations of how much limitation should be applied to the free manifestation of religion under the needs of democratic society, and there has tended to be a reluctance to consider cases under Article 9 unless it is not possible to avoid the issue.[9]

All three of the cases that have been successfully contested on Article 9 involved the Greek government, and two of these were brought by members of the Jehovah's Witness church. In fact, the prominence of Greece in the European Court's deliberations on this particular article during the 1990s, and particularly the large number of cases dealt with by the Commission and the Court which have involved the Jehovah's Witnesses in Greece is noteworthy in itself. The Jehovah's Witnesses would themselves argue that they have had to resort to the European Court because of the numerous problems which *all* minority religious groups face in Greece – primarily because of the aggressive attitude taken by the Greek Orthodox Church as the hegemonic state religious organisation – and this claim is backed up by groups such as the Church of Scientology (CoS 1997) and independent non-governmental agencies.[10] But the success that the Jehovah's Witnesses have had in taking cases to the European Court does suggest a fairly high degree of organisation and proficiency (and also money) in their dealings with and use of the ECHR to protect what they see as their rights. Within the discussion of cases at the European Court that I provide in this section, I follow this trend by looking particularly at Jehovah's Witnesses in Greece, mainly because the examples highlight some interesting points about judicial interpretations of Article 9.[11]

Kokkinakis and *Larissis*

The watershed case was that of *Kokkinakis v. Greece*, after which (it seems) it became possible for the Court to feel comfortable with upholding other claims of violation of religious freedom. Minos Kokkinakis was a Jehovah's Witness who brought a complaint against the Greek state to the Court on the grounds of a violation of his right to freely manifest his religion through teaching (and thus seeking to convert) members of other religious traditions.[12] Kokkinakis had been found guilty by a Greek court in 1986 of proselytising (a criminal offence under Greek law) and sentenced to a fine of 10,000 Greek drachmas and four months in jail. His appeal to the European Court was declared admissible by the Commission in 1991, and a judgment was reached by the Court in 1993. The Court found that there had been a violation of Article 9 of the Convention, which could not be justified by the limitations put on Article 9(1) by 9(2). The judgment of this case depended on the balance between the right of Kokkinakis to manifest his religion (through proselytising) and the right of the recipient of his teachings (a woman who happened to be the wife of the local cantor of the Greek Orthodox Church, which is the State Church, or 'prevailing religion') to maintain the convictions of her own religious tradition. In the case of Greek law, the criminalisation of all forms of 'proselytism' quite distinctly privileges the religious discourses of the majority religion, the Orthodox Church over those of other (minority) religions.[13]

In pursuit of finding this balance the judges of the Court made a distinction between what could be considered to be 'improper proselytism' and 'bearing Christian witness'. On this basis there was no evidence to suggest that Kokkinakis had done anything more than the latter, and for which he should be able to claim the right of manifestation under Article 9. As noted by one of the judges who ruled on this case, Judge Pettitti, the Court judgement failed to follow through its own argument, and define what could considered to be 'improper witness'. In doing so, the majority judges avoided making an attempt to 'define the difference between a legitimate and an illegitimate exercise of the right of manifestation' of religion (Evans 1997:334, Hamilton 1995:27). Pettitti argued that all proselytism, including 'improper proselytism' (however one may define such a thing), is also a proper manifestation of a person's religion, so long as it does not contravene the rights of others or the needs of a democratic society (Evans 1997:332; Hamilton 1995:27), and so in effect does not need defining. Therefore, in his view, the Greek law criminalising proselytism was contrary to Article 9.

The majority decision of the Court was upheld several years later in 1998 in a fairly similar case, of *Larissis and Others v. Greece*.[14] This involved several Greek air-force officers (including Dimitrios Larissis) who had been imprisoned by the military for proselytising (both to other airmen and to civilians). Unlike Kokkinakis and the other cases discussed in this section, however, Larissis and the other air-force officers were not members of the Jehovah's Witnesses but of the Pentecostal Church, which (like the Jehovah's Witnesses) is a minority religious organisation within a state dominated by the the Greek Orthodox Church. The case was complicated by the variety of circumstances under review, with several different contexts in which illegal proselytising was held to have occured. The Court held that in the cases of the proselytising of other airmen, the Greek military authorities had not violated Article 9 by imposing relatively minor punishments (fines in lieu of prison sentences). In these cases, the proselytised airmen were in subordinate positions, and so the officers who were doing the proselytising were exerting a degree of 'improper pressure' on their subordinates to convert.[15]

But separate to this, the Court also considered cases involving two applicants (Savvas Mandalarides and Ioannis Sarandia, both of whom has also been involved in the proselytising of their subordinates), who had been charged and fined for trying to convert civilians – two different women in domestic environments on separate occasions. In these cases, the Greek authorities had defined the attempts by the air-force officers to covert as 'improper proselytism'. However, taking into account the earlier Kokkinakis judgment, the European Court did not consider there to be any excessive obligation to convert or improper behaviour within these incidents. The Court also noted that it was of 'decisive significance that the civilians whom the applicants attempted to convert were not subject to pressures and constraints of the same kind as the airmen'.[16] On the basis of this, they rejected the argument that these were 'improper proselytism', and thus there had been a violation of Article 9 by the Greek government when the men had been punished for their actions.

In this ruling, there was no further effort by the Court to clarify within their main judgment the ambiguous distinction previously made in *Kokkinakis* between 'proper' and 'improper' proselytism, and so the *Larissis* judgment merely underlined the earlier one. That is, the European Court made clear that a law against proselytism (such as the one extant in Greece) could lead to violations of Article 9, but was not necessarily contrary to it in principle. However, as had been the case in Kokkinakis, some of the judges attached their concuring opinions. Judge de Meyer made a short statement in which he argued 'the [Greek] law in issue in the present case is contrary to the Convention in its very principle, since it directly encroaches on the very essence of the freedom everyone must have to manifest his religion'.[17] In a more detailed opinion, which was partly dissenting (since he argued that the proselytising of the airmen should not have been pubished), Judge Repik argued that the Greek law on proselytism was articulated so vaguely, and had built up so much inconsistent case-law, that it is very hard to foresee how the law will or can be applied, and as such contradicts article 7 of the ECHR.[18] This being the case, in Repik's opinion, 'a believer who tries to spread his religious beliefs can never be certain whether his conduct is illegal or not. The law is not sufficiently precise', and as such he argued that it did not satisfy the requirements of article 7.[19]

Valsalmis & Efstratiou and *Tsirlis & Kouloumpas*

The cases of *Kokkinakis* and *Larissis* have established, fairly vaguely, that it is possible for state authorities to violate Article 9 through legislation such as the law on proselytism, but despite this there has continued through the 1990s to be a reluctance to make substantial use of this article in situations where there has been any a level of contestability over whether a particular issue could be regarded as 'religious'. In two separate clusters of cases (again both involving Jehovah's Witnesses in Greece) circumstances were considered in the Court where people had been punished (in one case fairly lightly, but in the other quite severely) for taking actions which they had themselves felt to be religious motivated. In both cases the Court found the punishments to be unfair, inappropriate, and in violation of the ECHR, but in doing so refused to consider the argument that the violations were of the applicants' religious freedoms.

In the cases of *Valsalmis v. Greece*[20] and *Efstratiou v. Greece*[21] – which were held on the same day and, in fact, dealt with very similar circumstances – the Court considered the cases of two teenage girls in different schools in different parts of Greece. These girls had been expected to take part in a school parade on a national holiday which they felt was against their pacifist beliefs as Jehovah's Witnesses. After failing to attend National Day parades organised by their schools (in October in 1992 and 1993), Victoria Valsalmis and Sophia Efstratiou were disciplined by their schools and given suspensions of one and three days respectively. They, together with their families, appealed to the European Court alleging violations of their rights under Article 9 of the convention, along with a violation of article 13 (which stipulates that there should be 'an effective remedy before a national authority' for allegations of a violation of the convention), and several other articles.

The unanimous judgments by the Court on both these cases were that there had been breaches of article 13 – that is the applicants had had no effective means at the national level of challenging the suspensions as breaches of their rights as set out under the convention. However, the majority judgments were that the expectation of attendance at the National Day parades did not amount in themselves to a violation of Article 9. The girls' arguments had been that as Jehovah's Witnesses their religion expected them to practise pacifism in their daily lives, and thus it was against their beliefs to take part in parades which commemorated the outbreak of war (between Greece and Fascist Italy in 1940). However, having received detailed evidence on the parades and the beliefs of Jehovah's Witnesses on pacifism, the majority verdicts of the judges came to the conclusion that the Court:

> can discern nothing, either in the purpose of the parade or in the arrangements for it, which could offend the applicants' pacifist convictions ... Such commemorations of national events serve, in their way, both pacifist objectives and the public interest. The presence of military representatives at some of the parades which take place in Greece on the day in question does not in itself alter the nature of the parades.[22]

This was despite the fact that in both cases the girls and their families had clearly felt the parades were an affront to their pacifist convictions. In reaching this position the majority judges also took note of the fact that the schools exempted both girls from religious education lessons and Greek Orthodox Mass due to their religious beliefs (ibidem.:paras.37/38). It seemed that these concessions were enough to safeguard the religious freedoms of the girls, and that – although the suspensions did appear to the judges rather heavy-handed – this case did not really concern the question of religious freedom. In so doing, it appears, the Court did not want to consider a particular case of in which religious discourse extended beyond the realm of discussion (such as teaching, or attempted conversion – as in the previous case) into actual practice (going to, or boycotting, a parade).

For the Court, the disciplinary rules of the schools (and through them of the state) were applied generally and in a neutral manner so far as religion was concerned. Thus, the majority judges quoted, without refuting, the Greek government's submission that the state is 'not under an obligation to take positive measures to adapt its activities to the various manifestations of its citizens' philosophical or religious beliefs' (ibidem.:paras.35/36).

However, two dissenting judges appended their opinions to the Court judgments stating they considered there had been violations of Article 9 in both cases. For them, the perception of the applicants about the parades 'has to be accepted by the Court' unless those perceptions are 'obviously unfounded and unreasonable'.[23] As there was no reason to find the Valsalmis or Efstratiou families' opinions unfounded and unreasonable, these two dissenting judges therefore felt that it was the duty of the Court to accept that the 'character and symbolism' of the parades were contrary to the girls' religious beliefs, and so a violation of Article 9(1) did occur. For these two judges, no justification of this violation under Article 9(2) could be reasonable, since the girls' participation could not be described as 'necessary in a democratic society'.

A further case heard shortly after these, in May 1997, took the reticence to examine Article 9 even further. This was the case of *Tsirlis and Kouloumpas v. Greece*[24] which was brought to the European Court following the separate imprisonments of two Jehovah's Witness ministers who had refused to wear the Greek army uniforms issued to them. By Greek law, ministers of religion are exempted from military service, so long as the religious group they belong to is recognised by the Greek state as a 'known religion'. The Jehovah's Witnesses have indeed been recognised as a 'known religion' in Greece since 1975, and so, therefore, the exemption from military service for these two ministers should have been a relatively straightforward matter.

In 1989 and 1990 respectively Kouloumpas and Tsirlis had applications for exemption rejected by their local army Recruitment Office (Eastern Attica) on the grounds that Jehovah's Witnesses were *not* a 'known religion'. Appeals were subsequently made against these appeal to the Director for Recruitment at the General Headquarters for National Defence, but in both cases the appeal was rejected on the same grounds as the local office: the Jehovah's Witnesses were not a 'known religion'. When the men were subsequently ordered for duty at a military training centre, they refused to join the units to which they had been assigned, invoking their status as ministers of a 'known religion', and they again refused to wear the military uniform as ordered by a military officer. This refusal was considered as insubordination by the military authorities, and the men were arrested, tried and sentenced to four year's imprisonment each under military law. In fact, both men only served fifteen months of these sentences, since they were released in May 1991 following a successful appeal to the Greek Supreme Administrative Court and the Military Appeal Court. However, although the latter court came to the verdict (by three judges to two) that the men were ministers of a known religion, and so there had been no act of insubordination, they also ruled that 'The State is under no obligation to compensate' the men for their detention, because it had been 'due to [their] own gross negligence' (paras.24 & 41). Indeed the minority positions of the two dissenting judges were that the accused were *not* religious ministers.

The two men took the case to the European Court on the grounds that their rights under the convention had been violated: they claimed that their detention was unlawful and amounted to discrimination on account of their religious beliefs (para.49). When the Court reached its judgment in 1997, they ruled that there had indeed been an arbitrary and unlawful detention of the men, and that the Greek government should pay 8,000,000 drachma in compensation to Tsirlis, and 7,300,000 drachma to Kouloumpas. However, the judges declined to make a judgment on the religious dimension of the case. They noted that the treatment of the men by the military authorities was in contrast with the automatic exemptions granted to priests of the Greek Orthodox Church. But, having found that the detentions were unlawful and arbitrary, the judges ruled unanimously that 'the Court does not consider it necessary to examine the same facts also from the angle of Article 9, either taken alone or in conjunction with Article 14 of the Convention' (para.70).

While the main issue at stake in this particular case was the imprisonment of the two men when the legal procedures should have allowed them exemptions from military service, it does seem unfortunate that the judges did not address the issues of religious identity and practice in the case. The imprisonment of both men was the direct result of authorities refusing to accept the status of ministers of the Jehovah's Witnesses, and it was only when the Supreme Court ruled that the Witnesses were established as a 'known religion' that the men were released. The men would not have suffered the imprisonment if they had been priests of the Greek Orthodox Church, and so were, in effect, discriminated against *because* they were members of a minority religious group. This is further compounded by the fact that there was fairly unambiguous recognition of the Jehovah's Witnesses as a religion which should be accorded privileges and freedom under Greek law. On these grounds alone the Court judges should have offered up a view of whether or not the Convention's aim of protecting religious liberty and preventing discrimination based on religion was violated in the treatment of Tsirlis and Kouloumpas.

Manoussakis

In distinction to the cases of *Valsalmis*, *Efstratious*, and *Tsirlis and Kouloumpas*, the case of *Manoussakis and Others v. Greece*[25] provided the other occasion on which the Court judges did actually rule there had been a violation of Article 9. This case brought in issues of the manifestation of religion in a public context which most closely relate to ISKCON's dispute over Bhaktivedanta Manor.

Manoussakis encountered problems when he tried to make use of a large rented room as a place of meeting and worship for the local Jehovah's Witness congregation in Heraklion, Crete. In June 1983 he applied to the Minister of Education and Religious Affairs for authorisation to use the room as a place of worship. In response the Ministry failed to take a decision on the application, informing Manoussakis on a number of occasions over the next year that they were still considering the matter (more than ten years later, in 1996, the Ministry had still not reached a decision). However, in July 1983 a local Greek Orthodox parish church complained to the police that the room was being used as an unauthorised place of worship, and subsequent to this, in March 1986 Manoussakis and three other members of his congregation were charged with 'having established and operated a place of worship for religious meetings and ceremonies of followers of another denomination ... without authorisation from the recognised ecclesiastical authorities and the Minister of Education and Religious Affairs ...' (para.12).

Although the charges were initially dismissed by the Heraklion criminal court, an appeal against the verdict by the town's public prosecutor's office led to a verdict in 1987 that Manoussakis and his colleagues had been guilty of using the room as an unauthorised place of public worship. The four men were each sentenced to three months' imprisonment (which could be converted into a fine of 400 drachma per day of detention), plus a fine of 20,000 drachma. When a further appeal against this judgment was turned down by the Greek Court of Cassation, the men lodged an appeal to the European Court on the basis of a restriction of their religious freedom under Article 9. In 1993 the local police placed seals on the front door of the room to prevent any further use of the place for public worship.

Under Greek law, a 'temple' or place of public worship for religious groups other than the Greek Orthodox Church requires authorisation from the Minister of Education and Religious Affairs, who determine whether there are 'essential reasons' for the authorisation of such a place. The application for this authorisation must initially be submitted to the local ecclesiastical authorities (i.e. the Orthodox Metropolitan), who should then obtain a 'reasoned opinion' on the application from the local police authority before transmitting the application to the Ministry. The application must be made on behalf of a group 'of at least fifty families, from more or less the same neighbourhood and living in an area at a great distance from a temple of the same denomination, it being assumed that the distance makes it difficult for them to observe their religious duties'.[26]

The argument that Manoussakis and his fellow applicants made to the European Court was that these laws made the practice of a religion other than the state religion of Orthodoxy subject to the granting of authorisation by the government, and so thus constituted an 'impediment' to religious freedom, especially as the sanction against use of a place without authorisation was subject to quite severe criminal sanction (para.37). There was a further impediment in that the process of applying for authorisation was very complicated, and involved not only police and government authorities, but also the state religious authorities. The Court judges agreed to a large extent with this argument, noting that Greek law allows 'far-reaching interference by the political, administrative, and ecclesiastical authorities with the exercise of religious freedom' (para.45), although the main point for them to decide was whether such interference in the case before them was acceptable and 'necessary in a democratic society'. The judges stated quite clearly that insofar as the involvement of religious authorities should be allowed within the process of authorisation of minority groups' places of worship:

> The right to freedom of religion as guaranteed under the Convention excludes any discretion on the part of the State to determine whether

> religious beliefs or the means used to express such beliefs are legitimate (para.47).

Thus, in order to comply with the Convention, the process of authorisation should depend on the application of formal procedures as set out under the relevant legislation, and not on an evaluation of the legitimacy (or otherwise) of the minority religion's beliefs and practices. In fact, the judges found that the Greek state have tended:

> to use the possibilities afforded by the [legal] ... provisions to impose rigid, or indeed prohibitive, conditions on practice of religious beliefs by certain non-orthodox movements, in particular Jehovah's Witnesses ... [T]he extensive case-law in this field seems to show a clear tendency on the part of the administrative and ecclesiastical authorities to use these provisions to restrict the activities of faiths outside the Orthodox Church (para.48).

On this basis, they found in favour of Manoussakis' allegation of a violation of Article 9 for this particular case, but ruled that no fine on the Greek state was necessary, since for the Jehovah's Witnesses the 'finding of a violation of Article 9 constitutes sufficient reparation' (para.57). However, the judges stopped short of ruling on whether the relevant Greek laws in themselves constituted an impediment to the free practice of religion in Greece, instead noting that it was the implementation of the laws by the Ministry of Education and Religious Affairs and the courts which had led to the violation.

In an interesting statement attached to the main judgment, one of the judges gave his concurring but alternative opinion that some ruling about the Greek laws themselves should have been made. According to Judge Martens:

> the very essence of the applicants' [i.e. Manoussakis et al] complaints is not one of individual, but one of *general* injustice: what they complain of is not so much the harassment *they* have been subjected to, but, basically, the obstruction to setting up a Jehovah's Witnesses chapel in general.[27]

He argued that the Court should take an innovatory (but legitimate) approach by ruling that the Greek Law of Necessity quoted above (No. 1363/1938) was incompatible with Article 9. In deciding this question, he argued:

> It is conceivable that the operation – and *a fortiori* the construction – of a place of worship in a particular area may raise serious public order questions and that possibility, in my mind justifies not wholly excluding the acceptability of making such operation or construction depend on prior Governmental authorisation.

> Nevertheless, I think that here, where freedom of religion is at stake . . ., the question is very delicate, for public order arguments may easily disguise intolerance. It is all the more sensitive where there is an official State religion. In such cases it should be absolutely clear both from the wording of, *and* from the practice under the law in question that the requirement of a prior authorisation in no way whatsoever purports to enable the authorities to *evaluate* the tenets of the applicant community; as a matter of principle the requested authorisation should always be given, *unless* very exceptional, objective, and *insuperable* grounds of public order make that impossible.
>
> . . . In sum, I find that the applicants rightly say that the Law of Necessity No. 1363/1938 is *per se* incompatible with Article 9.[28]

As with the minority viewpoints expressed in the Valsalmis and Efstratiou judgments, this conclusion was not binding but only showed an alternative viewpoint to that put forward by the majority of judges. But it does provide a useful perspective to consider the application of the principles of Article 9 of the Convention to the question of use of a place for public worship. As outlined above in chapter six, the decision made on Bhaktivedanta Manor was reached in almost an opposite way to that suggested by Judge Martens. ISKCON were required to argue against established planning policies on land use which were practically silent about religious practice, and so within this claim their only course of redress was to present and demonstrate their case that the religious significance of the Manor constituted exceptional 'special circumstances'.

The ECHR and Article 9 in British law?

To sum up this extended discussion of some of the cases dealt with by the European Court, the overwhelming preponderance of cases involving Jehovah's Witnesses and the Greek state show the obvious imbalance of power between the national Greek Orthodox Church and religious minority groups. The relations of inequality have been expressed and used to such an extent that although the Jehovah's Witnesses have managed to obtain the officially registered status as a 'known religion' (and so are given a measure of legal protection from state interference) they have still found it necessary to contest their needs and seek redress when issues of religious identity and practice have led to individuals and groups being imprisoned or punished.

At the level of the European Court, it is worth noting Richardson's (1995) argument that both this institution and the European parliament have been very much involved in processes of extending the powers of central European bodies into the political domains of individual nation states, and particularly into arenas of social (rather than overtly political) life. Obviously the European Court has played a particular role within the intergovernmental and international politics of the European Union and the wider Council of Europe, as well as trying to play the role of a political and legal broker between individuals and their particular governments. As such a supranational and supragovernmental institution the Court has had an ambiguous but very powerful role in defining normative rights discourses across a wide political area. In this context, therefore, it is not altogether surprising to find the clear reluctance on the part of the judges to deal in any systematic way with issues of religious belief, religious practice, and religious discrimination. The judges of the Court have been faced with a number of problems – not least in the thorny issue of defining (or not defining) what is meant by 'religion' within Article 9 – which rather than being clearly addressed have tended to be fudged or avoided in favour of more obvious legal matters which can be resolved more easily.

I think it is fair to say that for the British context at least, the incorporation of the ECHR into British laws will provide a new and alternative forum for such discussions which has the potential for allowing a different kind of debate on how and in what ways religious liberty is relevant to contemporary culture. It will become necessary for political and judicial decision-makers to find ways in which the operation of discourses on freedom, and particularly religious freedom, which have developed in British contexts, can be matched up with the careful deliberations on Article 9 by the European Court. The most radical shift in this regard that will be brought about with the implementation of the HRA is that there will for the first time be an explicit articulation in law of what has previously been a very vague (albeit well used) principle of religious freedom or tolerance.

Discourses of Religious Freedom in English Law

As noted already, within British legal discourses there has not been, until 1999, any obvious mechanism for dealing with issues of religious liberty, particularly for challenging a law on the basis that it restricts religious freedoms. Any protection of religious freedom has only come from *within* laws which are generally framed without any specific regard for religious needs.[29] In fact, within English law there has been no clearly articulated attitude towards the principle of freedom of religion. Unlike the US there is an established church (the Church of England, in the Anglican Communion), and there has been no formal mechanism such as the First Amendment to safeguard religious rights and liberties.

Historically, the Church of England had an hegemonic role within England once it was established under Henry VIII and Elizabeth I, and the most blatant exercise of the church's power was the string of repressive laws introduced by Charles II between 1661–1666 against the practice of any faith other than Anglicanism. These included the Corporation Act (1661), the Act of Uniformity (1662), the Conventicle Act (1664), and the Five Mile Act (1666), all of which were very restrictive against non-Anglicans, being aimed at the perceived threat of the Dissenters, Puritans, and to a lesser extent Roman Catholics (Hamilton 1995:5–6). Charles' successor James II repealed all these acts a few years later in 1689, and the Toleration Act of the same year allowed dissenters (but not Roman Catholics) 'to have their own places of worship' under certain (fairly liberal) conditions (Hamilton 1995:6). However, it was not until 1828 that Roman Catholics in England were admitted into the legal profession, and allowed schools and places of worship (Hamilton 1995:8).[30]

According to Bruce and Wright, there was a gradual process of numerous dissenting movements successively challenging the political and cultural hegemony of the Church of England, encouraging the state to have an attitude of religious toleration to those outside the established church as a 'product of slow accommodation to reality' (Bruce & Wright 1995:103–120). This was, however, never systematic. Of course, in more recent years the social and religious make up of British society has become increasingly plural – with a number of non-Christian religious communities and traditions formed by migration and/or conversion – and the commonly held view is that all bona fide religious groups are free to practise their religions.[31]

The main legal issue, however, that religious groups (of all types) have had to face in Britain is the fact that there have been no clear legal protection for religious practice and religious freedom – such as the US First Amendment – to which religious groups can turn. According to Hamilton, in Britain there is an emphasis on tolerance of religion (and so of the practice of non-mainstream religious groups) rather than on the more rigorous principle of religious freedom. This religious tolerance, therefore, is 'a leave granted by a religious majority to a religious minority to practise some or all of their religious practices' (Hamilton 1995:11).[32] That is, the majority viewpoint of the established Church of England (and to some extent in Scotland it has been the Church of Scotland) has remained a dominant discourse, particularly as the frame of reference for legal decisions concerning religion.

What this has meant in practice is that contestation of policy implementation or legislation by minority individuals or groups has tended not to occur within the courts at all. Where cases have been examined by judges they have been in terms of deciding whether or not a group should be accorded the status of 'a religion' (such as those examined in the previous chapter) or whether or not a 'religious' identity is the same as an 'ethnic' identity and thus within the remit of the *Race Relations Act* 1976 (also discussed in the previous chapter). Other exceptions have been those concerned with the blasphemy laws. Although the 'Gay News' case in 1979 (*Whitehouse v. Lemon*) showed that the old common law of blasphemy could be used as a means of preventing certain defamations of religious identities, the subsequent judicial examination of the accusations of blasphemy against Salman Rushdie following the publication of *The Satanic Verses* (*R. v. Chief Metropolitan Stipendiary Magistrate, ex parte Choudhury* in 1991) made it clear that such legal protections did not extend beyond those who identified themselves as Anglican Christians (Bradney 1993:82–103, Edwards 1993, Poulter 1991, Webster 1990).

Instead of issuing from courts, most decisions tend to have been bound up with other matters (particularly with the implementation of planning policy), and so have been made by *politicians* and *bureaucrats*, either at the level of national or local government. Thus, religious organisations have had to rely on making representations concerning issues of use of buildings for religious practice within the forum of bureaucratic procedures which are to some degree less transparent than judicial considerations, and which rarely make any explicit consideration of issues which could be called religious. It is possible for a group to make a legal challenge of such a governmental decision. For example, it is possible to appeal against a planning decision made by the Secretary of State for the Environment, as ISKCON did in 1991. However, although such an appeal is made at a senior judicial level – in the High Court – the procedure only allows the challenge to be made on the basis of re-examining the procedures by which a governmental decision has been reached. It does not allow any examination of the substantive issues of a case.

Within such a context, a case such as that over Bhaktivedanta Manor shows that a minority, non-Anglican, religious organisation can successfully contest the implementation of policy when it has what they consider a negative effect on their religious practice. But in this case, ISKCON did not achieve any success by arguing in terms of a 'right to religious freedom' in the courts, primarily because prior to the incorporation of the ECHR such an argument held no legal weight, and also because the only point at which they could make such an argument in a British court was when they defending themselves against a criminal prosecution (in 1995). Instead, it was necessary to make a more subtle case using strategies which were far more indirect than presenting an argument through their lawyers and barristers in court. Although at a rhetorical level they were relatively successful in arguing in the public domain that they had a justifiable case of 'religious freedom', the only legal mechanism that ISKCON could invoke was that of *special circumstances* which were of sufficient weight to set aside normal policy guidance.

What this success by ISKCON suggests, therefore, is that under such circumstances, a minority religious group needs to make a case that: (i) there is a clearly identifiable 'religious' element which is important enough as special circumstances (that is, it is a significant factor), (ii) this element is special enough to outweigh more 'pure' legal matters, and (iii) the religion involved is indeed a *religion* (that is, the group comes within a suitable acceptance or definition, and that the activity, manifestation or belief is itself 'religious'). As I argued in the previous chapter, the third of these elements is perhaps the most contentious and requires considerable rethinking in order to avoid the problem of judges, politicians, and bureaucrats making theologically political judgements about what and who should be accorded the status of 'religion'. If, as I suggest, the emphasis is shifted from religious identity to religious practice, then a consideration of whether or not the practice conforms with the 'civil standard' and is in some obvious way in line with a notion of 'public benefit' can be the means by which the application of 'special circumstances' could or should be made. However, in practice the application of such special circumstances by politicians for cases where they can determine a public benefit will be the product of striking a political balance between majoritarian and minoritarian power interests.

In terms of Bhaktivedanta Manor, the timing of the Conservative Secretary of State's decision in 1996 showed how significant the political pressures (at both the local and national level) were on the 'purely planning' decision that he made. As I mentioned in chapter six, just one week before this decision was released, local elections for Hertsmere council had put the Labour group in power in the local authority, taking control from the local Conservative party. With the arrival of a Labour run administration in Hertsmere, who had already publicly pledged to allow the access driveway and public worship at the Manor if they came to power, a rejection of ISKCON's application could make the Secretary of State a hostage to future measures made by Hertsmere council (who could even find some way of granting permission for another similar application). Therefore, John Gummer's decision was pre-empting any action that Labour in Hertsmere could make, and so was taking credit for a decision that was becoming inevitable.

At the time of the decision in May 1996, the national Conservative government were well aware that a General Election would be happening within the next twelve months, and that the election was very likely to be closely contested.[33] The issue of Bhaktivedanta Manor was not something that could easily be ignored by any political party – the Hindu population of Britain, numbering around 500,000, were strongly involved with the campaign to save public worship at the Manor. It would of course have been naive for anyone to expect these Hindus to vote en bloc for any particular party, or that they would vote on a single issue, but any decision made on the Manor would clearly have considerable significance for many Hindus in Britain. For John Gummer, a decision to allow permission for public worship at the Manor would probably gain support for the Conservative party – particularly in some of the key marginal seats – whilst a decision against the Manor could well have a negative impact. In this sense, there was little for the Secretary of State and the Conservative government to lose by deciding in favour of ISKCON. Thus it was fair to say that this politician's decision on the balancing of planning issues against special circumstances was very heavily determined by straightforward party politicking.

Regardless of whether contests are determined by judges, politicians, or bureaucrats, one of the primary discursive frameworks for judging claims made by minority religious organisations is Christianity, and particularly Anglican Christianity. This is not surprising, perhaps, but such political christocentrism does have its limitations, especially when principles of multiculturalism and multi-religiosity are put into practice. Such principles can work fairly well so long as there are no cases of open dispute between those who consider themselves part of the majoritarian establishment, and those who are defined as outside of this as minorities. What decision makers find themselves having to decide (implicitly or explicitly) is the degree to which different cultural and religious perspectives and expectations should be stretched (or even accommodated).

In his discussion of legal discourse and practice on religious liberty in the US, Stephen Feldman (1997) argues that such decisions are made by people with vested power interests and particular perspectives, and are often done quite unreflexively. As Feldman shows, the application of laws that are believed to be fair and tolerant of all religions are in fact decisions which come out of judges', politicians', and bureaucrats' interpretations of the law. All laws are framed within and for a particular cultural/social context, which is itself the product of power relations. Thus, Feldman shows that the operation of the US Supreme Court in its decisions on violations of the First Amendment have privileged claims made by Christian groups, despite proclaiming the principle of freedom of religion for all. He shows how minority groups, such as Jews, have been most successful when they have made appeals to the court which emulate Christians and Christian discourses on religious matters. For example, the case *of Lee v. Weisman* – decided by the Supreme Court in 1992 – judged in favour of the Jewish parent of a high school student whose graduation ceremony had included religious prayers. In this case the successful Weisman was able to argue that his daughter was subject to religious coercion, which the judges accepted since it struck a chord with their Christian assumptions about the nature of faith and religious conscience (Feldman 1997:242–44 & 249). However, the case of *Goldman v. Weinberger*[34] failed in 1986, when an Orthodox Jewish rabbi argued that the US Air Force's requirement for him to remove his yarmulke (skullcap) when on duty was a violation of his religious need to wear this head covering. The judgment of the Supreme Court that the wearing of the yarmulke was a matter of 'personal preference' blatantly ignored expert evidence telling them that within Orthodox Judaism the wearing of a yarmulke is a religious requirement, not a matter of personal taste (pp. 237 & 247). Feldman argues that the concept of a religious requirement to cover the head was difficult for the all-Christian justices to grasp, 'because it did not easily translate into Christian terms' (p. 281). Thus he concludes that Jews are most likely to succeed with appeals based on the First Amendment if they appear to 'fit comfortably within the normal (meaning Christian) structures of American society' (p. 281).

To make a successful challenge of discrimination or violation of religious liberty, therefore, minority religious groups are required to accommodate to the dominant political/cultural/religious discourse, or at least to translate into it. Attempts to deal with this situation range from 'basic' issues such as notions of deity (can Buddhism be a religion?), to expectations of sacred texts (identifying suitable texts such as the *Bhagavad Gita* for swearing oaths), through to questions of what is appropriate at a temple, or a theological college, or (as in the case of the Hare Krishnas) whether a drama is 'public entertainment' or an 'act of worship. The point to bear in mind is not so much whether there is a 'correct' answer to any of these issues, but rather that the 'correct' (or successful) answer is the one that most approximately (and appropriately) translates the minority religious practice as clearly and unambiguously as possible to a Christian model. Thus, in 1973 Bhaktivedanta Manor was given its planning determination because it was fairly easy to translate the Vaishnavite concept of a Math into the dominant Christian conceptualisation of a 'theological college', although to a large degree this translation began to unravel in the subsequent legal debates over what was and was not 'ancillary' to a place defined under planning laws as a theological college. The debate over public entertainment was more contentious. Initially there was reluctance by authorities such as Hertsmere council to make any such translation, although it gradually became acceptable to argue that a Krishna *lila* drama is 'like a nativity play' (or perhaps a medieval mystery play).

US Constitutional developments on the free exercise clause

It was noted at the beginning of this chapter that, historically, the apparatus for considering and protecting religious freedoms in the US has been quite different to the UK. The First Amendment[35] has long been regarded as a useful vehicle for the protection of religious groups that fall outside the mainstream, particularly through the 'free exercise clause'. The role of the judiciary (the Supreme Court) as arbiters and upholders of the Constitution has meant that it has been Supreme Court judges in the main who have made decisions on alleged violations of religious freedom in the US. In recent years this has begun to change, but on the whole the model does appear to be very different to that offered in Britain.

Although the First Amendment became part of the US Constitution in 1791, it is probably fair to say that the use of this framework as a piece of dynamic legislation for upholding the rights of non-Christian religious minorities did not emerge until the twentieth century. The arguments by politicians such as William Jefferson for the 'free exercise' of religion in the eighteenth century were directed at a liberalisation of Christian sectarianism (see Clayton n.d.), and so twentieth century Supreme Court judges have had to reinterpret for a very new context the minimalist words of the First Amendment clauses. The case of *Sherbert v. Verner*[36] in 1963 marked a significant focus of use by the Supreme Court of the free exercise clause of the First Amendment, in a case relating to a woman (Sherbert) who as a Seventh-day Adventist had refused to work on a Saturday, and then was subsequently refused state unemployment benefit because she had refused to accept suitable work 'without good cause' (Feldman 1997:235). The Supreme Court ruled that this refusal of benefit was a violation of her rights under the free exercise clause, and in doing so the judges set out what became known as the 'balancing test', which was for nearly thirty years to be the means by which cases of religious discrimination would be considered. Under this formula, it would be necessary first for the plaintiff in the case to demonstrate that a state law restricted her religious practice, and then the burden of proof shifted to the government to show a 'compelling state interest which justified the substantial infringement of the appellant's First Amendment's rights' (*Sherbet v. Verner*, quoted in Breyer 1993:369).

Thus, in a number of cases, particularly in the 1970s and 1980s, the Supreme Court made their adjudications on this basis: on the principle of balancing between protecting against restrictions placed on individuals' religious practices and the compelling interests of state and federal government to implement laws which created such restrictions. It is particularly noteworthy that the Supreme Court judges felt that it was appropriate that it was their role to interpret the free exercise clause of the First Amendment to adjudicate such decisions. In many respects, this balancing test could be likened to the ways in which courts (particularly the European Court) have attempted to balance the free exercise/manifestation clause of Article 9(1) of the ECHR against the restrictions of Article 9(2). Thus, individuals' and groups' rights to religious freedom should only be restricted when authorities have a compelling interest which is 'necessary in a democratic society'.

In 1990 the Supreme Court was led into a significantly different approach by Justice Anthony Scalia, a conservative who had recently been appointed by President Ronald Reagan. In the case of *Oregon v. Smith*,[37] two members of the Native American Church were dismissed from their jobs for taking the narcotic substance peyote in the context of practising their religion. As with *Sherbet*, their dismissal made them ineligible for state unemployment benefit, although in this case the refusal was related to the fact that the dismissal was drugs related. Smith's appeal on the basis of the free exercise clause was dismissed by a majority (but not unanimous) decision, which upheld the Oregon state criminal law prohibiting the use of peyote even for religious purposes as *not* violating the First Amendment. More significantly, however, the judges overturned the general principle of compelling interest and the balancing test, and proposed in its place the 'strict neutrality test'. Thus, Scalia and the other majority judges argued that rather than balancing the interest of the state against the restrictions that the law imposes, the function of the Court should be to examine the particular law in question to determine whether or not the law in itself is 'generally applicable' and does not *intentionally* restrict the religious freedoms of minorities.[38] That is, according to this formula, the Supreme Court should only find a violation of the free exercise clause if a particular piece of legislation has been created with the intentional purpose of restricting a particular individual's, group's, or groups' religious liberties – if the restriction is a side-effect of an otherwise neutral law, then the court should not find any violation. As Chloe Breyer argues, this decision thus 'lends power to the legislature over the courts in deciding how much religious liberty is acceptable' (Breyer 1993:370).[39]

Fairly soon after this landmark ruling, a successful appeal to the Supreme Court appeared to go against this: in the *Church of Lukimi Babalu Aye v. City of Hialeah*[40] in 1993 the court overturned a law which has been issued by the city council of Hialeah in Florida which had made the ritual slaughter of animals a criminal offence. In a rather contradictory way, the court upheld the compelling interest test, but only insofar as it conflicted with the question of strict neutrality, with the verdict being that the city council's action had contravened such neutrality (Feldman 1997: 360fn.84). Thus the law in question had been intentionally framed to target a particular religious group, that is the African American followers of Santeria who are the main and most obvious practitioners of such ritual animal slaughter. Thus, according to Warburg, 'had the decree been phrased differently, it might well have been upheld because the majority of judges restated the "neutrality" principle' which had been established in *Smith* (Warburg 1998:266). This case, therefore, primarily served to affirm the position that in this respect it was the role of the Supreme Court to scrutinise the *intentionality* of legislation towards the free exercise of religious groups, but it was the role of legislators, and therefore politicians to be primarily concerned with ensuring that the legislation that they pass does not intentionally discriminate.

The Smith judgement prompted a political response led by the Catholic Senator Ted Kennedy and the conservative Mormon Senator Orrin Hatch, who together managed to pass the *Religious Freedom Restoration Act of 1993* through the US Senate, to be signed into law by President Bill Clinton in November 1993. This law proclaimed 'by statute that the State has the burden to prove its "compelling interest" and lack of alternatives before it can interfere with the practice of religion' (Introvigne 1998:282). In doing so, the purpose of the law was to restore the situation back to that which had prevailed before the *Smith* judgement in 1990.[41] However, in June 1997, a case which challenged the *Religious Freedom Restoration Act*[42] was heard by the Supreme Court, who ruled that the Act was unconstitutional and so struck it down (Introvigne 1998:283). In so doing, it was established that the *Smith* formula should prevail, and thus, in effect, gave little scope for the Supreme Court to give any substantial consideration of claims of violations of religious freedom, unless there was a clear intentionality on the part of legislators to restrict such freedoms without a compelling interest. Thus, the 'Court will not attempt to enforce any particular principle of religious freedom and instead will defer to the legislative decision, so long as it is not infected by discriminatory intent' (Feldman 1997:248). It is quite likely that this will remain the case until a new generation of judges replaces those who have maintained this position.

Locations of power within the decisions of rights discourses

The US constitutional settlement gives to the Supreme Court the ultimate power to decide on issues of the constitution, for example on how the free exercise clause of the First Amendment should be interpreted. The decision on *Smith* has in no way changed this situation, but what it has done is to delegate to legislators a large part of the responsibility for making decisions relevant to minority religious groups. It is interesting that the balance of decision-making appears to be going in an alternative direction, following the incorporation of the ECHR into British laws. That is, the ECHR will provide a legal framework through which challenges to state power (and legislation) can be made, and thus in courts rather than to politicians.

It can be argued that, in a democratic society, the most effective place for decisions on basic human rights should be made by elected politicians, rather than the judiciary. Thus, according to Andrew Marr, editor of the London based *Independent* newspaper, 'Human rights are not, unfortunately, for the courts but for the political arena ... The main stage for adjusting the balance between state and the individual has to be democratic politics.'[43] Similarly, the Supreme Court commented in the *Smith* case that the 'political process' was the most appropriate place for such considerations (Feldman 1997:238). One of the strengths (or weaknesses) of the ECHR is that it provides a framework in which discourses on rights to freedom of religion are located squarely within the context of the needs of a democracy.

But in doing so it places the religious minority in the hands of the majority (as indeed is the case with all minority groups within a democracy).

Although Feldman does not himself make such a point, one could argue that in many cases it is likely that politicians will be more sensitive than judges to the needs (and demands) of religious minorities, particularly minority groups which are substantial enough to have some political representation. This notwithstanding, the US judges in the *Smith* case did warn that: 'It may fairly be said that leaving accommodation to the political process will place at a relative disadvantage those religious practices that are not widely engaged in; but that [is an] unavoidable consequence of democratic government' (quoted in Feldman 1997:248).

ISKCON's experiences in 1995–96 may also suggest that politicians are better disposed to be accommodating to religious minorities than judges. It was in the court (Luton Crown Court) in November 1995 that ISKCON were severely fined for the criminal act of breaching the enforcement notice, and the judge in the case made quite clear his lack of sympathy with ISKCON's arguments (see chapter four). It was only a few months later, in May 1996, that the Secretary of State made the political decision to give ISKCON exactly what they wanted. The contrast between these two decisions is shown most extremely by the judge's prediction that the Secretary of State would *not* grant planning permission for the temple. Having failed at the European Commission on Human Rights, and then having faced this particular judge, I am sure ISKCON were very relieved that the fate of their temple was ultimately left for politicians to decide, even though they were fortuitous that the chance of political circumstances made it possible for national politicians to reach a decision that was favourable to them.

In many respects it is probably best not to valorise the judiciary too much in anticipation of the implementation of the *Human Rights Act 1998*. The Act will indeed open up a new area of legal discourses, and make available a far more accessible path for minority groups to challenge what they may consider to be heavy handedness and restriction by the hegemonic state and other public authorities. By having access through the British courts to the ECHR, there will be a substantially new arena for decisions to be made which affect the lives of large numbers of people who are defined as minorities by those who align themselves to the majority cultural values of the state and the establishment. But what needs to be remembered, is that the judiciary are themselves as much part of this establishment as politicians and civil servants. In fact, as perhaps the ISKCON court case showed, the judiciary tend to be more conservative in dealing with minority and alternative religious and cultural groups. For example, Werner Menski's discussion of the use of the *Race Relations Act 1976* shows clearly that the judges have produced a very patchy record on determining issues of cultural, ethnic, or religious identity, and there is no reason to expect that this will change overnight following the implementation of the HRA

(Menski 2000). Judges are not so subject to public opinion, even though they may unwittingly reproduce it, and they are also part of the political class who seek to shape and control public attitudes and behaviour. It could possibly be said that juries are more in line with majoritarian perspectives, but juries are usually strongly led by judges, and ultimately, case law is determined by senior judges and not juries. Politicians act on what they consider to be public opinion, whilst judges interpret and implement the law.

Ironically, as things are at present, another form of power can be mobilised for some minority groups through politicians. This is direct lobbying, if and when the minority group is a *significant* minority or, in other words, if it has demographic and political clout. A lobbying campaign that mobilises such minority group power can be *more* effective than a legal challenge – since a legal processes is very much constrained by court procedures and protocol. Even a successful court case will usually take a considerable amount of time and money, and will constantly run the risk of being defeated on appeal right up to its adjudication in the House of Lords.

As I discussed in chapter five, ISKCON became aware of the significance of such an approach only when their main legal campaigns had run to a standstill. They already had the support of a large section of people from Hindu backgrounds. The success of their campaign was dependent to a large part on their ability to mobilise the power that such a constituency of interest could have through lobbying establishment figures, politicians, and particularly the government. The campaign was successful, therefore, as a *collective* pressure strategy, and the success of this strategy can be compared with their failure to have their legal claim on the basis of the ECHR even considered by the European Court in Strasbourg. Thus providing a legal strategy for implementing rights discourses through court procedures under the HRA does not necessarily mean that this is the most effective means by which minority groups and people can achieve what they want.

Even so, the *idea* or rhetoric of a 'right to religious freedom' is in itself a powerful lobbying discourse which can be incorporated into a collective pressure strategy. The rhetoric of law spills over into the rhetoric of politics: politicians try to be seen as acting in accordance with the expressed normative cultural values which are enshrined in the laws of the land. Thus to have a 'Bill of Rights' – as the *Human Rights Act 1998* has been described – which make express discursive provision for freedom of religious practice is a useful strategic resource for any group that is attempting to make its case in an overtly political domain. What is more, such discourses may be even more effectively put to use by combining a campaign of collective action with a legal challenge through the courts on the basis of the ECHR.

Within such structures and strategies of majority-minority power relations, it is worth asking the reflexive question of where does 'freedom' actually come into all of this. The ECHR makes 'freedom of religion' axiomatic (within limits), but it is much harder to actually how these discourses or political possibilities actually translate into freedom for any of the religious organisations or people who mobilise such an idea. What is being said when it is claimed that worshipping at the *mandir* of one's choice is an expression of one's freedom of religion?

Once the argument is mobilised into the overtly political and legal sphere, such a claim by ISKCON devotees, other Hindus, or any of religious minority group is a mean of proposing a challenge to the existing balance of state power. A *claim* to religious freedom makes an accusation against a local government, or some other authority, that freedom is being denied and, thus, some means of redress needs to be found. Such a claim, however, is a 'higher level' discourse, inasmuch is it primarily articulated in this way by lawyers and lobbyists, rather than by the people who they have positioned themselves as representing. And, by locating this challenge within particular court procedures (as they are being set up through the HRA), the claim to freedom also links in with a mechanism by which the particularities of the power imbalance between majority and minority can be challenged, if not necessarily changed.

The discourse of freedom also can be used as means of protection for minority groups and individuals. Thus, although the claim for freedom might not resolve an imbalance of power, it can sometimes help to prevent that balance becoming unbearable or repressive. The Greek case of *Tsirlis and Kouloumpas* which I discussed above, shows this most clearly: the rights discourse of freedom did not help prevent these two Jehovah's Witnesses from being sent to prison, and nor indeed did it help them receive any compensation from the European Court, who refused to consider the application of Article 9 of the ECHR to their case. But the rhetoric of religious freedom gave the men some means of expressing their challenge to the injustice which they had suffered, and the presence of Article 9 made it easier for them to take their case to the European Court to be considered.

Closer to home, the discourse of freedom gives some measure of protection for minority religious groups to challenge public discourses, particularly for those who are labelled as 'dangerous cults'. By asking for 'religious freedom' (either through the courts, or through public media such as televisions and newspapers) minority religious groups can attempt to open up public discourses and redefine the negative images which they feel are unfairly put on them. In a country where religious freedom is enshrined in key legal documents, such as the ECHR, then it can be argued it is inappropriate to categorise some religious organisations in terms of the bizarreness of their religious practices. However, such a use of rights discourses can be a double edged weapon – a subtle use of the brainwashing debate can be used to accuse minority groups of taking away their own followers' fundamental rights and freedoms, particularly the right to liberty itself (or protection against unlawful imprisonment). But the argument by minority groups to have protection through a religious freedom discourse is, of course, dependent on the underlying discourses on definitions of religion. If a group is defined out of the rights discourse, as a non-religion (such as in the House of Lords debate on the Moonies discussed in the previous chapter), then such a 'right' is of no use at all and there are no appreciable freedoms to be won or fought for.

Thus, the discourse of freedom of religion is a means by which groups and people who are defined as disempowered within state structures can attempt to challenge or manifest what power they have. It may not necessarily be the most effective means of achieving a particular set of objectives, and it is not at all likely that use of a rights discourse will in any appreciable way alter the balance of power within a particular context. A dependence on judicial processes to administer and adjudicate on such a challenge may possibly make a more articulate statement of discontent and provide a neatly bounded field for pursuing redress. But the mobilisation of power can be achieved as effectively sometimes through more overtly political processes.

Even after *Smith*, it will still be possible to use the US Supreme Court structures to make a case of violation of the free exercise clause. But the current interpretation of the practice of this clause will mean such an appeal is very unlikely to be considered in depth, unless it can be shown that there was intent behind a particular law to cause such a violation. In the case of Britain, however, the introduction of a new judicial framework will mean that, until case law is established, the field will be open for litigants to explore quite how the balancing of articles 9(1) and 9(2) should be interpreted. The case law of the European Court to date has, of course, established a fairly conservative set of precedents, but it is also likely that litigants (and their barristers) will try to encourage judges to bring new interpretations to how a multicultural society should resolve the paradox of encouraging free manifestation of religious practice whilst also limiting such practices by the needs of democratic society.[44] Thus, it is interesting to note that the Labour government, in proposing the Human Rights Bill, described the Convention as a 'living instrument' which needs to be 'interpreted ... in the light of present day conditions and therefore reflects changing social attitudes and the changes in the circumstances of society' (RBH:para.2.5). What remains, perhaps, to be seen is the extent to which the judiciary wish to respond to such a challenge. To a large extent, perhaps, this will depend on whether judges decide (implicitly or explicitly) that their role is to uphold the needs of the majority against the needs of religious minorities, and how much value should be placed on using the discourses of religious freedom (particularly for minorities) as a safeguard against the 'demands of the general interest of the community' (ibid.)?

In this respect, the terms of the ECHR, when incorporated into British laws, will only be as good as the people (particularly the judges) who interpret particular cases. The terms of reference used for deciding what is a 'religion' will on the main be informed by Christian perspectives, and aggrieved parties will most likely be successful in demonstrating violations of the Convention if they frame their grievances in terms which can be understood by the judges as part of religious discourses. Thus, although the establishment of Article 9 does for the first time provide a written constitutional protection for religious groups in Britain, it does not necessarily alter the balance of religious interest and religious discourse within British cultures – the Anglican hegemony is still not challenged.

Notes

1 Alongside devolution of power to national authorities in Scotland and Wales, as well as a developing review of the shape and the electoral basis of the Westminster (London) houses of parliament.

2 See Home Office, *Rights Brought Home: The Human Rights Bill*, UK Government White Paper, (HMSO London, 24th October 1997); also available from the Home Office Internet Site (http://www.official-documents.co.uk/document/hoffice/rights/rights.htm).

3 *Human Rights Act 1998 Chapter 42*. The Stationery Office; also available from the HMSO internet site (http://www.hmso.gov.uk/acts/acts1998/19980042.htm). For discussion of the Act see Wadham and Mountfield (1999) and Betten (1999).

4 Full incorporation of the ECHR through the HRA was effected in Scotland in July 1999 with the institution of the devolved Scottish Parliament. In other parts of the UK – i.e. England, Wales, and Northern Ireland – the HRA did not come into effect until 2nd October 2000.

5 For a discussion of the history and workings of the Commission and Court of Human Rights, see Richardson (1995:39–59). In 1998, under Protocol 11 of the Convention, the European Court and the European Commission were merged into a new European Court, which will hopefully prove to be more efficient than its predecessor.

6 Case of Manoussakis and Others v. Greece, Judgment of European Court of Human Rights, 26th September 1996, (59/1995/565/651), para 44.

7 See Evans (1997:282–86,332–35); Hamilton (1995:26–30); Richardson (1995:47–49), and below.

8 Third Reading of the Human Rights Bill, House of Lords, 5th February 1998. Reported in *Hansard*, column 752–53 (available at <http://www.parliament.the-stationery-office.co.uk/pa/ld/ldhome.htm>).

9 For a detailed recent discussion of the operation of Article 9 in the European Court see Evans (1997:281–341). Most of the cases that he discusses relate to decisions made at the level of the Commission, since until the mid 1990s very few cases had made their way through to the Court.

10 For example, the Brussels based group Human Rights without Frontiers (Droits de l'Homme sans Frontieres) published a special issue of their bimonthly magazine in 1994 on 'Greece: religious intolerance and discrimination', highlighting contemporary Greek legislation which they considered to be in

violation of religious minorities' rights to religious freedom (Human Rights without Frontiers 1994).

11 This is not to say that there have been no cases brought before the European Court on the basis of Article 9 from other countries. See, for example, Kalac v. Turkey (61/1996/680/870, 1st July 1997) and Wingrove v. the UK (19/1995/525/611, 25th Nov 1996), and the summary discussion of cases in Evans (1997:281–341).

12 Case of Kokkinakis v. Greece, Judgment of European Court of Human Rights, 25th May 1993, (Ser.A, no.260-A, 1993), discussed in Evans (1997:282–284 & 331–35); see also Edge (1995), Hamilton (1995), and Richardson (1995).

13 Section 4 of Greek 4 no. 1368/1938 defines proselytism as 'any direct or indirect attempt to intrude on the religion or beliefs of a person of a different religious persuasion, with the aim of undermining those beliefs, either by any kind of inducement or promise of an inducement or moral support or material assistance, or by fraudulent means or by taking advantage of his inexperience, trust, need, low intellect or naivety.' (Quoted in Evans 1997:333). In principle this law does not cover the conversion of another by what could be considered 'rational discourse', but as there have many convictions under this law it looks quite evident that it is used in a rather heavy handed way. For example, Kokkinakis himself had been arrested more than sixty times in fifty years for proselytism (p. 282.), and in general between 1975 and 1992 there were 4,400 Jehovah's Witnesses arrested for proselytism, with 1,233 committed for trial, and 208 convicted (Richardson 1995:48).

14 Case of Larissis and Others v. Greece, Judgment of European Court of Human Rights, 24th February 1998, (140/1996/759/958–960).

15 *Larissis v. Greece*, paras.52–55.

16 Ibid., para.59.

17 Ibid., Concuring opinion of Judge de Meyer.

18 'No one shall be held guilty of any criminal offence on account of any act or omission which did not constitute a criminal offence under national or international law at the time when it was committed ...' (quoted in *Larissis*, para.32).

19 Ibid., Partly dissenting opinion of Judge Repik.

20 Case of Valsalmis v. Greece, Judgment of European Court of Human Rights, 18th December 1996, (74/1995/580/666).

21 Case of Efstratiou v. Greece, Judgment of European Court of Human Rights, 18th December 1996, (77/1996/696/888).

22 *Valsalmis v. Greece*, para.31; *Efstratiou v. Greece*, para.32. (The wording of the two judgments is almost identical.)

23 Ibidem, Joint dissenting opinion of Judges Thór Vilhájlmsson and Jambrek (Valsalmis *and* Efstratiou cases).

24 Case of Tsirlis and Kouloumpas v. Greece, Judgment of European Court of Human Rights, 29th May 1997, (54/1996/673/859–860).

25 Case of Manoussakis and Others v. Greece, Judgment of European Court of Human Rights, 26th September 1996, (59/19995/565/651).

26 Royal Decree of 20th May/2nd June 1939, also relevant is Section 1 of Law no. 1363/1938 (as amended by Law non. 1672/1939) which sets out the duties of the Ministry of Education and Religious Affairs to grant authorisation, the penalties for operating a place without such authorisation, and also the definition of a temple as 'any type of building open to the public for the purpose of divine worship'. Quoted in *Manoussakis v. Greece* judgment, paras. 21–23.

27 Ibid., Concurring Opinion of Judge Martens, para. 2; emphasis in original.

28 Ibid., Concurring Opinion of Judge Martens, paras.5, 6, & 8; emphasis in original.
29 This is not to say that a law cannot be changed on the basis that it conflicts with the free exercise of a person's religion. For example, *The Motor-Cycle Crash-Helmets (Religious Exemption) Act of 1976* allowed male Sikhs to be exempt from the legal requirement to wear a crash-helmet when riding a motor cycle, on the grounds that a helmet could not be worn if the Sikh was carrying out his religious duty to wear a turban over his hair, see Bradney (1993:5). But such exemptions are granted in an ad hoc manner, with some groups such as Sikhs succeeding in gaining exemptions whilst others such as Rastafarians being less successful. It has indeed been argued that rather than granting religious freedom on an equitable basis, this state of affairs is quite unfair and divisive since it privileges certain religious groups over others, see Menski (2000).
30 Even so, the Roman Catholic Relief Act of 1829 which opened up these concessions sought the 'suppression and final prohibition of Jesuits' and Roman Catholic religious orders (Bradney 1993:6).
31 As Wilson (1990a:71) puts it, 'the English law courts, today, regularly affirm that the law does not discriminate among religions, but deals with each impartially'. Wilson himself goes on to show that this is not strictly the case.
32 Bruce & Wright (1995), writing from a rather different perspective, make a similar distinction between religious toleration and religious freedom, likewise describing the situation in Britain as one of religious tolerance.
33 In retrospect, of course, this was far from the case, since the Conservatives were defeated heavily in May 1997. But it was certainly clear to the Conservative leadership that if they were to have any chance of remaining in power against the odds – as indeed that had succeeded in doing in the general election of 1992 – then they would have to make sure every available vote was won for them, and none lost.
34 Goldman v. Weinberger, 475 US 503, 507–10 (1986).
35 'Congress shall make no law respecting the establishment of religion or prohibiting the free exercise thereof', quoted in Hamilton (1995:10)
36 Sherbert v. Werner, 374 US 398 (1963).
37 Employment Division of Oregon Department of Human Resources v. Smith, 494 US 872, 877–879 (1990).
38 See Breyer (1993:370), Feldman (1997:238), Introvigne (1998:264), and Warburg (1998:265).
39 Although not directly relevant to the argument that I am presenting here, it should also be noted that the decision on *Smith* was also very much based on the assumption that legal considerations of religion could be based on a distinction between religious faith or belief and religious practice. A landmark case of *Reynolds v. United States* in 1879 (98 US 145 [1879]) had established that the First Amendment upheld the freedom of individuals to believe in anything they liked, but this freedom did not extend to action, their religious practice was subject to the laws of the country. Thus, in the *Reynolds* case the Supreme Court ruled that 'Mormons were free to believe that polygamy was superior to monogamy but not to practise it' (Introvigne 1998:281). Likewise, the consideration of *Smith* over a century later was based on the fact that there was no reason for governments to concern themselves with *beliefs* in the importance of peyote as a substance with religiously significant properties, but governments did have the right to restrict the actual practice of taking this substance, which as a hallucinogenic drug was criminalised. In using such a belief/practice dichotomy the Supreme Court is reproducing a particular

christocentric definition of religion which I critiqued in the previous chapter, and in doing so they are privileging religious groups who easily conform to it, and potentially excluding those where belief and practice are not so readily distinguished (see Feldman 1997:248–49).

40 Church of Lukimi Babalu Aye v. City of Hialeah, 113 StCt 2217 (1993).

41 It is probably also useful to bear in mind Feldman's critique of the general operation of Supreme Court decisions, even during the period between *Sherbet* and *Smith*. That is, even though the formula for deciding cases was based on the principle of compelling interest, the actual interpretation of this balance by the judges was very often christocentric. Thus 'regardless of the level of judicial scrutiny, between 1972 ... and 1990 ..., the Court held that a governmental action contravened the free exercise clause in only three cases. And each of those cases closely resembled *Sherbet*: the free exercise claims were brought by Christians (belonging either to a minority sect or to no sect at all) who had been denied unemployment benefits' (Feldman 1997:237). The case cited above, of *Goldman v. Weinberger* was considered on the basis that the US Air Force did have a compelling interest to prevent a Jewish officer to remove his yarmulke.

42 City of Boerne v. P.F. Floeres, Archbishop of San Antonio, and United States, (1997).

43 Editorial, *Independent*, (London, Saturday 25th October 1997), p. 20.

44 Interestingly, the introduction of the HRA will also encourage a change in the ways in which much litigation is argued in British courts. Thus 'because the Convention must be given effect wherever possible, and because Strasbourg case law must be taken into account, the Strasbourg method of judicial reasoning will gradually enter English legal practice. This involves an explicit balancing of the rights of individuals against the rights and freedoms of others and the general public interest. Judges and legal representatives will have to begin to structure their arguments in the systematic way that this is done in Strasbourg, namely to identify the broad prima facie right which may have been infringed, and then to consider limitations to it' (Wadham and Mountfield 1999:30).

CHAPTER NINE

Religion and the Politics of Multiculturalism

The political discourses over the campaign for Bhaktivedanta Manor can be located within a triangulation of three separate but related perspectives that together shape a large part of minority religious practice in contemporary Britain. These three discourses are that Britain (particularly England) is a nation-state with a *secularised* society, which is *multicultural*, and yet still has an *established* (Anglican) church.

That is, in crude graphic terms, the relationships can be understood as:

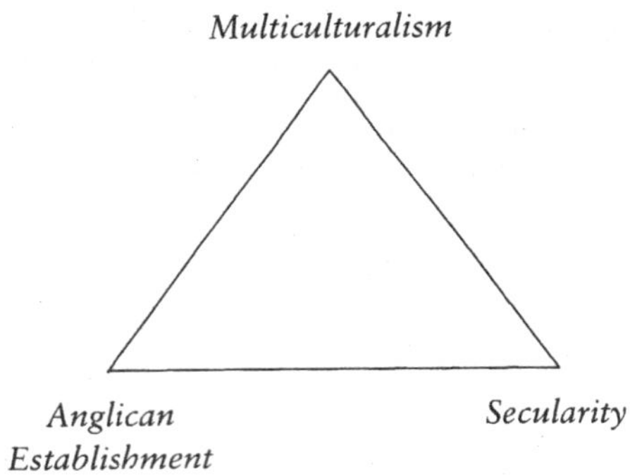

Within this triangulation, all political and cultural discourses on religious (and other forms of) plurality fall somewhere within grey areas of uncertainty. Indeed, because each point of this framework is in some ways at odds with the others, discourses on placing non-Anglican religious manifestations can often produce substantial and significant conflicts. The most obvious example of this is the case of the Rushdie conflict, when the discourse on multiculturalism (and tolerance) was very much at odds with a viewpoint that assumed a liberal Anglicanism as a norm both as a social ethic and as a legal basis for dealing with the issue of blasphemy.

I do not wish to suggest this is the only framework for mapping out some of the contours of the relationships between ideas and discourses of multiculturalism and religion. Gerd Baumann has very effectively helped to deconstruct some of the key assumptions of what he calls the 'multicultural riddle', in which there is a need to resolve the conflicting aims of national, ethnic, and religious identities (G. Baumann 1999). I would suggest that his triangulation easily maps onto my own, perhaps creating a three (or more) dimensional frame that shows some of the intense complexity of these issues, at both the theoretical and empirical levels.[1] The nation-state and issues of ethnic identity are very much bound up with discursive constructions of both Anglican establishment and secularity in British cultural contexts. British, and particularly English nationhood is located somewhere within the paradox of religious identities that are latent rather than manifest, and that are generally intolerant of explicit manifestation – to a degree summed up by Grace Davie's concept of 'believing without belonging' (Davie 1994).

In this chapter my intention is examine how, in theory and practice, the three conflicting discourses of secularity, establishment, and multiculturalism are separately framed and yet operate in a certain set of political fields in contemporary Britain. In doing so, these discourses not only shape the experiences of people living within minority cultural and religious groups – they also help to create and construct the identities of such individuals, and work to create and reinforce certain organisational structures. Thus, to a large degree, the presence and organisation of a *Hindu* community/population in Britain (on whose behalf, of course, the Bhaktivedanta Manor campaign was fought and won) is very much a product of multicultural politics in a secularised nation-state with an Anglican establishment.[2]

The Politics of Secularisation and Secularity

According to Peter van der Veer: 'In discourses about modern society from the Englightenment onwards one finds a strong concern with the neutrality of the state in relation to religious belief and organization' (van der Veer 1998:281).

Besides the seeming paradox of an established church operating at the heart of the English political establishment, there is a common assumption, and indeed expectation, that religion in Britain is on the 'decline' and has been for a long time. Academic sociologists of religion have also (for almost as long) been debating the evidence for and against this perspective, trying to find a conclusive ending to the long running (almost interminable) secularisation debate. The leading founders of this debate, such as Bryan Wilson (1966, 1982) and David Martin (1978) have even managed to produce and perpetuate a new generation of the antagonisms, so that where once student essays were set on comparing Wilson's and Martin's arguments, in the 1990s the contrast is between Steve Bruce (1996) and

Grace Davie (1994) – their respective students. As Gerd Baumann pithily observes: 'three decades of sociological and historical research have amassed a vast body of evidence, much of it statistical, concerned with rates of church attendance, the seating capacity of parish halls, and similar indicators of what is called "religious adherence". Precisely what these data can prove is still a matter of fundamental disagreement' (G. Baumann 1998:264).

I do not wish to enter too far into the murky depths of such a tedious debate, which is driven so much by the politics of academic sociology, as well as ideological assumptions about the place of 'religion' (usually meaning formal Christianity) in contemporary British cultures. Instead, the point I would like to raise follows on from van der Veer's comment, that is how much could it be argued that the academic discourse (and counter discourse) on secularisation is a *political strategy*.[3] It is worth asking in whose political interests is it to conceptualise contemporary British (and other western) cultures as secularised? The theory of secularisation certainly fits in well with the laissez faire liberal perspectives of Anglican establishment, which governs through allowing a semblance of consent, and still benefits largely from having a nation in which few people are actively 'religious' but the majority still identify themselves as 'Anglican' (and hence, to a certain degree still belong *as well* as believe). I would suggest, therefore, that sociologists consider the possibility that the keenly contested secularisation debate has been a product (as well as an agent) of a subtle political strategy in which the decline of religion, or the shift of religiosity from the 'public' to the 'private' sphere has been a means by which a nation-state such as Britain has constructed particular political identities and unities.

Thus, van der Veer continues in his paper to remark: 'One of the crucial issues facing the modern nation-state is how to deal with group differences. Historically, religion has been the most important foundation of group difference' (van der Veer 1998:281). Pursuing this line of argument, it appears that one of the means by which such religious identities can be (and often are) neutralised is by their dissolution, or at least by shifting their focus from the public (overtly political) sphere to the realm of private, internal belief. Indeed Asad (1993b) argues that it was this *public* political contestation of Islam by British Muslims that prompted such a backlash from the liberal British establishment. The theory of secularisation as a political strategy provides a rationale for assuming and creating national conformity: where once it was minority religious groups that posed the greatest challenge to national harmony, the shifting of all religious identities to the realm of 'private choice' neutralises such challenges, as well as fitting in very well with a theory of liberal economic capitalist values.

Gerd Baumann's largely rhetorical question 'Is there, perhaps, a secret systemic link between the largely successful project of creating "nation"-

states and the largely unsuccessful project of secularization?' (1998:265) can, therefore, be answered with a tentative 'yes'. Whether or not there has been (or is) a process of secularisation (instituted at a state or popular level), or whether any particular governments have been pro-actively secularist, there is certainly a case to argue that an ideology of secularity is in the interest of most contemporary nation-states.

If one can imagine secularity as somewhere between the *ideology* of secularism and the *theory* of secularisation, and thus as a political discursive practice, then the assumption of secularity as a basis of British cultural life allows for the practice of religiosity (in majoritarian and minoritarian forms). This is so long as such practice *appears* to operate outside of the public domain, and there is no substantial questioning of the political centrality of Anglican Christianity as both a foundational factor of English identity, and also as a strong element within the political apparatus of the state. That is, the secularisation argued by most sociologist allows for the anomaly of a 'secularised society' with an established church – and the political discourses which perpetuate this anomaly could be labelled (for want of a better term) as secularity.

The political and academic debates that have been focused around the issue of 'secularism' in India illustrate this approach very well. The Indian state has had a policy of secularism since its foundation. This has been intended to promote a fair treatment of all religious minorities in India, with the central state authorities taking a neutral attitude towards all religious communities. In practice, the legal structures within India for different religious groups are very complex, with separate laws in some cases for Hindus and Muslims. Within this social, legal, and cultural pluralism, however, there has been an ongoing problem of inter-community tensions and violence which has gone by the name of communalism. The most obvious and dramatic example of Hindu-Muslim communalism was the destruction of the Babri Masjid in Ayodhya in December 1992, and the riots and murders that immediately followed this action. The secularist policy of the Indian government is intended to provide a neutral state response to such communalistic conflict so that no cultural/religious community or faction is favoured over any others.

In practice, however, the operation of the Indian polity has not been so ideologically simple as this policy would suggest. Writers such as Madan (1987) and Nandy (1985, 1998) have argued that secularism has been a means by which the Hindu majority have established their agenda without resorting to explicit Hindu nationalism. In fact, the secularist policy of distancing religious identities from political discourses have favoured the Hindu ruling group (particularly the Congress party) who, although they define themselves as secularists, still operate very much within a Hindu nationalist worldview. Indeed, as Chatterjee (1998) argues, the discourses of secularism have not been seriously challenged by the right-wing Hindu nationalist Bhartiya Janata Party (BJP). Instead they have critiqued the 'pseduo-secularism' of the dominant Congress administrations which, by instituting separate laws and codes for different religious communities, have failed to live up to the fair ideals of secularism of treating all groups on an equal measure. In this sense, therefore, for Chatterjee the ideology of secularism in India is not necessarily at odds with extreme Hindu (majoritarian) chauvinism, even though Hindu political activists are making a lot of capital out of critiquing the practice of secularism.

The political structures and discourses of contemporary India are, of course, very different from Britain. In particular, the rise of a specific form of religious nationalism (Hindu) is far more reactionary and explicitly religious than any comparable forms of English nationalism that have emerged in recent decades. However, I would argue that the ideology of secularism in India is not altogether different from the practice of secularity in Britain. There is an important difference in Britain that its central government is tied politically to an established (Anglican) church, whilst the ideology of secularism in India is that there should be no religious establishment at the centre of government. But still, in both cases of majoritarian political responses to cultural pluralism (whether it is seen as multiculturalism or communalism) has been based on attempts to remove religious identities from public political discourses. And in both cases the promotion of secularity has been a means by which a certain form of cultural and religious hegemony has been sustained, at the expense of minority religiously-identified political groups. That is, a discursive lack of tolerance of religion can often be a means of creating and sustaining a particular religious hegemony within a nation-state, whether there is a political distinction (or 'wall of separation') between religious and state organisation or there is an established church which appears to be secularised.

The Politics of Establishment

It is perhaps confusing to talk of the English establishment, since the term refers to two quite distinct (but related) perspectives. On the one hand, the Establishment are the ruling class of the nation-state. They are the people who exert most control over political and cultural life in Britain and dominate institutions of power such as the civil service, the judiciary and legal professions, and (to a certain extent) dominate party political life. It is well known that this establishment is self-perpetuating, especially through public (independent) schooling, through ties of marriage and social activity, and through a common worldview as a class of people who are born to rule and dominate England (and Britain).

Alongside this, there is another establishment, the established Anglican church (the Church of England), which exercises particular social and political privileges – such as having the head of state (the monarch) as the head of the church, as well as having church and political activity intertwined (for example, church legislation is subject to certain parliamentary scrutiny, and bishops are appointed by the prime minister). On major state occasions, such as coronations and royal weddings, the Church of England are the chief officiaries, and there are twenty six seats set aside in the upper chamber of parliament (the House of Lords) for Anglican bishops (the 'Lords Spiritual'). One element of this establishment, which was brought into sharp focus in the early 1990s, was the practice of English law in terms of religious matters, insomuch as the laws of blasphemy were interpreted as being only relevant for members of the established church.

Despite this, the established church has no obvious power over the practice of British political life, and the presence of lord bishops at the heart of the legislative belies a situation in which the church is meant to have no formal power. Thus, on a number of occasions senior church leaders have been criticised by members of successive governments if they have been seen to cross over the imaginary line between 'religion and politics', or between church and state matters (the most particular example of this was the criticism by Richard Jenkins, the then Bishop of Durham, of the Conservative government's economic policy in the mid-1980s).

Although the established church is very much part of the establishment, the establishment extends considerably further than the church. Thus, participation in the politics of the establishment is no longer the exclusive preserve of Anglicans. For example, both religious and secular leaders from Hindu and Jewish groups have taken up lordships and are active members of the House of Lords. In this respect, the establishment is more multicultural and multireligious than the presence of the state Anglican church suggests. At the same time, the Church of England itself can no longer claim an English cultural homogeneity – two of its senior members are non-white clerics who were born outside of the UK (in Pakistan and the Caribbean respectively). These senior appointments reflect in a small way the changing demographics of English churches, where there has been increasing participation and leadership in local congregations of black Afro-Caribbean Christians.

Despite this, however, on an ideological level there is a very strong element of collusion between the two forms of establishment. That is, the Anglican worldview coincides to a large extent with the worldview of the political establishment. Both groups tend to subscribe to a view that essentialises and dehistoricises English identity, assuming that it is a culture and way of life that is to be celebrated and cherished. There is a relatively uncontested assumption that Britain is 'both a Christian *society* . . . and also a Christian *state*' (Parekh 1997:17, emphasis in orginal). The consequences of this hegemonic perspective are very strong, since not only do the two forms of establishment reproduce each other in the political structures of the nation-state, they are also the framework in which political and cultural debate have to operate, assuming that this perspective is normative.

Thus, as I will discuss later in this chapter, debates about multiculturalism become subsumed within a conceptualising of an essentialised 'Englishness', often emerging with essentialised viewpoints and expectations of *other* and essentialised cultures such as 'blacks', 'Asians', and 'Muslims' which only partially fit into normative Englishness. And in particular, the legal and political framework in which minorities have to operate is very much fixed and controlled by a white Anglican establishment who, having defined a particular form of multiculturalism, then expect British citizens (or subjects) to act accordingly. Thus, the 'continuance' of non-Anglican (and non-Christian) religions within a secularised Britain with an established church is permissible and encouraged so long as religious manifestations fit in with a viewpoint that expects religion to be well articulated (doctrinal), tolerant, private, and generally quietist and apolitical. Should any person or group try to force their way out of such a stereotyping, then they will find it hard to claim any advantages that are available within legal discourses for those that are recognised as 'religions'. Even those who seem to easily fit into the mould of what a religion should be find their endeavours most successful if they can translate their terms of reference into native Christian terms. Thus, most religious groups identify their leaders as ministers or priests, create clearly identifiable centres such as churches, and (at their most extreme) show some identity between their religious discourses (particularly on deities) and those within Anglican Christianity. As a rather simple example of this, Vaishnavites find there are political advantages from identifying Krishna as similar to the deity Christians call God. At a more subtle level, the Krishna-*lila* performances can be seen as more acceptable as a religious practice (rather than as public entertainment) if it is 'explained' that they are akin to Christian nativity plays.[4]

Within this clearly unequal field of power relations, therefore, it is not altogether surprising that there have been substantial debates in Britain about the role and future of the established church within nation-state politics (see in particular Modood 1997c, Parekh 1997). However, as Modood observes, much of the debate over disestablishment has given 'no recognition of Britain's non-Christian religious presence' (Modood 1997c:8), and so has been more centred on the question of whether or not there is still a role for a religious institution within the structures of contemporary British political life. Modood himself suggests that some minority perspectives go against the general tone of this disestablishment argument, since many of these minorities argue that establishment does at least treat religious practice seriously, and so for Modood 'multi-faithism leans much more towards establishment than abolition. The goal of a plural religious presence in the architecture of the state and our sense of national community is not served by severing the existing links' (Modood 1997c:13, see also Modood 1994).

I would not fully agree with Modood's argument that one of the benefits of establishment is that it potentially serves as a protection against all religious forms. He is probably correct that its absence could possibly help to create a climate of secularist intolerance for all religious manifestations (majoritarian or minoritarian). While it is evident that there needs to be some form of alternative structures to those currently in place (as Parekh 1997 argues), it appears that it is easier to argue against establishment than it is to argue for something to put in its place. To distill Modood's argument, there are two most likely options for change from the current situation of Anglican establishment. One is for the removal of the link between the Church of England and the British nation-state, and the other is for its evolution into a 'multicultural' form of benevolent establishment which is epitomised by Prince Charles'[5] argument for the monarch to become 'Defender of Faith' (that is, all faiths) rather than the traditional 'Defender of the Faith' (that is, Anglican Christianity).

Disestablishment would most probably lead to a legal/constitutional replacement of Anglican establishment with secularist neutrality. Such a policy of neutrality could be (and probably would be) interpreted in a number of different ways. It could create a framework for state hostility to all religious forms, in which the only forms of religiosity are expressed on the private level by individuals in ways that do not conflict with the obligations of the state. This type of pro-active secularity is probably best epitomised by French national discourses, where there has been an extremely strong state-led reaction against new and alternative forms of religiosity and an equally strong resistance to the Islamicisation of public spaces and action (c.f. G. Baumann 1999:48–51). Although the French model may be an extreme example, such a secularist world-view could drive a wedge between discourses on multiculturalism and religious plurality. That is, it may create a perspective that religious manifestations are anachronistic in contemporary society even if multi*cultural*ism is still valued. It may thus create an uncomfortable space between discourses of respect for cultural diversity, and indifference (or antipathy) towards minority forms of religion. Such a disestablishment based on secularism may also only serve to create an Anglican political 'secularism' which is akin to the Hindu secularism in India, where the political establishment maintain a particularly cultural/religious worldview which is disguised by an ideology of neutrality. In fact, this form of disestablishment is fairly similar to the dominance of Protestant churches in contemporary Germany.

The other alternative is to develop establishment in broad multi-faith direction, which maintains the centrality of Anglican to British (particularly English) cultural life but also gives some formal recognition and acceptance of religious diversity. This is in line with Prince Charles' suggestion noted above concerning the title 'Defender of the Faith'. Inherent in this suggestion are a great number of ambiguities of the extent to which the monarch would be the head of a particular church and also custodian of all (legitimate) religious manifestations, and indeed it suggests a strongly paternalist encompassment by the Anglican church of the plurality which would not be limited to 'spiritual' discourses. In particular, any political working out of exactly who the monarch is supposed to be 'defending' would require some definition of who and what sorts of practice are deserving of the title 'faith' (or religion), which brings the debate back to the issues raised in chapter seven. It is certain that some religious/faith groups would see no necessity for their interests to be defended by the state leader, whilst other (particularly those defined as having 'new' or supposedly 'crank' faiths) would be excluded from such discourses. Furthermore, the political relations between normative Anglicanism and the self perpetuating hegemonic worldview of the ruling establishment would not be altered in any tangible way.

It is, in fact, fairly certain that the connection between Anglicanism and the political establishment would not be dissolved merely by disestablishing the Church of England. What is required instead is a recognition of plurality and an innovative approach to multiculturalism that goes beyond tokenism and essentialism. It should account for the fact that all forms of British cultural practice are in the process of development, and that a seemingly homogeneous English Anglicanism is one of many ways of being British (and English) in contemporary Britain. I am, in fact, very much in agreement with another participant of the conference on establishment and religious minorities which Tariq Modood organised. That is Deepak Naik, who as public relations office for the NCHT (National Council for Hindu Temples) was asked to give a 'Hindu perspective' on the issue. Wisely admitting that his view (like any other) can only be partial and not representative of all British Hindus, Naik (1997) argued that rather than arguing about establishment or disestablishment of the church, the real issue is how minorities relate to the (political) Establishment:

> People of minority faiths need to be interwoven into the political body: as members of parliament, in the civil service, in dotted-line relationships parallel to Ministers of Parliament. Enabling them to be involved in the decision-making processes would mean that instead of being starved or neglected, minority cultural and religious needs and values would begin to be fulfilled ... [They] will not achieve a sense of belonging until true partnerships are created, established, and supported to make each partner equal to the other. (Naik 1997:79 & 80)

What this is suggesting is that any reform of the church establishment will be achieved by pursuing a political multiculturalism which takes some active account of the political relations between groups and people identified as minorities and those who have control over substantial issues of power within the contemporary nation-state. The practice of such a multiculturalism will need to take account of the multiciplicity of identities and cultural forms (including those that are considered to be religious) that are being actively created and manifest.

The Politics of Multiculturalism

In discussing the locating of religious identities and practices within multicultural discourses, however, I need to make a few points with regard to the applications of the term. In its various uses, multiculturalism can be mapped into frameworks of *legislation*, *ideology*, *theory*, and *practice*,[6] each of which construct and are constructed by certain expectations of what multiculturalism 'should be' about. At the base of most uses of the term is some sort of assumption that 'multiculturalism represents a demand for the dissociation (decentering) of the political community and its common social institutions from identification with any one cultural tradition' (Turner 1993:425). The perceived need for dissociation/decentring can of course vary considerably and depends to a large extent on who is articulating the term (and the discourse). Thus it may be a weak demand when articulated by those at the centre of a political community, and indeed for others such as right wing critics ('anti-multiculturalists') the rhetoric of decentring may be indeed meant in a perjorative sense. In the words of Susan Stanford Friedman:

> The term multicultural is highly problematic, without consistent meanings in its many usages and easily open to co-optation into celebrations of pluralist diversity that obscure underlying power relations. In its North American context, multicultural most often means nonwhite racial groups considered together, but it also sometimes refers to cultural diversity of all kinds (including white and western); to a group that is itself multicultural (e.g., African Americans or Asian Americans), and even to individuals of mixed heritage. (Friedman 1998: 252)

In many senses multiculturalism is an abstract concept with multiple, situational meanings depending on who is using the term, and how they are applying it. The point of conjunction between each of these perspectives is not altogether clear. Instead 'multiculturalism' is marked by considerable polysemy and ambiguity, and its use demonstrate how the term 'has become a slippery signifier onto which diverse groups project their hopes and fears' (Stam and Shohat 1994:299). As Yunus Samad argues:

> It seems that the hegemonic ascendancy of the concept as a slogan or paradigm has simultaneously resulted also in its fragmentation. ...

> multiculturalism has different implications and meanings depending on its social, political and disciplinary location. Multiculturalism can be conservative or radical, and social policy based upon it can have different implications and outcomes depending on the context in which cultural difference is negotiated. (Samad 1997:240)

At its most obvious, and perhaps most clearly (although not radically or innovatively) articulated, multiculturalism has been expressed in some nation-states through legislation. The two foremost states used as examplars of this are Canada and Australia. In Canada multiculturalism was adopted as an official policy by the federal government in 1971, although it took until 1988 for this policy to become law through the *Multiculturalism Act*. This Act had the express aim of ensuring that the Canadian government should work to 'preserve and enhance the multicultural heritage of Canadians while working to achieve the equality of all Canadians' (quoted in Bibby 1999). In Australia there has not been a comparable piece of legislation, but the development of policy since the late 1970s, by governments of differing political parties, has promoted 'a view of Australia as a multicultural society' (Spuler 1999). In both these cases the level of cultural diversity is probably not any greater than in most European nations, although the historical constructions of both Canada and Australia are derived from narratives of immigration (primarily of white Europeans).[7] The legislation and policy of multiculturalism does perhaps do no more than recognise that most Canadians and Australians are relatively recent arrivals (excepting of course the marginalised indigenous populations of both countries), whilst at the same time – despite the legislation – the political and cultural dominance of white European populations has been left largely unchallenged and unaffected.

Other nation-states have articulated a goal of multiculturalism, without making any explicit legislation in this respect. For example, the nation-state in Britain has an ideology and a vague self-definition of multiculturalism as a 'widely accepted goal' (Asad 1993b:260). Thus, in a speech made at the Policy Studies Institute in London in October 1997 the Home Secretary Jack Straw put forward the new Labour government's view that:

> The appreciation of diversity in our communities is right and proper in itself. It is also a source of enjoyment and inspiration in our cultural and social lives ...
>
> Ethnic minority communities are an integral part of British society ... This Government greatly values the contribution that they make to the country – economically, socially and culturally ...
>
> Today's Britain is unquestionably richer for the contribution made to it by its ethnic minority communities.

> And I am proud of a vision of Britain which both accommodates and celebrates diversity ...
>
> Britain has long been a multiracial and multicultural society ... (Straw n.d.)

A year and a half later, the government were required to further articulate their commitment to cultural diversity and pluralism, following a direct violent challenge by right wing racist elements. In April 1999, three nail bombs were exploded in Brixton (south London), Brick Lane (east London), and Soho (central London), all of which were directly targeted at obvious 'multicultural' sites. Brixton is a major centre for black (African-Caribbean) Londoners, Brick Lane has a large (Bangladeshi) Muslim population, and the target in Soho was one of a number of gay pubs in the area (it also has, incidentally, a large Chinese population). The third of these attacks proved to be the most shocking for media coverage: not so much because of the targets being ethnically white (gay) men and women, but because this bomb killed three people.[8] In response to the Soho bomb a number of government ministers felt it was necessary to affirm their commitment to multiculturalism and diversity, and to show the marginality of the bombers who were attempting to undermine this principle. Leading these discourses was the Prime Minister Tony Blair, who, according to a newspaper report 'said that the Britons took pride in their ethnic diversity and could be proud of a patriotism that united rather than divided the nation'. In a direct quote of Blair's words:

> The true outcasts today, the true minorities, those truly excluded are not the different races and religions of Briton but the racists, the bombers, the violent criminals who hate that vision of society and try to destroy it. But thay shall not win. The great decent majority of British people will not let them. We can defeat them and we can build the tolerant, multi-racial Britain the vast majority of us want to see ... In the past patriotism and national identity were defined by those excluded. Nationalism in this sense can be dangerous, you have to come from one colour, one religion, one ethnic background as opposed to others. Today we take pride in an identity limited by the geography of the country but within that country open to all, whatever their colour, religion or ethnic background.[9]

In a similar, although less sophisticated, vein Prince Charles also stated that 'this is not just an attack on particular groups but on all of us. It helps bring people together in a remarkable way and we must build on that fact. The British people are never going to be put down'.[10]

One of the reasons for this series of bomb attacks was that issues of multicultural Britain had already come to the fore a month earlier in March

1999, following the publication of the Macpherson Report (1999). This was a government sponsored report on the murder in 1993 of Stephen Lawrence, a young middle-class black man in south east London. Despite strong evidence presented to police investigators shortly after his death, implicating a group of five local white men in the murder, no prosecutions were brought by the Crown Prosecution Service.[11] A determined campaign by the dead man's parents exposed serious failings in the police investigation, which eventually led to the government inquiry and the Macpherson Report. As well as making specific recommendations for a police review of the persistence of 'institutional racism' within its ranks, the report also highlighted the significance of multicultural rhetoric within contemporary policing (and society in general) by placing a strong emphasis on 'valuing cultural diversity', with this phrase coming up in two of its recommendations (nos. 49 and 52, see Yuval-Davis 1999:2.1). However, as Nira Yuval-Davis points out, the Macpherson report failed to go beyond rather vague recommendations on this point, since it is nowhere elaborated 'what its authors mean by "cultural diversity", how one should value it and who would have the authority to determine what it means' (ibid.:2.2).

The ambiguity behind this rhetoric of multiculturalism is strongly characteristic of the knee-jerk responses generated by a series of crises that have arisen out of social and political changes in Britain. The right wing bombs, the murder of Stephen Lawrence, and the subsequent political exposure of the inadequacies and instituational racism of police officers were only one such set of crises. The governmental (and wider) response to the protests and Iranian *fatwa* against the publication of Salman Rushdie's *Satanic Verses* was another such crisis management reaction to multicultural challenges. Indeed, as Asad argues, the practice of multiculturalism in Britain has been pursued 'not in an ideological commitment to cultural diversity but in the attempt to deal with practical problems encountered in education and the social services – two major institutions of Britain's welfare state' (Asad 1993b:260). Further to this, Yunus Samad positions the rise of multicultural policy and rhetoric as a rearguard attempt to stave off social, cultural, and political unrest:

> so-called multiculturalist policies ... are not the product of misplaced magnanimity on the part of the Establishment. In Britain and the USA, social policies specifically designed to deal with racial discrimination were implemented as a result of social upheaval and political protest. Political mobilisation [and riots] ... *forced* the authorities to act. (Samad 1997:245, emphasis in original)

At one level, the ideology of multiculturalism in national discourses is as much motivated by the practicalities of nation-state politics as any 'magnanimity' or liberal enlightenment on the part of dominant majority cultural groups.

It is the theoreticians of multiculturalism who have provided the most ideological perspectives on how the concept, and the practice of multiculturalism, should be understood. Thus in academic circles, 'the term multiculturalism has come to be used primarily in connection with demands on behalf of black and other minority groups for separate and equal representation in college curriculums' (Turner 1993:411). This critical theoretical multiculturalism has developed as an important part of the wider cultural studies agenda, in which there has been a self-conscious attempt to use academic discourses 'to find the cultural and political norms appropriate to more heterogeneous societies within and across nations, including norms for the production and transmission of knowledges' (Chicago Cultural Studies Group 1994:114, see also Berlant and Warner 1994, Gilroy 1993, Clifford 1997). Thus academics are reacting to and challenging theoretical perspectives which assume (explicitly, or more usually implicitly) or promote a normative Eurocentric monoculturalism.

> The other key aim of multiculturalism, grounded theoretically in the work of Homi Bhabha (1994: chapter 8) is ideological: continuously to remind 'Europe', as it negotiates its internal differences, that the continent is fundamentally incomplete, a postcolonial locus of multiple diasporas; and by doing so to 'interrupt' or 'disrupt' singular narratives of nation and supranation ... (Werbner 1997b:263).

Alongside this, and indeed feeding off and interacting with more critical academic writers, is the ever growing academic literature which discusses and attempts to delimit political and social responses to social and cultural diversity (see Taylor 1994, Gutman 1994, G. Baumann 1999, Modood and Werbner 1997b). Quite where the boundary lies between these various forms of theorising multiculturalism is never clear, since any attempt to theorise the politics of multiculturalism occurs within a particular social context. It is possible to mark out some general boundaries within these academic approaches, such as between conservative, liberal, left-liberal, and critical/resistance multiculturalisms (McLaren 1994), between difference and critical multiculturalism (Turner 1993, see below), or liberal pluralism and polycentric multiculturalism (Stam and Shohat 1994:300). Thus, although academic discourses on multiculturalism may not always be ideologically motivated, they do still have ideological, or practical, applications and consequences. In this way, for one such writer, Pnina Werbner:

> multiculturalism is ultimately not a matter of theory, even critical theory, but of real politics; there are as many multiculturalisms as there are political arenas for collective action. ... Multiculturalism is always a specific negotiated order and no amount of abstract philosophical or legal reasoning can prescribe a single 'just' model. (Werbner 1997b:264)

This brings me on to the last of the frameworks for multiculturalism that I wish to highlight – that is, multicultural practice. In many respects, the other three frameworks are all forms of practice of multiculturalism: after all, legislation is the practice of governments (as well as civil servants, lawyers, barristers, judges, and state agencies). But multicultural practice takes place (as Werbner argues) in a variety of political arenas, and it is a significant part of the 'practice of everyday life' for all people living within contemporary nation-states. That is, multiculturalism is not only practised in countries where there is official recognition of such diversity (such as Australia and Canada), nor indeed is it only the preserve of people who identify themselves as belonging to minority cultural groups. The interweaving of diverse identities and cultural formations into all contemporary cultural milieu means that every person now engages with multiculturalism, whether they recognise this or not. Thus political articulations of monoculturalism and exclusionism (including the London bombings of 1999) are themselves a product of multicultural praxis, since without diversification these reactions would not be generated. But although this observation is significant inasmuch as it challenges hegemonic assumptions of cultural majority perspectives, at another level it is merely a trite recognition that diversity and hybridity adds up to no more than stating the obvious.

What recent theoretical debates have opened up in particular are questions of how issues of multiculturalism are used in political fields, as ways of *constructing* and *containing* diversity (c.f. Asad 1993b:260–266) and – to a large extent – fixing and reifying fluid processes of cultural identification and practice into rigid cultural types and groups. In his influential essay on multiculturalism and anthropology, Terence Turner (1993) makes a distinction between 'difference multiculturalism' and 'critical multiculturalism'. In these terms, difference multiculturalism is merely about the recognition (and possibly celebration) of difference, in which 'culture reduces to a tag for ethnic identity and a license for political and intellectual separatism' (1993:414).

This image of multiculturalism could be likened to a metaphor of many islands of culture existing together (in relative harmony) in a sea of plurality. A monoculturalist perspective may just see an archipelago or, worse still, a bloc of colonised lands all under the one authority, but a difference multiculturalist will delight in recognising the separateness, distrinctiveness, and uniqueness of each 'island culture'. Although laudable enough as a political agenda in itself, this difference multiculturalism is conceptually weak, and is open to challenge both from right wing critics (since it suggests the strong possibility of balkanisation), and from left wing activists for whom such a 'same but different' approach comes perilously close to apartheid. Another metaphor often used within difference multiculturalist discourses is of a mosaic of cultures. Here, a multicultural society is made up in patterns of diverse 'pieces' (cultures): each piece is well defined when examined in close detail, each piece has its place within the whole, and the summation of all the pieces is an ordered mosaic picture. A more complicated version of this metaphor is of tapestry, which does not give such a fixed perspective since most strands are interwoven with strands of other colours. What is quite obvious about both these metaphors is the reliance they place on *colour* as a representation for cultural diversity, and so both play precariously with issues of racial (skin colour) stereotyping.

In contrast to this, Turner suggests a more reflexive and rigorous 'critical multiculturalism' which 'seeks to use cultural diversity as a basis for challenging, revising, and relativizing basic notions and principles common to dominant and minority cultures alike, so as to construct a more vital, open and democratic common culture' (Turner 1993:413). The advocacy of such an approach should, according to Werbner, help to establish:

> a multiculturalism that aims not only to allow national, ethnic and immigrant minorities a voice, but to protect them from offensive symbolic as well as civic and material exclusions and violations. ... What a critical multiculturalism recognises is the rights of minorities to demand restitution for historical racialisations which disempowered them and suppressed their voice in the national sphere. (Werbner 1997b:263)

In this sense, multiculturalism should not be merely a recognition or celebration of cultural differences. Nor indeed should critical multiculturalism necessarily be limited to the processes described by Charles Taylor (1994) as the politics of recognition. In his carefully crafted essay, Taylor seeks to find a practical multicultural paradigm which is based on a powerful concept of recognition, rather than on bland generalisations such as an uncritical acceptance of homogenised differences or a totalising monoculturalism. Multiculturalism, in this philosophical framework, is therefore a matter of the politics of recognition, and is an active engagement between cultures premised on a conceptualisation of equal worth between deserving partners. Writing from an assumed majoritarian perspective (and addressing a similarly situated audience through the pronoun 'we') he articulates the summation of his argument as follows:

> it is reasonable to suppose that cultures that have provided the horizon of meaning for large numbers of human beings, of diverse characters and temperaments, over a long period of time – that have, in other words, articulated their sense of the good, the holy, the admirable – are almost certain to have something that deserves our admiration and respect, even if it is accompanied by much that we have to abhor and reject. (Taylor 1994:72)

This, however, is where Taylor leaves the reader: having defined a political agenda for knowing how to 'recognise' those cultures which are deserving of respect he abruptly avoids pursuing his argument to any easily identifiable end point. But Gerd Baumann points out, this is an extremely vague conclusion for such a densely argued essay. But it is perhaps the inevitable result of the fact that 'Taylor complicates the issues of recognition and simplifies the issue of culture' (G. Baumann 1999:109), and indeed judging by its content, the essay itself 'should be called not *The Politics of Recognition*, but *Recognizing Cultures*' (ibid.:116).

The recognition that Taylor is looking for is complex, since in particular it comes through a two way dialogic exchange (between 'us' and 'them' in Taylor's terminology):

> the last thing one wants ... from Eurocentered intellectuals is positive judgments of the worth of cultures that they have not intensively studied. For real judgments of worth suppose a fused horizon of standards ... they suppose that we have been transformed by the study of the other, so that we are not simply judging by our original familiar standards. (Taylor 1994:71)

But despite this exchange of both knowledge and perspective, there remains within this viewpoint an expectation that the politics of recognition will take place between two (or more) 'fixed "cultural identities", and these cultural identities are 'supposed to be ancient and continuous, proven and integral, and determining of people's entire horizons' (G. Baumann 1999: 116). Baumann's critique of this approach is that 'multicultural society is not a patchwork of five or ten fixed cultural identities, but an elastic web of crosscutting and always mutually situational, identifications' (ibid.: 118). 'What needs to be recognized, therefore, is not one reified culture as opposed to another one. Rather, it is the dialogical nature of all identities and, consequently, that different cultural identifications can and will, in a multicultural society, cut across each other's reified boundaries' (ibid.: 119). Thus although Taylor's own essay is intended as a critique of the 'unauthentic and homogenizing demand for recognition of equal worth' (Taylor 1994:72) which is so characteristic of most forms of 'difference multiculturalism', what he provides instead is a framework based on a similarly static set of interactions. The multiculturalisms suggested by such difference approaches seem to suggest frameworks based either on models of equal partners in a multicultural enterprise (various cultures existing side by side, ostensably in harmony), or otherwise a majority (or hegemonic) power group and various equal but different cultural minorities. Both of these options sound more preferable than monoculturalism, and an assumption (or expectation) of homogeneity – as defined by a ruling elite.

Thus according to Ayse Caglar, even in this form:

> Multiculturalism implies a decentralisation of the political community. It calls for a reformulation of the relations between its cultural collectivities, in order to create new forms of identity politics ... Hence, multiculturalism takes the form of a political movement for cultural empowerment. Culture becomes the idiom for resistance. (Caglar 1997: 178)

However, she continues immediately after this to point out: 'Yet what culture is, or who "owns" it, is left unanswered' (ibid.). This is where the problem lies with difference multiculturalism: whether one is looking at a celebration of cultural diversity, or the politics of recognising cultures, the 'culture' of such difference multiculturalism remains too essentialised:

> multiculturalism does not involve merely a recognitition of collective cultural differences but the need to guarantee politically the *survival* of the cultural communities bearing these differences. This implies an institutionalisation of cultures in the public sphere, a freezing of cultural differences and a reifying of cultural 'communities'. Moreover, as the assertion of rights is based on the identity of groups recognised within the multicultural framework, only those group identities will be publicly endowed and given 'rights'. (Caglar 1997: 179)

Although such multiculturalism is about respecting and expecting diversity between cultures, it is left broadly unexamined whether and to what extent these separate cultures are 'themselves' heterogeneous collections and abstractions of diverse individuals and interest groups. Hence, for Caglar 'the restrictive tendency of multicultural identity politics is deeply embedded in the idea of an integrated community, one that possesses a simple homogeneous "culture" – as the necessary basis for rights and identity claims' (ibid.:179–80). Her response to this is to suggest caution with respect to the term 'multiculturalism', and even to consider abandoning the term altogether. Likewise, Talal Asad is distinctly cool about the concept, although he does not outrightly reject or 'argue against' it (Asad 1993b:266).

The political analysis of situationally constructed cultural differences that is called for in Turner's work, and which Caglar is happy to accept under a name (and perhaps a process) other than multiculturalism,[12] is also pursued by Werbner (1997b) and Gerd Baumann (1999). They both call for a multicultural praxis which is based on a more sophisticated understanding of what culture 'is'. This is in itself following on from Turner's article, in which (using an unpublished paper by Fernanda Coronil) he suggests an approach to culture which is 'constituted by process of production of both the self and the other, and calls for a critical understanding of the way these processes produce representations that conceal the interdependence of the entitites involved, reifying difference as otherness and masking the nature of the entities thus representated as historical products' (Turner 1993:422).

Thus cultural differences must be located in fluid processes, which are politically embedded and for which in most cases the rhetoric of difference multiculturalism actually serves to obscure relations of hegemony and political/social exclusion. This exclusion is not merely of 'minority cultures' or bounded groups, but of people (collectively and individually) on the basis of perceived and projected cultural identities which can themselves be produced by multicultural rhetoric. Thus a 'celebration of diversity' creates an othering of the cultural groups that participate in this multiculturalism, and can thus reinforce their political and social marginality. In this sense multiculturalism becomes fixated on a problematic 'culturalism' which assumes that a person's (and a group's) culture is 'virtually burnt into the genes ... forever distinguishing and separating them' (Vertovec 1996:51).

Meanwhile, like everyone else, people within minority contexts are themselves actively engaged in the *processes* of culture, the making and doing of cultural forms. That is, cultures do not exist in essence, they are *done*,[13] or to put this another way 'culture is culturing' (White 1949, Lambek 1995: 275, Nye n.d.1). Where multiculturalism can provide a useful theoretical framework, as well as a useful praxis, is that these processes of doing and performing culture are situated in the two-way interactions that are talked about by Taylor, but elaborated to a much greater extent by Bhabha (1994, 1996) and others (e.g. Werbner and Modood 1997).[14] The abstraction of culture is produced through processes of hybridisation, creolisation, and syncretism, through dialogical interactions between people on a number of levels of practice and in a variety of contexts, and through diverse forms, performances, and manifestations.[15]

However, it is worth bearing in mind that, as Asad points out, there are limits to these discursive processes of hybridity: 'To argue that a culture must be seen as a process does not exclude the possibility that it is a coherent process' (Asad 1993b:263), and therefore 'in the sense of being the political *effect* of discursive traditions, "culture" does after all have boundaries, even though they are not eternally fixed' (ibid.:264, emphasis in original). Thus, although a theoretical discussion on the politics of multiculturalism should be founded on the recognition of the fluidity of interactions within and between groups and individuals who are making their cultural forms in various ways, the praxis of the politics of multiculturalism does at the same time have the effect of consolidating manifestations into particular forms (groups, organisations, categories, even 'cultures'). As Baumann argues, it should not be the task of the academic to bemoan such reifications and concretisations, especially not as they are often the products of the processual dynamics of the practice of culture (G. Baumann 1999: 90–91). Instead the 'double discursive processes' of simultaneously reifying and constructing/performing culture are all part of the realities lived by all people within multicultural contexts. Understanding the politics of multiculturalism in practice requires an acceptance of how such oscillations occur, who manages or controls them (if at all), and in whose interests.

Religious manifestations in critical multiculturalist perspective

As I quoted above, in 1997 the Labour Home Secretary gave a speech in which he said that he considered Britain to be 'a multiracial and multicultural society'. He drew attention to the fact that 'Britain is a multiracial, multireligious society where as many British people now attend a Mosque as an Anglican or Methodist church' (Straw n.d.). Quite where he intended the boundary to be between 'multicultural', 'multiracial', and 'multireligious' is by no means clear, but like many other commentators he demonstrated the common assumption that the recognition and praxis of multiculturalism also implicates a recognition of a dynamic religious plurality.

In contrast, Martin Baumann argues that discussions of multiculturalism, particularly within theoretical discourses, tend to exclude detailed consideration of religious practice, primarily because 'in rational, scientific modernity religion is perceived as obsolete' (M Baumann 1999).[16] Instead, there is a preponderance for the emphasis to be placed on ethnicity and ethnic identity as the principal element within multicultural theory and practice. Thus 'a perception of the significance of religion for a migrant group means recognition of religious identification within a multicultural setting. The plurality of cultures does not only consist of a plurality of ethnic styles, but also a plurality of faiths and religions' (ibid.). This point is most clearly illustrated by the case examined by Gerrie ter Haar (1999) in the collection of papers edited by Baumann, in which she argues that the marginalisation of black Christian groups in the Netherlands is substantially the result of the fact that they are defined/labelled as an *ethnic* community (as Afro-Caribbeans), rather than in terms of the religious identity which they would prefer to promote (as Christians).[17]

This criticism by Martin Baumann is one that I would only partially agree with. The last few years of the 1990s have, in fact, seen a strong development of discourses on religion and multiculturalism – most obviously shown by the publication of Gerd Baumann book in 1999, examining in considerable depth the 'multicultural riddle' of 'national, ethnic, and *religious* identities' (G. Baumann 1999). One point that is strongly noticable about much of the literature on multiculturalism and religion is that it is Islam as a religion/culture/way of life/identity that figures most prominently (as evidenced by Gerd Baumann's choice to focus on various forms of European Islam to illustrate his discussion of the 'multicultural riddle'). To a large extent this preponderance for Islam is easily accounted for – Muslims probably compose the most substantial minority religious (and ethnic) populations in Europe (albeit a very heterogeneous population). And a large part of the debates in various nation-states in Europe have arisen out of 'problems' of placing Muslims (or accommodating European cultures to the Islamic presences) – particularly the Salman Rushdie affair in Britain, the Gulf War, and other incidents such as the issue of schoolgirls wearing headscarves in France.[18]

A significant point that comes out of this inclusion of Islam within the politics and practice of multicultural theory, however, is that such religious identities are often very ambiguously placed within the rethinkings of culture. For example, as Tariq Modood argues (1997b:3–4), misrepresentations of Islam as 'fundamentalist' and 'barbaric' have formed the basis for writers such as Charles Taylor to exclude Islam (as a cultural entity) from his politics of recognition. And although there has developed a strong awareness that theorising multiculturalism should avoid a reification of cultures and cultural identities, this perspective has not been applied so readily to religious groups. Thus, whilst critical multicultural theory stresses issues of hybridity, diversity, and creolisation on the part of cultural manifestations, as we have seen, there has been far less discussion of similarly constructed religious manifestations.[19] This is probably partly because of widespread images of Islam in the west as static and monolithic (and thus Islam serves as a paradigm for all 'multicultural religions'), but also more subtly because so many minority religious groups are composed of obvious organisational structures (for example, mosques, *mandirs*, religious societies/parties) which create a clear appearance of ordered boundedness. The diversity of practice *within* such religious cultures and organisations is very easily overlooked – especially as many religious groups wish to create (both internally and externally) a sense of cohesion and stasis – and in fact diversity is sometimes only recognised by those who seek to critique the 'religion' (such as feminist critics of Islam, e.g. Sahgal and Yuval-Davis 1992).

According to Saba Mahood and Nancy Reynolds, despite the fact that debates 'on political inclusion and tolerance in Western liberal democracies [acknowledge] that racial, ethnic, gender, and sexual differences must be accommodated at the level of political systems', there is still a problem with religion:

> extending this public recognition of difference to include religious affiliations often makes those who argue for multiple public identities uncomfortable. Part of this discontent resides in a genuine fear arising from an awareness that a number of recently instituted theocracies have been oppressive of historically subordinate groups. Another part

> of the discomfort with making religion a public issue, however, lies in the way principles of liberal-humanism have become hegemonic and naturalized in discussions on modern politics. (Mahmood and Reynolds 1996).

In contrast to this perspective (which Mahmood and Reynolds are also critiquing), Gerd Baumann's attempt to place religious identities within the practice of multiculturalism is based on the argument that 'religion is not some cultural baggage that is taken along on migration wrapped, tied, and tagged. Rather . . . it provides a point of orientation . . . yet the bearings of religious conviction and action will change as the users themselves change positions, or see them changed in their new contexts' (G. Baumann 1999:78). As with the argument of culture as practice rather than essence, religiosity needs to be conceived of in these fluid terms – which I discussed in chapter seven as religious practice, or religioning, rather than as religion. The identities coming from such religious identities may well be different from those coming from other cultural identities, such as ethnicity. For example, many Muslims are eager to argue that their identity as Muslims is more important (in some contexts) than their identity as Pakistanis (or Turks, or whatever). The articulation of a Hindu identity is rather different from being Indian or Gujarati, and indeed there are the subtle and important identities being played within the distinctions between Hindu, Vaishnavite, or Krishna devotee.

Critical multiculturalism is, therefore, not at odds with religiosity – although the ideology of some critical multiculturalists may have problems with some 'fundamentalist' expressions of religiosity (as well as nationalist and monoculturalist identities). A critical multiculturalism is also a critical multireligionism. It is a theoretical approach that assumes religious and cultural identities to be situational, based on syncretic and hybrid processes of construction and innovation, and that manifestations of a particular religious tradition within a particular multicultural context will give rise to certain religious forms. Further to this, such religious manifestations will be involved in the processes of cultural and ethnic construction, there is often a creative interplay between such religious and cultural identities and practices within multicultural settings, not just within groups, but also between different groups. And indeed, ISKCON is an excellent example of the fluidity, and some of the boundaries of these processes.

'New religions' in multiculturalism

Having brought the discussion to this point, I think a very important point worth noting is that there are significant attitudes towards particular religious minorities which play extremely creatively with the politics of multiculturalism – including some groups/manifestations in, and excluding others. By this I mean that those perceived as 'new religious groups' are usually classified as irrelevent to multicultural debates, since they are not 'ethnically' constituted (inasmuch as they are very often defined, or stereotyped, as being predominantly ethnically white), and are thus not quite cultures in the sense that (difference) multiculturalism may propound.[20] Hence at a crude level, multiculturalism can often be taken as a celebration of *ethnic* diversity, whilst still creating an ambivalent climate concerning religious diversity, in which there is suspicion (and indeed some measure of hostility) towards *religiously* identified groups if they differ too much from majoritarian norms, particularly through innovation, rather than migration. To put this another way, the concepts of hybridity and cultural creativity are only acceptably multicultural for so long as the processes of hybridisation take place within the confines of a particular ethnic identity. British Hindus are allowed to hybridise and explore the boundaries between 'being' Hindu, British, Indian, Gujarati, etc., because that is where they are structurally placed. But someone who is ethnically 'white' has less choice: to hybridise and become a British convert to Hinduism, or Buddhism, or Islam is seen as an aberration which does not have any place within multiculturalism. Thus to take a share of the multicultural pie, alternative religious groups often find themselves having to ethnicise themselves, either by stressing non-white participation (such as in the case of the Indian following in ISKCON), or otherwise to align themselves with broad minority cultural discourses (such as the identification of Neo-Paganism with Celticism, and hence indirectly with the emergence of Scottish and Welsh identities, c.f. Bowman 1995).

One influential response to this has been what can be called a 'Religions' response, that is the assumption that there are certain major religions ('world religion') into which all (legitimate) religious groups can be categorised.[21] This approach is very much based on the assumption that religious manifestations can be classified into categories, almost in the same way as animal and plants can be classified into species. In fact it amounts to no more than a form of difference multireligionism which gives a list of the most important religions to which a Taylorian form of recognition has been given (usually it is academics who are at the leading edge of making such judgements on who should be recognised and what categories should be used). Some groups, such as ISKCON, may eventually gain recognition because they can be fitted into one of the categories (in this case Hinduism). Other groups are excluded because they do not obviously fit (or are politically excluded). Thus many groups which are called 'new religions' are categorised as such because they seem to be like Christianity, but are not accepted into the Christian classification by mainstream Christian groups. For example, the Unification Church is excluded as non-Christian because of its Moon-centred theology,[22] whilst the group called The Family (who are still recognised by their former title of the Children of God) are excluded because of their theological and social attitudes towards sexuality (see Lewis and Melton 1994).

I discussed a manifestation of this approach in chapter seven, when Baronness Young suggested it as a means of distinguishing 'principal' from 'crank' religions. One of the problems with this is that many of the groups and strands which are involved in such an exercise do not appear to fit in as easily as would be assumed, so it becomes a distinctly political decision as to whether a group is in or out. But more importantly, a critical perspective acknowledges that all manifestations are constructed on a continual basis, and thus to identify what is 'proper' Christianity, Islam, or Hinduism, etc., is to engage in processes of essentialism which homogenise difference and serve particular power interests over others. For example, most normative assumptions about Islam (and indeed Christianity) tend to privilege patriarchal assumptions about gender relations. Also, having a 'big league' also by definition excludes innovation outside of these terms. For example, it gives no place for Neo-Pagan groups. A difference multiculturalist perspective may say that if it can be shown to have a viable enough pedigree then Paganism should be added to the list (perhaps with other 'indigenous' or 'tribal/traditional' religions under a separate, expansive category, or in a 'minor league'). But from a critical multicultural perspective this would only be tinkering with a set of categories which are flawed in conception: the emergence of Neo-Pagan groups and identities in Britain in the second half of the twentieth century is (like all other religious manifestations) part of the dynamic processes of religious and cultural change. In this respect I would like to return to my earlier point that religion is more a matter of practice than one of essentialised groupings, and so placing particular manifestations into world religion classifications is an exercise that is thoroughly bound up with a particular christocentric type of political articulation of difference.

Following from this point, I would like to use a suggestion made by Terence Turner that the 'almost infinite malleability' of culture 'means that there are virtually no limits to the kinds of social groups, networks, or relations that can generate a cultural identity of their own' (1993:426). It is possible that some identities are 'naturally constructed',[23] but many such identities can be generated by 'self-consciously formed voluntary' groupings (ibid.). This suggests that not only should academics (and others) reconceive how such 'cultural groups' are self-consciously constructed, but also there are no obvious reasons why religious groups formed by conversion (those which are often labelled as new religious movements) should be excluded from these critical multiculturalist discourses. Thus although the examples which Gerd Baumann uses to explore his discussion of religion and multiuculturalism are predominantly of 'ethnic' religious groups (primarily South Asian and Turkish Muslims in western Europe), his general argument does suggest a substantial rethinking of the place of all religious minorities (including predominantly white conversion movements, which usually become segregated as 'new religions').

There are indeed some very important research questions which could be asked about the creations of ethnic and national identities that are produced by such minority religious perspectives (which feed into majority identities as well as minorities). One such question that could be raised is the role of ethnic identities within large-scale 'new religion' events such as the Branch Davidian siege and fatalities at Waco, Texas in spring 1993 and the mass suicides of Jim Jones' Peoples Temple group at Jonestown, Guyana in November 1978.[24] In both cases the majority of people who died were ethnically identified as black African-Americans, belonging to groups that had predominantly 'white' leaderships. Most portayals of the Peoples Temple and the Branch Davidians have placed them as ('white') 'cults' rather than as ('black') 'ethnic religions', and both cases have been used extensively by (white, mainly Protestant) religious leaders to highlight the 'dangers of cults' to (white) American society. I would suggest that in both cases the ethnic identities of those who died have helped to construct an otherness which feeds off and feeds into a construction of the groups as 'cults'. Thus the groups were defined in terms of their ethnically white leaders (and hence as cults, or more politely as new religions) rather than as expressions of multicultural religiosity within contemporary north America.

What I am arguing here, therefore, is that the boundaries of identity and group formation around these 'new' religious manifestations are much more fluid in practice than are perceived in public discourses. A critical multiculturalist perspective accepts that all cultural (and religious) manifestations are, in effect, 'new' since all such cultures are the discursive products of innovation, creolisation, hybridity, and so on. By dividing some cultural forms off as 'new religions' and some as 'ethnic religions', public discourses (popular views) play a very effective strategy of 'divide and rule'. Although it is possible that some 'ethnic religions' can cause serious challenges (such as with the Rushdie affair), there is a considerable climate of tolerance for them because they are perceived/constructed as part of a landscape of cultural diversity which the ideology of 'difference multiculturalism' is prepared to celebrate (so long as it is practised in moderation). In contrast, because 'new religions' are not conceived as 'ethnic minorities', attitudes towards them tend to be much harsher. There are periodical calls for legislation against them (in Britain) and governmental commissions, and even (in other countries) national agencies to investigate and/or control them.[25] Muslims (as a 'minority cultural group') might be thought of as fundamentalist, but they do not 'brainwash', and of course (as I quoted in chapter seven) a populist view is that in national discourses the 'Moonies are out, and the Muslims are in'.[26]

By breaking down the conceptual barrier between these various forms of minority religiosity I am not suggesting that they share any real common political interest. There is little common cultural, social, or economic ground between Deobandi, Wahhabi, or Ismaili Muslims, Vaishnavite Hindus, Neo-Pagans, and followers of Sun Myung Moon. Separately and together they do provide a critique of majority hegemonic cultural perceptions of Britain as a monocultural (English) entity, united by a single normative religious identity (Anglicanism), and indeed appear to challenge the perception that public discourse in contemporary Britain is secularised. This notwithstanding, a critical multicultural perspective needs to recognise that the people who identify with each of these groups (and who perhaps belong to organisations that are vehicles for the various forms of religious practice), are in their very different ways participating in strategies of innovation that derive from the particular political and cultural structures of contemporary British life.

There are, therefore, good conceptual reasons to break down the rigid academic distinction between 'ethnic minority' and 'new' religions, since both involve people who are actively engaged in cultural reconstructions working within similar contexts, albeit with rather different cultural materials. The dividing line which is set up between new and ethnic religions is probably too much a part of the divisive politics of British (difference) multiculturalism to allow academics to feel comfortable with perpetuating the distinction, and in practical, theoretical and ethnographic terms there should be a wider cross-over and reconceptualisation of how religious cultures are being reconstructed in such diverse ways.

Multiculturalism in the political and postcolonial domain

As an ideology and a form of political practice, multiculturalism is about more than having a society/nation-state which is made up of people with different cultural identities, and with various clusters and groups which can be called cultures and religions. A multicultural society does not simply have plurality: its political leadership needs to show a recognition of this and to operate with the diversity rather than against it, and thus the political structures need to give some expression of diverse minority perspectives against the hegemony of a majoritarian outlook. But multiculturalism is also about a political recognition of the challenge of creative diversification: that in the constructions of identity, each person and group is changed – British identities have not simply adapted to the presence of alternative cultural forms, they have themselves been transformed. Contemporary Britain is multicultural and middle England is created through interactions with 'others' who are now part of itself. Letchmore Heath is simultaneously a traditional English village and also a place of pilgrimage for thousands of Hindus. In this sense it is at the heart of what Britain has become, and the struggle against it was – on some levels – a struggle against this change, whilst also helping to adapt to it and bringing about the change.

However, critical multiculturalism also needs to take account of how such discourses actually work out in multicultural praxis, particularly with relation to intercultural dynamics. People and groups may be involved in complex creative processes of constructing ethnic, cultural, and religious identities, but they are all doing so within particular political fields, and in the case of contemporary Britain the field is set out with a certain set of hegemonic relationships in which one particular cultural (and religious) form is set out as normative. Within this set of relationships there are discourses of multiculturalism that are articulated (such as the Home Secretary's statement), but they are so often done so in terms of 'difference multiculturalism' that is cultural diversity is welcomed as a state of different 'mosaic pieces'. The creativity of the processes by which the diverse groups and individuals interact with each other, and with majoritarian cultural perspectives (based on relations of power), are left unexamined in the interests of multicultural harmony.

I mentioned earlier in this chapter the comment by Peter van der Veer that one of 'the crucial issues facing the modern nation-state is how to deal with group differences' (van der Veer 1998:281), and that group differences within the context of nation-states (that is, plurality, or multiculturalism) have very often been based on religious identities. However, the nation-state does not remain a neutral player merely observing the articulation of differences. Through various political strategies and fields nation-states not only recognise differences but actually work to construct them. One such example of this is the articulation of differences between 'ethnic minority' and 'new' religions. Thus the state does:

> not so much [have] to relate to pre-existing cultural and religious differences, but is involved in producing that difference ... The modern state is an interventionist state which identifies and targets populations in order to reform and improve them ... It is ... not possible for the state to leave 'minorities' out of its reach of improvement and participation.' (van der Veer 1998:283)

Similarly, Talal Asad argues that legislation such as the *Race Relations Act* 1976, and in particular its interpretation through the case of *Mandla v. Dowell Lee* in 1983 (see chapter seven), has been a device by which English courts have been able to normalise ethnic groups and ethnic customs 'as exemptions from the rule' and thus has legalistically helped to construct cultural minorities (Asad 1993b:258–59). 'Because fundamentally *different* traditions are described as in themselves *contradictory* (and therefore in need of regulation), state power extends itself by treating them as norms to be incorporated and coordinated' (ibid.:261, emphasis in original). Thus one very significant conclusion that Asad takes from the British governmental response to the Rushdie affair is that the Muslim campaign against the *Satanic Verses* was a direct challenge to the government's 'authority to define crucial homogeneities and differences' (ibid.:267).

Gerd Baumann takes this argument forward a little further, by arguing that the operation of nation-state policy towards 'ethnic minorities' has the direct effect of creating particular communities (and to a lesser extent identities). In this respect:

> former migrants do not organize themselves into religious 'communities' in isolation from the surrounding nation-state. On the contrary, the purportedly secular state is an active partner in what I call the encorporation of religious different into quasi-corporate 'communities' ... [However] the transformation of traditions and currents into putative bodies of people need not, and in the cases I describe certainly does not, entail their incorporation 'into' the political system. In fact, it usually works in the opposite direction by depicting the encorporated as an autonomous body placed beyond and outside the relevant boundaries. (G. Baumann 1998:267)

That is (difference) multiculturalist discourses at the level of the ruling agencies of the nation-state (particularly through local authorities, but through other agencies, such as the courts) can help to create distinctive cultural groups, as well as the substantive discourses of differences between groups and individuals.

Although the Rushdie affair had the particular effect of helping to place British Muslims outside of majoritarian notions of British-ness (c.f. Asad 1993b, also Bhabha 1990), it also set up a number of complex distinctions between Muslims and other 'ethnic/religious' categories. In particular, it created clusters of responses that could be categorised into two distinct forms: that is between those who identified with the 'upset to Islam' (this category is composed predominantly but not exclusively of Muslims) and those who had similar experiences but disputed the notion of blasphemy (I am intending here to mean particularly those who identify as Hindus). Although the destruction of the Ayodhya mosque in India three and a half years later (in 1992) was to consolidate these differences most particularly, the setting up of activist British Muslims as pariahs of British cultural liberalism certainly served a purpose of dividing 'good tolerant' Hindus from 'intolerant Muslims', both in terms of external perceptions and also within Muslims' and Hindus' own perceptions of themselves and others. Thus, the particular demonisation of Muslims at the expense of other, similarly identified groups was a useful strategy for dividing the two categories and helping to reinforce the segregation of the two into distinct camps.

The parallels between British governmental responses to diversity by creating and reinforcing strategies of 'divide and rule' in India and in Britain are interesting to observe, in this case, as well as in the issues of similarity drawn from the debates on secularism which I discussed above. As Peter van der Veer observes:

> What is especially interesting is the extent to which the nation-state produces its own internal differences and actually works not through unification, but diversification ... For an Indianist like me it is fascinating to see how much of what postcolonial theory has been arguing about colonial India can also be shown in political processes in contemporary Britain. (van der Veer 1998:284).

Such a realisation should not be as startling as it is. On one level the relations between the English political establishment and South Asian Muslim and Hindu responses are themselves part of a developing history which began long before the migrations from the Indian subcontinent to Britain in the post-world war two (postcolonial) era. It is well known that many British people of South Asian descent will answer the question of what they are doing in Britain with the response 'we are over here because you were over there'. Conflicts over Rushdie's characterisations of Islam, and over the use of the religious site at Bhaktivedanta Manor are very much products of this long history of interaction and unequal power relations, and so could be said to be a continuation of a colonial frontier into a postcolonial and diasporic context. In this respect, the study of all minority religious manifestations in Britain ('new', 'ethnic', or whatever) needs to be included, in some way or other, within the emerging discourses of postcolonial theory.

Notes

1 I should also be possible to place within such a multidimensional frame liberal conceptualisations of *tolerance* and *human rights*, the latter of which I discussed in more depth in chapter seven, and the former operates (in varying degrees) within articulations of *multiculturalism* and *secularisation*.

2 For a related argument on the construction of a Hindu community out of national and nationalist (and supernationalist) discourses see Bhatt (1996).

3 As such, this is not necessarily the same as the discourse of *secularism*, which is the active propagation of an anti-religious perspective, or at least the propagation of the argument for the separation of religious institutions from governmental structures (for a discussion of the difference between secularisation and secularism, see Wilson 1991). But on the other hand, the use of the secularisation theory is not necessarily as distinct from secularism as is commonly assumed by sociologists. This may be the possible reason why a generation of students have had such problems with distinguishing between secularisation and secularism, because the difference between the two is more subtle than this dichotomy assumes.

4 This was indeed an analogy I used at Luton Crown Court when giving evidence in the case of *R. v W.M. Fleming and* ISKCON, 6th November 1995 when I was asked by the judge (Justice Rodwell) to explain how such performances could be

religious when they involved such a high degree of entertainment. The jury's verdict that the performances were *not* entertainment shows that such a translation may well have been quite effective.

5 Prince Charles is currently the heir to the monarchy, and is expected to become king at the death of his mother Queen Elizabeth II.

6 Christine Inglis makes a similar division of usages of the term multiculturalism as 'demographic descriptive', 'ideology and norms', and 'programme and policy' (quoted in Wievorka 1998:883). However, this breakdown ignores the various forms of practice of multicultural discourse, and appears to subsume academic discourses within the category of 'demographic descriptive'.

7 In the case of Canada, the primary motivation behind the policy of multiculturalism was not concerned with political accommodation to non-European minorities, but was in fact an attempt to deal with Québecois separation (see Wieviorka 199:884–85).

8 The nail bomb in Brixton on 17th April left 45 people injured, whilst the one in Brick Lane on 24th April had a more limited effect of injuring seven people because it was spotted before it went off. The bomb in Soho on 30th April, however, was placed in a crowded pub and not only killed three people sitting at one table, it caused injuries to another 65 people in the immediate vicinity. Responsibility for the first two bombs was claimed by several individuals representing different organisations, in particular two known far right fringe groups called Combat 18 and the White Wolves. However, on 1st May (the day after the Soho bomb) David Copeland was arrested and subsequently charged with causing all three explosions, and the police involved in this arrest made a public statement that they did not think he was an actual member of any far right organisation, and was working on his own (*The Independent*, Monday 3rd May 1999, p. 1).

9 Reported in *The Independent*, Monday 3rd May 1999, p. 2. Tony Blair made these comments in a speech to a conference of British Sikhs which had been arranged to celebrate the 300th anniversary of the Guru Gobind Singh's foundation of the Khalsa in 1699.

10 Quoted in *The Independent*, Tuesday 4th May 1999, p. 7. There are, of course, strong ambiguities in this speech which suggest it could be read in a number of ways. His invocation of 'the British people' makes a strong assumption that 'all of us' are the same, despite differences of ethnicity, religion, class, or sexual identity and thus could be read as asserting a weak monoculturalism, against the violent, strong and exclusive monoculturalism of those behind the bombs. However, Prince Charles' support in other contexts for discourses of cultural diversity suggests that his comments should be read as supporting the multiculturalism that was under attack.

11 Furthermore a privately sponsored prosecution, brought by Lawrence's parents, failed on the grounds that the police had not been able to provide enough evidence against the alleged murderers.

12 Robert Stam and Ella Shohat argue for a similar approach to diversification by introducing the term 'polycentric multiculturalism', which they argue 'envisions a restructuring of intercommunal relations within and beyond the nation state according to the internal and partially overlapping imperatives of diverse communities ... The emphasis in 'polycentrism', for us, is not on spatial points of origin but on fields of power, energy, and struggle. The 'poly', for us, does not refer to a finite list of centers of power but rather introduces a systematic principles of differentiation, relationality, and linkage (Stam and Shohat 1994:300).

13 C.f. Keesing (1997), Turner (1993), Stolcke (1995), G. Baumann (1999:87–90).

14 For example, in his reflections on Taylor's *Politics of Recognition*, Bhabha writes: 'Taylor always presents the multicultural or minority position as an imposition coming from the 'outside' and making its demands from there ... In fact the challenge is to deal not with them/us but with the historically and temporally disjunct positions that minorities occupy ambivalently within the nation's space. Taylor's evaluative scheme, which locates the presumptions of equality and the recognition of value (the before and the after of liberal judgement) in the *long dureé* of national and nationalizing cultures, is in fact antithetical to the Bakhtinian hybrid, which precisely undermines such claims to cultural totalization' (Bhabha 1996: 58).

15 However, Homi Bhabha's stress on the importance of literary texts as loci of hybridity is rather limiting in this respect, since such hybridisations occur and come out of a range of discursive and non-discursive practices. Thus 'Bhabha's claim that one can bring newness into the world, that one can reinvent oneself when one is writing from the cultural interstices, is a conceit of the literature-producing and consuming world ... [I]t is crucial to go beyond the analysis of literary discourses and representations to the social, political and economic contexts in which they are embedded. There may be nothing outside of the text, as Derrida proposes, but there is certainly something outside the literary text' (van der Veer 1997:102, 103).

16 Indeed, Chetan Bhatt's recent book *Liberation and Purity* gives an extended treatment of Hindu and Muslim identities, including a detailed consideration of religious practice from a multiculturalist perspective, and yet argues very much from a strongly rationalist position (Bhatt 1997).

17 Gerd Baumann makes an interesting point in this respect that majoritarian perspectives in Britain of black Afro-Caribbean groups do tend to be more ethnicised and less religionised than South Asians. 'While strong religious and congregational loyalties are commonly recognized among both these categories, the former are seen as 'Blacks' or 'West Indians', 'Jamaicans' or 'not Jamaicans'. They are hardly ever identified as Methodists or Church of England, Pentecostalists or Adventists, Spiritualists or Rastafarians, and few if any local councils would even think about providing their public services through any of the latter, and 'ethnically' exclusive, congregations. Citizens of South Asian backgrounds, by contrast, are most readily distinguished as Muslims, Hindus, and Sikhs ...' (G. Baumann 1998:275). Although I can claim no quantitative support for this, my impression is that academic literature (in sociology, anthropology, religious studies, and perhaps even cultural studies) has also represented this dichotomous reification. That is, most papers and books on South Asians discuss religious identities, whilst those on black Afro-Caribbeans concentrate more on ethnic and cultural identities.

18 It appears to me that contemporary academics (and other things) have decided that Islam (as a category/stereotype) is good to *think with* (c.f. Levi-Strauss 1964), whether in positive or negative terms. Indeed Islam provides perhaps the easiest multiculturalist contrast to majoritarian western perspectives – as a religion and culture, 'it' is perhaps seen to be (more than any other cultural manifestation) as the 'other' of 'contemporary western liberal culture'. One possible further reflection from this is that the success of the ISKCON campaign was because Hindus managed to convince the important decision-makers that they were *not the same* as Muslims.

19 For an excellent collection of papers on religious hybridity, or syncretism, see Stewart and Shaw (1994). See also Bhatt (1997) and Vishvanathan (1996).

20 This notwithstanding, some 'new religions' have managed to come into the wider politics of multiculturalism through inter-faith dialogue (which could be seen as a religious adjunct of multiculturalism) although even here many alternative religious groups tend to be wary of the context and politics of inter-faith praxis. Most alternative religious groups which are active in inter-faith circles are either proponents of a liberal inclusive philosophy that matches well (even if not theologically) with the liberal Christians who form the backbone of inter-faith activity, or otherwise who can establish their credentials as adherents of an authentic world religion.

21 The list can show some variations, but it is usually based around Christianity, Judaism, Islam, Buddhism, Hinduism, and Sikhism in particular, and perhaps also Shintoism, Daoism, and Jainism. It is interesting to note that in a number of academic Religious Studies departments (in Britain and north America) there are now a number of courses (and appointments) which are centred on 'New Religions' and which are taught alongside other 'Religions' courses (such as Buddhism, Hinduism, Judaism, Islam, etc.) as though the category New Religions has now gained academic credibility as new type of western based 'world religion'. Although this does give some measure of academic credibility to such new and alternative forms of religiosity, the assumption underlying this is pretty nonsensical. Categorising the diverse manifestations into a separate class of 'new religions' belies both the diversity and the fluidity of many of these manifestations in a similar way to the classification of diverse practices into the category of 'Hinduism'.

22 The central doctrine of the Unification Church that Sun Myung Moon is the Lord of the Second Coming, and the exposition on the nature of this redemptive messiah which is outlined in the *Divine Principle* are considered to be unacceptable for most 'mainstream' Christians for the Unification Church to be classed as part of the Christian tradition. However, the Korean cultural background of Revd Moon, some of which is incorporated into the Unification Church, does give the church some measure of legitimacy in this respect as an internationalised member of the category of 'Korean religions', which could be seen as belonging to a 'minor league' of world religions.

23 Turner recognises that this is a problematic term. In this context he intends to mean that such identities are produced in a relatively unself-conscious manner, and to clarify this he argues that most 'ethnic' groupings in contemporary multicultural society do not come under this category.

24 For a detailed consideration of ethnicity in relation to the Peoples Temple suicides, see Maaga (1998), who also gives an excellent account of the many voices that helped to create the final tragedy in Guyana. For discussions of Waco, see Tabor and Gallagher (1995) and Wright (1995).

25 Such as in France, Belgium, Germany, and Sweden.

26 It is hard to imagine the much publicised visit by Princes Charles, the future king of Great Britain, to the Swaminarayan temple in Neasden in 1996 being repeated to Bhaktivedanta Manor. Both the Swaminarayan Hindu Mission and ISKCON are sectarian forms of Vaishnavism, and both predominantly attack Gujaratis, but the former is classed as ethnic Hinduism, whilst the latter is still too much associated with cultishness to make a royal visit (and hence endorsement) likely.

CHAPTER TEN

Postcolonial Conflict in an English Village: Some Concluding Reflections

The long and complex history of the Bhaktivedanta Manor dispute suggests that there cannot be any simple or straightforward explanations for why ISKCON found themselves in such a protracted dispute over what they considered their 'right' to use the place for worship. At a fairly straightforward level it could be explained as the result of a racist attempt to exclude Asians or Hindus from what is perceived as a quintessentially (white) English village. Otherwise, it was the result of a lack of tolerance of diversity, or difference, and particularly the religious difference expressed by a group who were identified as a 'new religion', a 'cult', or (sometimes) an 'ethnic religion'. The explanation given by the villagers, and other local residents, was also a partial truth – that ISKCON were encouraging to their fairly limited facilities the numbers of worshippers that would be far better accommodated in a large purpose-built venue with suitable access. Indeed, it was ISKCON's eventual recognition of this that led them to pursue a successful alternative campaign, resulting in the construction of the access driveway.

No matter how one looks at this particular dispute, one sees it through a particular perspective and sees it caused and maintained by certain factors. There can be no political neutrality with respect to the issue, since in a campaign that was fought out through national media publications, and at the highest level of British politics all participation in the debate helped to shape its direction. Sebastian Poulter's extended treatment of the case in his volume on ethnic minority rights and laws (1998:237–276), although written after the decision in 1996 to build the access driveway, does itself enter this political domain. Thus, after an extended reportage of the details of the two major planning inquiries, Poulter decides to conclude his discussion with some very simplistic generalisations:

> Fortunately, planning permission for the construction of a new access driveway ultimately enabled a long-standing problem to be resolved in a manner in which the reasonable requirements of both

> worshippers and villagers could be satisfactorily accommodated. In the end, the English legal system proved capable of settling the dispute through the flexible application of its ordinary planning principles, without any need for a specific provision designed for the exclusive benefit of ISKCON or Hindus. Religious freedom was properly accorded considerable weight ... (Poulter 1998:276)

Thus, he shows his sympathies to lie with the essential practicality and robustness of 'English Law', and more generally in the rhetorical discourse of 'religious freedom'.

In making such a claim about lack of neutral ground, I am not intending to exclude myself from this analysis. As a researcher, I began visiting the Manor in autumn 1993, and on my first visit to the Manor I remember being part of a procession which included at one stage an invocation to Krishna to help smooth the path towards the purchase of lands adjacent to the Manor grounds, which could hopefully be the site of the access driveway solution. On the same visit it was suggested to me in plain language that the existing temple facilities were not enough, that one day a proper hall would be needed if the place was to meet the full needs of the visiting devotees. During the midst of the public inquiry, in late 1994/early 1995 the person who had said these words made a firm statement to me that he would never have made such a suggestion, worried that my quotation of the statement in a research paper which I had then written would be used as evidence against ISKCON by Hertsmere council. In deference to his wishes I decided to exclude this passage from the paper, which within a matter of weeks I had in fact sent to the chief planning officer at Hertsmere, who was at the time preparing her case to fight ISKCON at the public inquiry. The decision I made, based on personal and academic reasons (I saw no reason to quote a statement that was later denied and had been said 'off the record'), obviously had political implications for ISKCON's case.

From December 1994, however, I found myself very clearly implicated within the conflict. Quite by accident Gill Gowing, Hertsmere's chief planning officer, phoned up the college where I was then working, asking to speak to someone in the religious studies department who might have some knowledge of Hinduism. I was in my office to take the call, and so readily accepted her offer to act as an academic consultant for Hertsmere on the religious issues of the case (ISKCON were already making use of Kim Knott, of the University of Leeds, in this respect). With some knowledge of ISKCON, Hindu traditions in Britain, and the history of the campaign, I felt I was well qualified to give them advice. I made it clear from my initial conversation with them that I had sympathies with ISKCON's position, and that particularly I would like to see the access driveway constructed to solve the traffic problems and to keep the Manor open. I was also very aware that they could have found some other academic who had a quite different opinion on the legitimacy and status of ISKCON, and who could have made some aspects of the public inquiry more difficult for ISKCON. However, from my conversations with the team of planners at Hertsmere council at that time, I quickly gained the impression that although their interpretation of planning policy in respect to the Manor was different from my own, we did in fact share fairly similar perspectives on evaluating ISKCON as a generally sincere and well intentioned religious organisation. It was on this basis that I agreed to give detailed advice to Hertsmere during their preparation for the public inquiry in 1995, although they decided that there would be no use for me to give any testimony within the context of the proceedings of the inquiry itself.

However a few months later in October 1995 I was called to give expert witness in court on behalf of Hertsmere planning authority in the criminal prosecution of ISKCON over the breach of the enforcement notice (see chapter four). In this case, I found that my role was not so much to provide any direct evidence against ISKCON (beyond the fact that large scale worship had occurred at Janmasthami in August 1994, something which was clearly evident and established by all concerned). Instead it fell to me to give an academic, and therefore politically 'normative' perspective[1] that ISKCON are an established religious group who are derived from a certain cultural and sectarian strand of 'Hinduism', and are thus are not necessarily a 'freakish' or dangerous 'cult'. In such terms, I was therefore arguing that ISKCON should be viewed as much as an 'ethnic religion' as a 'new religion', and that any decisions made by the jury and judge should be on this basis. Thus within an adversarial legal system in which all testimony and witness is given by those for and against a prosecution, I saw my role as someone who could provide perspectives on both sides of this conflict, and that my own testimony did not compromise the generally good will I felt towards ISKCON and the campaign they were fighting for Bhaktivedanta Manor. Because of this, I was not altogether surprised when ISKCON lost the case and were found guilty of violating the planning laws (nor indeed were ISKCON all that surprised either, see chapter four), but I was somewhat amazed by the scale of the fine imposed on ISKCON by a judge who took a pragmatically sceptical view of ISKCON's activities over the years. Indeed, one part of the financial penalty imposed upon ISKCON was half of the prosecution's (that is, Hertsmere's) costs, which included half of my own fees and expenses.

The intention behind my writing up these small vignettes on some of my engagements within the campaign for the Manor is to show how I do not intend to bypass the issue of personal detachment from the analysis. I have been writing this book as someone with experience of ISKCON, but no direct alignment with the personal, political, and spiritual agendas that attachment to Krishna consciousness usually involves. I am not a devotee, and of the many identities that I have there are not many that would situate me within the broad constituency of political interests that fought so vigorously to 'save the Manor'. What I have been trying to present in this book, therefore, is my own engagement with and analysis of the series of events that emerged out of the interactions between ISKCON (both as an organisation, and individual devotees) and various elements of the social and political structures in which they are placed. In so doing I have sought to bring to the foreground in particular aspects of the campaign and the debates which I have found most interesting, and from which I have been able to generalise to some degree or other (over issues such as multiculturalism, human rights, and general perspectives on evaluating religious identities).

On arriving in this final chapter, however, I also feel there is some place for exercising an attempt at interpretation of the events that I have analysed: albeit an interpretation which is situated in my own engagement with some of the characters, texts, and situations which I have tried to describe. And it is from this perspective that I would argue that, for a large extent, the dispute was fuelled by the breakdown (on both sides) of multicultural rhetoric; or rather, the politics of multiculturalism was used in an hegemonic and racist manner by certain 'white British' power groups against a religious/cultural minority. Thus, the conflict very much revolved around issues of minoritarianism, or subalternity, in which a collection of people became defined as a minority group vis-à-vis a powerful, hegemonic majority, and through the processes of such constructions came to exercise a measure of power by challenging, opposing, and succumbing to the determining influences of the political establishment. In as much as this minority group was an historical result of migrations from India (of people, practices, and ideas), the Manor became a (post)colonial frontier in the English countryside.

Postcolonial theory and minority religious forms

By introducing some aspects of postcolonial theory at this point I do not intend to produce a neat conceptual package that can tie up all the loose ends left over from the foregoing analysis of the Bhaktivedanta Manor campaign. Instead, my intention is to raise a few possibilities that tend to be overlooked when analyses are made of 'new religions': that is the international dimensions which are based not only on ease of communication and travel but also on discrepancies of power and access to material resources.

However, as I discussed in the previous chapter, one of my intentions in this book is to conflate the two categories of 'new religion' and 'minority religion', not only by questioning the designation of the term 'religion', but also by placing both types of religious manifestations (and organisations) within multicultural conceptual categories. Therefore my dalliance here with postcolonial theory is intended not only to open up *obviously* 'colonially'-derived religious groups (such as British Indians) to such analysis, but also to introduce the same analysis to the field of study which is marked out as 'new religious movement' studies. Thus a considerable number of groups identified as 'new religions' in the west derive from non-western ('third' or 'developing world') contexts (ISKCON from India and the Unification Church from Korea are the two most obvious examples) or have otherwise substantially involved themselves in non-western countries (for example, the missionary work of The Family and many emerging evangelical Christian groups). Indeed, other groups and practices which do not fit in so easily within such a framework can never be 'immune' from postcolonial analysis, since western cultural life is intrinsically bound up with (and ultimately shaped by) histories of colonisation and exploitation of non-European countries.[2] This is particularly true of all the main Christian religious organisations in Britain (including of course the Churches of England and Scotland) who were actively engaged for many years in colonial projects through their missionary efforts.

Although in recent years there has been some analysis of the global dimensions of the study of 'new religions', for a large part this has focused on global interconnections and dissemination within particular international contexts, and where substantial power relations have been examined they have primarily been concerned with nation-state politics, rather than hegemonic power structures that set up complex transnational interactions around the basic dichotomy of 'the west versus the rest'. Thus globalisation theory as applied to the study of 'new religions' has, for a large, part left out the crucial dimensions of non-western politics, and particularly western countries' historical and contemporary relations of domination and exploitation of a large part of the non-western world. Although questions about the class background of north American practitioners of alternative forms of religiosity are important ones to ask – for example, why so many are from comfortable middle-class backgrounds which have been working through various manifestations of counter-culture for the past thirty years – international postcolonial questions shift the emphasis away from the parochialisation of seeing such classes merely on the level of nations. What sorts of global factors (particularly of exploitation) have produced such affluent but 'disaffected' (or experimental) populations in western countries, and what produced – what can be characterised as – the plundering of 'Eastern spirituality' by bourgeois hippies from the late 1960s onwards? This is one contribution that I would argue postcolonial theoretical approaches can make to the study of alternative forms of religiosity (and indeed vice versa). Such a theoretical perspective tries to contextualise contemporary and historical events through a series of frames derived from a recognition that global power relations are unequal, and have been for a very long time, and yet the terms of engagement between interlocutors within these various locations of the colonial and postcolonial world have been produced by a number of factors which are partly but not wholly material.[3]

It is with some hesitation that I am introducing these approaches to my analysis, primarily because 'postcolonial theory' does have its problems. Although Edward Said's *Orientalism* (1978) has long been an established classic, the writings of the other two members of the 'Holy Trinity' of postcolonial theory – Gayatri Spivak and Homi Bhabha – are regarded as obscure texts, not only in terms of their writing styles and use of theory in quite eclectic ways, but also because of their heavy dependence on literature as a source and subject of theory. On top of this, postcolonial theory can often appear as a faddish development within academic disciplines which involves privileged white western academics in comfortable economic situations trying to 'get a bit of the other' (Pile and Thrift 1995:15) by taking on board the perspectives (and sometimes politics) of less privileged non-western subalterns. On the other hard, exactly where the boundaries lie between postcolonial approaches and globalisation theory are extremely hard to map – if it is done well, globalisation theory could and should produce the types of critical questions and analysis that postcolonial writers are keenly pursuing. Most particularly, the emphasis that Said, Spivak, and Bhabha all place on literary texts over other discursive and non-discursive practices is a problem that can alienate many who are working outside of the area of literature studies. In this respect, I would be wary of a too enthusiastic or fundamentalist adaptation of postcolonial theory within the study of religion, fearing that the theoretical foci of Spivak, Bhabha, and Said would encourage a retreat into the excessive textuality which has been for so long one of the key *problems* of the discipline of religious studies.

However, I do think that there are theoretical innovations that can be drawn from some elements of postcolonial theory that can be employed (perhaps catechristically) regardless of whether one accepts any of the writers' primary methodological approaches. Or, to put this another way, one does not have to be a postcolonial theorist to make use of postcolonial theory. Indeed, postcolonial theory is an open, fluid, and indeed very much situated concept (c.f. Mani and Frankenberg 1993) which should not be reduced to any one particular disciplinary approach or area of study. What such an approach can give to this study is the types of questions that are raised, and perhaps some of the theoretical images or frameworks that help to contextualise relationships of inequality in transnational contexts. In particular, postcolonial theory encourages a mapping out of the silences that are contained in any text, asking awkward questions about how constructions and relations of 'otherness' are implicit within discourses, bringing to the fore the silenced 'others' whose actions (and often labour) have helped to produce European/North American global hegemony. For a large part, this strategy has been focused on trying to recover the silenced voices of subalterns from historical records (predominantly in Indian contexts).[4] But it has also sought to raise questions of where the silences are to be found and explored within narratives and discourses of colonialism and neo-colonialism (for example Bhabha 1994, Spivak 1993, Suleri 1992). One such example of this is Spivak's catechristic use of major works of English literature, exploring the linkages of characters such as the creole Jamaican Bertha Mason (the first Mrs Rochester) in Charlotte Brontë's *Jane Eyre* and the reliance of the great house on slave plantations in Antigua in Jane Austen's *Mansfield Park* (Spivak 1996). That is, because of the long history of colonialism in western countries it has become a significant political strategy to ignore and erase the linkages with colonised cultures that have perpetuated (and sometimes disrupted) western discourses. These global connections are as significant in contemporary contexts as at any other time since European colonial expansions into Asia and Africa began, and a very significant point made by postcolonial theorists is that western cultures (and western academia) cannot be understood without reference to the colonial and postcolonial legacy.

Postcolonial studies of British South Asians are not altogether new – one significant focus for discourse within this field has been reactions to the Rushdie affair, and the narratives of migrancy, diaspora, and colonial legacy that are expressed in Rushdie's work, particularly *The Satanic Verses*. Indeed, it could be argued that the post-Rushdie industry has taken Rushdie as the first major (still living) martyr of the postcolonial era. Rushdie himself did do some interesting things with his narrativisations of hybridity, transculturalism, and postcolonial contexts in *The Satanic Verses*, and this of course has been eclipsed by the Islamic opposition to the passages in his book which were read as blasphemous insults to the Prophet Mohammed. However, Rushdie's approach to cultural translation and adaptation among British people of South Asian ancestry is one perspective out of many, and the criticisms made by Aijaz Ahmad that his characterisation is severely weakened by his representation of women and sexuality are in my opinion quite justified (Ahmad 1992). What I think is more important, however, is that the furore provoked in Britain following publication of *The Satanic Verses* (particularly prior to Ayatollah Khomeini's *fatwa* against him) demonstrates a manifest inability of Rushdie to *speak to* those who he wrote about – instead his literary style, form, and subject matter reached a quite different audience of white, liberal, middle-class intelligentsia.

By raising postcolonial theory in the context of British Indians, British Hindus, and British Vaishnavas, my intention is to show that it embraces other aspects of South Asian cultural and religious practices in Britain which are silenced or ignored in Rushdie's narratives (as well as postcolonialist discourses on Rushdie). That is, the presence of various forms, transplantations, and recreations of religiosity from India (and other parts of the subcontinent) in British contexts in the last part of the twentieth century is very much bound up with postcolonial inheritances which have been directly and indirectly disrupting and challenging normative ideas and assumptions of what Britishness and Englishness mean. However, these disruptions are not only occurring through creolisations and hybridisations that create obvious syncretic blends (such as the disco-isation of Panjabi *bhangra* music). These postcolonial disruptions are also happening through traditionalisations and anti-syncretisations (or anti-hybridisations) which were most obviously manifest in the Islamic reactions to Rushdie's work. In the context of British manifestations of Hindu religious identities, similar traditionalisations have occurred (working in different ways) through recreations of conceptions of Hindu practices. In some cases this has tied in with developments of Hindutva (Hindu nationalism) within the Indian political scene, but I would also like to question the common assumption that reconstructions of Hinduism in Britain are tied in completely with such Hindu revivalism (c.f. Bhatt 1997). In particular, ISKCON's avowedly non-political stance, and the distance ISKCON leaders and devotees try to put between themselves (theological and politically) and groups such as the VHP do suggest that Hindu forms of revivalism and retraditionalisation in British contexts are not wholly derivative of Indian political developments.[5] That is, reconstructions of Hindu practice in Britain, particularly around the concept of Hinduism (rather than other religious or cultural identities), are part of the postcolonial context of multiculturalist and secularist Britain. Such reconstructed British Hindus have created (and have had created) for themselves new forms of subalternity, being located as a significant minority 'group' or constituency who are very much defined as other, and yet also are able to collectively articulate a very powerful political voice (as the success of ISKCON's campaign clearly suggests). This is very much because of the material empowerment of a significant number of British Hindus – their strength lies more in their considerable wealth than in their numbers. However, this has to be balanced against the fact that such powerful subalternity is not distributed equitably among those who consider themselves Hindu. There are significant differences among the general group according to caste, class, gender, age, sectarian affiliation, and regional origin, all of which serve to privilege certain Hindu voices in contemporary Britain over others.

I will explore below how (from my perspective) it appears that the processes of mimicry that Bhabha analyses with respect to Indian discourses in nineteenth century India can be applied to the legal and political practices of ISKCON and Hindus within the campaign to keep Bhaktivedanta Manor open. But more generally, I would argue that (from what could be called a postcolonial perspective) the campaign for the Manor was, in large part, a peaceful challenge made by Hindus as a minority, subaltern group against the British nation-state.

The campaign was of course fought on the basis of Hindus' right to freedom of religion, and was concerned primarily with the issue of access to worship at the Radha-Gokulananda temple. However, underlying these discourses there were also issues arising directly from the racist exclusions that I alluded to at the beginning of this chapter. There were few reported instances of overt racism directed against ISKCON and devotees: the case of the ethnic monitoring that I mentioned in chapter four is the most obvious example of this (when separate counts were made in 1985 of the number of 'white' and 'coloured' visitors to the Manor), but there is even here a measure of subtlety involved in such racism and the instance has been subsequently contested (as the investigators' own initiative rather than any direction from the council planning authority). There have been other contested incidents, such as reports of the British National Party (an extreme right wing political party) canvassing for support in Letchmore Heath (unsuccessfully), and Councillor Frank Ward told me once informally of the racist bigotry he had found amongst Conservative and Liberal councillors on Hertsmere council (although such allegations have been denied strongly by those so accused within the council chamber). In general, the experience and discourses on racism have worked in more implicit and subtle ways, such as through the common acknowledgement by devotees that one of the crucial elements in the opposition in Letchmore Heath was not so much an intolerance of ISKCON or of religion, but rather worries about the effect the temple (if given full planning status) could have on property prices.[6] This is, in effect, a variation on the common white British middle-class fear that the arrival of an 'Asian family' in a street will lower prices because of a fear of 'swamping' and mass influx of other Asians. On a yet more subtle level, the feeling has been that the British political system (particularly the planning system) was throughout the conflict insensitive to and intolerant of differences, not merely cultural or 'racial' differences, but also different articulations of religious concepts, such as what constitutes 'public entertainment' and what is the role of a 'theological college'.

All of these perceptions of racism helped to fuel Hindus' determination to fight for the temple, and particularly struck a chord with the late-teenage/early-adult men and women who formed groups such as Hindu Youths Saving Our Temple and Pandava Sena. Through this medium the fight for the temple was a fight *against* white, Anglo-Saxon Anglican racism, and so was very much a challenge by a minority, subaltern group against cultural and political hegemony. And, through making the challenge, it is clear that such Hindus were empowered on a number of different levels. Obviously, ISKCON's eventual victory was a significant empowerment, since it showed that the 'system' could be challenged and beaten (however, as I will discuss below, the planning system was also victorious by deciding to give permission to the road and the temple). But the fact that a challenge could be made – and made in such a powerful way through very important media of the British political apparatus – were also crucial expressions of this subaltern empowerment. Hindus and Krishna devotees were able to fight racism (and English cultural hegemony) through courts, public inquiries, through newspaper columns, television and radio, and even into the lobbying corridors of centralised political power in Westminster. All of these are locations of considerable symbolic capital in British cultural life, through which a self-consciously minority group could express their outrage and challenge, and thus could create a sense (if not necessarily an actualisation) of empowerment.

ISKCON is, like many such religious movements, a manifestation of cultural hybridity which is self-conceived as traditional, orthodox, and (to a large degree) pure. The organisation is not simply a hybrid 'cross' between Prabhupada's unchanged, traditional Gaudiya Vaishnavism and the white personnel who joined ISKCON after its foundation in 1966. Prabhupada's religious inheritance came to him through an organisation (the Gaudiya Math) which was formed in colonial Bengal in the early twentieth century, itself a generation after the reconstitution of Gaudiya Vaishnavism by an employee of the colonial government (Bhaktivinod Thakur). That is, the religious and cultural formulations that Prabhupada brought with him to North America in 1965, and which he used as the basis for recreating the Gaudiya Math in an international context as ISKCON, were themselves hybridisations emerging out of colonial encounters. The impetus for Prabhupada's travel was the instruction by his spiritual teacher Bhaktisiddanta Saraswati to take Krishna consciousness to the English.

This is not to challenge the authenticity or purity of the Vaishnavism that has been carried and mediated through these various manifestations. Instead what I am trying to show here is that the encounter between Gaudiya Vaishnavism and western cultures did not begin with the setting up of Prabhupada's shop in the lower East Side of New York. The creation and spread of ISKCON was rather a dramatically significant development within a history of interactions, shaped very much by late nineteenth/early twentieth century Bengali Vaishnavites' recognition of and reactions to the British political and cultural hegemony of the then colonial era, and their manifest desire to counter such hegemony through active proselytisation. The acting out of this desire finally produced – in a postcolonial era, nearly twenty years after Indian Independence, with the USA now as the global superpower – the particular result of a recreation of certain forms of Vaishnavism (and thus Hinduism) within western contexts. The blending of these cultural forms took another twist in Britain with the rapid involvement of recent immigrants (originally from India) at Bhaktivedanta Manor in the mid-1970s, who soon became a very important constituency (and congregation) of support for ISKCON.

The well defined and well packaged Vaishnavism that Prabhupada incorporated into ISKCON became a popular option for many newly located British Indians, who were themselves trying to come to terms with issues of reformulating identities and practices out of their hybrid experiences of British, western, Hindu, and Indian cultural forms. In some respects, ISKCON provided a form of Hinduism for westerners – whether they be indigenous (or native) white westerners, or westerners of Indian ancestry. The campaign for Bhaktivedanta Manor, I think, came to be used as important symbolic capital in such renegotiations of identity and practice: by fighting for Krishna and ISKCON, Hindu supporters were themselves helped to recreate and encourage a reconstruction of Hindu/Indian/diaspora identities in British contexts. This was particularly true for younger Hindus, who had little or no experience of life beyond Britain – who formed the basis of the youth groups such Pandava Sena – but it was also true among older (migrated) generations in a different way. The conflict very much involved a *placing* (in terms of physically siting as well as cultural negotiation) of their conceptualisations of Hinduism in their present locations: as Hindus in London, in England, and in Britain. The fight to establish the legitimacy of the Radha-Gokulananda temple helped to create for them an establishment of their religious conceptions of personal and cultural identities.

At the same time, though, the development of the campaign became an obviously political action to place 'Hinduism' in an essentially English location (in a quiet country village). Thus the conflict was very much an ideological clash: between a white/powerful/secularist perspective and what could be called Indian/subaltern/religious. However, in setting up this contrast, it is important to point out Homi Bhabha's point that such dichotomies are never absolute, and that in fact the negotiations between and across such contrasts are the means by which they are worked out. There was indeed a lot of playing between these two positions – for example, there was considerable Christian church support for ISKCON, and ISKCON made considerable use of the legal mechanisms, discourses, and procedures of the dominant majority. And of course by using such mechanisms, ISKCON actually achieved a subaltern victory. Also, ironically, the subaltern victory of placing Hinduism and Vaishnavism in this essentially English site was only achieved by taking the Manor (almost literally) out of the village, by cutting the point of access between the Manor and Letchmore Heath. Following construction of the access road, very few visitors to the Manor now interact with the village (entering the grounds along the road which goes across open fields), and conversely very few villagers now have any of the direct experiences of the visitors that were so much a part of life in Letchmore Heath for over twenty years (from 1973 to 1996). Although the Manor has not, of course, actually moved, its location has in fact been re-placed with respect to its immediate neighbourhood.

Religion in the political field of planning

One very important legacy of the writings of Michel Foucault is that contemporary analysts of social and historical contexts need to ask certain types of questions about the 'hidden' circumstances of action that look beyond the obviousness of the events themselves. One such set of questions moves away from asking about the how and the why of the particularities, and instead looks towards the underlying themes working within discourses and fields of power. In particular, it becomes necessary to ask how do certain fields and practices of power create certain ways of thinking and practice?

Within any social or political context there are of course many different fields of power, operating across each other (very often in opposition, sometimes helping to produce each other). Here I would like to return to a theme that I began to discuss in chapter three, that is a point touched upon by Foucault that the use and control of space is one such very important field of power within a number of nation-states. In the context of Britain, this is encapsulated in the planning system: the framework of laws, policies, guidelines, and planning practitioners whose role is designated by the state to determine how (and which) people practise particular places (that is, how buildings are used, by whom, in what ways, where, etc.). This type of power is what Foucault (1984:247–48) alludes to, but dismisses, with respect to the role of architects, since once an architect's plans have been actualised s/he can have no direct control over how the space is used. In contrast, it is planning officers who have the power to accept or reject architect's suggestions, and also to monitor (directly and panoptically) the continual use of a place and to take action if the place is used in any way which is different from its authorised planning determination.

This type of power is quite obvious and manifest. It is a direct means through which the state regulates the lives of individual people and groups at a local level. However, the practice of this power is more complicated than this suggests, since although (as the Bhaktivedanta Manor conflict shows) the planning authorities do have a lot of power, it is the operationalisations (and internalisations) of such power forms within the planning field that determine practice more than any direct exercise of legislative or judicial power. That is, the planning apparatus creates certain types of spatial practice which are very much determined by planning legislation and planning practice. At its most extreme, perhaps, one could argue that planning practice is a very effective means of colonising living space, and particularly of homogenising the uses of space by groups and individuals who may otherwise differ from majoritarian expectations.

To employ the Manor conflict as an example of this: ISKCON found it necessary to fit into a legal system which defined land use into categories which separated out a domestic residence from a place of public worship and a theological (educational) college. Although at times ISKCON wished to challenge these categories, and to step outside of them, they found they also had to engage with and become determined by them in order to put forward such a challenge. Thus, at an early stage (that is, when the Manor was being created in 1973) a decision had to be made that it would serve ISKCON's purposes if they defined the Manor's purpose as a *math* (a place of education and training of temple priests) as roughly equivalent to other forms of training colleges (particularly theological colleges) with respect to planning regulations. This was, of course, an expedient decision to make, since it meant that the creation of the Manor could go ahead in 1973 without becoming too delayed by negotiations (and probably applications) with the local planning authority. In due course, as it became clear in later years that ISKCON were not using the building according to what the local planning authority considered to be appropriate for a training college, ISKCON found themselves entering a debate on the extent to which public worship should or could be ancillary to the activities of a theological college.

At the level of the discourses that they participated in through the courts, planning structures, and through lobbying channels, the use that ISKCON were making of Bhaktivedanta Manor came to be directed more and more to the expectations put on them by planning criteria. At this level, the only appropriate strategy that ISKCON could pursue in planning terms was that the Manor should be recognised as a place of public worship. And the only way they could achieve such recognition was by arguing *through* planning discourses and not *against* them. Thus, they argued (eventually successfully) that the Manor should be a place which was both a theological college (use class C2) and a place of worship (use class D1) – which as a combination of different use classes was considered by planning officials as *sui generis* (and hence something of a hotchpotch). Indeed, the success of ISKCON at achieving this planning status has meant that they are now required to incorporate their uses of the place more closely to those expected of them by the planning guidelines. Now that conformity with their planning status has been achieved for the Manor, it has become harder to use the place in ways which are not defined by the planning authority as legitimate. In this sense, by requiring ISKCON to apply for and then be given planning permission for certain 'authorised uses', the planning authority have now been able to create more compliance on the part of this subaltern group (and so at last bring them more under their authority).

This success out of defeat by the planning officers can be seen by looking at the situation prior to the completion of the access road. ISKCON had for a long time decided to avoid, as far as possible, arguments that strayed too far out of planning discourses. Thus, they fought the campaign mainly in terms of the planning benefits and challenges offered by the alternatives of closure of the Manor or the building of the road, and they made a strong effort to play down arguments within the public domain that were based on allegations of racism or intolerance motivating their opponents. However, whilst they were involved with these engagements with planning procedures and locations (such as courts and public inquiries) they were also very much involved in promoting practices that challenged the authority of this planning system. From 1973 through to 1996, Bhaktivedanta Manor was continually used in the ways that Krishna devotees and leaders intended it to be used: small scale and large scale worship took place on regular bases, despite the fact that throughout this time the planning determination explicitly defined the Manor as a place where public worship should *not* take place. (Arguably this was not explicit until Chris Patten made his decision following the first main public inquiry in 1990, or perhaps the collapse of the final appeal in 1992.) It was only during the brief period between 1983 and 1985 – when the Section 52 agreement permitted worship exceeding 1,000 visitors on six festival days each year – that the planning authority gave ISKCON any leeway in this respect, and even then it was clear that ISKCON were prepared to allow use of the Manor which exceeded these quotas.

I am highlighting this point not so much to suggest any bad grace on the part of ISKCON, or some crafty flouting or avoidance of the planning legislation, but rather to underline the point made by Michel de Certeau about the mismatch between the regulation and use of space, or in this particular example between the discourses of planning authority and the actual practices of place (de Certeau 1984:95–98). This is summed up in de Certeau's concept of 'walking': that the gridlines of planning authorities may set out the ways in which a space should be practised, and indeed those who make such practices are happy to enter the discourses that are set out by these authorities. At the same time, however, the practices that took place within the planning apparatus, under the noses of the planners, was in direct contrast to what *should be*. Even when the Manor should not have been used for large scale worship – particularly at the end of the legal line in 1994 when every available challenge had been made and lost by ISKCON – what actually occurred at the Manor was exactly that: large scale worship. The thousands of visitors (including myself) who attended at Janmasthami in late August 1994, and on many other occasions, were walking within gaps in the planning apparatus, walking over the best endeavours of the planning authority to prevent them being at the place and using the Manor in such a way. In this sense, whether directly or intentionally, or merely by being in that place, these people, and particularly the leaders of ISKCON who facilitated and encouraged their presence, were challenging the power of the planning authority. The seriousness of this challenge was, I would argue, a motivating factor behind Justice Rodwell taking a very hard line against ISKCON in November 1995 by setting such a high fine for this criminal activity (organising the Janmasthami festival and hence violating their permitted planning use). He saw ISKCON as deliberately 'flouting the law' and trying time and again to 'push its luck' (LCC:sentence, see chapter four). His role, as a judge asked to adjudicate on a specific criminal violation, also became one of making clear the seriousness of the challenge of such a systematic violation.

The challenge offered was both an obvious and a subtle one. In many respects it fits in very much with Homi Bhabha's concept of hybridity (Bhabha 1994). What ISKCON managed to get away with for a long time was a sort of mimicry of planning power: they put a lot of effort into fighting within the planning system, whilst at the same time flagrantly challenging it. This was very much an exercise of subaltern power, the system was challenged without being directly challenged. The same can also be said for the use made of the other major discursive strand of ISKCON's appeal: that is the reliance on the discourse of rights and 'religious freedom'. On the one level it is quite obvious why ISKCON chose to employ this strategy – it is a commonly held perspective across many different manifestations of British culture that there should be 'free practice of religion' (within unspecifiable limits). The vagueness of such a discourse (particularly prior to the HRA in 1998) made it an ideal strategy to use to contest a situation in which the planning authority appeared to consider the 'pure planning' issues as (relatively) straightforward. The question of whether or not such a discourse of 'rights' and 'freedoms' is compatible with the idioms of Gaudiya Vaishnavism is a moot point, but one which is not particularly relevant – since the practice of ISKCON devotees at the Manor was to *make* it compatible (or to ignore or downplay any incompatibilities).

What seems more important than this, however, is the apparent challenge to state authority that is effected through the mobilisation of this discourse by a religious minority organisation who otherwise advocate a rather ambivalent attitude towards the principles of liberal secularist democracy. As Talal Asad argues about reactions to Muslim activism in 1988 and 1989:

> the fear aroused in the Rushdie affair (and the often unrestrained language it has generated among normally staid persons) has to do with a perceived threat to authority, not to power: more precisely, the fear is generated by the fact that people who do not accept the secular liberal values of the governing classes are nevertheless able to use the liberal language of equal rights in rational argument against the secular British elite, and to avail themselves of liberal law for instituting their own strongly held religious traditions. (Asad 1993b:267)

In ISKCON's case it is certainly true that the Hindu groups making such a challenge were harder for the establishment to place outside of 'secular liberal values'. For example, it was hard for the most part to portray the Hindu campaigners as intolerant, violent, or fundamentalist. Even so, they (devotees and other campaigners) were very much defined as 'other' – either because of their skin colour, their dress, their religious practice, or simply the sense that Hare Krishnas are not 'quite us'. But, nonetheless, the processes of challenge were a subordination of British liberalism for the purposes of a minority group. In the Rushdie case this produced a situation in which Muslims were significantly demonised and thus excluded and marginalised. Perhaps because the Hindu campaigners for the Manor managed to play across this divisions without being trapped within it – primarily by dissociating their campaign from violence, and thus making themselves appear more amenable and acceptable to multicultural liberals – this may be a possible reason for their success in eventually pushing the government to accept their planning case. In a sense, ISKCON were becoming too successful at arguing their case on a popular level through the language of rights and multiculturalism.

But perhaps one of the largest ironies of this case is the fact that a significant cause of ISKCON's victory was that they had been fighting for something they already had. That is, the campaign was fought as a way of placing ISKCON/Hinduism in England, whilst their continual involvement in the dispute and final victory could not have been achieved if they had not already been empowered by being *in place* at the Manor. ISKCON had become placed in Letchmore Heath in 1973 when they converted the country house into offices, dormitories, and temple rooms. The immediate connection between the Manor and Prabhupada helped to establish the place within just a few years as very significant for ISKCON devotees, and within a decade the Manor had also become a *de facto* site of great religious/sacred importance to many local Hindus.

The years of legal conflict, especially from 1982 onwards, were thus fought on the basis of the planning authorities attempting to *dis*place what was already firmly in place. Although ISKCON were forced to enter the disputes on the basis of a threat of closure, the most serious threat was in fact related to access to the site – in particular the fact that ISKCON were encouraging too many people to the temple. Closure, or movement to another place, were never a serious option, since even when there was a proposal in the late 1980s to create a new temple building nearby, ISKCON leaders were firmly resolved to maintain the Manor too. At the same time, therefore, the campaign was based on an attempt to create the Manor as a place invested with significance (as a location of Vaishnavism, Hinduism, and Indian rootedness in Britain), whilst it had already become such a place. Furthermore, the ability of ISKCON to mobilise the support for their campaign and legal disputes, and also have the financial resources to do so, were all dependent on their location at the Manor – and so being in place was a necessary condition for them to eventually achieve victory.

The issues of the campaign, however, went further than the Manor and how (in what ways) its space should be practised. For those fighting this campaign a crucial issue was the placing of Hinduism within the fabric of British cultural life: that is a recognition of the distinctiveness of what Hindus themselves saw as their religion and culture. At one level, this meant finding a place for tolerance of diversity within planning structures, as well as tolerance of disruption in a quiet English village. It was, of course, advantageous for ISKCON that the discourse of religious freedom has been commonly used and invoked in British cultural life – although courts and politicians have been struggling for years to decide what such a discourse means in practical terms. This debate will of course continue, as the discourse becomes more explicitly placed within legal structures with the introduction of the Human Rights Act. As this case shows, I believe, the political implementations and consequences of multicultural diversities and religious practice are issues that have a profound place within many contemporary democratic nation-states.

Notes

1 I use the term normative in this respect to mean that I was arguing as a salaried academic working within a respected institution of higher education (University of Stirling) with a formal qualification (a PhD), and the experiential qualifications of having published a monograph and conducted several years of research in the field. Together these factors were taken by the judge, and much of the court, to put me in a position where I could/should be able to provide an authoritative, considered, and liberal viewpoint on how ISKCON should be considered. It was also, however, very much taken as normative in the sense that my location was (and of course remains) firmly within the apparatus of a liberal political establishment that is white, middle class, predominantly male, and to a large extent influenced by Anglican and English cultural and religious values. (My own personal and professional responses to such a location do not in any substantial way effect any challenge to being socially and politically located in such a way.)

2 As a small example of this, a leading English bank has in 1999 decided to rename itself to be identified with the international banking company that has owned it for the past decade. Thus, what was once known as the Midland Bank has now become the Hong Kong and Shanghai Bank (or HSBC). A friend of mine recently commented on his regret at the loss of a name which suggests the cosy familiarity of an old English regional identity (the English midlands) to the anonymity and unfamiliarity of the letters HSBC. However, I can think of nothing more quintessentially 'British' than the two Chinese trading colonies of Hong Kong and Shanghai, whose wealth for many years formed a substantial basis of Britain's own economic strength. And thus although the renaming of Midland Bank as HSBC is at one level simply an internationalisation (or globalisation) of the identity of a small part of England's banking market, at another level it is recognising that historically Englishness (and particularly English trading) has been misrepresented as parochially concerned with regions within its own boundaries, instead of aggressive strategies across the globe.

Or to put this another way, although much of English (and British) cultural life has been represented as narrowly confined within the relatively narrow boundaries of the islands of Britain, all British people have for several centuries been very much involved within a global political economy which they have chosen to ignore for the large part.

3 For good introductions to postcolonial theory, both written from the perspective of literary studies, see Moore-Gilbert (1997) and Loomba (1998). For general overviews of the field, see also Aschroft et al (1995), Chambers and Curtis (1996), Rattansi (1997), Williams and Chrisman (1993), and Young (1990, 1995). For an introduction to the application of postcolonial theory to theoretical debates in religious studies and the study of Indian religions, see King (1999).

4 For example, Chakrabarty (1993), Guha and Spivak (1988), Prakash (1990), Schwartz (1997).

5 Nor are they wholly separate either, and studies of Hindu practice in Britain should not (and cannot) ignore the wider Hindu diasporic and Indian contexts.

6 This is in fact a fear which has proven significantly ungrounded, since property prices in Letchmore Heath have in fact risen in the years since 1996 when the access road was completed and public worship was allowed. It is unknowable, however, if prices would have risen even more if the temple had not been there.

ABBREVIATIONS FOR SOURCES USED

AdPE Akhandadhi das, *Proof of Evidence* for a Public Inquiry held in January–May 1995, The Venue, Borehamwood, Hertfordshire.

AgHBC *Agenda & Report* for Hertsmere Borough Council meeting, Wednesday 19th October 1994, Council Chamber, Civic Offices, Borehamwood, Hertfordshire.

AgHBC/A *Agenda & Report* for Hertsmere Borough Council meeting, Wednesday 19th October 1994, Council Chamber, Civic Offices, Borehamwood, Hertfordshire. Appendix 1.

BT *Borehamwood Times.*

DoE90a Decision letter by P. Pascoe on behalf of Chris Patten, Secretary of State for the Environment, Tolgate House, Bristol, 20th March 1990, reference App/C/87/N1920/1. (Decision on ISKCON's appeal against the enforcement notice.)

DoE90b Decision by letter by P. Pascoe on behalf of Chris Patten, Secretary of State for the Environment, issued by the Depts of the Environment and Transport, Eastern Regional Office (Environment), Bedford, 20th March 1990, concerning appeal applications nos: 0626/88 and 0390/88. (Decision on planning application for Dagger Lane site temple.)

DoE96 Decision letter by Andrew Hayes on behalf of John Gummer, Secretary of State for the Environment, Government Office for Eastern Region, Bedford, 10th May 1996. (Decision on planning application for access driveway.)

EHRR European Commission of Human Rights, First Chamber, *Decision of the Commission.* Private sitting, 8th March 1994, Application no: 20490/92 by ISKCON and 8 others against the United Kingdom.

ICAP — Anonymous document titled 'ICAP – the Indian Community Affairs Programme', c.1982, in archive of the Oxford Centre for Vaishnava and Hindu Studies, Oxford.

IR89a — Inspector's Report: Inspector C. Russell, *Report of an Inquiry into appeals by the International Society for Krishna Consciousness against an enforcement notice*, for Public Inquiry held in November 1987-December 1988, The Venue, Borehamwood, Hertfordshire, April 1989. File no.: APP/C/87/N1920/00001.

IR89b — Inspector's Report: Inspector C. Russell, *Report of an Inquiry into appeals by the International Society for Krishna Consciousness and London Regional Transport against the refusal for planning permission for a Temple and Business Park on land between Dagger Lane and Elstree Road, Elstree, Herts*, for Public Inquiry held in December 1988, The Venue, Borehamwood, Hertfordshire, April 1989. Files nos.: APP/N1920/A/88/100747, APP/N1920/A/88/10997.

IR96 — Inspector's Report: Inspector D. Hanchet, *Hertsmere Borough Council Appeal by the International Society for Krishna*, for Public Inquiry held in January-June 1995, The Venue, Borehamwood, Hertfordshire. File no.: APP/N1920/A/94/241083.

IWR — *ISKCON World Recorder.*

JB93 — *Shree Krishna Janmasthami 1993 Magazine/Brochure*, (Bhaktivedanta Manor, Hertfordshire: Bhaktivedanta Manor Foundation, August 1993).

JB94 — *Shree Krishna Janmasthami 1994 Magazine/Brochure*, (Bhaktivedanta Manor, Hertfordshire: Bhaktivedanta Manor Foundation, August 1994).

JB95 — *Shree Krishna Janmasthami 1995 Magazine/Brochure*, (Bhaktivedanta Manor, Hertfordshire: Bhaktivedanta Manor Foundation, August 1995).

JB96 — *Shree Krishna Janmasthami 1996 Magazine/Brochure*, (Bhaktivedanta Manor, Hertfordshire: Bhaktivedanta Manor Foundation, September 1996).

JB97 — *Shree Krishna Janmasthami 1997 Magazine/Brochure*, (Bhaktivedanta Manor, Hertfordshire: Bhaktivedanta Manor Foundation, August 1997).

LCC	Regina v. W.M. Fleming & International Society for Krishna Consciousness, 6th November 1995, Luton Crown Court, Bedford. Transcript provided by Barnett, Lenton & Co., 61 Carey Street, London WC2A 2JG.
MYF	*Manor Youth Forum.*
NH	*Nama Hatta.*
PPG	Department of the Environment. *Planning Policy Guidance*, PPG2 (Revised): Green Belts. January 1995. London:HMSO.
RBA	*Radlett and Borehamwood Advertiser.*
RBH	Home Office, *Rights Brought Home: The Human Rights Bill*, UK Government White Paper, (HMSO London, 24th October 1997); also available from the Home Office Internet Site (http://www.official-documents.co.uk/document/hoffice/rights/rights.htm).
TCN	*Temple Campaign Newsletter.*
VTE 1994	The European Working Party on Vaishnava Training and Education. Report, June 29th 1994. (EWPVTE, Bhaktivedanta Manor, Herts).
WHWO	*West Herts and Watford Observer.*

BIBLIOGRAPHY

Abu-Lughod, Lila. 1991. 'Writing Against Culture', in *Recapturing Anthropology: Working in the Present*, ed. R. Fox. Santa Fe: School of American Research Press.

Ackermann, Andreas. 1999. 'The Social Engineering of Culture and Religion in Singapore', *Diskus: a disembodied journal of religion*. vol. 5, located at website url: <http://www.uni-marburg.de/fb03/religionswissenschaft/journal/diskus>

Ahmad, Aijaz. 1992. 'Salman Rushdie's *Shame*: Postmodern Migrancy and the Representation of Women', in *In Theory: Classes, Nations, Literatures*. London: Verso.

Appardurai, Arjun. 1986. 'Theory in Anthropology: center and periphery', *Comparative Studies in Society and History*, vol. XX: 356–361.

Appardurai, Arjun. 1990. 'Disjuncture and Difference in the Global Cultural Economy', in *Public Culture*, 2(2): 1–24.

Appardurai, Arjun. 1991. 'Global Ethnoscapes: Notes and Queries for a Transnational Anthropology', in *Recapturing Anthropology: Working in the Present*, ed. R. Fox. Santa Fe: School of American Research Press.

Appardurai, Arjun. 1996a. 'Here and Now', in *Modernity at Large: Cultural Dimensions of Globalization*. Minneapolis: University of Minnesota Press.

Appardurai, Arjun. 1996b. 'The Production of Locality', in *Modernity at Large: Cultural Dimensions of Globalization*. Minneapolis: University of Minnesota Press.

Arnal, William. 1999. 'Definition', in *Guide to the Study of Religion*, eds. W. Braun & R. McCutcheon. London Cassell.

Asad, Talal. 1986. 'The Concept of Cultural Translation in British Social Anthropology', in *Writing Culture: the poetics and politics of ethnography*, eds. J. Clifford and G. Marcus. London: University of California Press.

Asad, Talal. 1993a, 'The Construction of Religion as an Anthropological Category', *Genealogies of Religion: discipline and reasons of power in Christianity and Islam*. London: Johns Hopkins Press.

Asad, Talal. 1993b, 'Multiculturalism and British identity in the wake of the Rushdie affair', *Genealogies of Religion: discipline and reasons of power in Christianity and Islam*. London: Johns Hopkins Press.

Asad, Talal. 1997. 'Remarks on the anthropology of the body', *Religion and the body*, ed. S. Coakley. Cambridge: Cambridge University Press.

Ashcroft, Bill, Gareth Griffiths, and Helen Tiffin (eds.). 1995. *The Post-Colonial Studies Reader*. London: Routledge.

Babb, Lawrence A. 1986. *Redemptive Encounters: three modern styles in the Hindu tradition*. Berkeley, California. University of California Press.

Barker, Eileen. 1984. *The Making of a Moonie: choice or brainwashing?* Oxford: Basil Blackwell.

Barker, Eileen. 1995. *New Religious Movements: a practical introduction*, (amended edition), London: HMSO.

Barker, Eileen. 1993. 'Charismatization: the social production of an ethos propitious to the mobilisation of sentiments', *Secularization, rationalism and sectarianism*, ed. E. Barker, J. Beckford, and K. Dobbelaere. Oxford: Clarendon Press.

Barot, Rohit (ed.). 1993. *Religion and Identity: minorities and social change in the Metropolis*. Kampen: Kok Pharos.

Barot, Rohit. 1993. 'Religion, ethnicity, and change: an introduction', in *Religion and Ethnicity: minorities and social change in the Metropolis*, ed R. Barot. Kampen, The Netherlands: Kok Pharos Publishing. pp. 1–16.

Barth, Fredrik. 1969. 'Introduction', in *Ethnic Groups and Boundaries: The social organisation of cultural difference*, ed F. Barth. Allen and Unwin.

Baumann, Gerd. 1996. *Contesting Culture: Discourses of Identity in Multi-Ethnic London*. Cambridge: Cambridge University Press.

Baumann, Gerd. 1998. 'Body Politics or Bodies of Culture? How Nation-State Practices Turn Citizens into Cultural Minorities', *Cultural Dynamics*, 10 (3): 263–280.

Baumann, Gerd. 1999. *The Multicultural Riddle: rethinking national, ethnic, and religious identities*. New York: Routledge.

Baumann, Martin. 1998. 'Channelling Information: the stigmatization of religious studies as an aspect of the debate about the new religious movements in Germany', in *New Religions and New Religiosity*, ed. E. Barker & M. Warburg. Aarhus: Aarhus University Press.

Baumann, Martin. 1999. 'Multiculturalism and the Ambiguity of Recognizing Religion', *Diskus: a disembodied journal of religion*. vol. 5, located at website url: <http://www.uni-marburg.de/fb03/religionswissenschaft/journal/diskus>

Baxi, Upendra. 1989. 'From Human Rights to the Right to be Human: Some Heresies', *Rethinking Human Rights: challenges for theory and action*, ed. S. Kothari and H. Kothari. New York: New Horizons Press.

Beckford, James. 1993. 'States, Governments, and the Management of Controversial New Religious Movements', *Securalization, Rationalism, and Sectarianism*, eds. E. Barker, J. Beckford, & K. Dobbelaere. Oxford: Clarendon.

Bell, Catherine. 1992. *Ritual Theory, Ritual Practice*. Oxford: Oxford University Press.

Berlant, Lauren and Michael Warner. 1994. 'Introduction to "Critical Multiculturalism"', in *Multiculturalism: a Critical Reader*, ed. D.T. Goldberg. Oxford: Blackwell.

Betten, Lammy (ed.). 1999. *The Human Rights Act 1998 – What It Means*. The Hague: Martinus Nijhoff.

Bhabha, Homi. 1990. 'The Third Space', in *Identity: community, culture, difference*, ed. J. Rutherford. London: Lawrence and Wishart.

Bhabha, Homi. 1994. *The Location of Culture*. London: Routledge.

Bhabha, Homi. 1996. 'Culture's In-Between', in *Questions of Cultural Identity*, ed. S. Hall and Paul du Gay. London: Sage.

Bhatt, Chetan. 1997. *Liberation and Purity: race, new religious movements, and the ethics of postmodernity*. London: UCL Press.

Bibby, Reginald W. 1999. 'Multiculturalism in Canada: a methodologically inadequate political virtue', *Diskus: a disembodied journal of religion*. vol. 5, located at website url: <http://www.uni-marburg.de/fb03/religionswissenschaft/journal/diskus>

Bourdieu, Pierre. 1977. *Outline of a Theory of Practice.* Translated by Richard Nice. Cambridge: Cambridge University Press.

Bourdieu, Pierre. 1992. *The Logic of Practice.* Translated by Richard Nice. Cambridge: Polity Press.

Bowen, David. G. 1988. *The Sathya Sai Baba community in Bradford: its origin and development, religious beliefs and practices.* Leeds. University of Leeds Department of Theology and Religious Studies.

Bowman, Marion. 'The Noble Savage and the Global Village: cultural evolution in the New Age and neo-Pagan thought', *Journal of Contemporary Religin.* 10(2): 139–149.

Bradney, Anthony. 1993. *Religions, Rights, and Laws.* Leicester: Leicester University Press.

Breyer, C. 1993. 'Religious Liberty in Law and Practice: Vietnamese home temples and the First Amendment', *Journal of Church and State,* 35: pp. 367–401

Bromley, David. 1998. 'Listing (in black and white) some observations on (sociological) thought reform', in *Nova Religio* vol. 1 (2).

Bromley, David and Larry Shinn (edd.). 1989. *Krishna consciousness in the West.* Lewisburg, PA.: Bucknell University Press. Brooks, Charles. 1989. *The Hare Krishnas in India,* Princeton: Princeton University Press.

Brooks, Charles. 1996. 'Understanding ISKCON', *ISKCON Communications Journal.* 3 (2): 77–81.

Bruce, Steve. 1996. *Religion in the modern world: from cathedrals to cults.* Oxford: Oxford University Press.

Bruce, Steve. and C. Wright, 'Law, Social Change, and Religious Toleration', *Journal of Church and State* 37 (1995): 103–120.

Brzezinski, Jan. 1998. 'What was Srila Prabhupada's Position: the Hare Krishna Movement and Hinduism', *ISKCON Communications Journal,* vol. 6 (2): 27–49.

Burghart, Richard. 1987. 'Introduction: The diffusion of Hinduism to Great Britain', in *Hinduism in Great Britain: the perpetuation of religion in an alien cultural milieu,* ed. R. Burghart. London. Tavistock.

Burr, Angela. 1984. *I am not my body: a study of the International Hare Krishna sect.* New Delhi. Vikas Publishing House.

Caglar, Ayse. 1997. 'Hyphenated Identities and the Limits of "Culture"', in *The Politics of Multiculturalism in the New Europe: Racism, Identity and Community,* ed T. Modood and P. Werbner. London: Zed Books.

Carey, Sean. 1987. 'The Indianization of the Hare Krishna movement in Britain', in R. Burghart (ed.), *Hinduism in Great Britain: the perpetuation of religion in an alien cultural milieu,.* London: Tavistock.

Carrette, Jeremy & Richard King. 1998. 'Giving 'Birth' to Theory: Critical Perspectives on Religion and the Body', *Scottish Journal of Religious Studies.* vol. 19 (1): 123–143.

Carter, Lewis. 1990. *Charisma and control in Rajneeshpuram: the role of shared values in the creation of a community.* Cambridge: Cambridge University Press.

Chakrabarty, D. 1993. 'Provincializing Europe: postocoloniality and the critique of history', *Cultural Studies.*

Chambers, I. and L. Curtis. 1996. *The Post-Colonial Question.* London: Routledge.

Chatterjee, Partha. 1998. 'Secularism and Tolerance', in *Secularism and its Critics,* ed. R. Bhargava. New Delhi: Oxford University Press. (First published in *Economic and Political Weekly,* 9th July 1994, xxix no. 28).

Chicago Cultural Studies Group. 1994. 'Critical Multiculturalism', in *Multiculturalism: a Critical Reader,* ed. D.T. Goldberg. Oxford: Blackwell.

Chidester, David and Edward Linenthal (eds). 1995. 'Introduction', in *American Sacred Space*. Bloomington: Indiana University Press.

Chidester, David. 1996. *Savage Systems: Colonialism and Comparative Religion in Southern Africa*. Charlottesville: University Press of Virginia.

Clarke, C., Peach, C. & Vertovec, S. (eds). 1990. *South Asians Overseas: Migration and Ethnicity*. Cambridge. Cambridge University Press.

Clarke, Peter B. and Peter Byrne. 1993. *Religion defined and explained*. Basingstoke: Macmillan.

Clayton, John. n.d. *Religious Diversity and Public Reason*. Inaugral lecture for the Chair to the Department of Religion, Boston University. 25th March 1998. Published on internet site: <http://www.bu.edu/religion/Faculty/Clayton/inaug.htm>

Clifford, James. 1986. 'Introduction: Partial Truths', in *Writing Culture: the poetics and politics of ethnography*, eds. J. Clifford and G. Marcus. London: University of California Press.

Clifford, James. 1997. *Routes: Travel and Translation in the Late Twentieth Century*. Cambridge, Massacheusetts and London: Harvard University Press.

Clothey, F.W. 1983. *Rhythm and Intent: Ritual Studies from South India*. Madras. Blackie and Sons.

Coakley, Sarah. 1997. 'Introduction: religion and the body', *Religion and the body*, ed. S. Coakley. Cambridge: Cambridge University Press.

Cohen, Anthony P. 1985. *The Symbolic Construction of Community*. London. Tavistock.

Coote, Nicholas. 1998. 'A Response by the Catholic Church in England' in *ISKCON Communications Journal*, vol. 6 (2): 67–69.

Cracknell, Kenneth. 1996. 'Conference report on the Nature of the Self, a Vaishnava-Christian conference', *ISKCON Communications Journal* 4 (1): 72–82.

Cullingworth, J.B. & V. Nadin. 1994. *Town and Country Planning in Britain*, 11th edition. London: Routledge.

Cumper, Peter. 1996. 'Religious Liberty in the United Kingdom', in *Religious Human Rights in Global Perspective*, ed. J.D. van der Vyver and J. Witte, Jr. The Hague: Martin Nijhoff Publishers.

D'Costa, Gavin. 1996. 'The Nature of the Self: report of a two-day Christian-Vaishnava conference', *Journal of Contemporary Religion* 11 (3): 355–6.

das, Akhandadhi. 1994. 'Vaishnava Training and Education', *ISKCON Communications Journal*. Issue 3: 67–73).

das, Bharata Shreshta. 1998. 'ISKCON's Response to Child Abuse: 1990–1998', *ISKCON Communications Journal*, vol. 6 (1): 71–79.

das, Kripamoya. 1994. 'Congregation in Conflict', *ISKCON Communications Journal*. Issue 3: 5–15.

das, Krishna Dharma. 1994. 'Integrating into Local Communities', *ISKCON Communications Journal*. Issue 3: 59–66.

das, Rasamandala. 1994. 'An Analysis of ISKCON Membership in the UK: Moving into Phase Three', *ISKCON Communications Journal*. 3 (2): 83–92.

das, Ravindra Svarupa. 1989. 'Patterns in ISKCON's historical self-perception', in *Krishna Consciousness in the West*, ed. D. Bromley and L. Shinn. London: Associated University Press.

das, Ravindra Svarupa. 1994a. 'Cleaning House and Cleaning Hearts: Reform and Renewal in ISKCON: Part One', *ISKCON Communications Journal*. Issue 3: 43–52.

das, Ravindra Svarupa. 1994b. 'Cleaning House and Cleaning Hearts: Reform and Renewal in ISKCON: Part Two', *ISKCON Communications Journal*. Issue 4: 25–33.

das, Subhananda. 1995. 'ISKCON after Prabhupada: an update on the Hare Krishna Movement', *ISKCON Review*. 1 (1): 7–14.

dasa, Dhira Govinda. 1998. 'Response' in *ISKCON Communications Journal*, vol. 6 (2): 61–64.

Davie, Grace. 1994. *Religion in Britain since 1945: believing without belonging*. Oxford: Blackwell.

de Certeau, Michel. 1984. *The Practice of Everyday Life*. Translated by Steven Rendall. Berkeley: University of California Press.

Deadwyler, William (Ravindra-svarupa das). 1995. 'The Devotee and the Deity: Living a Personalistic Theology', in *Gods of Flesh, Gods of Stone: the Embodiment of Divinity in India*, ed. J. Waghorne and N. Cutler. Chambersburg, PA: Anima Press.

devi dasi, Radha. 1998. 'Fundamental Human Rights in ISKCON', *ISKCON Communications Journal*, vol. 6 (2): 7–14.

Douglas, Mary. 1966. *Purity and danger: an analysis of concepts of pollution and taboo*. Routledge & K Paul.

Durkheim, Emile. 1964 [1915]. *The Elementary Forms of the Religious Life*. London: Allen & Unwin.

Eade, John and Michael Sallnow (eds.). 1991. *Contesting the Sacred: the anthropology of Christian pilgrimage*. London: Routledge.

Eade, John. 1993. 'The polictical articulation of community and the Islamisation of space in London', in *Religion and Ethnicity: minorities and social change in the Metropolis*, ed R. Barot. Kampen, The Netherlands: Kok Pharos Publishing. pp. 29–42.

Edge, Peter W. n.d. 'Sacred Spaces: Planning Law and Religion', unpublished paper presented to Dept of Legal Studies, University of Central Lancaster, 28th May 1998.

Edge, Peter. 1995. 'The Missionary's Position after *Kokkinakis v Greece*', *Web Journal of Current Legal Issues*, located at website url: <http:www.ncl.ac.uk/~nlawwww/articles2/edge2.html>

Edwards, D. 1993. 'The History of Blasphemy and the Rushdie Affair', in *Liberalism, Multiculturalism, and Toleration* ed. J. Horton. London: Macmillan. pp. 157–177

Eliade, Mircea. 1959. *The Sacred and the Profane: the nature of religion*. San Diego: Harcourt Brace Jovanovich.

Eliade, Mircea. 1963. *Patterns in Comparative Religion*. New York: World Publishing Co.

Evans, Malcolm. 1997. *Religious Liberty and International Law in Europe*. Cambridge: Cambridge University Press.

Faure, Bernard. 1987. 'Space and place in Chinese religious traditions'. *History of Religions*, vol. XX: 339–356.

Featherstone, Mike, Mike Hepworth and Bryan Turner (eds.). 1990. *The body: social process and cultural theory*. London: Sage.

Feldman, Stephen M. 1997. *Please Don't Wish Me A Merry Christmas: a critical history of the separation of Church and State*. New York: New York University Press.

Fitzgerald, Tim. 1995. 'Religious Studies as Cultural Studies: a philosophical and anthropological critique of the concept of religion', in *Diskus: a disembodied journal of religion*. vol. 3 (1): 35–47, located at website url: <http://www.uni-marburg.de/fb03/religionswissenschaft/journal/diskus>

Flood, Gavin. 1996. 'Hinduism, Vaishnavism, and ISKCON', Authentic Traditions or Scholarly Constructions?', *ISKCON Communications Journal*. 3 (2): 5–15.

Foucault, Michel. 1967. *Madness and Civilization: a history of insanity in the Age of Reason*. Translated by Richard Howard. London: Tavistock.

Foucault, Michel. 1979. *Discipline and Punish: the birth of the prison*. Translated by Alan Sheridan. Harmondsworth: Penguin.

Foucault, Michel. 1984. 'Space, Knowledge, and Power', in *The Foucault Reader*, ed. P. Rabinow. New York: Pantheon.

Fox, Richard G. 1991. 'Introduction: Working in the Present', in *Recapturing Anthropology: Working in the Present*, ed. R. Fox. Santa Fe: School of American Research Press.

Friedman, Susan Stanford. 1998. *Mappings: feminism and the cultural geographies of encounter*. Princeton, New Jersey: Princeton University Press.

Fuller, Chris. 1994. *Servants of the Goddess: the priests of a South Indian temple*. Cambridge: Cambridge University Press.

Gale, Richard. n.d. *Pride of Place and Places: South Asian Religious Groups and the City Planning Authority in Leicester*. MA dissertation in South Asian Studies, School of Oriental and African Studies, University of London, 1998.

Geertz, Clifford. 1973. 'Religion as a Cultural System', in *The Interpretation of Culture*. London: Fontana.

Gell, Alfred. 1985. 'How to Read a Map: remarks on the practical logic of navigation', *Man: the Journal of the Royal Anthropological Institute*, 20 (3): 271–86.

Ghai, D.P. & Ghai, Y.P. 1970. *Portrait of a Minority: Asians in East Africa*. (Revised edition). Nairobi: Oxford University Press.

Gill, Sam. 1998. *Storytracking: texts, stories, and histories in Central Australia*. Oxford: Oxford University Press.

Gilroy, Paul. 1987.*'There ain't no black in the Union Jack': the cultural politics of race and nation*. London: Hutchinson.

Gilroy, Paul. 1993. *The Black Atlantic: Modernity and Double Consciousness*. London: Verso.

Gooding, Susan Staiger. 1996. 'At the Boundaries of Religious Identity: Native American Religions and American Legal Culture', *Numen: International Review for the History of Religions*. XLIII(2): 157–183.

Goswami, Mukunanda. 1996. 'NRM is a Four-letter Word: the Language of Oppression', *ISKCON Communications Journal*. 3 (2): 73–75.

Goswami, Satsvarupa das. 1983. *Prabhupada: he built a house in which the world can live*. (The Authorized Biography). Los Angeles: Bhaktivedanta Book Trust.

Goswami, Tamal Krishna. 1997. 'The Perils of Succession: heresies of authority and continuity in the Hare Krishna movement', *ISKCON Communications Journal*, vol. 5 (1): 13–44

Graves, Pamela C. 1989. 'Social space in the English medieval parish church', *Economy and Society*, 18 (3): 297–332.

Greed, Clara. 1996a. *Introducing Town Planning*, 2nd edition. Harlow: Longman.

Greed, Clara. 1996b. 'Introduction: the question of 'what is town planning' revisited', in *Investigating Town Planning: changing perspectives and agendas* ed. C. Greed. Harlow: Longman.

Gregory, R.G. 1971. *India and East Africa: a history of race relations within the British Empire 1890–1939*. Oxford: Clarendon Press.

Guha, Ranajit and Gayatri Spivak (eds.). 1988. *Selected Subaltern studies*. New York: Oxford University Press.

Gupta, Akhil and James Ferguson. 1997. 'Beyond 'Culture': Space, Identity, and the Politics of Difference', in *Culture, Power, Place: Explorations in Critical Anthropology*, ed. A. Gupta and J. Ferguson. London: Duke University Press.

Gupta, Akhil and James Ferguson. 1997. 'Culture, Power, Place: Ethnography at the End of an Era', in *Culture, Power, Place: Explorations in Critical Anthropology*, ed. A. Gupta and J. Ferguson. London: Duke University Press.

Guttman, Amy (ed.). 1994. *Multiculturalism and the Politics of Recognition.* (New edition). Princeton, NJ: Princeton University Press.

Haar, Gerrie ter. 1999. 'Imposing Identity: the case of African Christians in the Netherlands', *Diskus: a disembodied journal of religion.* vol. 5, located at website url: <http://www.uni-marburg.de/fb03/religionswissenschaft/journal/diskus>

Hall, Stuart. 1996. 'Introduction: Who Needs 'Identity'?', in *Questions of Cultural Identity*, ed. S. Hall and Paul du Gay. London: Sage.

Hall, Stuart. 1996. 'Identity and Difference', *Culture, Identity and Politics: Ethnic Minorities in Britain*, ed. T. Ranger, Y. Samad, and O. Stuart. Aldershot: Avebury.

Hamilton, Caroline. 1995. *Family, Law and Religion.* London: Sweet & Maxwell.

Hannerz, Ulf. 1992. *Cultural Complexity: studies in the social organization of meaning.* New York: Columbia University Press.

Hardy, Friedhelm. 1990. 'The classical religions of Asia', in *The World's Religions: the religions of Asia*, ed. F. Hardy. London: Routledge.

Harvey, David. 1989. *The Condition of Postmodernity.* Oxford: Blackwell.

Harvey, David. 1993. 'Class Relations, Social Justice and the Politics of Difference', in *Place and the Politics of Identity*, ed. M. Keith and S. Pile (eds.). London: Routledge.

Hastrup, Kirsten and Karen Fog Olwig. 1997. 'Introduction', in *Siting Culture: the shifting anthropological object*, ed. Olwig & Hastrup. London: Routledge.

Heap, D. 1978. *An Outline of Planning Law.* London: Sweet and Maxwell.

Hesse, Barnor. 1993. 'Black to Front and Black Again: racialization through contested times and spaces', in *Place and the Politics of Identity*, ed. M. Keith and S. Pile (eds.). London: Routledge.

Hollingsworth, L.W. 1960. *The Asians of East Africa.* London: Macmillan.

Hopkins, Thomas J. 1998. 'Why Should ISKCON Study its own History?', *ISKCON Communications Journal*, vol. 6 (2): 1–6.

Humphrey, D. & M. Ward. 1974. *Passports and Politics.* Harmondsworth: Penguin.

Inden, Ronald. 1986. 'Orientalist Constructions of India', *Modern Asian Studies.* 20 (3): 101–446.

Inden, Ronald. 1990. *Imagining India.* Oxford. Basil Blackwell.

Introvigne, Massimo. 1997. 'Religious Liberty in Western Europe', *ISKCON Communications Journal.* 5 (2): 37–48.

Jackson, Robert. and Nesbitt, Eleanor. 1993. *Hindu Children in Britain.* Stoke on Trent: Trentham Books.

Jones, K.W. 1976. *Arya Dharm: Hindu consciousness in nineteenth century Panjab.* Berkeley: University of California Press.

Judah, J. Stilson 1974. *Hare Krishna and the Counterculture*, New York: John Wiley & Sons.

Keesing, Roger. 1994. 'Theories of Culture Revisited', in *Assessing Cultural Anthropology*, ed. Robert Borofsky, New York: McGraw-Hill Inc. (pp. 301–312)

Keith, Michael and Steve Pile. 1993. 'Introduction Part 1: The Politics of Place' and 'Introduction Part 2: The Place of Politics', in *Place and the Politics of Identity*, ed. M. Keith and S. Pile (eds.). London: Routledge.

Kelly, John D. 1995. '*Bhakti* and Postcolonial Politics: Hindu Missions to Fiji' in *Nation and Migration: the Politics of Space in the South Asian Diaspora*, ed. P. van der Veer. Philadelphia: University of Pennsylvania Press.

King, Richard. 1999. *Orientalism and Religion: postcolonial theory, India and 'the mystic East'*. London: Routledge

Knott, K. 1986. *Hinduism in Leeds: A study of religious practices in the Indian Hindu community and in Hindu related groups.* Monograph Series, Community Religions Project. Dept of Theology and Religious Studies, University of Leeds.

Knott, Kim. 1987. *My Sweet Lord: the Hare Krishna Movement.* Northampton: Aquarian Press.

Knott, Kim. 1996. 'The Debate about Women in the Hare Krishna Movement', *ISKCON Communications Journal.* 3 (2): 33–49.

Knott, Kim. 1997. 'Insider and Outsider Perceptions of Prabhupada', *ISKCON Communications Journal*, vol. 5 (1): 59–71.

Knott, Kim. 1998. 'Issues in the study of religions and locality', *Method and Theory in the Study of Religion.* 10: 279–290.

Knott, Kim. 1999. 'Hinduism in Britain', in *The South Asian Diaspora in Great Britain, Canada, and the US*, ed H. Coward and J. Hinnells. New York: State University of New York Press.

Knott, Kim. n.d. 'In Every Town And Village: adaptive strategies in the communication of Krishna Consciousness in the UK, the first thirty years', *Social Compass* (forthcoming).

Kothari, Smitu. 1989. 'The Human Rights Movement in India: a Critical Overview', *Rethinking Human Rights: challenges for theory and action*, ed. S. Kothari and H. Kothari. New York: New Horizons Press.

Kuepper, W.G., G.L. Lackey & E.N. Swinterton. 1975. *Ugandan Asians in Britain: Forced Migration and Social Absorption.* London: Croom Helm.

Lambek, Michael. 1995. 'Choking on the Quran, and other consuming parables from the western Indian Ocean front', in *The Pursuit of Certainty* ed. Wendy James. London: Routledge. pp. 258–281.

Lefebvre, Henri. 1984. *The Production of Space.* Translated by Donald Nicholson-Smith. (1st edition in 1974). Oxford: Blackwell.

Levi-Strauss, Claude. 1964. *Totemism.* (translated by R. Needham). London: Merlin Press.

Lewis, James and J Gordon Melton (eds.). 1994. *Sex, Slander and Salvation: Investigating The Family/Children of God.* Stanford, CA: Center for Academic Publication.

Lewis, Philip. 1994. *Islamic Britain.* London: I.B. Tauris.

Lipner, Julius. 1994. *Hindus: their religious beliefs and practices.* London: Routledge.

Littell, Franklin Hamlin. 1989. 'Religious Freedom in Contemporary America', *Journal of Church and State*, 31(2): 219–230.

Lock, M. 1993. 'Cultivating the Body: anthropology and the epistemologies of body practice and knowledge', *Annual Review of Anthropology.* 22: 133–155.

Loomba, Ania. 1998. *Colonialism/postcolonialism.* London: Routledge.

Lord Bingham of Cornhill. 1998. 'The Way We Live Now: Human Rights in the New Millennium', *Web Journal of Current Legal Issues.* located at web site <http://webjcli.ncl.ac.uk/1998/issue1/bingham1.html>

Maaga, Mary McCormick. 1998. *Hearing the Voices of Jonestown.* Syracuse: Syracuse University Press.

Madan, T.N. 1987. 'Secularization in its place', in *Journal of Asian Studies.* 46: 747–59.

Mahmood, Saba and Nancy Reynolds. 1996. 'Introduction', *Stanford Electronic Humanities Review*, vol. 5 (1), special issue: *Contested Politics.* located at website url: <http://shr.stanford.edu/shreview/5-1/text/introduction.html>

Mangat, J.S. 1969. *A History of Asians in East Africa, 1886 to 1945*. Oxford: Clarendon Press.

Mani, L and R. Frankenberg. 1993. 'Crosscurrents, crosstalk, race, 'postcoloniality' and the politics of location', *Cultural Studies*, 7(2): 292–30.

Marcus, George. 1995. 'Ethnography In/Of the World System: the emergence of multi-sited ethnography', *Annual Review of Anthropology*, vol. 24, pp. 95–117.

Marret, V. 1989. *Immigrants Settling in the City*. Cambridge: Cambridge University Press.

Martin, David. 1978. *A General Theory of Secularization*. Oxford: Blackwell.

Massey, Doreen. 1993. 'Politics and Space/Time', in *Place and the Politics of Identity*, ed. M. Keith and S. Pile (eds.). London: Routledge.

McLaren, Peter. 1994. 'White Terror and Oppositional Agency: Towards a Critical Multiculturalism', in *Multiculturalism: a Critical Reader*, ed. D.T. Goldberg. Oxford: Blackwell.

Melady, T.B. & M.B. Melady. 1976. *Uganda: The Asian Exiles*. New York: Orbis.

Menski, Werner. 1993. 'Asians in Britain and the Question of Adaptation to a New Legal Order: Asian Laws in Britain?', in *Ethnicity, Identity, Migration: the South Asian Context*, ed. M. Israel & N.K. Wagle, South Asian Studies Papers, no.6 (University of Toronto: Centre for South Asian Studies, 1993), pp. 238–268;

Menski, Werner. 2000. 'Law, Religion and South Asians', in *From Generation to Generation: religious reconstruction in the South Asian diaspora*, eds. J. Hinnells & W. Menski. Basingstoke: Macmillan.

Michaelson, Maureen. 1987. 'Domestic Hinduism in a Gujarati trading caste', in *Hinduism in Great Britain: the perpetuation of religion in an alien cultural milieu*, ed. R. Burghart. London: Tavistock.

Modood, Tariq and Pnina Werbner. 1997a. *Debating Cultural Hybridity: Multi-Cultural Identities and the Politics of Anti-Racism*. London: Zed Books.

Modood, Tariq and Pnina Werbner. 1997b. *The Politics of Multiculturalism in the New Europe: Racism, Identity and Community*. London: Zed Books.

Modood, Tariq et al (ed.). 1997. *Ethnic Minorities in Britain: diversity and disadvantage, the fourth national survey of ethnic minorities*. London: Policy Studies Institute.

Modood, Tariq. 1994. 'Establishment, Multiculturalism and British Citizenship'. *Political Quarterly*, LV (1): 53–73.

Modood, Tariq. 1997a. ''Difference', Cultural Racism, and Anti-Racism', in *Debating Cultural Hybridity: Multi-Cultural Identities and the Politics of Anti-Racism*, ed. T. Modood and P. Werbner. London: Zed Books.

Modood, Tariq. 1997b. 'Introduction: The Politics of Multiculturalism in the New Europe', in *The Politics of Multiculturalism in the New Europe: Racism, Identity and Community*, ed T. Modood and P. Werbner. London: Zed Books.

Modood, Tariq. 1997c. 'Introduction: Establishment, Reform and Multiculturalism', in *Church, State, and Religious Minorities*, ed. T. Modood. London: Policy Studies Institute.

Moore-Gilbert, Bart. 1997. *Postcolonial Theory: Contexts, Practices, Politics*. London: Verso.

Morris, Brian. 1987. *Anthropological studies of religion: an introductory text*. Cambridge: Cambridge University Press.

Morris, H.S. 1968. *The Indians of Uganda*. London: Weidenfield and Nicholson.

Moser, Mary Theresa. 1988. 'Revising the Constitution? The Problem of Religious Freedom', *Journal of Religious Ethnics*. 16(2):325–344

Naik, Deepak. 1997. 'A Hindu Perspective', in *Church, State, and Religious Minorities*, ed. T. Modood. London: Policy Studies Institute.
Nandy, Ashis. 1985. 'An Anti-Secularist Manifesto', in *Seminar.* 314: 14–24.
Nandy, Ashis. 1998. 'The Politics of Secularism and the Recovery of Religious Tolerance', in *Secularism and its Critics*, ed. R. Bhargava. New Delhi: Oxford University Press. (First published in *Mirrors of Violence: Communities, Riots and Survivors in South Asia*, ed. V. Das, 1990, New Delhi: OUP)
Nye, Malory. 1993a. 'Temple congregations and communities: Hindu constructions in Edinburgh', *New Community*, 1993. 19 (2): 201–215
Nye, Malory. 1993b. 'A place for our gods: tradition and change among Hindus in Edinburgh', in *Religion and Ethnicity: minorities and social change in the Metropolis*, ed R. Barot. Kampen, The Netherlands: Kok Pharos Publishing. pp. 123–37.
Nye, Malory. 1995. *A Place for our Gods: the construction of an Edinburgh Hindu temple community.* London: Curzon Press.
Nye, Malory. 1996. 'Hare Krishna and Sanatan Dharm in Britain: the campaign for Bhaktivedanta Manor', *Journal of Contemporary Religion* 11 (1): 37–56.
Nye, Malory. 1997. 'ISKCON and Hindus in Britain: some thoughts on a developing relationship', *ISKCON Communications Journal.* 5 (2): 5–13.
Nye, Malory. 1998. 'Hindus old and new: problems of sacred space', in *New Religions and New Religiosity in Europe*, ed. E. Barker & M. Warburg. Aarhus: Aarhus University Press.
Nye, Malory. 2000. 'The Iskconisation of British Hinduisms', in *From Generation to Generation: religious reconstruction in the South Asian diaspora*, ed. J. Hinnells & W. Menski. Basingstoke: Macmillan.
Nye, Malory. n.d.1. 'Religion, Post-Religionism, and Religioning: Religious Studies and Contemporary Cultural Debates', *Method and Theory in the Study of Religion* (forthcoming).
Nye, Malory. n.d.2. *'A Place For Our Gods': the construction of a Hindu temple community in Edinburgh.* PhD thesis presented to Department of Social Anthropology, University of Edinburgh. 1992.
O'Connell, Joseph T. 1997. 'Does the Caitanya Vaishnava Movement Reinforce or Resist Hindu Communal Politics?', *ISKCON Communications Journal*, vol. 5 (1): 45–57.
Okely, Judith. 1983. *The traveller-gypsies.* Cambridge: Cambridge University Press.
Okely, Judith. 1996. *Own or other culture.* London: Routledge.
Olwig, Karen Fog & Kirsten Hastrup (eds). 1997. *Siting Culture: the shifting anthropological object.* London: Routledge.
Olwig, Karen Fog. 1997. 'Cultural sites: sustaining a home in a deterritorialized world', in *Siting Culture: the shifting anthropological object*, ed. Olwig & Hastrup. London: Routledge.
Oomen, T.K. 1997. *Citizenship, Nationality, and Ethnicity: reconciling competing identities.* Cambridge: Polity Press.
Paden, W. 1991. 'Before the 'sacred' became theological', *Method and Theory in the Study of Religion.*
Palmer, Susan J. 1994. *Moon Sisters, Krishna Mothers, Rajneesh Lovers: women's roles innew religions.* Syracuse: Syracuse University Press.
Parekh, Bhikkhu. 1997. 'Religion and Public Life', in *Church, State, and Religious Minorities*, ed. T. Modood. London: Policy Studies Institute.
Peabody, Norbert. 1991. 'In Whose Turban Does the Lord Reside?: the objectification of charisma and fetishism of objects in the Hindu kingdom of Kota', *Comparative Studies in Society and History*, vol. XXX: 726–754.

Pile, Steve and Nigel Thrift. 1995. 'Introduction' and 'Mapping the Subject', in *Mapping the Subject: geographies of cultural transformation*. London: Routledge.

Pocock, David. 1976. 'The preservation of the religious life', *Contributions to Indian Sociology* 10 (2): 342–365.

Poulter, Sebastian. 1986. *English Law and Ethnic Minority Customs*. London: Butterworths.

Poulter, Sebastian. 1991. 'Towards legislative reform of the blasphemy and racial hatred laws', *Public Law* 371–85.

Poulter, Sebastian. 1998. *Ethnicity, Law and Human Rights: the English experience*. Oxford: Clarendon Press.

Prabhupada, A.C. Bhaktivedanta Swami. 1977. 'Krishna Consciousness: Hindu cult or divine culture?', *The Science of Self Realization*, Watford: Bhaktivedanta Book Trust, pp. 117–123.

Prabhupada, A.C. Bhaktivedanta Swami. 1977. *The Science of Self-Realization*. Watford: Bhaktivedanta Book Trust.

Prabhupada, A.C. Bhaktivedanta Swami. 1983. *Bhagavad-Gita as it is*, Watford: Bhaktivedanta Book Trust.

Prakash, Gyan. 1990. 'Writing post-Orientalism in the Third World', *Comparative Studies in Society and History*, 32(2):383–408.

Purdue, M. 1977. *Cases and Materials on Planning Law*. London: Sweet & Maxwell.

Puttick, Elizabeth. 1997. *Women in new religions: gender, power and sexuality and spiritual power*. Basingstoke: Macmillan.

Rattansi, Ali. 1997. 'Postcolonialism and its discontents', *Economy and Society* 26 (4): 480–500.

Reid, Jennifer. 1998. 'The Politics of Ahimsa', *Scottish Journal of Religious Studies*, 19(2): 185–209.

Richardson, James. 1995. 'Minority Religions, Religious Freedom, and the new Pan-European Political and Judicial Institutions', *Journal of Church and State*, 37.

Robbins, Thomas. 1988. *Cults, converts and charisma: the sociology of new religious movements*. London: Sage.

Robbins, Thomas. 1997. 'Krsna and Culture: Cultural Exclusivity and the Debate Over 'Mind Control', *ISKCON Communications Journal*, vol. 5 (1): 77–84.

Rochford, E. Burke with Jennifer Heinlein. 1998. 'Child Abuse in the Hare Krishna Movement: 1971–1986', *ISKCON Communications Journal*, vol. 6 (1): 43–69.

Rochford, E. Burke. 1985. *Hare Krishna in America*. New Brunswick: Rutgers University Press.

Rochford, E. Burke. 1987. 'Dialectical processes in the development of Hare Krishna: tension, public definition, and strategy', in*The Future of New Religious Movements*, ed. D.G. Bromley & P.E. Hammond. Macon, GA. Mercer University Press.

Rochford, E. Burke. 1988. 'Movement and Public in Conflict: Values, Finances and the Decline of Hare Krishnas', *Money and Power in the New Religions*, ed. J.T. Richardson. Lampeter: Edwin Mellen Press.

Rochford, E. Burke. 1989. 'Factionalism, group defection, and schism in the Hare Krishna movement', *Journal for the Scientitic Study of Religion*, 28(2): 162–79.

Rochford, E. Burke. 1998. 'Response' in *ISKCON Communications Journal*, vol. 6 (2): 64–67.

Rochford, E. Burke. 1998b. 'Reactions of Hare Krishna Devotees to Scandals of Leaders' Misconduct', in *Wolves Within the Fold*, ed. A. Shupe. New Brunswick, NJ: Rutgers University Press.

Rochford, E. Burke. 1999. 'Prabhupada Centennial Survey: A Summary of the Final Report', in *ISKCON Communications Journal*, vol. 7 (1): 11–26.

Rose, Nikolas. 1996. 'Identity, Genealogy, History', in *Questions of Cultural Identity*, ed. S. Hall and Paul du Gay. London: Sage.

Roseberry, William. 1992. 'Multiculturalism and the Challenge of Anthropology', *Social Research*. 59 (4): 841–58.

Sadurski, W. 1993. 'On Legal Definitions of "Religion"', *Australian Law Journal*, 63: 834–839.

Sahgal, Gita and Yuval-Davis, Nira (eds.). 1992. *Refusing Holy Orders: Women and Fundamentalism in Britain*. London: Virago Press.

Said, Edward. 1978. *Orientalism*. London: Routledge and Kegan Paul.

Samad, Yunas. 1997. 'The Plural Guises of Multiculturalism: Conceptualising a Fragmented Paradigm', in *The Politics of Multiculturalism in the New Europe: Racism, Identity and Community*, ed T. Modood and P. Werbner. London: Zed Books.

Sardar, Ziauddin. 1998. *Postmodernism and the Other: the new imperialism of western culture*. London: Pluto Press.

Schwartz, Henry. 1997. *Writing Colonial History in Colonial and Postcolonial India*. Philadelphia: University of Pennsylvania Press.

Shelton, Dinah & Alexandra Kiss. 1996. 'A Draft Model Law on Freedom of Religion', in *Religious Human Rights in Global Perspective*, ed. J.D. van der Vyver and J. Witte, Jr. The Hague: Martin Nijhoff Publishers.

Shinn, Larry. 1987. *The dark lord: cult images and the Hare Krishnas in America*. Philadelphia. Westminster Press.

Shinn, Larry. 1994. 'The Maturation of the Hare Krishnas in America', *ISKCON Communications Journal*. Issue 3: 25–36.

Shinn, Larry. 1987. *The Dark Lord: cults images and the Hare Krishnas in America*, Philadelphia: Westminster.

Smith, Jonathan Z. 1978a. *Map is Not Territory: Studies in the History of Religions*. Leiden: E.J. Brill.

Smith, Jonathan Z. 1978b. *To Take Place: toward theory in ritual*. Chicago, University of Chicago Press.

Smith, Neil and Cindi Katz. 1993. 'Grounding Metaphor: towards a spatialized politics', in *Place and the Politics of Identity*, ed. M. Keith and S. Pile (eds.). London: Routledge.

Smith, W.C. 1978. *The Meaning and End of Religion*. London: SPCK.

Soja, Edward and Barbara Hooper. 1993. 'The Space that Difference Makes: some notes on the geographical margins of the new cultural politics', in *Place and the Politics of Identity*, ed. M. Keith and S. Pile (eds.). London: Routledge.

Spivak, Gayatri. 1993. 'Can the Subaltern Speak?', *Colonial Discourse and Post-colonial Theory: A Reader*, ed. P. Williams and L. Chrisman. New York: Harvest Wheatsheaf.

Spivak, Gayatri. 1996. *The Spivak Reader: selected works of Gayatri Chakravorty Spivak*, ed. D. Landry and G. MacLean. London: Routledge.

Spuler, Michelle. 1999. 'The Impact of Multiculturalism on Australian Religious Traditions', *Diskus: a disembodied journal of religion*. vol. 5, located at website url: <http://www.uni-marburg.de/fb03/religionswissenschaft/journal/diskus>

Stam, Robert and Ella Shohat. 1994. 'Contested Histories: Eurocentrism, Multi-culturalism, and the Media', in *Multiculturalism: a Critical Reader*, ed. D.T. Goldberg. Oxford: Blackwell.

Stanner, W. 1967. 'Relections on Durkheim and Aboriginal Religion' *Social Organisation*.

Stewart, Charles and Rosalind Shaw (eds.). 1994. *Syncretism/Anti-Syncretism: the politics of religious synthesis*. London: Routledge.

Stirrat, R.L. 1984. 'Sacred Models', *Man: the journal of the Royal Anthropological Institute*. 19: 199–215.

Stirrat, R.L. 1992. *Power and Religiosity in a Post-Colonial Setting: Sinhala Catholics in Contemporary Sri Lanka*. Cambridge: Cambridge University Press.

Stolcke, V. 1995. 'Talking Culture', *Current Anthropology*, 36 (1): 1–13.

Suleri, Sara. 1992. *The Rhetoric of English India*. Chicago: University of Chicago Press.

Sullivan, Donna. 1988. 'Advancing the Freedom of Religion or Belief through the UN Declaration on the Elimination of Religous Intolerance and Discrimination', *American Journal of International Law*, vol. 882: 487–520.

Sullivan, Lawrence. 1991. 'Body Works: knowledge of the body in the study of religion', *History of Religions*, vol. 30: 86–99.

Sullivan, Winnifred Fallers. 1994. *Paying the Words Extra: Religious Discourse in the Supreme Court of the United States*, Harvard University Press.

Sullivan, Winnifred Fallers. 1996. 'Competing Theories of Religion and Law in the Supreme Court of the United States: an Hasidic Case', *Numen: International Review for the History of Religions*. XLIII(2): 184–212.

Tabor, James and Eugene V. Gallagher. 1995. *Why Waco?: cults and the battle for religious freedom in America*. Berkeley, California: University of California Press.

Taylor, Charles. 1994. 'The Politics of Recognition', *Multiculturalism: Examining the Politics of Recognition*, ed. A. Gutman. Princeton: Princeton University Press.

Taylor, David. 1989. 'Citizenship and Social Power', *Critical Social Policy* vol. 9 (2): 19–31.

Thompson, Judith. & Paul Heelas. 1986 *The way of the heart: the Rajneesh movement*. Aquarian. Wellingborough, Northampton.

Turner, Bryan. 1984. *The body and society: explorations in social theory*. Oxford: Blackwell.

Turner, Bryan. 1990. 'Outline of a Theory of Citizenship', *Sociology* vol. 24 (2): 189–217.

Turner, Terence. 1993. 'Anthropology and Multiculturalism: What is Anthropology That Multiculturalists Should be Mindful of It?', *Cultural Anthropology*, 8 (4): 411–429.

Twaddle, M. (ed.). 1975. *Expulsion of a Minority*. London. Athlone.

van der Veer, Peter (ed.). 1995. *Nation and Migration: the Politics of Space in the South Asian Diaspora*. Philadelphia: University of Pennsylvania Press.

van der Veer, Peter. 1997. ''The Enigma of Arrival': Hybridity and Authenticity in the Global Space', in *Debating Cultural Hybridity: Multi-Cultural Identities and the Politics of Anti-Racism*, ed. P. Werbner and T. Modood. London: Zed Books.

van der Veer, Peter. 1998. 'Cultural Politics and the State', *Cultural Dynamics*, 10 (3): 281–286.

van der Vyver, Johan. 1996. 'Introduction, Legal Dimensions of Rleigious Human Rights: Constitutional Texts', in *Religious Human Rights in Global Perspective*, ed. J.D. van der Vyver and J. Witte, Jr. The Hague: Martin Nijhoff Publishers.

Vertovec, Steve. 1992. 'Community and Congregation in London Hindu Temples: divergent trends'. *New Community*. 18 (2): 251–264.

Vertovec, Steve. 1995. 'Hindus in Trinidad and Britain: Ethnic Religion, Reification, and the Politics of Public Space', in *Nation and Migration: the Politics of Space in the South Asian Diaspora*, ed. P. van der Veer. Philadelphia: University of Pennsylvania Press.

Vertovec, Steve. 1996. 'Multiculturalism, Culturalism, and Public Incorporation', *Ethnic and Racial Studies*. 19 (1): 49–69.

Vertovec, Steve. n.d. '*Comparative Issues in the Hindu diaspora*'. Paper presented to the conference on communal polarisation, UK South Asian Anthropologists' Group, London, 26th–27th September 1991.

Vishvanathan, Gauri. 1996. 'Beyond Syncretism'. *Stanford Electronic Humanities Review*, vol. 5 (1), special issue: *Contested Politics*. located at website url: <http://shr.stanford.edu/shreview/5-1/text/introduction.html>

von Stietencron, H. 1989. 'Hinduism: the proper use of a descriptive term', in *Hinduism Reconsidered*, ed. G.D. Sontheimer & H. Kulke. Delhi: Manohar.

Wadham, John and Helen Mountfield. 1999. *Blackstone's Guide to the Human Rights Act 1998*. London: Blackstones.

Waghorne, J. and N. Cutler. 1995. *Gods of Flesh, Gods of Stone: the Embodiment of Divinity in India*. Chambersburg, PA: Anima Press.

Wallis, Roy. 1984. *The Elementary Forms of the New Religious Life*. London: Routledge and Kegan Paul.

Wallis, Roy. 1993. 'Charisma as explanation', *Secularization, rationalism and sectarianism*, ed. E. Barker, J. Beckford, and K. Dobbelaere. Oxford: Clarendon Press.

Wallman, Sandra. 1979. 'Preface' and 'Introduction', in *Ethnicity at Work*, ed. S. Wallman. London: Macmillan.

Warburg, Margit. 1998. 'Restrictions and Privileges: the legal and administrative practice towards minority religions in the USA and Denmark', in *New Religions and New Religiosity in Europe*, ed. E. Barker & M. Warburg. Aarhus: Aarhus University Press

Weber, Max. 1968. *On charisma and institution building: selected papers*, ed. S.N. Eisenstadt. Chicago: University of Chicago Press.

Webster, Richard. 1990. *A Short History of Blasphemy*. Southwold: Orwell Press.

Weightman, Martin. n.d. 'The Definition of Religion', unpublished paper presented to conference on *Taking Religious Convictions Seriously: the impact of incorporation of the European Convention on Human Rights*, Imperial College London, 6th–7th January 1999.

Weller, Paul (ed.). 1997. *Religions in the UK: a Multi-Faith Directory*. Published by the University of Derby in association with the Inter Faith Network for the United Kingdom.

Werbner, Pnina and Tariq Modood. 1997. *Debating Cultural Hybridity: Multi-Cultural Identities and the Politics of Anti-Racism*. London: Zed Books.

Werbner, Pnina. 1997b. 'Afterword: Writing Multiculturalism and Politics in the New Europe', in *The Politics of Multiculturalism in the New Europe: Racism, Identity and Community*, ed T. Modood and P. Werbner. London: Zed Books.

White, Leslie. 1949. *The Science of Culture*. New York: Farrar, Straus and Giroux.

Wiebe, Donald. 1999. *The Politics of Religious Studies*. Basingstoke: Macmillan.

Wiener, M.J. 1981. *English culture and the decline of the industrial spirit, 1850–1980*. London: Cambridge University Press.

Wieviorka, Michel. 1998. 'Is multiculturalism the solution?', *Ethnic and Racial Studies*. 21 (5): 881–910.

Williams, Patrick and Laura Chrisman. 1993. *Colonial Discourse and Post-colonial Theory: A Reader*. New York: Harvest Wheatsheaf.

Williams, Raymond Brady. 1984. *A New Face of Hinduism: the Swaminarayan Religion*. Cambridge: Cambridge University Press.

Williams, Raymond Brady. 1994. *The Religions of Immigrants from India and Pakistan: new threads in the American tapestry*, Cambridge: CUP.

Williams, Raymond. 1985 (1973). *The Country and the City.* London: Hogarth Press.

Wilson, Bryan. 1966. *Religion in Secular Society.* London: Watts.

Wilson, Bryan. 1982. *Religion in Sociological Perspective.* Oxford: Oxford University Press.

Wilson, Bryan. 1990a. 'Old Laws and New Religions', *The Social Dimensions of Sectarianism: sects and new religious movements in contemporary society.* Oxford: Clarendon. pp. 69–86.

Wilson, Bryan. 1990b. 'Scientology: a secularized religion', in *The Social Dimensions of Sectarianism: sects and new religious movements in contemporary society.* Oxford: Clarendon. pp. 267–288.

Wilson, Bryan. 1991. 'Secularization', in *The study of religion, traditional and new religions*, ed. P.B. Clarke & S. Sutherland. London: Routledge.

Wilson, Richard (ed.). 1997. *Human Rights, Culture and Context: anthropological perspectives.* London: Pluto Press.

Wilson, Elizabeth. 1991. *The Sphinx in the City: Urban Life, the Control of Disorder, and Women.* London: Virago Press.

Wood, James E. 1989. 'Editorial: Religious Pluralism and Religious Freedom', *Journal of Church and State*, 31(1): 7–14.

Wright, Stuart A. (ed.). 1995. *Armageddon in Waco: critical perspectives on the Branch Davidian conflict.* Chicago: University of Chicago Press.

Young, Iris M. 1995. 'Togetherness in Difference', in *The Rights of Minority Cultures*, ed. W. Kymlicka. Oxford: Oxford University Press.

Young, Robert. 1990. *White Mythologies: Writing History and the West.* London: Routledge.

Young, Robert. 1995. *Colonial Desire: Hybridity in Theory, Culture, and Race.* London: Routledge.

Yuval-Davis, Nira. 1999. 'Institutional Racism, Cultural Diversity and Citizenship: Some Reflections on Reading The Stephen Lawrence Inquiry Report', *Sociological Research Online*, vol. 4, no. 1, <http://www.socresonline.org.uk/socresonline/4/1/yuval-davis.html>

Zablocki, Benjamin. 1997. 'The blacklisting of a concept: the strange history of the brainwashing conjecture in the history of religions' in *Nova Religio* vol. 1 (1), pp. 96–121.

Zablocki, Benjamin. 1998. 'Exit Cost Analysis: a new approach to the scientific study of brainwashing', in *Nova Religio* vol. 1 (2).

Zaidman-Dvir, Nurit. n.d. *When the Deities are Asleep: processes of change in the Hare Krishna temple*, PhD submitted to the Temple University Graduate Board, May 1994.

Miscellaneous documents and web pages

'ISKCON World Wide, GBC Members and BBT Trustees', Directory of Contact names and addresses for GBC members, on ISKCON web pages <http://iskcon.org/txt-only/main/address/boss.htm>.

Bhardwaj, P. n.d. Letter by P. Bhardwaj, President of the NCHT to the Director General of the BBC, part of a press release from the NCHT, 14th March 1983.

Campaign leaflet produced by Hare Krishna Temple Defence Movement, for Rally on 16th March. 1994.

Campaign leaflet produced by ISKCON, titled 'Return Religious and Racial Tolerance to Britain', c.1976, in archive of the Oxford Centre for Vaishnava and Hindu Studies, Oxford.

Case of Efstratiou v. Greece, Judgment of European Court of Human Rights, 18th December 1996, (77/1996/696/888), on ECHR web pages <http://www.dhcour.coe.fr>.

Case of International Society for Krishna Consciousness v. Secretary of State for the Environment and Hertsmere Borough Council (Queen's Bench Division, Kennedy J., October 31 1991).

Case of Kokkinakis v. Greece, Judgment of European Court of Human Rights, 25th May 1993, (Ser.A, no.260-A, 1993), on ECHR web pages <http://www.dhcour.coe.fr>.

Case of Larissis and Others v. Greece, Judgment of European Court of Human Rights, 24th February 1998, (140/1996/759/958–960), on ECHR web pages <http://www.dhcour.coe.fr>.

Case of Manoussakis and Others v. Greece, Judgment of European Court of Human Rights, 26th September 1996, (59/1995/565/651), on ECHR web pages <http://www.dhcour.coe.fr>.

Case of Regina v. W.M. Fleming & International Society for Krishna Consciousness, 6th November 1995, Luton Crown Court, Bedford. Transcript provided by Barnett, Lenton & Co., 61 Carey Street, London WC2A 2JG.

Case of Tsirlis and Kouloumpas v. Greece, Judgment of European Court of Human Rights, 29th May 1997, (54/1996/673/859–860), on ECHR web pages <http://www.dhcour.coe.fr>.

Case of Valsalmis v. Greece, Judgment of European Court of Human Rights, 18th December 1996, (74/1995/580/666), on ECHR web pages <http://www.dhcour.coe.fr>.

CoS. 1997. *Restoring and Safeguarding Religious Freedom: how to protect your human rights in Europe*. Brochure produced by the Church of Scientology, European Human Rights and Public Affairs Office.

Council of Europe. 1968. *The European Convention on Human Rights* (Strasbourg: Council of Europe, Directorate of Information.

Department of the Environment. *Planning Policy Guidance*, PPG2 (Revised): Green Belts. January 1995. London:HMSO.

Everyman, 'The Road to Hare Krishna', BBC TV, 2nd October 1994.

Home Office, *Rights Brought Home: The Human Rights Bill*, UK Government White Paper, (HMSO London, 24th October 1997); also available from the Home Office Internet Site (http://www.official-documents.co.uk/document/hoffice/rights/rights.htm).

Human Rights Act 1998 Chapter 42. The Stationery Office; also available from the HMSO internet site (http://www.hmso.gov.uk/acts/acts1998/19980042.htm).

Human Rights without Frontiers. 1994. *Greece: religious intolerance and discrimination*. Special double issue of the *European Magazine of Human Rights*. Brussels, Belgium: Brussels-Human Rights.

ICAP. Anonymous document titled 'ICAP – the Indian Community Affairs Programme', c.1982, in archive of the Oxford Centre for Vaishnava and Hindu Studies, Oxford.

Introvigne, Massimo, 'The Italian Supreme Court Decision on Scientology', CESNUR (the Center for Studies on New Religions), CESNUR web site at <http://www.cesnur.org/testi.htm>

ISKCON. n.d. *Inviting Krishna Into My Life*. Bhaktivedanta Manor Foundation Publication.

Journal of Planning Law, 1st October 1992, p. 963.

Leaflet produced by Hare Krishna Temple Defence Movement, for Rally on 16th March 1994.

Letter from P. Bhardwaj, President of NCHT to XXX. (Part of Press release from NCHT, 14th March 1983.)

Macpherson of Cluny, Sir William. 1999. *The Stephen Lawrence Inquiry: Report of an Inquiry by Sir William Macpherson of Cluny.* London: The Stationery Office; <http://www.official-documents.co.uk/document/cm42/4262/4262.htm>.

Media Release from ISKCON communications, 2 St James Rd, Watford, 28.8.91.

Minutes of 'A special meeting to discuss the way forward for the Manor campaign', held at Bhaktivedanta Manor, 8th September 1990, in the archive of the Oxford Centre for Vaishnava and Hindu Studies, Oxford.

Press release from National Council of Hindu Temples, 14th March 1983 and 25th March 1983.

Straw, Jack. (n.d.) British Home Secretary, 'Diverse Britain: the Rewards and the Challenge', speech made to the Policy Studies Institute, London, 8th October 1997, from PSI website: http://www.psi.org.uk/news/j_straw.htm)

INDEX